YUKON:
PLACES & NAMES

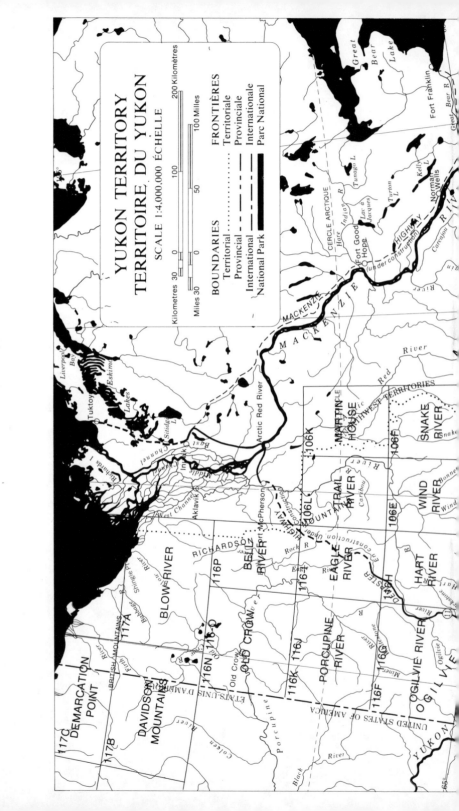

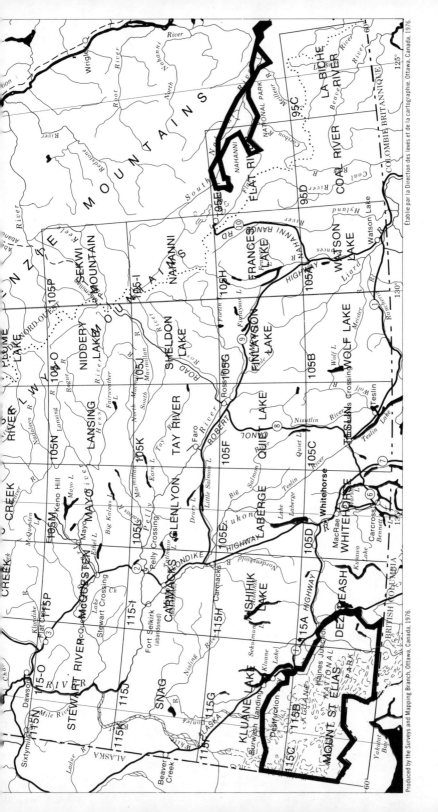

Produced by the Surveys and Mapping Branch, Ottawa, Canada, 1976.

Établie par la Direction des levés et de la cartographie, Ottawa, Canada, 1976.

YUKON:
PLACES & NAMES

R.C. Coutts

Gray's Publishing Limited,
Sidney, British Columbia,
Canada.

Cover photograph courtesy of Public Affairs Bureau, Yukon Government.

Design and typesetting by The Typeworks, Mayne Island, B.C.

Index map reproduced with permission of the Surveys and Mapping Branch, Department of Energy, Mines and Resources, Ottawa.

Names listed in this book are normally found on maps of the National Topographic Series, scale 1:250,000.

Indexes and ordering instructions can be obtained free of charge from:

>   Canada Map Office,
>   Surveys and Mapping Branch,
>   Department of Energy, Mines & Resources,
>   615 Booth Street,
>   Ottawa, Ontario.
>   K1A 0E9

Canadian Cataloguing in Publication Data

Coutts, Robert C., 1918–
  Yukon: Places & Names

  ISBN 0-88826-085-7 hardcover
  ISBN 0-88826-082-2 paperback
  1. Names, Geographical — Yukon Territory.
2. Yukon Territory — History, Local. I. Title.
FC4006.C68   917.19′1′0032   C80-091167-9
F1093.C68

FOREWORD

For any country, its names are a part of its history. From the beginning they have been a necessity; they are the means by which inhabitants and particularly explorers tell others where they have been and what they have seen. Indeed, without names, maps, records and books would be unintelligible.

When we see names in books or on maps we often take them for granted, thoughtless of asking ourselves whence they came or whether there is a meaningful story in their origin; but if we are curious, where do we find out? Heretofore, there has been no handy reference for this information on names of the Yukon Territory which, with its growth of population and expanding development, badly needs a published record of the history of its names. In *Yukon: Places & Names*, Robert C. Coutts gives us a book which fills this need admirably.

For him, its compilation has been a labour of love, occupying years of research through old manuscripts, maps, books and all sorts of sources of information including mining records and private diaries. This work has taken him to many parts of Canada and to the United States in his hunt for original sources of names. From this he has produced a convenient alphabetical list of Yukon names, giving the features they apply to, their locations and historical background. In many instances this includes tales of the men who discovered the features, how they chose the names and who or what the names commemorate, in addition to accounts of those whose names the features bear. The author gives historical accounts not only of the well known, established names in common usage but also of lonely creeks and hills, and long-abandoned localities in the hinterlands rarely now remembered, whose stories fade with passing years.

Besides supplying the history of these out-of-the-way places, this volume will make a most useful contribution to resurrecting these old names. When new strikes are made on old ground, where the early names were in obscure records and generally unknown, newcomers are prone to introduce new names. But here is a bulwark against such errors. Throughout its length the book by its very nature supplies a store of historical notes and fills an important place among the historical references for the Yukon Territory.

Five years of experience as representative for the Yukon Territory on the Canadian Board on Geographical Names gave me a very real appreciation of the need for such a work as this book and it gives me great satisfaction that this need has now been so well filled. The author points out that a number of names are omitted for lack of information and almost daily we see more new names established. It is my earnest hope that as time goes on, revised editions, in the same style but containing the missing names and giving the new ones, will follow, keeping the record up to date.

Hugh S. Bostock

Ottawa

INTRODUCTION

"Names are the pegs from which history is hung."
Henry Schoolcraft.

The work contained in this book began about ten years ago as a hobby. When first prospecting in the southwest Yukon and Cassiar country, I was naturally interested in the history of an area about which I had read and been told so much. Becoming curious about the origin or meaning of a Yukon place name, I found that there was often no answer, or conflicting ones. Alone of Canada's provinces and territories almost nothing has been written on this subject. On reading the early literature it often appeared that the modern name was often not that given originally and that in many cases the name and its meaning had been altered or changed. I began to search for the true origins of these names. Gradually, the people and the stories behind the names began to live for me and many were more interesting than much of the fiction written about the territory. As the stories unfolded and extended, my interest became more serious but no less enjoyable. Many newly learned facts revealed other stories and puzzles to be traced and solved.

The stories set down here are almost entirely contained in the written accounts of those who took part in or were close to the events. Little is from hearsay, unless confirmed by other statements or accounts. In cases of conflict the earliest or most obvious story is given; in some cases, two or more equally reliable but differing accounts are recorded and the reader may choose between them.

The stories of most of the early explorers are well known, but those of the common people who opened and developed the country are often remembered only in the name of a feature where they pioneered. As the builders of a country their lives should not be forgotten. This is an attempt to record some of these stories.

This Yukon is a hard and demanding country. For the most part it has always attracted the more self-reliant, individualistic and adventurous types of people. Most asked little of others but gave freely of themselves. They were people worth knowing and people worth remembering.

The first known white man to set foot in the Yukon Territory was John Franklin, the famous English Arctic explorer. During his second expedition, in 1826, he travelled the Arctic coast from the mouth of the Mackenzie River westward into what is now Alaska. Many of the Yukon's coastal features, including Herschel Island, were named by him at that time. However, the first feature in the Yukon to be given a name by white men was Mount St. Elias in the southwest corner of the territory. Seen from the sea on St. Elias Day, 16 July, 1741, it was named by Vitus Bering while he was exploring the coast of Alaska for the Russian government.

The next group of names was given in the period between 1839 and 1850. Robert Campbell of the Hudson's Bay Company entered the central Yukon by way of the Liard, Frances and Pelly Rivers. Campbell established the courses of the Frances, Pelly and Yukon Rivers and built trading posts on or near each of them. He named these rivers and many of their tributaries. Later in the same period John Bell and Alexander Hunter Murray, of the same company, crossed the northern Yukon from the Mackenzie River and established Lapierre's House and later Fort Yukon.

From 1880 on, the early prospector-miners arrived, and in their wanderings gave names to many of the streams where they won gold and to the mountains they used as landmarks. Up to this time the prospectors and explorers retained many of the old native names.

Lieutenant Frederick Schwatka of the United States Army came over the Chilkoot Pass and rafted quickly down the Yukon River in June and July 1883, conducting the first rough survey of its course. Ignoring the names known to the natives, traders and miners he renamed most of the principal streams, lakes and outstanding features along the river after his army superiors and prominent academicians of his day.

Dr. George M. Dawson, Director of the Geological and Natural History Survey of Canada (and one of Canada's outstanding explorer-geologists), in 1887 ascended the Liard and Frances Rivers from the Stikine, and descended the Pelly to its junction with the Yukon, surveying the river and topography as he went. His maps and reports, which included all available information concerning the territory and its inhabitants, were of such high quality that they are still classics of their kind today. He repudiated much of Schwatka's nomenclature, retaining many of the original names.

William Ogilvie, DLS, of the Department of the Interior, ran a precise survey in 1887–88 from Pyramid Harbor near Haines, Alaska, up Chilkoot Inlet to Dyea and over the Chilkoot Pass to Lake Bennett. From Bennett he carried his survey down the Yukon River to the Yukon-Alaska boundary below Fortymile; these were the first accurate surveys made of the route through the central Yukon. He then cut the Yukon-Alaska boundary line from the Yukon River south through the Fortymile and Sixtymile Rivers country, thus settling any disputes as to the national ownership of the rich placer goldfields then being exploited there. He later settled the first disputes as to claim ownership on Bonanza Creek in the Klondike in the fall of 1896. Ogilvie, who was to become the first Commissioner of the Yukon Territory, named a number of prominent peaks after the pioneer prospectors of the Yukon whom he admired, and a number of streams after geological phenomena observed on them.

The Klondike Gold Rush years of 1896–99 saw hundreds of names added to the maps as thousands of gold-seekers overran the country. The custom of the times allowed the first man who found gold and staked the Discovery claim on any creek (the first claim on a stream was double the size of a regular claim) to give it any name he chose. In many cases where the miner was ignorant of this custom the Mining Recorder supplied the name for him.

Other and later mining rushes and stampedes to various parts of the territory added still more names to the maps. Many creeks and lakes were named locally after the trappers, traders and prospectors who made their homes on them. The Geological Survey of Canada has, since Dawson's time, added many names as its geologists mapped the rocks of the region. The Alpine Club of Canada and various institutional mountaineering expeditions have named many of the peaks in the St. Elias Range of the southwestern Yukon. Construction workers of the Alaska Highway and the Canol Pipeline added their share of new names.

The last large group of names was acquired in the 1960–70 period, when the Surveys and Mapping Branch of the Department of Energy, Mines and Resources was preparing its 1:50,000 scale topographical maps. (This project has yet to be completed). As each sheet is titled by the name of a central feature, any that were without such names were given those of early Yukoners. Gordon McIntyre, Yukon Lands Titles Agent and later Member of the Yukon Legislative Assembly was responsible for most of the research. He ensured the perpetuation of the names of many nearly forgotten pioneers.

A continuing class of names is that honouring many Yukoners who died in foreign wars. Individual names have been and are being proposed and adopted with the approval of the Territorial Government and the Canada Permanent Committee on Geographical Names (also known as the Canadian Board on Geographical Names or the Geographical Board).

In no way is this book anything but a beginning. There are still many names for which no information has been found. There are many gaps yet to be filled. Over the years many records have been lost or misplaced and are no longer available. It is my earnest hope that any readers who possess any part of this missing information will share it with the Yukon Archives or with me: it will be received with appreciation. With this help, in time a new and more comprehensive work can be prepared.

R.C. Coutts
Atlin, B.C.

ACKNOWLEDGEMENTS

It is doubtful if any book is solely the work of any one person. Certainly this one is not. Although I have gathered the material together, it would have been a much smaller work without the active help and encouragement of many other people.

My good friend Hugh S. Bostock, Ph.D., gentleman, scientist and bushman, whose 40 years work with the Geological Survey of Canada in the Yukon Territory makes him an authority which he is quick to disclaim, encouraged me steadily. His expert advice and incisive criticism kept me searching for the right answers.

Mrs. Helen Akrigg, herself an authority on such matters, took an interest at the beginning and sponsored my application for a Canada Council grant.

Brian Speirs, the first Archivist of the Yukon Territory and my second sponsor, has encouraged this work from the start and helped in every way to obtain obscure material as well as providing facilities for working. His successor, Linda Johnson, has continued this interest. Diane Johnston, Assistant Archivist, has given much of her own time and thought to finding necessary material over the past four years.

Ron D'Altroy, Curator of Photography at the Vancouver Public Library and an old and valued friend, has contributed much both in ideas and material over the years, for which I thank him.

My gratitude must be expressed to the Explorations Programme of the Canada Council and in particular to Paul-Emile Leblac, Executive Officer, whose patience with amateur writers seems endless. The grant enabled me to do much of the original research for this work.

Appreciation must be expressed to my friends the rare-book dealers, whose advice and assistance in finding almost-unknown material was and is invaluable, particularly to John W. Todd, Jr. of Shorey's in Seattle, David Moon of West Vancouver, Stephen McIntyre and Bill Hoffer of Vancouver and the late R. Hilton Smith of Victoria. Each one has persistently searched for and found material previously unknown to bibliographers.

My gratitude also goes to the many institutions which gave me access to their northern collections, especially to Ann Yandel of UBC and Andy Johnson of the University of Washington, the BC Provincial and the Public Archives of Canada, the people of the Glenbow-Alberta Institute in Calgary and others too numerous to list here.

The foundation for this work was laid at the offices of the Canada Permanent Committee for Geographical Names in Ottawa with the active encouragement and help of Gordon Delaney, the Executive Secretary and his assistant Frank Stevenson who bore with my many questions and requests for many weeks. This interest and help has been continued by Allan Rayburn, the present Executive Secretary.

Mrs. Shirley Connolly, founder and past president of the Atlin Historical Society, aided materially from her own personal knowledge of the Yukon and the people in the Ross River country. Mrs. Sue Morhun, the present president of the society, gave me sound professional advice in putting the material into manuscript form.

To all these friends, thank you.

LOCATING THE FEATURES LISTED

All features named in this work are listed alphabetically. Their positions are based on the National Topographic Series of maps, scale 1:250,000 (1 inch = 4 miles), which gives a complete coverage of the Yukon Territory using 45 separate map sheets. They are available at most territorial government offices. Each of these sheets is known by sheet name and sheet number, e.g. Dawson 116-B&C, Whitehorse 105D.

These maps are plotted in degrees and minutes of latitude and longitude which increase to the north and west from the bottom right-hand corner of the sheet. Using these figures the location of any place is easily and quickly obtained. Settlement locations are pin-pointed. The figures given for a mountain are those of its highest point. Those for lakes are at the centre of the lake; those for rivers and creeks are given at the mouth of the stream.

In this work a rough description of the location is given after the map sheet number.

ABBREVIATIONS USED IN THE TEXT

ACC	The Alaska Commercial Company
CEF	Canadian Expeditionary Forces. (The Canadian Army overseas during the First World War.)
CPCGN	Canada Permanent Committee on Geographical Names.
CIMM	Canadian Institute of Mining and Metallurgy.
CMG	Companion of the Order of St. Michael and St. George. (A British Order of Chivalry.) This is a sort of Long Service and Good Conduct Medal awarded to senior civil servants and their equivalents in the armed forces.
DFC	Distinguished Flying Cross. Awarded for bravery in action by officers of British Air Forces.
DFM	Distinguished Flying Medal. Awarded for bravery in action by non-commissioned officers of British Air Forces.
DLS	Dominion Land Surveyor.
DSM	Distinguished Service Medal. An American decoration for service, both civilian and military.
DSO	Distinguished Service Order. A British award for exceptional leadership by officers against an enemy.

DTS	Dominion Topographical Surveyor. The most highly qualified degree for Canadian surveyors.
FASAS	Fellow of the American Society for the Advancement of Science.
FRGS	Fellow of the Royal Geographical Society.
FRS	Fellow of the Royal Society. This is Britian's most prestigious society for science and scholarship.
FRSC	Fellow of the Royal Society of Canada. (The Canadian equivalent of the Royal Society.)
G&NHSC	Geological and Natural History Survey of Canada.
GSC	The Geological Survey of Canada.
HBC	The Governor and Company of Adventurers of England Trading into Hudson's Bay. As a business title it was more simply called The Hudson's Bay Company: colloquially called "The Bay".
KCMG	Knight Commander of the Order of St. Michael and St. George. A British Order of Chivalry awarded for most distinguished services in any field. It carries a knighthood.
MC	The Military Cross. Awarded to officers of the British armies for bravery in action.
MID	Mentioned in Dispatches. A citation for outstanding conduct during a military operation by any member of the British forces.
MM	The Military Medal. Awarded to non-commissioned officers and men of the British armies for bravery in action.
MP	Member of Parliament.
NAT&TC	North American Transportation and Trading Company. They built Fort Cudahy at Fortymile in 1893.
NCO	Non-Commissioned Officer. (Corporals, Sergeants, Warrant Officers, etc. in any police or armed force.)
NWMP	North-West Mounted Police (1873–1904).
NWT	North West Territories. Before June 1898 the Yukon Territory was part of the NWT.
OBE	Order of the British Empire.
PEng	Professional Engineer. A member of the association of Professional Engineers.
RCMP	Royal Canadian Mounted Police (1920–).
RGS	The Royal Geographical Society. A prestigious British society for the advancement of geographical exploration.

RN	Royal Navy.
RNWMP	The Royal North-West Mounted Police (1904–1920).
RCN	Royal Canadian Navy.
RCAF	Royal Canadian Air Force.
T&D	Taylor and Drury's. A retail store company.
USCGS	The United States Coast and Geodetic Survey.
USGS	United States Geological Survey.
YOOP	The Yukon Order of Pioneers. A society or brotherhood formed by early Yukoners at Fortymile in 1894, of those who had come in the country before 1887. Still active, its membership requirement is now 11 years residence in the Yukon watershed.

HOW TO NAME A FEATURE IN THE YUKON TERRITORY

It is the privilege of any person or organization to ask that a chosen name be given to any feature in the Yukon Territory. There are definite rules of procedure to be followed to make the name official. A booklet prepared by the Committee on Geographical Names, which outlines advice and requirements, may be obtained by writing to:

The Secretary,

Canada Permanent Committee on Geographical Names,

Department of Energy, Mines and Resources,

615 Booth Street,

Ottawa, Ontario, Canada.

Briefly, the requirements for naming a feature are as follows:

1. Names proposed must be for specific geographic features. The committee does not normally select features for naming;

2. The following information should be supplied for all names or name changes proposed:

(a) Location—by latitude and longitude (specify the map you are using), map reference, sketch or photograph;

(b) Feature identification—indicate the extent as precisely as possible by colour, arrows, or description relative to adjoining features;

(c) If new name(s), supply also

1. origin,

2. reasons for proposing,

3. evidence that the feature is unnamed;

(d) If changing existing name(s), supply also

1. alternate name(s),

2. reasons for proposed change(s).

ABRAHAM CREEK 63°32′N 139°57′W (115-O).A tributary to the Sixtymile River.

This stream was named after Harry ABRAHAM who mined 27 placer gold claims here from 1913 to 1925 and who had probably prospected in the area much earlier.

ACLAND CREEK 60°18′N 127°29′W (95-D). Flows into the Coal River.

In 1956 G. Rowley named this stream in honour of Sgt. Arthur Edward ACLAND, RNWMP, who was in this area about 1910. He was later in charge of the police post at Kluane in 1912–14.

MOUNT ADAMI 4,158′ 63°19′N 138°02′W (115-O).45 miles up the Stewart River on the south side.

F.A. Stretch, Warden at Carmacks, named this hill after Frank ADAMI, long-time Yukoner who had trapped this area from 1936–57. Adami came from a good background, holding three degrees in chemistry and physics from Milwaukee and the Sorbonne but he preferred the solitary life of a trapper to any other. He died in Vancouver, BC, in 1958.

ADAMS CREEK 63°56′N 139°20′W (115-O&N). A small stream entering Bonanza Creek from the west, a short distance above the mouth.

Orginally called ADAMS Gulch, probably by Carlo Tilly who was the first man to stake a claim on it on 31 August, 1896, this little stream was staked immediately after Bonanza and at the same time as Eldorado. The first miners found little gold on it, showing the chanciness of placer mining. However, two years later in 1898 new miners tried again and did find payable gold.

AFE CREEK 62°17′N 135°53′W (105-L). Flows into the Tatchun River.

This was named about 1954 after AFE Brown, pioneer packer, trapper and miner in this area for many years. Acknowledged a superior man by his contemporaries, he was well-liked and respected by all who knew him. He died in 1952 at a sawmill owned by his two sons, at the mouth of the nearby Tatchun River. This creek had been called by his name by the local people long before he died.

AFE PEAK 5,662′ 62°15′N 135°22′W (105-L). At the headwaters of Afe Creek.

AFE Brown was further commemorated by the giving of his name to this peak in 1954.

AHVEE MOUNTAIN   3,701′ 67°10′N 139°47′W (116-O&N). 28 miles south of Old Crow.

Long known to the people of Old Crow, this is a Vanta Kutchin Indian word meaning "Weasel".

AISHIHIK LAKE   61°25′N 137°07′W (115-H). 100 miles northwest of Whitehorse.

This is an old Indian name meaning "High Place." The lake is 35 miles long and, at an elevation of 3,001′ above sea level, is the highest lake of comparable size in all of Canada. A long-time Indian community of the same name on the north shore was abandoned after 1967.

A hydro-electric power dam was recently built at the foot of the lake and, since early 1976, has supplied electricity to the Yukon power grid.

Other sources claim the Indian name means "Big Lake". This is unlikely but if so, it makes the present name redundant.

ALASKA HIGHWAY   1523 miles from Mile "O" at Dawson Creek, BC to Fairbanks, Alaska, of which 1221 miles are in Canada. A paved road in Alaska, the Canadian section is about 90% an all-weather, 30-foot-wide, gravel highway traversing some of the most beautiful scenery in North America.

Since the early 1900′s various groups in Canada and the US had pressed for a highway to Alaska. In 1930 the US government established the Alaska International Highway Commission and in 1931 a similar body was set up by the Canadian government to study the location, financing and construction of such a road.

Finally, two major routes were chosen. Route "A" started from Vancouver, BC and went through Prince George, Hazelton, Telegraph Creek and Atlin to Whitehorse: 1275 miles approximately. Route "B" went through Prince George, Fort St. James, Dease Lake, and Atlin to Whitehorse: 1250 miles approximately. Several other routes were proposed for special or local reasons. The major reason advanced for constructing such a road was the advantage of a land link to Alaska in time of war. The major problem was always financing.

In February 1942, the American armed forces, ignoring all previous studies and plans, chose the present and, until then, unconsidered route. The need for an access and service road for the string of airfields being built between Edmonton and Fairbanks to supply Russia with aircraft was immediate; local and future economic needs of the region were of no importance. An agreement with the Canadian government was quickly reached.

Surveys were started the same month and by April 1942 construction had begun. Round-the-clock work by 9,000 US Army Engineers saw a usable truck road pushed through by late November. Following the troops came the civilian contractors, 77 of them; 62 American and 15 Canadian firms employed 12,000 men to bring the road up to standard by late 1943. In all, 7,000 pieces of equipment were used.

The US government paid all construction costs and the cost of maintenance up to 1 April, 1946, when the Canadian section was turned over to the Canadian Army Engineers. The airfields and land communication systems were turned over to the RCAF at the same time. The road was maintained until 1965 by the Canadian Army Engineers and from that date by the Departments of Highways of the Yukon Territory and British Columbia, with federal assistance. The total cost of the highway to April 1946 was never revealed but estimates place it above $138,000,000.

Officially and originally named the "Alaska Military Highway", the men on the job soon shortened this to "The Alcan". Neither name was popular with the public, which had followed the construction with great interest. On 25 March, 1943, Anthony J. Dimond, Congressman from Alaska, proposed the name "The Alaska Highway", which was officially adopted by both governments on 19 July, 1943. (Dimond had been a long-time backer of Route "A").

The speed of construction, the location and climate all make this project one of the great engineering feats of our time. As shorter and more economical routes are being built closer to the Pacific coast, the highway will gradually lose its overall importance but never its history or impact on the Yukon and central Alaska, where its opening heralded the end of an era.

ALBERT CREEK 60°03′N 128°54′W(105–A). A tributary of the Liard River, crossing the Alaska Highway at mile 643 (K1029).
This is a long-known local name after ALBERT Death, an old-time packer and trapper in the area for many years.

MOUNT ALBERTA 10,985′ 60°56′N 140°51′W(115–B&C). In the Centennial Range of the St. Elias Mountains.
This was named in 1967 to celebrate Canada's Centennial year. (See the Centennial Range.)

3

ALKI CREEK   64°04′N 138°59′W(116-B&C). A small stream entering the Klondike River 20 miles from Dawson.

A.E. Elliott, who had come from Seattle to Skagway in the old steamer *ALKI* found gold, staked the Discovery claim and named this creek on 24 November, 1897.

ALLAN CREEK   60°30′N 129°45′W(105-A). Flows into the Liard River 40 miles northwest of Watson Lake.

This was a long-used local name after Fred ALLAN who trapped here for many years. A striking character, he resembled Buffalo Bill Cody, was a crack shot with pistol or rifle and preferred an isolated life in the bush. In the early 1900's he and George Adsit (reputed to have been a member of Butch Cassidy's Hole-in-the-Wall Gang) drove a herd of horses overland from Montana to Teslin Lake.

ALLGOLD CREEK   63°57′N 136°27′W(115-O&N). A short creek running from King Solomon's Dome to the Klondike River.

Clinton Jones staked and optimistically named this creek on 10 September, 1897. He was mistaken. Although it is in the Klondike and lies between rich placer gold creeks, it produced almost no gold at all.

ALMSTROM CREEK   68°07′N 136°27′W(117-A). A tributary to Cache Creek from the east.

This stream was named in 1973 after Edward ALMSTROM, officer in charge of Water Surveys in the Yukon from 1949 to 52 and Mining Inspector until 1972.

ALSEK RIVER   59°27′N 137°53′W(115-A). Flows from the Kluane Ranges through the St. Elias Mountains and into the Pacific south of Yakutat Bay.

It is a rough and almost impassable stream. The native name "Alsekh" was reported by the Russian Captain Tebenkov in 1825. Earlier, La Pérouse, the French explorer, in 1786 had named it "Rivière du Behring". The New York Times Expedition in 1886 (led by Lt. F. Schwatka) had named it the "Jones" River after one of Schwatka's sponsors. The USCGS called it the "Harrison" River in honour of a president of the US. The US and Canadian governments in 1891 officially gave it back its original and present name.

The first white men to explore the river were the members of the Frank Leslie Illustrated Newspaper Expedition, Edward James Glave and Jack

4

Dalton, who travelled it by canoe from Neskataheen (near Dalton House) to the sea in 1890, the only men ever to do so.

ALVERSON GULCH   64°06'N 135°02'W(106–D). A small tributary of Scougale Creek in the Davidson Range.

Jack Alverson, who came into the Yukon in 1899, lived and prospected on this creek. Originally from Oregon, he spent most of his life here and about the upper Stewart River country. In 1910 he and his partner, Grant Hoffman, mined 59 tons of high-grade, silver-lead ore, the first ever mined in the Mayo district. The ore body had been found in 1906 by H.W. McWhorter and was the first such ore found in the Mayo area.

MOUNT ALVERSTONE   14,565' 60°22'N 139°02'W(115–B&C). In the St. Elias Range close to the Yukon-Alaska boundary.

This was named in 1908 by the Canadian government after Baron ALVERSTONE, Lord Chief Justice of England and the British member of the Canadian-Alaskan Boundary Tribunal of 1903. He cast the vote which established the present boundary between Canada and Alaska, effectively cutting off the Yukon and the northern half of British Columbia from access to the Pacific except through US territory. He was acting on orders from the British government which had been informed secretly by American President Theodore Roosevelt that if the vote went against the US he would send troops to seize all the disputed areas. Alverstone voted as ordered.

AMERICAN GULCH   63°57'N 139°16'W(115–O & N). Just ¼ mile long, this little brook enters Bonanza Creek on the west side, a mile below Eldorado Creek.

It was staked entirely by American prospectors. B.H. Laughlin and his brother Chester made the discovery and staked the first two claims on 20 August, 1897.

On 15 June, 1904, a gold nugget was found here which, it was claimed, weighed 450 ounces. This would be by far the largest nugget ever found in the Yukon except that a certain amount of quartz was associated with the gold in the nugget and no true weight was ever announced.

AMMERMAN MOUNTAIN   68°23'N 141°00'W(117–B). A high ridge running east-west and centred on the Yukon-Alaska border.

This is a local name, probably after a trapper-prospector in the area, reported in 1911 by the International Boundary Control Survey crew, from the name of a creek which flows along the base of the ridge.

ANDERSON CREEK 61°34'N 129°25'W(105-H). Joins the Thomas River at the head of the east arm of Frances Lake.

Although this area was travelled from the 1840's and smaller streams named, no one found this creek until, in 1949, it was named to honour the memory of First Lt. P.M. ANDERSON RN, DSC, MID, killed in action in the Second World War.

Anderson Lake received its name at the same time.

ANDERSON GLACIER 61°11'N 141°00'W(115-G & F). Straddles the International Boundary in the St. Elias Range.

This was named in 1912–13 by the International Boundary Control Survey party after P. Chandler ANDERSON (1866–1936), of New York; he was arbiter of the Pecuniary Claims Commission of 1910 and a counsel for the US before the Yukon-Alaska Boundary Tribunal in 1903.

MOUNT ANDERSON 60°13'N 135°09'W(105-D). South of the Wheaton River.

John ANDERSON was a well-known prospector in this area for many years. The hill was given his name when he found the first mineral, — gold, silver and others, none in economic quantities — on it in 1910.

ANGEL LAKE 64°49'N 134°39'W(106-D). A very small lake on the Wind River, three miles north of Bond Creek.

It was named by L.H. Green in 1970. About 1960 two prospectors, John Berry O'Neil and John J. O'Neil (not related) crashed here on take-off. Somehow they survived and from this incident the lake was named.

ANIK ISLAND 66°53'N 137°38'W(116-I). An island in the Porcupine River.

The word ANIK means "brother" in the Inuit (Eskimo) language. It was given to the first northern communications satellite, Anik 1, which was launched on 9 November, 1972. Anik 2 was put up in April 1973 and Anik 3 two years later.

The satellites are owned by the Telesat Canada Corporation, a company half owned by the Canadian government and half by ten telephone and communications companies. The purpose of the corporation is to make television and telephone service available throughout Canada's north.

Each satellite can carry 12 colour TV channels (only ten are used — two are spares) or 960 one-way telephone calls at the same time. No direct signals are received except through earth stations which are leased to communities by the corporation.

The name was proposed by Gordon McIntyre, MLA.

ANKER CREEK   68°43′N 137°27′W(117-A). A tributary of the Blow River near the Arctic coast.

This stream was probably named about 1962 by F.G. Young of the Alberta Geological Survey while he was exploring in this area for oil-bearing rock formations.

ANKER Hoidal trapped and prospected for many years on the Arctic slope and was of great service to the geologists mapping the area. (See Mount HOIDAL).

ANN GULCH   64°02′N 135°50′W(106-D). A small tributary to Dublin Gulch, Mayo area.

Fred Taylor mined longer on Dublin Gulch than anyone else. His wife ANN and their two sons lived near here for several years and the name is used locally.

ANNETT CREEK   68°35′N 137°52′W(117-A). Flows into Anker Creek near the Arctic coast.

In 1909 William ANNETT (or ANNET) and David Lord, two trapper-prospectors, claimed to have found placer gold here. In 1916 Annett enlisted with the Black contingent of the Yukon Infantry Company and fought in the First World War.

ANTONE CREEK   60°06′N 128°23′W(105-A). A tributary to the Hyland River, ten miles east of Watson Lake.

A local Indian of this name lived and trapped here for many years.

AQUILA CREEK   66°49′N 137°05′W(116-I). A short tributary to the Eagle River.

This was named during the wilderness study in 1973. The name is a play on words, being Latin for "eagle".

ARCH CREEK   61°30′N 139°43′W(115–G&F). Flows into the Donjek River, ten miles south of the Alaska Highway.

Placer gold was found here during the rush to the Burwash Creek and Kluane goldfields in May 1904, by Henry Flaherty, Morley Bones and Fred Ater. They named the stream because of a peculiar, arch-like opening in the limestone rocks of the canyon.

MOUNT ARCHIBALD   8,400′ 60°47′N 137°52′W(115–A). 15 miles west of Haines Junction.

In 1971 this mountain was named after Dr. E.S. ARCHIBALD, sometime director of the Experimental Farm Service of the Department of Agriculture. He was instrumental in setting up the Pine Creek Experimental Farm near here.

ARK MOUNTAIN   60°14′N 136°10′W(115–A). On the southwest side of Kusawa Lake.

Many years ago local Indians hunting on the mountain found the rotted remains of an old log cabin, built by prospectors far above the timber line. Uneducated except for missionary teachings, and unable to find any reason for anyone to carry logs this far and high, they thought them to be the remains of Noah's ARK.

Dr. E. Kindle, GSC, who explored the mountain in 1950 was told this story and confirmed the name.

ARKELL CREEK   60°48′N 135°43′W(105–D). Flows into the Ibex Creek and to the Takhini River.

In 1890, E.J. Glave and Jack Dalton of the first Frank Leslie Illustrated Newspaper Expedition, after separating from the other two members of the party at Lake Kusawa, travelled in this area and named this creek and also Lake Kusawa after the owner of the paper, W.J. ARKELL of New York. Arkell also owned the humour magazine *Judge* and was secretary and part owner of a patent medicine company. Arkell had organized this expedition to cash in on the publicity value of the recent news of rich gold finds in the Yukon at Fortymile. In 1891 he sent Glave and Dalton back again to explore more of the country.

It was from these two journeys that Dalton conceived the idea of the Dalton Trail to the Yukon. (See Dalton Trail.)

An interesting sequel to these expeditions was that in 1897 when news of the fabulous wealth of the Klondike reached the outside world, Arkell instituted legal claims to the whole of the Klondike, based on these travels. His brother-in-law offered A.B. Schanz, one of the four members of the expedition, $50,000 for any rights he might have to such a claim. So great was the euphoria engendered by the Klondike riches that Schanz turned the offer down. Needless to say, the lawsuit came to nothing.

LAKE ARKELL   (See Kusawa Lake.)

MOUNT ARKELL   7,246′ 60°36′N 135°37′W(105–D). At the head of Arkell Creek, 20 miles southwest of Whitehorse.

This was named in the 1950's in association with the creek.

MOUNT ARMSTRONG   7,083′ 63°12′N 133°15′W(105–N). The highest peak in the Russell Range.

This was named in 1954 under the auspices of the Hon. George Black, MP for the Yukon, after Lt. Col. Neville Alexander Drummond ARMSTRONG, OBE, FRGS, 98′er, prospector, miner, geographer, big-game hunter and conservationist, soldier and gentleman.

Born in England in 1874, Armstrong at the age of 17 spent three years in Texas and New Mexico as a day labourer. In 1898 he came to the Klondike via St. Michaels as assistant manager of the Yukon Goldfields Company. He acquired rich claims for the. company on Bonanza Creek and Cheechako Hill and became manager of the company. In 1901 he made a deal with Duncan Gillies, the discoverer, for a placer concession on Russell Creek on the MacMillan River. On 3 August, 1901, together with his crew of six, he took the first steamboat, the *Prospector*, up the MacMillan River to Russell Creek. For this journey he was made a Fellow of the Royal Geographical Society.

In 1904 and 1905 he was appointed Game Warden for the MacMillan River country. Until 1914 he spent almost every summer and several winters on Russell Creek, searching for the elusive gold with little success. In 1914 Armstrong joined the Canadian Expeditionary Forces in France. Given the rank of major he trained scouts and snipers and was awarded the OBE for his outstanding services. Returning to Russell Creek in 1920 he worked until 1926 before giving up the quest. In 1928 he left for England, never to return.

In 1939, at the age of 65 he joined the British army and organized a sniping school. He served in France in early 1940, missing Dunkirk. Transferring to the Canadian First Division he was later retired because of his age. The British army, with better judgment, promoted him to lieutenant-colonel and placed him in command of the Royal Marines Small Arms School.

He died in November 1954. For most of 30 years he was part of the Yukon, believing in its bounty, studying its animals and features and gaining the respect of all who knew him. His two books are Yukon history.

ARMSTRONG'S LANDING   63°05'N 133°25'W(105-N). At the mouth of Russell Creek.

This was a landing place with storage cabins, built by Neville ARMSTRONG in 1901 and later, to service his operations on Russell Creek. No one lived here, and it fell into disuse in 1926 when he abandoned operations.

ARMSTRONG   63°05'N 133°25'W(105-N).

This was a small trading post established in 1919 by Alec Coward and Arthur Zimmerlee of Fort Selkirk, about half a mile downstream from Armstrong's Landing. They were in business here until the 1930's.

MOUNT ARTHUR WHEELER   61°11'N 140°09'W(115-G&F). Above the Steele Glacier in the St. Elias Range.

This was named by the Alpine Club of Canada in memory of their first President, Arthur Oliver WHEELER (1906-1910). Born in Kilkenny, Ireland on 1 May, 1860, he came to Canada in 1876. He became a surveyor and a founder of the Alpine Club in 1906. He died in 1945.

ART LEWIS GLACIER   60°00'N 139°00'W(115-B&C). On the Yukon-Alaska boundary.

This small glacier was named jointly by the US and Canadian governments in 1922 in memory of Arthur LEWIS, a member of the Canadian Boundary Survey parties in 1912 and 1914. He was killed in action in France while serving with the 72nd Highlanders of Canada in the First World War.

ASKIN LAKE   61°56'N 133°14'W(105-F). 25 miles west of Ross River.

In 1951 this little lake was chosen to honour the memory of Gunner C.D. ASKIN, Royal Canadian Artillery, MID. He was killed in action in the Second World War.

MOUNT ATHERTON   62°02'N 133°44'W(105-K). 17 miles southwest of Faro, in the Pelly Mountains.

This was recently named after Charles T. ATHERTON, long-time Yukoner at Whitehorse and a Territorial Councillor in the mid-1930's.

ATLAS CREEK   61°14′N 139°12′W(115–G&F). A short tributary of the Duke River from the south.

This was named in 1973 by the Scenic and Wilderness Study Group for no particular reason.

ATLIN LAKE   60°00′N 133°50′W(105–C). Straddles the BC-Yukon boundary, 20 miles east of Carcross.

With its surrounding mountains, ATLIN Lake is one of the most beautiful in North America. It is 70 miles long and, so far, unpolluted. The Tlinkit Indians who came here for centuries from the Taku River region called it "Ahklen" or "Aht'lah", meaning "Big Water". Dr. G.M. Dawson of the GSC officially adopted the Indian name in 1887.

Probably the first white man to see the lake was Michael Byrne, an explorer working for the Western Union Telegraph Company, who is now believed to have reached the south end of the lake from the Taku River in 1867.

In August 1898, Fritz Miller and Kenneth MacLaren of Juneau found rich placer goldfields on the east side of the lake, second in importance only to the Klondike itself. Of the many people bound to the Klondike via the White and Chilkoot Passes, 10,000 to 15,000 were diverted to this discovery. The White Pass and Yukon Railway, under construction at the time, lost 80% of its workmen almost overnight as they deserted with their tools. Gold has been mined here ever since.

MOUNT AUGUSTA   14,070′   60°19′N 140°27′W (115–B&C). One of the boundary markers in the St. Elias Range.

The mountain was named in 1891 by Professor Israel C. Russell of the USGS after his wife J. AUGUSTA Olmstead Russell. Russell was the first scientist to explore the topography and geology of the St. Elias area with an expedition sponsored jointly by the National Geographical Society and the USGS in 1890–91. Augusta Glacier was named at the same time. (See Russell Col.)

AUSSIE CREEK   64°02′N 137°56′W (116–A). Flows into the Klondike River from the north.

It was originally named Australia Creek in 1897 by Australian miners, of whom there were many in the stampede to the Klondike. The name was changed by W.H. Miller GSC in 1935 to avoid confusion with the earlier-named creek of the same name flowing into the Indian River.

MOUNT AUSTON 64°26'N 136°25'W (116–A). In the south Wernecke Mountains, 12 miles west of Worm Lake.

This was named recently by G.W. Rowley after the late Robert AUSTON, long-time prospector and big-game guide, who discovered and tried to develop copper deposits at nearby Worm Lake.

AUSTRALIA CREEK 63°37'N 138°42'W (115–O&N). A tributary of the Indian River in the south part of the Klondike.

Although Robert Henderson was the first recorded prospector on this stream it is very likely that it was named by other prospectors about 1891–94.

AXEMAN CREEK 64°28'N 138°27'W (116–B). A tributary to the North Klondike River.

In 1968, Dr. Dirk Tempelman-Kluit, GSC, named this creek because of the very old blazed trail he found on it.

BABBAGE RIVER 69°14'N 138°27'W (117–D). Flows north into the Beaufort Sea near Herschel Island.

It was one of the earliest features named in the Yukon Territory when it was found by John Franklin, RN (later Sir), during his second Arctic expedition in 1826. Charles BABBAGE (1792–1871) was a noted British mathematician and a founder of the Astronomical Society.

The Eskimos called it "Cook-Keaktok" or "Rocky River".

BABICHE MOUNTAIN 60°17'N 124°22'W (95–C). In the far south-eastern corner of the territory in a bend of the La Biche River.

This feature was probably named for or by Bobby La Biche, a Mackenzie Indian from Fort Simpson and Fort Liard in the NWT, who trapped in this area for many years.

BABICHE is a northern word used to described raw, or untanned, leather from moose, caribou or deer hides. It is used to string snowshoes and to bind tools, as it shrinks when drying.

MOUNT BACH 61°08'N 136°31'W (115–H). An isolated peak east of the Hutchi Lakes at the head of the Nordenskiold River.

This was named in 1897 after Frank BACH who helped Jack Dalton make a pack trail through here to the Yukon River.

BACK CREEK 62°03'N 137°04'W (115-I). A tributary of Victoria Creek, ten miles southeast of Mount Nansen.

Captain Henry Seymour BACK and his son Frank prospected this creek and named it in 1910. (See Mount Nansen.)

BACKE GLACIER 61°13'N 140°19'W (115-G&F). On the east side of Mount Wood in the St. Elias Range.

In 1971 this mountain was named to honour a pioneer. John BACKE lived and mined for many years in the Mayo district before moving to Haines Junction in 1945 where he built the first lodge. He died in 1970.

BACKHOUSE RIVER 69°36'N 140°32'W (117-C). A small river entering the Beaufort Sea east of Clarence Lagoon.

This was named in 1826 by John Franklin, (later Sir), early British Arctic explorer, after his friend John BACKHOUSE, the Under-Secretary of State for Foreign Affairs of Great Britain at that time.

MOUNT BADHAM 12,625' 60°52'N 139°52'W (115-B&C). At the head of the Donjek Glacier in the St. Elias Range.

This was named in 1919 to honour the memory of Francis Molyneaux BADHAM, a member of various International Boundary Surveys. Enlisting in the Canadian army in 1914, one of the first, he was killed in action in France in 1915.

MOUNT BAIRD 60°19'N 140°30'W (115-B&C). A high peak five miles northwest of Mount Augusta.

Named by Prof. I.C. Russell, USGS, in 1890 after Prof. Spencer Fullerton BAIRD, Secretary of the Smithsonian Institution.

BAKER CREEK 64°00'N 139°37'W (115-O & N). A small tributary of the Yukon River from the east side, eight miles above Dawson.

J.A. BAKER named this stream in 1897-98. He later prospected for many years in the Livingstone Creek and Boswell River districts.

BAKER LAKE 60°12'N 128°28'W (105-A). 12 miles northeast of Watson Lake.

This was named after Jack W. BAKER, the first weather observer and radio-wireless operator for the Yukon Southern Transport Ltd. at Watson Lake. Baker was an all-round bushman and, in 1941 before the Alaska highway was built, he and his wife and daughters were the only white inhabitants of what is now Watson Lake airport.

MOUNT BAKER   62°34′N   140°09′W   (115-J&K). On the west side of the White River, three miles north of Ten Mile Creek.

William J. Peters and Arthur H. Brooks of the USGS named this peak in early June 1898 while on their expedition up the White River and into the Tanana River basin.

It was named after one of their packers, H.B. BAKER.

BALLARAT CREEK   64°17′N   139°39′W   (116-B&C). A tributary of the Chandindu River.

W.F. Woodward named this stream after the famous goldfields in southwestern Australia when he found gold and staked the Discovery claim on 9 March, 1898. The Dawson Mining Recorder allowed another Discovery claim to be recorded on 14 October, 1899 by J.A. Kirkman.

At the time this took place a person staking a claim was allowed 40 days to record it at the Mining Recorder's office for that district. Owing to the lack of maps of the area and to the distance to the recorder's office it sometimes happened that two men found gold on different parts of the same creek at about the same time, unknown to each other. In such a case the Mining Recorder had the option to allow both Discovery claims. Discovery claims were twice the size of regular claims. This happened on Quartz and Dominion Creeks in the Klondike and at several other places in the Yukon. (See Touleary Creek.)

BALLARD   CREEK   63°56′N   136°28′W   (115-P). A tributary to the North McQuesten River.

A prospector named BALLARD lived here from the early 1900's to the 1930's

MOUNT   BARK   61°05′N   137°30′W   (115-H).   15 miles south of Sekulmun Lake.

This mountain was named in 1958 to honour the name of 0-04450 Sub-Lt. Wilfred BARK, RCN, MID. He was born in Toronto, Ontario on 1 March, 1922 and enlisted in the RCN on 13 January, 1942 at Montréal. He served in Canada and at sea and was missing, presumed to have died, on 22 February, 1943.

BARKER CREEK   63°11′N 138°54′W (115-O&N). Tributary to the Stewart River, 20 miles above its mouth.

This was named on 8 November, 1898 by F.M. BARKER who staked the lower half of the Discovery claim that day. Little gold was found and all claims were soon abandoned. In 1903 Louis Marret found good prospects and staked a new Discovery claim. There was another and later stampede on this creek in 1906 but it never lived up to its early promise.

MOUNT BARKER   60°23′N 137°13′W (115-A). Five miles west of Beloud Post.

Edward Herman BARKER was a dredgemaster in the Klondike and Mayo districts as well as for a period in Siberia. He and his partner, Irvine Ray, mined on Haggart Creek in the 1930's and on Shorty Creek about 1946. This mountain was named about 1973.

BARLOW   63°37′N 137°38′W (115-P). At the junction of Clear Creek and the Stewart River.

A small settlement was started here in 1903 when placer mining began on Clear Creek and its tributaries. A steamboat landing, roadhouse and trading post to supply the miners were built. It was abandoned in the 1920's.

BARLOW CITY   63°45′N 137°38′W (115-P). At the junction of Barlow and Clear Creeks.

A small settlement, connected to Barlow by a rough trail, was built here in 1903 with a roadhouse and trading post to supply local miners. It also was abandoned in the 1920's.

MOUNT BARLOW   65°21′N 141°00′W (116-G&F). On the inter-national boundary.

This was named in 1912 by D.D. Cairnes, GSC, after his assistant, F.J. BARLOW, who helped him map the geology along this portion of the Yukon-Alaska boundary that year.

BARNEY CREEK   63°59′N 135°10′W (105-M). A small stream flowing into the Keno Ladue River, north of Keno Hill.

This creek was one of the first to be named in this part of the country when BARNEY Hill found gold in its gravels in 1890.

BARNEY LAKE 60°00′N 127°24′W (95-D). On the Yukon-BC boundary, ten miles west of the Coal River.

Kenneth MacMillan trapped for many years in this area. He made his camp on this lake and named it after his son BARNEY, who was born here.

BARR CREEK 63°04′N 132°48′W (105-N). Tributary to the North MacMillan River.

This was named around 1900 because John BARR had his cabin at the mouth of the stream. Barr came into the country in 1898 and ranged this area for a great many years, trapping and prospecting. Tall, rugged, a supreme bushman, he was known as the "King of the MacMillan Country" by both white and Indian. Courteous and ever-helpful, he was liked and respected by all.

BARWELL LAKE 62°39′N 133°05′W (105-K). 35 miles north of Faro, near the Tay River.

A young Englishman, Charles S.W. BARWELL, became a Dominion Land Surveyor. Coming into the Yukon in the spring of 1897 he worked for the government for several years in many parts of the territory, mostly on claim and route surveys. A friend of his may have given the lake his name.

BATTLE CREEK 62°42′N 138°18′W (155-J & K). A tributary of the Selwyn River.

Pontius Servus Larson and Charles J. Brown found gold here and named the creek on 28 September, 1915. They had just heard the news of heavy fighting in France involving Canadian troops.

BAULTOFF CREEK 62°09′N 140°59′W (115-J & K). A tributary to Beaver Creek.

W.M. BAULTOFF came into the Yukon in 1898 and prospected in the Klondike and western region for many years. He found lode-gold (veins) prospects here in 1903–04. His find led to a minor rush in which other vein deposits were discovered as well as placer gold on some nearby streams in the area.

Baultoff Mountain above the creek was probably named by D.D. Cairnes, GSC, while mapping the geology along the Yukon-Alaska boundary in 1911-12.

BAWN BOY GULCH   64°02'N 135°47'W (106–D). A very small tributary to Dublin Gulch.

Rich silver-lead ore was found here by Robert Fisher in 1916. He gave his Discovery claim an old Celtic name meaning "Cowherd" or "Cowboy". The name was locally corrupted to "Bum Boy" and was so used for many years in the literature and on mining maps. (See Fisher Creek.)

BEAR CREEK   64°02'N 139°15'W (116–B & C). A small stream entering the Klondike River from the south about six miles east of Dawson.

On 24 September, 1896, shortly after George Carmack found the Bonanza gold, Salmo Manberg, too late to find a claim on either Bonanza or Eldorado, had prospected this little stream, finding gold and staking a Discovery claim that day. He and his partners, William Corley and Frank Johnson, who staked Nos. 1 and 2 Below Discovery, called the stream BEAR Creek because of the number of black bears that found them and their camp.

The creek gave up considerable wealth although it was not nearly as rich as Bonanza or Eldorado. A settlement was later established at the mouth of the creek by the Yukon Consolidated Gold Corporation Ltd. and was their main headquarters and shops until the cessation of their operations in 1966, when it was abandoned.

Parks Canada has lately taken over the old camps of the YCGC and is developing a complex to house its headquarters as well as a centre to display methods of mining in the Klondike and a museum of mining machinery.

BEAR RIVER   64°55'N 134°43'W (106–D). A tributary to the Wind River.

This is the translation of an old Loucheaux Indian word meaning "Bear Killed One of Us Here". The full title was shortened over the years.

BEARFEED CREEK   62°11'N 135°08'W (105–L). Tributary to the Little Salmon River.

In 1925 W.E. Cockfield, GSC, gave this name because of the large number of bears attracted to the stream and the extensive berry patches on its banks.

MOUNT BEATON   60°01'N 137°02'W (115–A). An isolated peak seven miles south of Dalton Post.

J.N. Wallace, DLS, named this peak after P. BEATON, a member of his International Boundary Survey party in 1908.

BEAUFORT SEA (117-D). The Beaufort Sea is that part of the Arctic Ocean touching the northern shores of Alaska and the Yukon. It is bounded by Cape Barrow on the west and Prince Patrick Island on the east.

l received its name in 1826 when John Franklin, (later Sir), named it after his friend Captain (later Admiral) Sir Francis BEAUFORT, RN (1774–1857), at that time hydrographer to the British Admiralty. He is best remembered for the scale of wind velocities which he invented, still in general use by all sailors. Several other features on the Arctic slope in Alaska are also named for him.

BEAUVETTE HILL 63°57′N 135°06′W (105–M). The farthest east of the five summits of Keno Hill.

Louis BEAUVETTE (often spelled Bouvette or Bovette) discovered rich silver-lead ore on this hill in 1919. (See Mount Bouvette.)

BEAVER CITY 64°28′N 135°15′W (106–D).At the junction of Carpenter and Settlemier Creeks.

This small settlement was established here in 1923 when silver-lead veins were found in the vicinity. It was a distribution point to supply the prospectors. The ore found was not rich enough to mine in this isolated area and the place was abandoned by 1925. It received its name because many of the prospectors came to the area by way of the BEAVER River. (See Carpenter and Settlemier Creeks.)

BEAVER CREEK 62°27′N 140°38′W (115–J & K). A tributary to Snag Creek.

The whole stream was called Snag Creek until 1902 when this part was renamed BEAVER, leaving the lower part with the original name.

The Beaver Creek area was first prospected by Frederick W. Best, Peter Nelson and William James between 1909 and 1914. Nelson and James went on to discover the rich placer goldfields of the Chisana, Alaska, district just over the boundary, in 1913. This creek was used as a supply route and winter trail between the steamboat landing on the White River and the Chisana diggings.

James B. Hendryx, the western novelist, used this creek as the setting for his series of Yukon short stories and novels concerning Corporal Downey,

Black John Smith, Cushing's Fort and Halfaday Creek which are still read and enjoyed.

The small settlement where the stream crosses the Alaska Highway at mile 1196 (K1914) was started about 1955 and had a post office in 1958. Canada Customs and other businesses have enlarged the community since then. This place is also the scene of the contact point of the northern and southern construction crews building the Alaska Highway. On 20 October, 1942, bulldozer operator Cpl. Refines Sims Jr. of Philadelphia and the 18th US Army Engineers was working south on the section from Fairbanks. He met his opposite number, Pte. Alfred Jalufka of Kennedy, Texas and the 97th Engineers, who was working north from Whitehorse. (See Contact Creek.)

BECKER CREEK 60°14′N 135°10′W (105-D). Tributary to the Wheaton River, 15 miles west of Carcross.

Theodore BECKER was an active prospector for many years in this district and found good mineral showings near this creek in 1906, when he named it. The silver and lead proved uneconomic.

BELIVEAU CREEK 63°48′N 135°29′W (105-M). Tributary to Duncan Creek on the southwest side of Mount Beliveau.

Discovery of good placer gold was made on this stream and the Discovery claim was staked on 7 January, 1902, by Ernest BELIVEAU of Québec, an active prospector who was connected with many of the early finds in the district.

Mount Beliveau was later named for the same man.

MOUNT BELL 6,328′ 60°10′N 135°11′W (105-D). 17 miles west of Carcross.

D.D. Cairnes, GSC, named this feature after his assistant, W.A. BELL of Queen's University, Kingston, Ontario. Bell had done much of the surveying when Cairnes mapped the geology of the Wheaton River district in the summer of 1909.

Dr. Walter Andrew Bell, BSc (Queen's), MA (Cambridge), PhD (Yale) joined the GSC in 1909 and enlisted in the army 1916–19. After the First World War he continued his education and his work with the GSC. He was appointed Chief Palaeontologist in 1938 and Director of the GSC from 1949 to 1953. He was awarded the Logan Medal, the Gold Medal of the Professional Institute of Public Services of Canada, the Inco Medal of the CIMM and the Honorary Degree of LLD from St. Xavier University. He died in 1969.

BELL RIVER   67°17′N 137°46′W (116–P). Flows from the MacDougall Pass to the Porcupine River.

John BELL, Chief Trader of the Hudson's Bay Company, explored this river in 1839 seeking new sources of furs. He was in charge of Fort Good Hope on the Mackenzie River at the time and was married to a daughter of Peter Warren Dease, a famous Arctic explorer of the HBC.

The stream was originally known as the West Rat River and sometimes as Bell's River. R.G. McConnell of the GSC while on his survey of 1887–88, mapped it as the Bell River to avoid confusion with the East Rat River flowing to the Mackenzie from the same source on the Continental Divide. The eastern branch of the Bell is still called the Rat River.

This isolated river was the main trade route into the Yukon for many years, servicing Fort Yukon from 1847 and Rampart House from 1867 to about 1890 when the HBC abandoned the route as uneconomic. Shortly after this time, the company gave up all its business in the territory.

BELOUD CREEK 60°25′N 137°27′W (115–A). Flows into Victoria Creek about 11 miles south of Louise Lake.

B. BELOUD found placer gold here in 1938 and mined till 1939. He found many copper nuggets weighing up to 28 pounds.

BELOUD POST   60°22′N 137°04′W (115–A). 34 miles from Haines Junction at the south end of Dezeadash Lake.

In 1938 B. BELOUD made camp here to explore and mine placer gold. He also began to carry on limited trading. Today it is a resort and lodge.

BENNETT CREEK   63°43′N 136°03′W (115–P). A tributary to Minto Creek from the north.

On 25 May, 1903, Charles E. BENNETT found placer gold and staked the Discovery claim on this stream.

LAKE BENNETT   60°06′N 134°52′W (105–D). Straddles the Yukon – BC boundary below Carcross.

This is "Kusooa"Lake of the Tagish Indians and "Boat" Lake of the early miners, for here it was that they stopped after the back-breaking toil of the Chilkoot Pass. Cutting the spruce trees on the shores of the lake, they laboriously hand-sawed planking and built their boats for the long voyage down the Yukon to the goldfields. Dr. Aurel Krause of the Bremen Geographical Society led an expedition through the Chilkat Pass in 1881 and gave the name "East Kussooa" Lake.

Lt. Frederick Schwatka, US Army, on his expedition in 1883 from Dyea over the Chilkoot Pass and down the length of the Yukon River blithely ignored all previous explorers' and miners' names. He made the first, rough survey of the river's course and named most of the features after superior officers and contemporary and prominent academicians and patrons of exploration. Some of his nomenclature was allowed to remain in use.

He named Lake Bennett after James Gordon BENNETT, editor of the *New York Herald* and a supporter of American exploration. It became one of the best-known names in the north because of its position and part in the stampede to the Klondike in 1897–99. The scene here during that period was one of intense activity as tens of thousands funnelled through the Chilkoot and White Passes, stopping here to organize themselves and build boats for the remainder of the journey to the Klondike. In the winter of 1897–98 the largest tent city in the world was at the head of the lake. Standing now at Carcross bridge it is hard to imagine that over 7,000 craft of all sorts and sizes passed here in 48 hours on 29 and 30 May, 1898, and many more afterwards.

A town was built; sawmills and boat yards sprang up on these shores. Steamboats, their boilers and engines hauled with heart-breaking effort over the passes, were built here in a matter of weeks and, until the White Pass and Yukon Railway was completed to Whitehorse in July 1900, they transported most of the passengers and freight to the territory.

BERNEY CREEK   60°11′N 135°20′W (105–D). Flows into the Wheaton River near Carbon Hill.

This was named about 1906 after Adam BIRNIE (correct spelling), one of a group of English prospectors who were known as "The Tally-ho Boys". (See Tally-ho Mountain.)

BERTHA CREEK   63°47′N 139°30′W (115–O & N). A tributary of the Indian River.

On 11 August, 1898, James E. Fairbairn and George B. Perry found placer gold and staked the Discovery claim, naming the stream. A stampede from Dawson saw the whole creek and its main tributaries staked in a few days. Little gold was found and the creek was soon abandoned. In 1902

Fred E. Envoldsen and his partner recorded a new Discovery claim and a new rush ensued. They renamed the stream "Gladstone" Creek but the Mining Recorder refused the name, retaining the original.

BIG CAMPBELL CREEK   61°46′N 131°07′W (105–G). A tributary of the Pelly River at Pelly Banks.

This was named shortly after 1887 by miners who could not distinguish it from Campbell Creek, as they join into a common stream stream a few yards from the Pelly.

BIG CREEK   62°37′N 137°00′W (115–I). Enters the Yukon four miles below Minto.

This stream, quite a large one, entered the Yukon behind an island which has since been eroded and so was missed by William Ogilvie on his survey in 1887.

A soldier named McMartin entered the Yukon with the Yukon Field Force in 1898, served at Fort Selkirk and took his discharge from the army there in 1899. When he took up the first homestead at the mouth of this stream he asked the local Indians for its name. Their reply was that it was a big creek — by which they meant that it was too large for a creek and was really a river. McMartin filed his application for his homestead under this name, which remains.

BIG CREEK   62°53′N 140°11′W (115–J&K). A tributary to the Indian River.

A staking rush took place on this creek in June 1898 from Dawson, when the whole creek was staked and named.

There are five Big Creeks in the Yukon.

BIG GOLD CREEK   64°01′N 140°42′W (116–B&C). Flows into the Sixtymile River.

This was originally named Gold Creek in 1891 during the rush to the newly-found, Sixtymile River goldfields, the second major gold discovery in the Yukon. Although tributaries of this stream produced good gold, little was found on the main stream itself until, in 1905, John Stockton found the pay-streak and the creek was restaked and renamed "BIG GOLD" Creek.

BIG HORN CREEK   61°09′N 139°24′W (115–G&F).Tributary to the Donjek River.

Edward Benson, with W.R. and W.B. Lamb, named this creek when they found and mined gold on it in August 1914.

BIG KALZAS LAKE   63°15′N   134°35′W   (105-M). Between the Stewart and MacMillan Rivers.

It is highly probable that this is the lake named "Gauche" Lake by Robert Campbell in 1849–50. It is shown as such on the earliest map of the territory. Gauche was one of Campbell's Indian employees. He was an able and reliable man and was noted, even by Campbell, for his clairvoyant powers.

This was one of the lakes which supplied fish for Fort Selkirk.

BIG SALMON   61°53′N   134°55′W   (105-E). At the mouth of Big Salmon River.

This is a now-abandoned settlement on the Yukon. Before the white men came there was an ancient Indian fishing village here. By 1898 it was a steamboat landing, a woodcutter's camp and a supply point for the people up the Big Salmon. For many years it was a station on the Yukon Telegraph.

BIG SALMON LAKE   61°16′N   133°17′W   (105-F). Five miles northwest of Quiet Lake on the Big Salmon River.

This was originally called "Island Lake" by John McCormack, prospector, in 1887. The name was forgotten and changed to the present one sometime about 1898.

BIG SALMON RIVER   61°53′N   134°55′W   (105-E). A major tributary of the Yukon River.

In 1881 a party of four prospectors, including George G. Langtry and Patrick McGlinchy of Juneau, ascended this river 200 miles above its mouth. They were the first white men to explore the stream. Gold prospects were found along the whole length of the river and two of the party won a fair amount of fine gold from the river bars. These men named the river the "Iyon", from the name of the Indian tribe living near its mouth.

In 1883 Lt. F. Schwatka, US Army, rafting down the Yukon, was told by his Chilkat interpreter that the Indian name meant "Big Salmon". The Tagish or local Indian name was "Ta-Tlin-Hini". Schwatka called it the "d'Abbadie" after M. Antoine d'Abbadie, Membre d'Institut and noted French explorer.

Dr. George M. Dawson, GSC, when reviewing his own notes of the

23

locality and William Ogilvie's survey of the river, disallowed the name and retained the original as used by the natives and the miners. Dawson was given much information on the river by John McCormack, a New Brunswick prospector, who had, with three partners, prospected the river in 1887 and had named several features including Quiet Lake.

H.S. Bostock, GSC, while mapping the area in 1935 applied the name "d'Abbadie" to a small branch of the North Fork of the Big Salmon River.

BIG SITDOWN CREEK 65°41′N 141°00′W (116–G&F). Flows into the Kandik River in Alaska.

In 1910 an International Boundary Survey crew was camp-bound by weather for several days, giving the creek its name.

BIG THING CREEK 60°03′N 134°34′W (105–D). Flows into Windy Arm, Tagish Lake.

In 1905 a large, wide vein of gold-and silver-bearing ore was found on the headwaters of this creek. The finder was extremely proud of his discovery. Payable in the first years, it has been worked unprofitably several times since.

MOUNT BILLINGS 6,909′ 61°14′N 128°54′W (105–D). In the Logan Mountains, southeast of Frances Lake.

This was probably named in 1887 by Dr. G.M. Dawson, GSC, after Elkanah BILLINGS (1820–1876), palaeontologist with the Geological and Natural History Survey of Canada.

MOUNT BISEL 61°37′N 137°07′W (115–H). A small hill northeast of the head of Aishihik Lake.

This was named in 1897, probably by J.J. McArthur, GSC, after a member of Jack Dalton's crew.

MOUNT BLACK 7,044′ 61°12′N 134°04′W (105–E). At the headwaters of the South Big Salmon River in the Livingstone Creek area.

George BLACK was born in Woodstock, New Brunswick in 1872. He qualified as a lawyer but soon was involved in the Klondike Gold Rush. He came into the Yukon in 1897. He had little success in the Klondike area and tried other places. In 1898 he and his partner found good gold on Livingstone Creek. However, in 1901 he was forced to get to Dawson by working as a deckhand on a riverboat.

In Dawson he again engaged in the practice of criminal law. He also became active in politics. He served three terms on the Yukon Council (1905–12) as a member from the Klondike Riding and then represented South Dawson.

In February 1912 he was appointed Commissioner of the Yukon Teritory. He served with distinction, his term being marked by progressive reforms in the civil service, increased road building and better labour and mining laws. He and C.A. Thomas, Manager of the Yukon Gold Company, drove the first automobile from Whitehorse to Dawson in December 1912.

He was given leave of absence in 1916 to enlist for service in the First World War. He formed the Yukon Infantry Company and raised 226 men whom he led to England in January 1917. They were reformed into the 17th Canadian Machine Gun Company and served with distinction. Black was severely wounded in the Battle of Amiens in France during August 1917.

Returning to the Yukon, he was elected in 1921 to sit in parliament as member from the Yukon. He represented the Conservative party. He sat continuously until forced to retire due to ill-health caused by war wounds. His wife, Martha Louise Black, ran in his stead and was elected. He recovered and was again elected in 1940, serving two terms as Speaker of the House of Commons. On his retirement in 1949 he returned to Dawson and his law practice. In August 1951 he was appointed a member for life of the King's Privy Council for Canada, by Prime Minister Louis St. Laurent. He entered politics once more in the election of 1953, losing to J. Aubrey Simmons, a Liberal. He died in Vancouver, BC on 23 September, 1965, at the age of 94.

George Black, BA, LLB, PC was a capable, unassuming, well-liked man. It would be hard to find a more worthy Canadian to honour with a permanent landmark memorial.

The mountain was mapped by H.S. Bostock, GSC, in 1935 and is the highest point in the Big Salmon Range. He also suggested the name, as he was a long-time friend of George Black.

BLACK HILLS CREEK   63°15′N 138°41′W (115–O&N). A tributary to the Stewart River.

One of the earliest miners' names in the territory, this creek was apparently named about 1883–85 by miners who had been in the gold rush to the Black Hills of South Dakota in the late 1870's. Although prospected earlier, payable gold was not found here until July 1898 when a stampede took place and the whole creek was staked in a few days. (See Rosebud Creek.)

BLACKSTONE RIVER   65°51'N 137°15'W (116-H). Tributary to the Peel River.

Indians many years ago named this isolated river because of the deep, extensive seams of coal (lignite) on both sides of a canyon on the stream.

BLANCHARD RIVER 60°02'N 136°53'W (115-A). Crosses the Yukon-BC boundary and joins the Tatshenshini River near Dalton Post.

This was originally called the "Kleheela" River by the NWMP who were here in 1898. They learned the name from the local Indians. It was renamed about 1915 after G. BLANCHARD Dodge, DLS, who was born in Halifax, Nova Scotia, in 1874 and educated at Dalhousie University. He served with the Topographical Survey of Canada from 1900 to 1932. He was in charge of survey parties that delineated much of the Yukon-BC boundary and died in Ottawa in 1945.

BLOOMFIELD LAKE   69°12'N 138°36'W (117-D). A small lake near Phillips Bay on the Arctic coast.

This lake was named in 1958 to honour the memory of B-67396 Pte. George Page BLOOMFIELD, MID. Born in Toronto, Ontario, on 24 August, 1914, he enlisted in the Canadian army at Toronto on 5 March, 1940, and served in Canada, Iceland, Great Britain and France. He was killed in action at Dieppe, France, on 19 August, 1942.

BLUEBERRY CREEK   63°05'N 139°11'W (115-O&N). A small tributary of Thistle Creek.

During the Klondike Gold Rush there were many smaller rushes and stampedes to other areas in the Yukon. One of these was the stampede to Thistle Creek in late 1898. A syndicate of Swedes from Minnesota, who called themselves the "Monitors", staked, named and unsuccessfully worked on this creek that year. (See Monitor Creek.)

MOUNT BOMPAS   10,027' 61°24'N 140°36'W (115-G&F). On the west side of Mount Constantine in the St. Elias Range.

This was named in 1918 to perpetuate the name of the most remarkable churchman in Yukon history, the Right Reverend William Carpenter BOMPAS, DD, first Bishop of Athabaska (1874–1884), first Bishop of the

Mackenzie River (1884–1891), and first Bishop of Selkirk (Yukon) (1891–1906). He was born in London, England, in 1834 and died, still serving at Carcross, in 1906.

His father, Charles Carpenter Bompas, Serjent-at-Law and eminent advocate before the British Bar, was said to be the original of Charles Dickens' Serjent Buzfuz in *Pickwick Papers.*

William Bompas first entered the Yukon in 1873, visiting the Indians at LaPierre House from the Mackenzie River. In 1874 he went to Fort Yukon to encourage and enlarge his Anglican Church missionary services to the natives. He spent 1891 to 1892 at Rampart House on the Porcupine River and having heard of the needs of the miners and natives in the Fortymile district, he set up a mission there. (See Buxton Mission.) He established missions at Fort Selkirk and later at Carcross and, in 1897, erected the original St. Paul's Church in Dawson. His greatest efforts were always for the native people and his school for Indian children at Carcross is still continuing in spirit, although it is neither church-run nor for Indians only.

He served for 43 years in the Mackenzie and Yukon, returning only once to England in all that time.

BONANZA CREEK   64°03′N 139°25′W (115–B&C). A tributary to the Klondike River about three miles east of Dawson.

This is one of the richest and most famous gold-bearing streams in the world. The name was a synonym for immediate and vast wealth. The word BONANZA was in former times used by Spanish miners and *conquistadors* to denote rich ore deposits.

On 16 August, 1896, George Carmack, Skookum Jim Mason and Tagish (later called Dawson) Charlie found rich, coarse gold in the gravels of this stream when they were returning from an inspection of Robert Henderson's diggings on Gold Bottom Creek. On 17 August, 1896, George Carmack staked the Discovery claim, wrote the name "Bonanza" on a piece of bark and nailed it to his discovery post.

On 22 August, on a hillside opposite claim No. 17 Below Discovery, a miners' meeting was held by 25 men, all those who had staked claims on the creek to that time. They agreed to a rough survey to avoid further confusion in claim staking; they elected one of their number, David McKay, to be Mining Recorder and they confirmed the name of the creek as Bonanza. It had previously been called "Rabbit" Creek by the miners and "Tha-Tat-Dik", meaning "Muffler" Creek, by the local Indians.

This is the creek that started a controversy which has never been settled to this day. Did Carmack on this creek or Henderson on Gold Bottom Creek first discover the Klondike gold? Henderson, after 1901, claimed this honour for the rest of his life, backed by local Canadian officials, and was finally awarded a pension and other concessions and proclaimed the discoverer by the Canadian government. Carmack never made any claim other than that he had found the rich gold of Bonanza, but his cause was taken up by the predominant American element in the Yukon and else-where. The Canadian government, in 1962, erected a bronze plaque on Carmack's Discovery claim giving the honour to Carmack, Skookum Jim and Tagish Charlie. Oddly enough, it has never been established just who was there at the discovery. Kate Carmack, George's wife, and the boy Patsy Henderson both claimed to have been the first one to find the gold. No matter who found the gold, one thing is certain: the Bonanza Creek find touched off the Klondike stampede.

From 1897 to 1905, as the whole creek was being mined, a number of reports were made of finding older, earlier workings.

Bonanza was phenomenally productive for a length of nearly 12 miles. Counting Eldorado Creek, a tributary, extremely rich gold deposits were mined for nearly 17 miles. A remarkable fact of this discovery was that few of the original claims were staked by experienced miners. The creek had been cursorily prospected by a number of prospectors as early as 1883 and passed by. At the time of Carmack's find nearly all the miners in the Yukon were busy on the productive creeks at the head of the Fortymile River and on the Sixtymile River diggings. As a result, when Carmack made the announcement of his find at Fortymile, only the local tradesmen and lay-abouts had the first news. With newly-arrived prospectors he met travelling up and down the river, these comprised the men who staked Bonanza and Eldorado. Many of them were inexperienced and when the true miners arrived on the scene and evaluated the find they quickly bought claims from the *cheechakos* (newcomers) at low prices.

The first mining on Bonanza was done by hand; pick, shovel and fire were used to thaw and gouge out the frozen gold-bearing gravels that lay above bedrock. This was the period from 1897–1900 that was the hey-day of the Klondike, when the suddenly rich, free-wheeling, big-spending miners made Dawson the "Paris of the North", where gold dust could purchase anything.

Then, as steam-thawing and machinery became available, larger and poorer quantities of gravel were worked, still yielding large profits. Finally, large capital was interested and millions of dollars were invested in large-scale water supply (flumes and ditches stretching in places for over 50 miles), dredges and large hydraulic equipment. In this, the final and longest phase of mining, nearly all the gravel of the valley bottoms was processed. Huge quantities carrying values in gold as low as 40 cents to the cubic yard were handled, still at a profit. This phase lasted until 1966 when the last dredge shut down. Every year since, several people still mine the creek in a small way.

It is impossible to arrive at the correct figure for the total value of the gold taken from this stream but the estimate for the Klondike for 68 years is well over $200,000,000; most of this was mined when gold was valued at $20 per ounce.

BONNET PLUME RIVER 65°56'N 134°57'W (106-E). A large tributary to the Peel River.

Andrew Flett, "BONNET PLUME", was a Loucheaux Indian chief. He had worked for many years as an interpreter for the HBC. He and his band made their home on this river. During the Klondike Gold Rush many of the stampeders from Edmonton made their way through this part of the country. Bonnet Plume gave assistance to many of these unfortunates caught by winter on the trail to Dawson and they named the river after him.

The Loucheaux themselves called it "The Black Sands" River, from the large amounts of black magnetite sand (iron ore) found in its bed.

BONNEVILLE LAKES 60°37'N 135°18'W (105-D). Three small lakes on the west side of Fish Lake, southwest of Whitehorse.

In 1948 these lakes were honoured with the name of A-61080 L/Cpl. Hector BONNEVILLE MM. He was born in Ottawa on 5 June, 1912 and enlisted in the Canadian army at Windsor, Ontario on 10 August 1942. He served in Canada, Great Britain and the Central Mediterranean Theatre. He was killed in action during the attack on the Gothic Line in Italy on 31 August, 1944.

BORDEN CREEK 63°31'N 140°28'W (115-O&N). A small tributary to Matson Creek in the Sixtymile River area.

BORONITE CITY 62°23'N 136°37'W (115-I). A short-lived settlement at the mouth of Williams Creek on the banks of the Yukon River.

This was built in 1907 to service the many prospectors on the new, hardrock copper finds on Williams and adjacent creeks. The WP&YR laid up their steamboat *Whitehorse* here for the winter of 1907–08. About 20 people lived here, running a store, hotel and a blacksmith shop. No commercial copper deposits were found and the settlement was abandoned by 1909.

BORTHWICK LAKE 61°28′N 137°27′W (115–H). Lies between Aishihik and Sekulmun Lakes.

In 1956 this lake was named to perpetuate the memory of A-105676 Pte. George Ross BORTHWICK MID who was born 18 June, 1923 at Thedford, Ontario. He enlisted in the Canadian army at London, Ontario on 6 January, 1943. Serving in Canada, Great Britain and Northwest Europe, he was killed in action on 29 July, 1944.

BOSWELL RIVER 61°03′N 134°13′W (105–E). Tributary to the Teslin River.

This was named by miners in 1887 after the two BOSWELL brothers, Thomas and George, of Peterborough, Ontario, who were the first to prospect the Teslin River. The Boswells were among the first prospectors in the Yukon watershed; records show that Thomas came over the Chilkoot Pass in the spring of 1882 and George came either then or the following year. They were active men and among the first to find the rich bar gold on the Stewart River at Chapman's Bar. A major tributary of the Stewart was given their name at the time. (See Nadaleen River.)

They ranged widely across the Yukon and Alaska for years, always in the forefront of the pioneers. Thomas lost a leg to a grizzly bear in Alaska in 1891 but he and his brother still joined in the Klondike stampede.

BOSSUYT LAKE 66°38′N 135°13′W (106–L). East of Road River.

Charles BOSSUYT was a Yukon Councillor for North Dawson 1912–15. His name is used as the title on the new topographical map of this area, printed in 1973. His name was proposed by Gordon McIntyre.

BOUCHER CREEK 64°01′N 140°20′W (116–B&C). Flows north into Sixtymile River.

Felix BOUCHER, of Québec, had prospected the Sixtymile country in 1891 when the first discoveries were made. At that time this stream was staked and called Larsen Creek and Larsen worked on it with fair results until he was called away in 1896 by news of far richer ground in the Klondike. The creek was abandoned.

In July 1902 Felix Boucher and his partner, James Huot, returned, prospected and staked a new Discovery claim. The Mining Recorder renamed the stream after Boucher. (See Huot Gulch.)

BOUTELLIER CREEK 60°59′N 138°13′W (115–B&C). Tributary to Christmas Creek, southwest of Kluane Lake.

Charles BOUTELLIER, of Québec, prospected and mined on this stream in 1903 when it received its name. He spent many years in the Yukon, prospecting, cutting wood for riverboats, and trapping; in 1914 he owned and operated a roadhouse at Lower Laberge.

MOUNT BOUVETTE 65°17′N 138°37′W (116–G&F). South of the Ogilvie River.

In 1973 this feature was named by the Topographical Surveys Branch as a map sheet title for their new series. Louis BOUVETTE was a pioneer prospector of the district; he found the first of the rich silver-lead ore deposits in 1919 on Keno Hill while hunting mountain sheep. (See Beauvette Hill.)

BOVE ISLAND 60°07′N 134°32′W (105–D). The island in Tagish Lake at the mouth of Windy Arm.

Lt. F. Schwatka, US Army, in 1883 renamed Tagish Lake "Bove" after Lt. BOVE of the Italian navy, who had served with the Austro-Hungarian Expedition of 1872–74.

Dr. G.M. Dawson, GSC, in 1887 gave Tagish Lake its original name and left Bove's name on this island.

BOW CREEK 62°18′N 137°13′W (115–I). Tributary to Seymour Creek near Mt. Freegold.

P.F. Guder of Carmacks assisted the GSC in this area in the summer of 1930. While travelling this stream he commented on its shape, almost a perfect arc, whence its name.

Previously, Captain H.S. Back had named the stream "Rogers" Creek after one of his men in the summer of 1917. They never worked the creek and the name had been forgotten. (See Back, Guder, Nansen and Seymour Creeks.)

BRABAZON GLACIER 61°21′N 140°37′W (115–G&F). Feeds into the huge Klutlan Glacier west of Mt. Bompas.

Alfred James BRABAZON, DLS, was in charge of surveys for the International Boundary Survey Commission from 1895–1906 and again in 1909. This glacier was named in his memory in 1925.

BRADEN'S CANYON   62°50'N 136°51'W (115-I). On the Pelly River about 15 miles below Pelly Crossing.

A trapper of this name settled here in 1898 with his native wife and children. They trapped, and for many years supplied cordwood to the riverboats.

BRAEBURN   60°31'N 135°50'W (105-E).

A roadhouse was established here in 1899 on the old winter trail from Whitehorse to Dawson. A small settlement remained here until the 1950's.

MOUNT BRAGG   65°38'N 140°18'W (116-G&F). West of the Porcupine River.

T.G. BRAGG was the principal of the Dawson Public School during 1904–05. In 1973 his name was used to denote the new topographical map sheet of this area.

BRAINE CREEK   64°22'N 134°59'W (106-D). Tributary to the Beaver River in the Wernecke Mountains.

This was named about 1898 after Frank BRAINE who lived in this area at the time. Braine Pass at the head of the creek was discovered and used by Braine in journeys to Fort Good Hope on the Mackenzie River. (See Lansing.)

MOUNT BRATNOBER   6,313' 60°44'N 136°40'W (115-A). In the bend of the Dezeadash River about ten miles southwest of Champagne.

This mountain was named in July 1897 by J.J. McArthur, DLS, a Canadian government surveyor who made an extremely cursory survey of the Dalton Trail that year. He was assisted by Jack Dalton and Henry BRATNOBER, who was one of Dalton's axmen at the time.

Henry Bratnober, of San Francisco, played more than an ordinary part in the Yukon. He was an accredited riverboat captain and had prospected and mined widely in the western United States. He took part in the Klondike rush, was a partner with Dalton during 1901–04 prospecting in the Alsek and White River regions, built and captained the riverboat *Ella* in 1905 and was operating it on the Tanana River in 1910. He was an agent and "mining expert" for the Rothschilds for many years in their mining ventures in the north.

BREFALT CREEK   63°55′N 135°30′W (105–M). A small creek flowing into Flat Creek from Galena Hill near Elsa.

This was named in the late 1920's after C. BREFALT, who first found high-grade, silver-lead ore here.

MOUNT   BRENNER   64°27′N 138°46′W (116–B&C).   Five   miles northwest of Tombstone Mountain, in the Klondike district.

This was named after Otto BRENNER, of London, Ontario, pioneer Yukoner and an active and successful prospector and miner.

BREWER   CREEK   63°11′N 138°59′W (115–O&N).   A   tributary   to Barker Creek.

In June 1906, Charles N. Graham staked a Discovery claim here when he found workable gold. In 1898 a prospector named BREWER had tried but failed.

BREWER   LAKE   60°40′N 133°26′W (105–C).   12   miles   north   of Johnson's Crossing.

Joseph BREWER, pioneer trapper and prospector, made his home on this lake for many years.

BREWERY CREEK   64°01′N 138°01′W (116–B). Tributary to the South Klondike River.

Until 1965 this was known as O'Brien Creek. It had been named in 1897–98. The name was changed to avoid conflict with one of a similar name in the White River district which had been named later.

Thomas W. O'Brien came to the Yukon in 1886 and mined in the Fortymile diggings. He gained business interests in Fortymile and in Circle City. He was an early staker in the Klondike and is said to have carried the first news of the find to Circle City. He and J.M. Wilson of the ACC arrived there on 15 December, 1896, and their tidings started a stampede to Dawson which left Circle City virtually deserted. He was one of the founders of the Yukon Order of Pioneers at Fortymile on 1 December, 1894.

Becoming prominent in the business and political life of Dawson and the territory, he built the first brewery in 1898 and, in the same year was instrumental, with Big Alex McDonald, in establishing the first electrical plant and telephone system in Dawson. He owned the first newspaper, the *Yukon Midnight Sun*, a pro-government paper. He was the promoter and financier of the Klondike Mines Railway which ran from Dawson to Sulphur Springs and he sought federal aid to extend it to Fort McLeod in British Columbia.

He served several terms as a Yukon Councillor in the early 1900's. The Liberal Party in the Yukon was known for a number of years as the "Steam Beers" because of O'Brien's prominence in their affairs.

Thomas O'Brien died in Dawson on 24 August, 1916.

MOUNT BRIMSTON 65°33′N 139°06′W (116-G&F). In the Nahoni Range, north of the Ogilvie River.

In 1973 the Topographical Surveys Branch named this feature after George BRIMSTON, former Klondiker and for many years Sheriff of the Yukon. He was also a past president of the YOOP. (See Brimstone Gulch.)

BRIMSTONE GULCH 63°43′N 138°51′W (115-O&N). Flows into Sulphur Creek in the south Klondike district.

This short creek was staked and named in late 1897 by George BRIMSTON. The name was a play on his own and that of Sulphur Creek. By November 1898 he was working his claim and had built and was operating a roadhouse at the mouth of this stream. He worked the stream for a number of years before moving to Dawson.

BRITANNIA CREEK 62°52′N 138°41′W (115-J&K). Tributary to the Yukon River.

This was named by E.L.C. de la Pole and C.M. Printz who staked the Discovery claim on 18 April, 1911.

MOUNT BRITISH COLUMBIA 10,200′ 60°57′N 140°57′W (115-B&C). Near the Yukon-Alaska boundary in the western St. Elias Range.

This is one of the group of mountains named to celebrate Canada's Centennial Year in 1967. (See Centennial Range.)

BRITISH MOUNTAINS 68°50′N 140°20′W (117-C). Range of mountains which crosses the Yukon-Alaska boundary 40 miles south of the Arctic coast.

These were named by John Franklin, (later Sir), the famous English Arctic explorer, in 1826, in honour of his native land.

BRITTON RIDGE 5,286′ 62°22′N 138°51′W (115-J&K). The high ridge between the Nisling and Klotassin Rivers.

This hill was named in 1973 after J.C. BRITTON, a pioneer prospector and miner in the region for many years.

MOUNT BROOKE 10,791′ 61°30′N 140°57′W (115-G&F). Near the Yukon-Alaska boundary, north of the Klutlan Glacier in the St. Elias Range.

This was dedicated in 1918 to the memory of 8186 Pte. William BROOKE. He was born 15 August, 1893, at Huntingdon, Québec and enlisted in the 2nd Battalion CEF on 13 September, 1914 — one of the very first. He died a prisoner of war in Germany on 13 March, 1917.

BROOKS ARM 61°28′N 139°02′W (115-G&F). A large bay on the north end of Kluane Lake.

This bay received its name in 1945 from Hugh S. Bostock, GSC, when he was mapping the geology of the area that year. Formerly called "Little Arm", he changed it to commemorate Alfred Hulse BROOKS (1871-1924), who served the USGS in Alaska from 1898 to 1923. Brooks travelled this way on an expedition from Pyramid Harbour to Eagle, Alaska, in 1899 and wrote the first geological report about the area. He was appointed chief of the USGS in Alaska in 1903 and later appointed Chief Alaskan Geologist. He was the Chief Geologist for the American Expeditionary Forces in the First World War. He contributed greatly and widely to the knowledge and mapping of Alaskan geology.

Brooks Creek and Brooks Valley were named later.

BROOKS BROOK 60°25′N 133°12′W (105-C). A small stream flowing into Teslin Lake about mile 829 (K1326) of the Alaska Highway.

This little stream was named in 1942 by black troops of the US Army Engineers. They constructed this section of the highway and named the stream after their company officer, Lt. BROOKS.

BROWN LAKE 60°19′N 124°39′W (95-C). In the southeast corner of the Yukon Territory.

In 1963 this lake was given the name of V-19206 Leading Seaman David Henry BROWN, MID. He was born 30 April, 1916, at Perth, Ontario and enlisted in the RCNVR on 20 November, 1940, at Windsor, Ontario. He served in Canada and was missing, presumed to have been killed in action on the high seas, 7 May, 1944.

MOUNT BROWN 60°01′N 135°03′W (105-D). On the east side of Munroe Lake.

This hill was probably used as a survey point by A. St. Cyr, DLS, in 1901 while surveying the Yukon-BC boundary and named after one of his crew.

BROWNS CREEK 64°19′N 140°53′W (116-B&C). A tributary to the Fortymile River.

In late 1886 or early 1887, "Shoemaker" BROWN found and mined gold on this stream, giving it his name. When the rush to the district started in the summer of 1887 he sold his claim for $140.00 and a Winchester rifle, "Because the country is getting too damn crowded."

In the spring of 1893 J.A. Howard and Frank Montgomery rafted logs down the Fortymile River from Sam Patch's Bar to Brown's Creek. They built and ran a roadhouse to service the traffic between Fortymile and the new diggings in the Sixtymile country as the trail between the two ran along this stream. They called it the Brown's Creek Roadhouse.

The Fortymile country lay dormant after 1896, most miners being in the Klondike. By 1906 the old goldfields were again being prospected and in September that year George L. Gates staked a Discovery claim on the abandoned creek. The Mining Recorder thought the claim was on Bear Creek (now Bruin) and decided to change the name, as there were too many Bear Creeks in the country. He named it Gates Creek and the mistake was allowed to stand, although it was referred to by both names on different maps.

In December 1958 the Geographical Board rectified the error and restored the name Browns Creek to the stream.

BRYANT CREEK 64°01′N 139°32′W (116-B&C). Flows into the Yukon six miles above Dawson.

J.H. Howell of Seattle found gold in the gravels of this stream and staked the Discovery claim on 8 September, 1897. When recording it, he named it after his schoolmate, three-time presidential candidate, William Jennings Bryan. The "t" was added in error by the Mining Recorder.

BUCKLANDS HILLS 69°17′N 139°40′W (117-D). The first range of hills on the Arctic coast facing Herschel Island.

36

These were originally named the Buckland Range by John Franklin in 1826 after Professor William BUCKLAND (1784–1865), an English geologist and clergyman, and Dean of Westminster in 1845.

BUFFALO MOUNTAIN 5,650' 61°54'N 136°46'W (115-H). 30 miles northeast of Aishihik Lake.

This was named by C.W. Rowley, as some of the last buffalo in the Yukon ranged here one winter. Buffalo have since been re-introduced into the area.

BULL CREEK 61°32'N 140°22'W (115-F). A tributary of St. Clare Creek, east of the Klutlan Glacier.

This was named in the 1900's by Tom Dickson, 98'er, ex-NWMP and noted big-game guide in the area around Kluane and the White River region for many years. He had killed a number of very fine caribou on this stream.

BULLION CITY 60°57'N 138°36'W (115-B&C). On Slim's River, five miles from Kluane Lake.

This was a short-lived mining camp, established in 1903 to serve the local miners. A post office was opened in 1905. The name was changed to Kluane in the following year, and the settlement lasted only a few more years.

BULLION CREEK 60°58'N 138°36'W (115-B&C). A tributary to Slim's River, five miles from Kluane Lake.

On 28 September, 1903, Frank Altemose, Joseph W. Smith, Fred Ater and Morley Bones found rich placer gold on this creek. J.W. Smith made the discovery. They took out 40 ounces of coarse gold in a few hours but never again found as rich a pocket. This discovery in a new area started a major rush to the district which continued to the fall of 1905. As many as 8,000–10,000 people were in the area.

MOUNT BURGESS 66°02'N 139°38'W (116-J&K). In the Ogilvie Mountains near Miner River.

William Ogilvie, DLS, named this peak in April 1888 after A.M. BURGESS, the Deputy Minister of the Interior from 1883–97, who had been extremely helpful in organizing Ogilvie's and Dawson's 1887–88 expedition to the Yukon.

BURKE CREEK   60°52'N 130°36'W (105-B). A tributary to the Liard River south of Wasson Lake.

In February 1936, J.A. Jeckell, Controller of the Yukon Territory and Livingstone Wernecke, of the Treadwell Yukon Mining Co., requested this name. Captain E.J.A. (Paddy) BURKE, formerly of the Royal Flying Corps, died near here.

While flying in to a mining property he crashed on the frozen Liard River. Being uninjured, he and his two companions, Emil Kading and Robert Martin, decided to walk north on the Liard River to Junkers Lake where they had established a food and fuel cache. Deep snow and unseasonably cold weather (it was 11 October, 1930,) together with the lack of snowshoes made travel extremely difficult. Burke died of exhaustion and exposure on 20 November, the first aircraft pilot to die in the Yukon.

Pilot Everett Wasson found the party after an extensive search. (See Wasson Lake and Junkers Lake)

The oddest part of the story is that although Burke's name has been officially given to a creek in the vicinity near where he landed, the exact creek has not yet been located. Here is an official name with no place.

Burke is buried in Atlin, BC.

BURNHAM CREEK   63°43'N 138°32'W (115-O&N). A tributary to Dominion Creek from the east, eight miles above its mouth.

On 26 January, 1898, John Hafler staked the Discovery claim on this creek. He was probably one of the group which included Major Frederick R. BURNHAM DSO, a noted American scout and frontiersman. Burnham distinguished himself in the American west and in the Matabele Wars in Southern Africa. He came into the Klondike in 1897 and was active in this area. After leaving the Yukon he returned to South Africa as Chief of Scouts for the British Forces and served with great distinction.

BURWASH CREEK   61°30'N 139°16'W (115-G&F). Flows to the Kluane River near Kluane Lake.

This was named on 28 May, 1904, by the well-known team of prospectors, Frank Altemose, Joseph W. Smith, Fred Ater and Morley Bones. On that day they discovered the rich, gold placers of this creek and named the stream after their friend, the Mining Recorder at Silver City, Lachlin Taylor BURWASH. The pay streak of the creek was elusive and sporadic, and consistent deposits were not found until 1909. The creek since then has produced steadily up to the present.

Burwash, born in Coburg, Ontario, was the son of the Rev. J. Burwash, Chancellor of Victoria College in Toronto in 1896. He came to the Yukon in 1897 as a prospector for the NAT&TC — but soon was appointed Mining Recorder at Stewart City in 1900, at Silver City in 1903 and later was named Government Mining Engineer and Mines Inspector for the territory. He served in the First World War in the 1st Pioneer Battalion, CEF from 1915–19, rising to the rank of major. In later years he explored much of Arctic Canada for the Department of the Interior. He died in 1940.

BURWASH LANDING 61°22′N 139°00′W (115–G&F). On the northwestern shore of Kluane Lake at mile 1095 of the Alaska Highway.

This small settlement was started in 1904, shortly after the discovery of Burwash Creek, by the brothers Louis and Eugene Jacquot who were from Alsace-Lorraine. It was a supply centre, serviced by boat, for the miners on the various creeks in the district. The brothers named it after their friend Lachlin Taylor BURWASH. It later became the supply point for the gold rush to the Chisana River placer fields in Alaska during 1913–15.

The Jacquots, who originally were miners, homesteaded here and, after the First World War and for many years, became outstanding big-game guides and outfitters.

MOUNT BUSH 60°19′N 135°05′W (105–D). The ridge between Perkins and Schnabel Creeks.

This was probably named in 1898–99 after Charles J. BUSH, pioneer prospector in the Wheaton River region and a partner of William Schnabel. They discovered and owned the Nevada Mines property on this ridge.

BUTLER GULCH 63°58′N 140°33′W (115–O&N). Tributary to Boucher Creek in the Sixtymile district.

This was named by a man called BUTLER who staked the Discovery claim in July 1902 during the stampede to the new gold discoveries on Boucher Creek. His full name is not known.

BUTTLE CREEK 62°11′N 133°20′W (105–K). Flows into the Pelly River near Faro.

Roy E. BUTTLE was a trapper, prospector and trader who lived on this stream for many years from the early 1900's to the 1920's and had a trading post at Ross River in the 1930's.

BUXTON MISSION 64°26′N 140°33′W (116-B&C). About one-half mile above the town of Fortymile on the Yukon River.

In 1887, Bishop Bompas of the Anglican Church, in response to requests from miners and natives, sent the Rev. J.W. Ellington to Fortymile to start an Anglican mission. The sum of £100 had been contributed for this purpose by T. Fowell BUXTON of Easneye, Ware, England.

Ellington, a young man and the son of missionaries, was evidently humourless and quite incompatible with the rough and ready miners. They found him an easy butt for their practical jokes, many of them crude. His health and his mind gave way and he was soon returned to Winnipeg.

The mission was unoccupied until Bishop Bompas re-opened it in 1892. Its main purpose was always the education of Indian children. He stayed here until 1896 when Fortymile was almost completely abandoned because of the Klondike discovery. He moved to Dawson in early 1897 and built the first church there, St. Paul's.

An attempt was made by Bompas to change the name of Fortymile to Buxton but the miners refused to use the name. The mission is separated from the town by a deep ravine, flooded in high water and crossed by a bridge, which led some to describe it as being on an island in the Yukon.

CABIN CREEK 60°15′N 129°08′W (105-A). Tributary to the Liard River just below the Frances River.

In 1949 the Board on Geographical Names recorded this name, as the cabin and the grave of an old trapper named Stewart are at the mouth of the stream.

CABIN CREEK 60°44′N 130°16′W (105-B). Tributary to the upper Liard River.

In the winter of 1874–75 miners from the Cassiar found and mined gold on this stream, the first payable gold ever found in the Yukon Territory. They built cabins here, giving the stream its name. (See Sayyea and Scurvy Creeks.)

CACHE LAKE 61°13′N 139°04′W (115-G&F). At the headwaters of Halfbreed Creek.

This small lake was named in the summer of 1973 by the personnel of the Yukon Wilderness and Scenic Study Group who left supplies here.

CADZOW LAKE 67°34′N 138°58′W (116-O&N). On the south side of the Porcupine River, 25 miles east of Old Crow.

In 1897 Daniel CADZOW, a Scot, left Edmonton for the Klondike. He took the Mackenzie—Peel River—Rat River route and reached Dawson in the summer of 1899, only to find the Klondike rush was over. Soon afterwards he returned to the northern rivers and settled at Rampart House. He set up as a small trader in 1903 or 04. After the smallpox epidemic of 1911-12 the post was abandoned and Cadzow moved with the Indians and built anew at Old Crow. He married an Indian woman. His trading post, supplied by water from Dawson, was the only base of supplies in the northern Yukon for many years. His family is still in the north.

CAESAR LAKES   61°26′N 127°54′W (95-E). At the headwaters of the Coal River.

On 20 August, 1968, Dr. H. Gabrielse, GSC, gave this name to these small lakes for an Indian family of this name who had lived here for many years.

MOUNT CAIRNES   9,150′ 60°52′N 138°16′W (115-B&C). In the Kluane Range, 15 miles southeast of Kluane Lake.

This mountain was named in the 1920's for D.D. CAIRNES, GSC, (1879-1917), noted pioneer Yukon geologist who explored and mapped much of this area. His explorations added enormously to the knowledge of the Yukon's geology.

Cairnes graduated from Queen's University in Kingston, Ontario. He worked in the Yukon from 1905 to 1917 when he died at the age of 37 in Ottawa.

MOUNT CAIRNES   64°26′N 138°18′W (116-B&C). In the Ogilvie Mountains at the headwaters of the North Klondike River.

This was named in July 1968 by Dr. D. Tempelman-Kluit, GSC, while mapping this area. He greatly admired the work done previously by D.D. CAIRNES, GSC. (See above.)

There is also a Mount Cairnes in BC named for the same man.

CALAMITES CREEK   65°56′N 134°29′W (106-E). Tributary to the Peel River.

About 1944 Dr. Stelck, GSC, found many of these fossil plants in the rock along this stream.

CALDER CREEK   63°47′N 139°07′W (115-O&N). A small tributary to Quartz Creek in the Klondike.

This was named by the first discoverer of gold on the creek, Alex

CALDER, who staked on 21 October, 1897, starting a staking rush to Quartz Creek. He was a partner of "Big Alex" McDonald. From Cape Breton, Nova Scotia, he came into the Yukon in 1896 and was one of the lucky men to stake a claim on Eldorado Creek. He died on 30 March, 1900 at Fort Selkirk.

CALEDONIA CREEK 62°42′N 140°05′W (115-J&K). Tributary to the Donjek River, one mile below Donjek City.

On 1 November, 1913, David Edwards and his partner Burnett Middleton discovered placer gold on this stream, staked the Discovery claim and probably named it after their native Scotland.

CALIFORNIA CREEK 64°01′N 140°21′W (116-B&C). Tributary to the Sixtymile River.

This creek was named in 1892 when coarse gold was first found in the Sixtymile district. In 1905 a Klondiker named Leonard found payable gold on one of the small tributaries which he named after himself. In June 1905 further finds caused another stampede and the whole stream was named Leonard Creek. The new name reverted to California Creek when the excitement died down and most of the stakers abandoned the stream.

CAMERON GULCH 64°06′N 135°03′W (106-D). A small brook running into Scougale Creek, in the Davidson Range.

This was named before 1910 by the prospector, CAMERON, who found and mined gold on this little gulch. This is probably the same Cameron who died one winter in his cabin on the banks of the Stewart River below Russell Creek. His body lay in the cabin for six years before the river changed course and swept both away.

CAMPBELL CREEK 61°46′N 131°07′W (105-G). Tributary to the Pelly River.

Robert CAMPBELL of the HBC, the first explorer of the central Yukon, travelled this creek on his famous journey of exploration in July 1840, when he discovered the Pelly River. Dr. G.M. Dawson, GSC, named this stream when he retraced Campbell's route on the first geological expedition to the Yukon in 1887.

Robert Campbell was born in Perthshire, Scotland on 21 February, 1808, the son of a sheep farmer. At the age of 22, he was hired by the HBC as a sub-manager of their experimental farm at Fort Garry in what is now Manitoba.

In 1833 he left the farm and was sent to Fort Resolution where he traded for the next four years. 1838 saw Campbell starting the series of explorations for which he became noted. The first journey was from Fort Halkett on the Liard River to Dease Lake where he and his Indian companions nearly starved to death the following winter. In early 1840 he ascended the Liard River to the Frances River (which he named), up to Frances Lake, and up the Finlayson River to its lake and then to the Pelly River at Campbell Creek, where he established Pelly Banks Post in 1846.

In 1843 he descended the Pelly River to its junction with the Yukon (the upper part of which he named the Lewes). In 1848 he again made this journey and built Fort Selkirk where the two rivers meet. This first post was moved to the west bank of the Yukon the following year because of flooding problems. It was raided and pillaged by the Chilkat Indians in 1852.

Due to this catastrophe, Campbell made, in the winter of 1852–53, one of the longest snowshoe journeys on record: from Fort Simpson on the Mackenzie River to Crow Wing, Minnesota on the Mississippi River, about 3300 miles, between 30 November, 1852, and 13 March, 1853. (This record stood for 24 years until exceeded by J.S. Camsell, Chief Factor at Fort Simpson, who retraced Campbell's route plus an additional 180 miles from Fort Liard to Fort Simpson.)

Although he was promoted to command the Peace River and Athabaska country, Campbell never was allowed to return to the Yukon. After 41 years service he was abruptly dismissed by the company in 1871. He died and was buried in Winnipeg on 9 May, 1894.

Fort Pelly Banks was built on the Pelly River opposite the mouth of this stream. The stream was first prospected by a man named Theakson who came up from Fort Liard in 1878–79.

MOUNT CAMPBELL 8,200' 64°23'N 138°45'W (116-B&C). 33 miles northeast of Dawson on the headwaters of the Tombstone River.

In 1896 William Ogilvie, DLS, was surveying the Yukon-Alaska boundary near Fortymile and while doing so, named many mountains to the east after Yukon pioneers. He named one, due east about 60 miles, after Robert CAMPBELL of the HBC, the first explorer of the central Yukon Territory. He described it in his report as "the most remarkable peak in the country, a black shaft about 600 feet wide and rising about 1,000 feet above the rest of the mountain ridge."

The early miners of the area and the people of Dawson, knowing nothing of Ogilvie's designation due to the fact that the name Campbell had not appeared on any map available to them, called it "Tombstone Mountain" from its eerie resemblance. In later years some maps showed this name, while others called it Campbell Mountain. A field investigation by the GSC failed to differentiate the two and the name Campbell was dropped and "Tombstone" adopted. Maps are still being printed showing it as Campbell. (See Tombstone Mountain.)

CAMPBELL GULCH 64°02′N 139°24′W (116-B&C). A tributary to Boulder Creek.

This stream was named on 7 September, 1897, when Alex CAMPBELL staked claim No. 6.

CAMPBELL RANGE 61°23′N 130°00′W (105-G&H). On the west side of Frances Lake.

This was named in 1887 by Dr. G.M. Dawson, GSC, after Chief Factor Robert CAMPBELL of the HBC. (See Campbell Creek.)

CANADIAN CREEK 62°48′N 138°43′W (115-J&K). Flows into Britannia Creek.

Named, for obvious reasons, by Joseph Britton and Charles C. Brown on 21 April, 1911 when they discovered gold here. (See Britton Ridge.)

CANALASKA MOUNTAIN 2,260′ 67°22′N 141°00′W (116-O&N). On the Yukon-Alaska boundary.

This composite name was given by J.H. Turner USC&GS, in 1890. It had previously been called Boundary Mountain.

THE CANOL ROAD AND PIPELINE

This road, 513 miles long, was built to provide access for the construction of a wartime emergency oil pipeline from the oil fields at Fort Norman, NWT, on the lower Mackenzie River, to Whitehorse. It ran from Johnson's Crossing past Quiet Lake to Ross River and through the MacMillan Pass to Fort Norman. From Johnson's Crossing the pipeline was built along the Alaska Highway to a refinery at Whitehorse. The gasoline from the Whitehorse refinery was to power the aircraft being flown to Russia and to provide for military needs in Alaska, which was expecting a Japanese invasion at the time. Later, it could help to mount air strikes against Japan.

The line laid was four inches in diameter and supplied about 3,000 gallons of oil per day. The project started in April 1942 and was carried through to completion in April 1944, when the first oil flowed through the line. The road was officially opened to traffic in September 1944 but it and the pipeline were abandoned shortly after the war.

The CANOL Project's total cost was $134,000,000, which includes the road, the pipeline, the refinery and the cost of sinking 26 oil wells at Fort Norman.

In recent years the Yukon government has gradually reopened portions of the road until it is now a good summer road in use by tourists and mining exploration companies searching for minerals.

CANTLIE LAKE   60°40′N   134°49′W   (104-D). Eight miles southeast of Whitehorse.

In 1948 this lake was given the name of Lt. Col. Stuart Stephen Tuffnell CANTLIE, MID, CEM. He was born in Winnipeg, Manitoba on 5 October, 1907 and enlisted on 4 September, 1939 at Montréal. He served in Canada, Great Britain and northwest Europe with the Black Watch (the Royal Highland Regiment) of Canada and died of wounds received in action in France on 25 July, 1944.

CANYON   60°52′N   137°03′W   (115-A). About mile 996.5 (K1604) on the Alaska Highway, on the east side of the Aishihik River.

During the stampede to the Kluane Lake goldfields in 1903, a wagon road was built from Whitehorse to Kluane Lake. A roadhouse and stores were built here and the small community existed until 1935. It gained its name from the stream beside it; it was called CANYON Creek until the 1940's when it was changed to the Aishihik River. The original bridge across the stream was built by Gilbert Skelly and Sam McGee (of Robert Service fame).

Tourist services were rebuilt here after the opening of the Alaska Highway.

CANYON CITY   61°48′N   140°47′W   (115-G&F). On the White River, ten miles east of the Yukon-Alaska boundary.

A now-abandoned mining settlement was started here in 1905 as a supply centre and winter quarters for the prospectors who were developing the new copper finds in the vicinity. It was the head of water transportation and became active when the rich placer gold of the Chisana was found in

1913, which attracted thousands to the area. Much prospecting was done in the area after Solomon Albert found promising deposits of native copper near here in May 1905.

After roads were built in Alaska to serve the Chisana and the deposits themselves were declining, this village lost its reason for being and was abandoned in the 1920's.

CANYON CITY 60°40′N 135°03′W (105-D). On the east side of the Yukon River at the head of Miles Canyon.

This settlement grew up in the summer and fall of 1897 due to the need to portage goods around the dangerous waters of Miles Canyon and the Whitehorse Rapids. Between 1897 and 1899 numerous people were drowned and large quantities of supplies lost in trying to ferry boats through these waters.

In the winter of 1897–98 two tramways were built around these obstructions. The one on the west bank was built by John Hepburn and was 6½ miles long. The one on the east bank was five miles long and was built by Norman MacAuley. The toll on both was three cents per pound and $25 per boat. (Most boats were usually taken through the canyon and rapids by professional pilots for less.) Goods were transported by the tramway by horse-drawn cars which carried about a ton.

MacAuley bought out Hepburn and concentrated his operations on the east bank of the river. Here he built offices, freight sheds and a hotel to serve the travellers. Others built stores and dwellings.

The settlement thrived until July 1900 when the WP&YR arrived in what is now Whitehorse. Canyon City was quickly abandoned and the business men moved their operations to Whitehorse.

CANYON MOUNTAIN   60°41′N 134°54′W (105-D). Four miles east of Miles Canyon and opposite Whitehorse.

This hill was named by the earliest miners travelling down the river in the 1880's. It was a good landmark to warn them of their approach to the dangerous waterway.

Local people now call it Grey Hill or Mountain.

CARBON HILL   60°10′N 135°16′W (105-D). On the south side of the Wheaton River.

In 1893, well before the Klondike rush, two prospectors from Juneau,

Frank Corwin and Thomas Rickman, investigated this area and found veins with rich gold, copper and silver-antimony ore in a number of places.

They found the black, silver-antimony ore on this hill. Returning to Juneau in the fall they both died within a short time and the exact location (there were no maps of the area at that time) of their finds was lost. In August 1906 H.E. Porter (see Porter Creek) rediscovered their old workings and gave the hill its name from the colour of the ore. (See Mount Hodnett and Gold Hill.)

CARCROSS   60°10′N 134°42′W (105-D). At the junction of Bennett and Tagish Lakes.

This was first known as Caribou Crossing, from the time of the earliest miners to come across the Chilkoot Pass, because large herds of caribou crossed the narrows here twice a year on their annual migration. A major way point on the route to the Yukon goldfields and later to the Atlin, BC, goldfields, the townsite was pre-empted by the WP&YR in September 1898. The largest sawmill on the Yukon was near here, owned by Mike King, who also built boats and scows from early 1897. The Caribou Hotel, built in 1898, is still in operation, the oldest continuing hotel in the Yukon Territory.

In 1903 Bishop Bompas, who had established a school here for Indian children in 1901, petitioned the Dominion government to change the name of the community to CARCROSS because of the confusion in mail services due to the duplication of names in Alaska and British Columbia as well as in the Klondike. The post office made the change official the following year but the good bishop had to fight longer with the WP&YR, which retained the name of the station until 1916.

Numerous Yukon pioneers are buried here including Bishop Bompas, Kate Carmack, Skookum Jim Mason, and Tagish Charlie.

CARIBOU CITY   63°50′N 138°44′W (115-O&N). At the junction of Caribou Creek and Dominion Creek in the Klondike.

A settlement sprang up here in early 1897 as a supply point and stopping place for the many miners on the surrounding creeks. Several hotels gave accommodation and amusement to the local miners, among them the Gold Run, the Driard and the Caribou Hotels. A post office was opened in November 1899 but after 1905 the settlement and the post office became known as Dominion.

The place died out during the First World War due to the end of the pick-and-shovel mining and with it the loss of people and business.

CARIBOU CREEK   61°18′N 133°20′W (105–F). Flows into Big Salmon Lake.

This was one of the earliest streams to be named by miners. John McCormack, of New Brunswick, and his partners prospected it for gold and named it in the summer of 1887.

CARLSON CREEK   63°39′N 136°22′W (115–P). A tributary to Bear Creek.

Louis Beauvette and Charles Johnson staked the first placer gold claim on this stream on 10 March, 1911, and named it for a friend.

CARMACKS   62°05′N 136°17′W (115–I). A settlement on the Yukon River at the mouth of the Nordenskiold River.

George Washington CARMACK was born at Port Costa, California, on 24 September, 1860, after his parents had crossed the continent by ox team and Conestoga wagon. In 1885 he went north to Juneau and in April the same year joined a party of seven miners and went over the Chilkoot Pass to prospect the Stewart and other Yukon rivers.

He met and liked the Tagish Indians of the region and, to a certain extent, adopted their life-style. About this time he became associated with Skookum Jim Mason and his sister Kate. In 1887 they worked for William Ogilvie, DLS, packing his supplies over the Chilkoot Pass and travelling from Dyea to Fortymile. In the next few years they prospected the Big Salmon River, the Hootalinqua (Teslin) River and the Stewart.

In 1893 Carmack found a seam of coal near Five Fingers Rapids and another near Tantalus Butte. He built a cabin here while he tried to develop the coal and carried on a certain amount of fur trading with the local Indians. Arthur Harper backed his coal ventures and owned a 50% interest in them. This was the beginning of present day Carmacks.

The settlement grew and became a riverboat stop during the gold rush and later a supply point for various mining operations in the district. After the building of the Dawson—Whitehorse highway it continued to grow.

Carmack, Skookum Jim and Tagish Charlie went on to uncover the golden wealth of Bonanza Creek in August 1896. Carmack died on 5 June, 1922, in Vancouver, BC, a relatively wealthy man. Contrary to the many stories showing him to be renegade white man, he was well-educated and intelligent. His cabin at Carmacks contained an organ which he played and many volumes of classical literature. He subscribed to *Scientific American* and other literate journals and was in the way of being a romantic poet. In all the controversy regarding the discovery of gold in the Klondike he was the only principal who did not attack the stories or characters of the others.

CARMACK'S FORK   63°55′N 139°09′W (115-O&N). The north fork of Bonanza Creek.

This small section of the famous Bonanza Creek is the only feature in the Klondike to perpetuate the name of the discoverer. Very little gold was ever found on it.

CARMACKS – FREEGOLD ROAD

This road was built by the N.A. Timmins mining interests in 1934 to explore and develop the LaForma Gold Mine on Mount Freegold. It was quickly extended by prospectors and the territorial government to other parts of this mineral-rich district.

CARPENTER CREEK   64°23′N 135°11′W (106-D). Flows into Beaver Creek.

Jack CARPENTER was an enterprising prospector who found the first, rich, silver-lead ore in this district. The find sparked a sizeable rush to the area in 1920–23 but, as the mineral finds were not economic at the time, the rush petered out and the country was deserted again. The big ridge to the northwest of the creek was later named Carpenter Ridge.

MOUNT CARTER   4,751′   65°40′N 137°03′W (116-H). Between the Blackstone and Hart Rivers.

In 1973 this mountain was named after Special Constable Sam CARTER, RCMP, a member of the lost Fitzgerald patrol in 1911. (See Dempster Highway.)

CASCADE   CREEK   63°38′N 134°51′W (105-M). Flows into the southeast end of Mayo Lake.

Gold was first discovered here by Thomas Heney about August 1903. He was one of a party of four Australians who first prospected the area at that time and found rich gold on this and several adjacent creeks. (See Ledge and Steep Creeks.)

CASINO CREEK   62°38'N   138°52'W   (115–J&K).   A tributary to Dip Creek in the Dawson Range.

This was named on or shortly before 28 November, 1915, by two prospectors, Jack O'Hara and Frank Farnan, who discovered placer gold on the stream and named it after their favourite card game.

CASSIAR BAR   61°48'N   135°00'W   (105–E).   One of a group of gravel bars in the Yukon River, six miles above the Big Salmon River and opposite the mouth of Fyfe Creek.

This series of gravel bars was the first and richest found on the Lewes (Yukon) River. Found in the summer of 1884 by Thomas Boswell, Howard Franklin and Michael Hess, it produced the first considerable amount of gold taken out of the upper Yukon region.

In 1886 over $30 (almost two ounces) per man per day were taken from here by many of the miners. The deposits, being shallow, were soon worked out but they gave encouragement to further prospecting in the territory. The miners who found it named it after the country they had come from previously, the CASSIAR, in northern BC.

CASSIAR CREEK   64°20'N   140°10'W   (116–B&C).   Tributary to the Yukon about 16 miles above the Fortymile River.

This name was applied by miners from the Cassiar country in northern BC when they moved into the Yukon in the 1880's. Although no gold was ever found on this stream in paying quantities, it has another claim to fame. It was the scene of the famous "Nigger Jim" Daugherty stampede of January 1899.

Daugherty, a Virginian, had wagered that he could start a staking stampede at any time he wished. He did, in extremely cold weather in January and several of the duped stampeders were severely frozen. The story, written in many accounts of the Klondike Gold Rush, epitomized the whole spirit and character of the Klondike stampede itself, in miniature.

CASSIAR MOUNTAINS   60°20'N   130°50'W   (105–B).   On the north side of the Alaskan Highway between mile 690 and 760.

This is a corruption of the Indian name "Kaska" which was applied to two tribes occupying the country to the east of the Stikine River in northern BC.

CATHEDRAL CREEK   65°12'N   141°00'W   (116–G&F).   Runs across the Yukon-Alaska boundary into Hardluck Creek in Alaska.

In 1909 surveyors on the International Boundary Survey named this creek because of the beautiful, cathedral-like mountains along its course.

CATHEDRAL ROCKS 66°08′N 138°45′W (116-J&K). On the east side of the Miner River.

In May 1888 William Ogilvie, DLS, passed down this river and thought this feature interesting enough to name. He described it as a large rock exposure extending for a half a mile. It rises 300 to 400 feet from the river and as it is weathered into resemblances to old buildings, he gave it this name.

CENTENNIAL RANGE 60°58′N 140°39′W (115-B&C). In the north-west corner of the St. Elias Range.

This group of 13 peaks was first selected in 1967 (although the idea was first thought about in 1965) to become the locale for perhaps the most unusual centennial project in Canada's Centennial Year.

It was organized mainly by David R. Fisher of the Alpine Club of Canada, David Judd, Executive Assistant to the Commissioner of the Yukon Territory, and Monty Alford of the Water Resources Board at Whitehorse and a co-ordinator of the Polar Shelf Project. The proposal was accepted by the Centennial Committee and was named the Yukon Alpine Centennial Expedition.

As 1967 also marked the Alaska Purchase Centennial it was decided to have a team of four Americans and four Canadians climb the highest, unclimbed peak on the Yukon-Alaska border. This peak, situated two miles north of Mount Vancouver, was to be named "Good Neighbour" Peak. This was the first part of the project to be carried out on 25 June, 1967.

The second and much more ambitious part of the project was the attempted ascent of the 13 Centennial Peaks in a two-week period. None had been climbed before.

Thirteen teams of four climbers each were organized and, with support personnel, more than 250 people took part in the project. It was the largest effort of its kind known in North America.

The attempt was nearly a total success. Nine peaks were scaled for the first time and climbers came within feet of conquering each of the others. All this was accomplished between 8 July and 13 August. The nine ascents were all made in the period 13–24 July.

CHADBURN LAKE 60°39′N 134°57′W (105-D). One mile east of Miles Canyon.

This little lake was named in October 1948 to perpetuate the name of a Canadian hero, Wing Commander Lloyd Vernon CHADBURN, DSO and Bar, DFC. He was born on 21 August, 1919, in Montréal. Québec and enlisted in the RCAF on 16 April, 1940, at Toronto, Ontario. He served in Canada and overseas and died of wounds suffered in action on 19 June, 1944.

MOUNT CHAMBERS   5,301'   65°10'N 138°48'W (116-G&F). South of the Ogilvie River.

In 1973 the Topographical Surveys Branch named this hill for Harlow "Shorty" CHAMBERS, who built the first trading post at Champagne and served as postmaster there.

CHAMPAGNE   60°47'N 136°29'W (115-A). At the junction of the Dalton Trail and Dezeadash River near mile 974 (K1658) on the Alaska Highway.

This little settlement, nearly abandoned now, was the centre of activity of the area for many years until the Alaska Highway was built. There are several different stories concerning the origin of the name.

Champagne was originally a camping spot on the Dalton Trail to Rink Rapids. The Klondike Gold Rush brought a great increase in travel and a demand for more horses for a longer part of the year. Jack Dalton wintered stock here as well as at Dalton Post, farther south.

In 1897 Gordon Bounds was taking a herd of 40 cattle to Dawson. He was probably working for Dalton at the time. When this point was reached, the worst of the trail was over and it was said that they opened a case of French champagne from the freight they were carrying to Dawson and celebrated the end of their hardships.

The place assumed some importance in 1902 when Harlow "Shorty" Chambers built his roadhouse and trading post. It became a supply centre the next year when the rush to the Bullion Creek finds started and gained again from the rush to the Burwash Creek diggings in 1904. During these days it was usually called Champagne Landing and, sometimes, Champlain or Champlain's Landing. Chambers' family still owned and ran the roadhouse when it burned in March 1962.

Since the end of placer gold mining in this district and the end of highway construction, the settlement has gradually shrunk to its present size.

CHANDINDU RIVER 64°15'N 139°43'W (116-B&C). Tributary of the Yukon River, 12 miles below Dawson.

52

This river was named by Lt. F. Schwatka, US Army, in 1883. It is a local Indian name and Schwatka did not obtain the meaning of the word. The early miners however, called it the Twelve Mile River because of its distance from Dawson. After 1900 large ditches were built by the Yukon Gold Company from its headwaters to supply hydraulic mining operations on the Klondike creeks.

CHAPPIE LAKE 65°47′N 134°56′W (106–E). Near the Bonnet Plume River, below its junction with the Peel River.

Ernest CHAPMAN was a trader, trapper and prospector for many years in this area. His home and trading post were on this lake in the 1930–40's. He was killed in an aircraft crash at Dawson on 31 January, 1941.

CHEECHAKO HILL 63°56′N 139°21′W (115–O&N). On the west side of Bonanza Creek between Grand Forks and Adams Creek.

Oliver B. Millet from Lunenburg, Nova Scotia, while working a lay on Eldorado Creek, formed a theory regarding an ancient and different stream channel crossing Bonanza Creek. Acting upon his idea he prospected above Tagish Charlie's claim in the winter of 1897–98 and on 14 April, 1898, he struck the White Channel gravels and their riches. The Bonanza and Eldorado miners, watching his efforts that winter, called the hill "CHEECHAKO Hill", for only a green newcomer, in their estimation, would look for gold on a hill top. Millet, sick with scurvy and nearly penniless, took $20,000 in gold from a small part of his claim (which was only 100 feet square) and then sold it for $60,000. The new owner took a further $500,000 from the ground. (The scoffers still worked for wages on the claims below).

The remainder of the hill, also staked mainly by newly arrived "cheechakos", was almost as rich and many fortunes were dug from its gravels.

CHIEF GULCH 63°52′N 139°14′W (115–O&N). The last tributary to Eldorado Creek.

CHIEF Isaac and men of his Moosehide Band of Indians were in at the beginning of the Klondike discovery. Several of them staked claims on Bonanza and other creeks. Chief Isaac found gold and staked the Discovery claim on this short stream on 4 December, 1896. He and his people were the first to trade with McQuesten when he built Fort Reliance. An able man and a good leader, he was respected by both peoples of that time. The stream was originally named Chief Isaac Creek. (See Mount Chief Isaac.)

MOUNT CHIEF ISAAC 5,280' 65°27'N 139°25'W (116–G&F). North of the Ogilvie River.

This was named in 1973 after CHIEF ISAAC, Chief of the Moosehide Indian Band at Dawson before and after the Klondike Gold Rush. Much mentioned in the literature of the time, he was helpful and friendly to the early miners. The Moosehide Band received its name from the rockslide on the hill behind Dawson, which resembles a moosehide stretched to dry.

CHITINA GLACIER 61°01'N 141°00'W (115–G&F). Lies across the Yukon-Alaska boundary in the St. Elias Mountains.

The glacier was named in 1912 by the International Boundary Survey team, from its closeness to the Copper River in Alaska. The name CHITINA is an Indian word meaning "Copper", as reported by Dall in 1870. There are variations in spelling such as Chettyna, Chitennah, Chechitna, etc.

CHOHO HILL 67°27'N 138°41'W (116–O&N). A long, low ridge ten miles southeast of Cadzow Lake.

Long known locally, this is a Vanta Kutchin Indian word meaning "Egg".

CHRISTAL CREEK 63°56'N 135°32'W (105–M). A small tributary to the South McQuesten River.

Charles CHRISTAL found and staked the first gold here on 14 November, 1902.

CHRISTIE PASS 63°03'N 129°41'W (105–P). The pass through the Selwyn Mountains, connecting the Gravel (Keele) River in the NWT to the headwaters of the Ross River.

James Murdoch "Jim" CHRISTIE was born on 22 October, 1874, in Perth, Scotland. He came to the prairies as a young man and in early 1898, left Carman, Manitoba to take the Edmonton Trail to the Klondike. He found and used this pass on the way. He prospected the NWT and the Yukon for years, mainly interested in a vast stretch of territory centring on the Rogue River.

In 1907 Joseph Keele, GSC, whom Christie assisted in his geological survey of the area, named the pass and the mountain after him.

It was near here, in late October 1909, that a huge grizzly bear attacked him. With his skull and jaw fractured, his right arm broken and his right thigh terribly bitten, this courageous man made his way, in sub-zero temperatures, seven miles to a temporary camp. His partner, George Crissfield, tended his wounds with the only medicine they had, some Scotch whisky. Crissfield obtained the help of some nearby Indians and their dogs and after four long and terrible days, over rugged mountain country, got Christie to the small settlement of Lansing on the Stewart River. There, the trader, J.E. Ferrell, who had some medical knowledge, tended his injuries and set his arm and jaw. He and his wife nursed Christie for two months. On New Years Day he was taken by dog-sled to Dawson, a journey of 17 days. Later he went to Victoria, BC, where his jaw was re-set and his other injuries given further attention. He was back prospecting in the summer of 1910.

Christie went to Ottawa and enlisted as a private in the famous Princess Patricia's Canadian Light Infantry on 24 August, 1914, one of the very first. He served with great distinction throughout the First World War. He fought in France and was first mentioned in dispatches and then won the DCM. He was commissioned in the field and won the MC and further Allied decorations.

His courage, integrity and good humour were appreciated by all who knew him. As a bushman he was almost without an equal; he once took a party from Dawson to Edmonton by a new route in a remarkably short time, in the dead of winter.

In later life, bothered by his old wounds, he retired with his wife to Saltspring Island, BC, where he died.

MOUNT CHRISTIE   61°01′N 129°41′W (105–P). On the south side of Christie Pass.

This peak was also named by Joseph Keele, GSC, in 1909, after Jim Christie.

CHRISTMAS CREEK 61°03′N 138°21′W (115–G&F). Tributary to Kluane Lake in Christmas Bay.

The Rev. John Pringle was an outstanding figure of the Klondike with his down-to-earth brand of Presbyterianism. He did not believe in turning the other cheek and had a helping hand for every unfortunate. He was active in community life and was a member of the Yukon Council. He was an active prospector when he had time and he and Richard Fullerton found gold and staked the Discovery claim on this creek on Christmas Day 1903. He served as a chaplain with the CEF in the First World War.

CHRISTMAS CREEK 63°31′N 140°30′W (115-O&N). **A tributary of Matson Creek in the Sixtymile River district.**

This creek was discovered, i.e. gold was found, on Christmas Day 1911.

CHUNGKLEE LAKE 67°50′N 139°12′W (116-O&N). **Between the forks of Johnson and Little Flat Creeks.**

This is a Vanta Kutchin Indian word meaning "Open Place".

CHUNGKUCH LAKE 67°57′N 138°55′W (116-O&N). **Near the headwaters of Johnson Creek.**

This is an old Vanta Kutchin Indian name meaning "No Timber".

CHURCHWARD HILL 2,875′ 65°34′N 138°12′W (116-G&F). **West of the Ogilvie River.**

This was named in 1973 after Guy S. CHURCHWARD, Dawson's first tinsmith in 1898. He later moved to Mayo in the 1920's. He invented and produced the Yukon Airtight Heater stove.

CLAIRE CREEK 61°59′N 135°25′W (105-E). **A short creek connecting Claire Lake (named later) with the Yukon River.**

This was probably named by or for Thomas CLAIRE, a prospector well known in this district for many years after 1900.

CLARENCE LAGOON 69°38′N 140°49′W (117-C). **On the Arctic coast about five miles east of the Yukon-Alaska border.**

This enclosed, shallow bay was named by John Franklin, (later Sir), in 1826 after Prince William Henry, Duke of CLARENCE, and afterward King William IV of Great Britain. The Clarence River was named at the same time.

CLARK LAKES 64°08′N 134°56′W (106-D). **Four small lakes on Scougale Creek.**

These were named in 1950 to honour the memory of C-19545 Gunner Arthur Raymond CLARK MID, who was born in Brockville, Ontario on 17 December, 1919. He enlisted in the Canadian army on 4 September, 1939, one of the first, at Ottawa, Ontario. He served in Canada, Great Britain and northwest Europe and was killed in action on 31 July, 1944.

CLEAR CREEK 63°37′N 137°38′W (115-P). **A tributary of the Stewart River about ten miles below the McQuesten River.**

This stream was known and named by prospectors in the early 1880's but it was not until 1900 that payable gold was discovered on it.

It was on this creek on 8 January, 1909, that "Big Alex" McDonald, the "King of the Klondike", died alone.

A bear of a man, he was slow moving and slow of speech but his expert knowledge of placer mining, combined with his phenomenal memory for facts and figures and his appetite for mining deals built him the largest fortune in the Klondike in just three years between 1896 and 1899. At his peak he was estimated to be worth in excess of $20,000,000.

Born in Antigonish, Nova Scotia, in November 1854, he went to school and mined there until 1880. For the next 13 years he mined in Colorado, early becoming a mine superintendent. The depression of 1893 broke him, along with most of the mines in the country. He went to Alaska following the stories of gold. After working for a year in the Mexican Mine at Douglas, he went over the Chilkoot Pass in April 1895. He was mining on the headwaters of the Fortymile River when he got word of Carmack's find on Bonanza Creek.

Arriving in Dawson on 22 September he located claim No. 89 Above on Bonanza and No. 11 Below on Hunker Creek. Grasping the potential of the district well before most of the men there he acted quickly to acquire interests in as many claims as possible before development work could disclose their unbelievable riches. His methods were simple: as little cash down as would be acceptable and a further sum to be paid after the spring clean-up, when the gravel mined during the winter would be sluiced and the gold recovered. After making such a deal he then found miners who had been unsuccessful in locating good claims of their own or who were short of money. To these he offered a percentage partnership, or a "lay", as they called such an arrangement. They were to mine the claim, or a portion of it and in the spring would return to him an agreed percentage of the gold they recovered. In this way and by staking, he acquired interests and claims on every gold-bearing stream in the Klondike.

At the same time he quickly bought land in Dawson City at the first, low prices. His ability to persuade others to invest their money and labour with him enabled him to build the McDonald Hotel, the Pioneer Drug Store Block, the Post Office Building and many other business establishments in the town. These he immediately rented to others.

The spring clean-up of 1897 vindicated his judgment and made him a multi-millionaire within weeks. His estimate of the amount of gold in the creeks was proven correct and the value of his holdings, both mining and business, appreciated by hundreds of percent overnight.

Through it all he remained the same man. He continued to buy and acquire more claims. He contributed major financing to build the Dawson Electric Plant, the Telephone Company, an iron works and a brewery among others. He gave $40,000, a large fortune at the time, to build the Roman Catholic Church. He was the largest supporter of the hospital and never refused financial help to any civic cause or needy friends. He was entertained by the highest circles in New York and London, where he met and married his wife.

The depopulation of the Klondike in late 1899 and 1900, caused by the discovery of the rich Nome goldfields, started his downfall. Miners became unavailable to work his claims and further, the richest ground on Bonanza and Eldorado was nearly worked out. His returns dropped and he had to buy extensions of time. His unfaltering belief in the Klondike would not let him sell any of his holdings and kept him acquiring others. By 1900 he was unable to meet some of his commitments and his financial pyramid began to crumble. The population of Dawson had halved and his businesses began to lose money. His efforts to consolidate came too late and by 1904 he had lost almost the whole of his fortune.

He repaid every debt. Nearly penniless, he returned to the simple life of the prospector on the creeks. His wife and son were supported by the income of a small insurance policy he had earlier purchased at the insistence of Belinda Mulroney. (See Grand Forks.)

On this creek, on 8 January, 1909, while chopping wood at his lonely cabin, the King of the Klondike died of a heart attack.

MOUNT CLEMENT 68°26′N 139°24′W (117-A). East of Timber Creek.

This was named in 1973 by the Topographical Surveys Branch after W.H.P. CLEMENT, who was the legal adviser and Registrar of Lands and Titles in Dawson from 1898–1900.

CLINTON CREEK 64°24′N 140°36′W (116-B&C). Tributary to the Fortymile River, three miles above its mouth.

CLINTON Felcht first prospected this stream in late 1886 or early 1887. Having prospected in Africa his friends nicknamed him "The African Hunter". He died of heart disease on 16 August, 1897, the first white man to die in Dawson.

No payable gold was ever found on the creek but it later gave its name to a thriving settlement and an asbestos mine.

CLINTON CREEK 64°27′N 140°37′W (116-B&C). On Clinton Creek, four miles above its mouth.

In 1957, Arthur Anderson, an Indian trapper at Dawson, found the large and valuable asbestos deposits which were worked here. He was born in Fortymile in 1912. This town was built in 1967 to house the employees of the Cassiar Asbestos Corp. Ltd.

This was the most northerly open-pit mine in Canada and the mill had the largest eccentric-jaw crusher ever made at the time. The mine was opened in October 1967 and closed in 1979.

MOUNT CLOSE 68°20′N 137°24′W (117-A). 13 miles northwest of Bonnet Lake in the Richardson Mountains.

This was named in 1973 after Robert CLOSE, born in Mayo and killed in a training accident at Penhold, Alberta, in 1957 while serving in the RCAF.

CLOSELEIGH

In September 1899 the WP&YR proposed this name for the settlement which would be constructed around their railroad terminus at the foot of the Whitehorse Rapids, on the west bank of the Yukon River. The only settlement at the time was on the east bank of the river and was already known as Whitehorse.

W.B. CLOSE, of Close Brothers, financiers of London, England, had raised the majority of the capital to build the railway. The name was used from September 1899 to April 1900 when the WP&YR bowed to public pressure and changed the name to Whitehorse. The east bank settlement was abandoned by then. (See Whitehorse.)

CLOUTIER CREEK 61°43′N 132°10′W (105-F). A small creek emptying into the Ketza River in the St. Cyr Range.

This perpetuates the memory of D-61181 Fusilier Gerard Ludger CLOUTIER MID who was born 1 January, 1917, in Montréal, Québec. He served in Canada, Iceland, Great Britain and France and was killed in action at Dieppe on 19 August, 1942.

CLUETT CREEK 61°16′N 138°47′W (115-G&F). This creek flows into the west side of Kluane Lake at Destruction Bay.

Albert CLUETT was born in the county of Dorset, England in 1875. He came to Canada in 1895 and joined the stampede to the Klondike in 1897.

He met the Jacquot brothers on the trail to the Kluane Lake goldfields on

Christmas Day, 1903, and helped them build their trading post at Burwash Landing the following spring. He worked there for many years when he was not prospecting or trapping. He cooked in a US Army Engineers camp nearby during the construction of the Alaska Highway and was instrumental in having the memorial plaque erected at Destruction Bay.

In 1954, when conflict arose over the name of a water feature in the area, his name was suggested. Everyone knew Bert but few knew or could spell his last name. He was away prospecting at the time and could not be reached, so another name was adopted. However, in 1957 it was decided to name this stream in Bert's territory and after some investigation it was called Klewitt Creek. In 1959 Dr. J.E. Muller, GSC, saw Bert and found the correct spelling. In 1960 the name was officially changed to Cluett Creek.

Bert died at Burwash on 15 December, 1972, a cheerful, friendly and energetic little man.

MOUNT CLUETT   65°36′N 138°46′W (116-G&F). East of the Whitestone River.

This was named in September 1973 after Hubert CLUETT. This was the same man as above except that a different government department checked the name and came up with this variation. However, Bert was never in this part of the country.

CLUM CREEK   64°04′N 137°28′W (116-A). A tributary to the Klondike River.

This was named in 1897 by four brothers who first prospected the creek. They were Peter, Charles, Joseph and Phillip CLUM (or Coulombe) from Massachusetts. They went on after the Klondike to mine in Alaska.

COAL CREEK   64°29′N 140°25′W (116-B&C). A tributary to the Yukon River about six miles below the Fortymile.

This creek was named by William Ogilvie, DLS, in 1887–88 for the coal seams previously found there by prospectors, which he examined.

The first workable coal deposits were found here by Henry Seimer in 1900. By 1904 English capital had formed a company to mine the coal and produce thermal electricity for the large gold dredges in the Klondike. They built a plant here and a 38-mile power line to Dawson. They also built a 12-mile-long, narrow-gauge railway along the creek from the mine to the Yukon River to supply coal to the riverboats.

The company ceased business in 1908 when cheaper hydro-electric power was developed nearer Dawson.

COAL GULCH 63°39′N 139°15′W (116–O&N). Flows into Ruby Creek.

The MacKinnon brothers, Archibald and Donald, who were trying to develop huge tonnages of low-grade gold ore in the Indian River conglomerates near here (see MacKinnon Creek), attempted to develop the coal seams on this gulch as a source of cheap power. Their gold property failing to produce, they also shut down work on the coal, although they had worked from 1910–15.

COAL LAKE 60°30′N 135°10′W (105–D). 15 miles southwest of Whitehorse at the foot of Mount Granger.

Several seams of anthracite coal from three to ten feet thick are located in this area. They were developed for some years after 1905 to supply the copper mines at Whitehorse.

The lake was given its name in 1900 by R.G. McConnell, GSC, when he mapped the area.

COARSE GOLD PUP 63°50′N 138°47′W (115–O&N). A very short valley entering Eldorado Creek from Cheechako Hill.

J.J. Rutledge staked the first claim here on 23 September, 1897, and optimistically named it at that time.

COBALT HILL 63°59′N 134°57′W (105–M). Just east of Keno Hill.

This hill was named by Jim MacDonald when he found rich, silver-lead ore here in 1922. He named it after COBALT, Ontario, a silver-mining camp which flourished from 1905 to 1927. He had prospected and mined there before he came to the Yukon.

MOUNT COCKFIELD 62°39′N 138°27′W (115–J&K). In the Selwyn River area of the Dawson Range.

This was named in 1915 after William E. COCKFIELD by D.D. Cairnes, GSC. He was a long-time member of the GSC and especially active in the Yukon. In 1915 he started as an assistant packer with Cairnes on a geological survey party in this area. He became senior assistant to Cairnes and later, in charge of his own operations, mapped and explored many parts of the Yukon.

COFFEE CREEK 62°55'N 139°03'W (115-J&K). A tributary of the Yukon River from the west.

"COFFEE Jack" was an Indian trapper well-known in this country at the turn of the century. Noted for his dry humour he was once accused of allowing his dogs to rob a white trapper's supplies. The trapper informed Jack that at the next offense he would poison Jack's dogs. Jack replied, "In that case I might shoot you and tell the Mountie I thought you were a moose!"

The creek was mined for gold intermittently over the years, giving reasonable returns but no bonanzas.

COFFEE CREEK POST 62°55'N 139°05'W (115-J&K). At the mouth of Coffee Creek.

Jim Derry ran a small trading post here in the 1920's and 1930's to serve the local miners and trappers.

COGHLAN LAKE 61°33'N 135°29'W (105-E). Ten miles north of Lake Laberge, on the old winter trail to Dawson.

Charles COGHLAN lived and trapped here for many years. He came to the Klondike in 1898 and remained. He accompanied F.C. Selous, a "white hunter" of African fame, on his big-game hunting expeditions to the upper MacMillan River in 1904.

MOUNT COLEMAN 61°10'N 140°08'W (115-G). At the head of the Steele Glacier in the St. Elias Mountains.

This was named by the Alpine Club of Canada after Arthur Philomen COLEMAN (1852–1939), geologist and past president of the club.

MOUNT COLLEY 65°05'N 133°12'W (106-F). West of the head of Snake River.

This was named by the Topographical Surveys Branch in 1973 after Howard "Harry" COLLEY, a well-known and successful prospector in the Dawson and Mayo districts from 1920–55.

COLORADO CREEK 63°58'N 139°00'W (115-O&N). One of the larger tributaries to Hunker Creek, from the west.

This creek was staked and named by Max Scanzon on 26 May, 1898. He, like many other Klondikers, had mined in Colorado.

COLUMBUS GLACIER 60°24′N 139°52′W (115-B&C). On the Yukon-Alaska boundary, west of the Seward Glacier in the St. Elias Range.

This glacier was named by H.R.H. Prince Luigi Amadeo, Duke of Abruzzi, on 31 July, 1897, for Christopher COLUMBUS. Prince Luigi led the Italian expedition which first climbed Mount St. Elias.

CONE HILL 64°24′N 140°35′W (116-B&C). On the south side of the Fortymile River, three miles upstream from the Yukon.

This cone-shaped hill was named by Lt. F. Schwatka, US Army, on his trip down the river in 1883. From the hill he also renamed the Fortymile River the "Cone Hill" River. Although the hill is still known locally by his name, it has been officially abandoned by the Board on Geographical Names as there are another Cone Hill and a Cone Mountain in the territory, both named much later.

CONGDON CREEK 61°09′N 138°33′W (115-G&F). Flows into the southwest end of Kluane Lake.

This stream was probably named after Frederick Tennyson CONGDON by a miner whom he had grubstaked, in February 1904.

F.T. Congdon, a lawyer from Nova Scotia, came to the Yukon in early 1898 as Legal Adviser to the Commissioner of the Yukon. This post he held until 1901. He quickly became the leader of the Liberal Party in the Yukon and was appointed Commissioner of the Yukon Territory in March 1903, a post he held until May 1905. He established the newspaper *The Yukon World* as a party mouthpiece. His tenure was marked by political graft and corruption and extreme political patronage, even in a day when this was common everywhere. In 1908 he was elected to parliament, losing the seat in the next election in 1911. He left the Yukon and engaged in law practice in Vancouver. He died in Ottawa on 13 March, 1932.

CONNOLLY LAKE 62°32′N 132°10′W (105-K). Four miles east of Mount Connolly.

Both this lake and the mountain to the west were known locally by this name for a number of years previous to the official designation in June 1978.

MOUNT CONNOLLY 7,018′ 62°32′N 132°20′W (105-K). 35 miles northeast of Faro.

Thomas Osborne CONNOLLY was born in Prince Albert, Saskatchewan, on 4 July, 1918. He was a born bushman and in his late teens went to Goldfields and then to Yellowknife where he earned his living mining and freighting. He and his lifelong friend, John Dewhurst, spent two years trapping in the Nahanni country and worked their way to the Pelly River country.

He enlisted in the Royal Canadian Naval Fishermen's Reserve in 1942 and soon was sent overseas on combined operations. He took part in the invasion of France, landing 3rd Division Canadian troops on the beach on D Day. He was engaged in numerous other landings and was discharged in March 1945.

Returning to the Yukon he took over the Taylor and Drury trading post at Ross River for a year and then set up his own store. Until 1964 he combined this with outfitting and guiding big-game hunters to the area. In 1964 he moved his family to Atlin, BC, and continued to guide in the Taku River region until his death in Vancouver, BC, on 21 July, 1975.

His fearlessness combined with his outgoing personality made him a true example of the northern pioneer.

CONRAD 60°04′N 134°34′W (105–D). On the west side of Windy Arm, Tagish Lake, about eight miles southwest of Carcross.

On 13 July, 1899, Ira Petty and W.R. Young had found and staked the silver-gold deposits that were to spark an intensive mining era in this section of the Yukon.

By 1905 Colonel John Howard CONRAD, an American mining promoter, had acquired control of most of the newly-discovered gold-silver-lead deposits on the west side of Windy Arm. He organized this settlement which at first was intended as a supply base for his operations. By 1909 it was a thriving town with stores, hotels, chuches and a District Mining Recorder. Steamboats ran schedules between here and Carcross.

The ore in the various mines, — The Big Thing, Montana, Joe Petty, Aurora, The Venus, all under Conrad Consolidated Mines Ltd., — was actively being developed but extensive work showed the erratic nature of the deposits. By 1914, with a drop in the world price for silver, the mines closed down and the town was abandoned. Several attempts have been made to reopen the mines but, so far, without success.

White Mountain, across the lake on the east side of Windy Arm, was locally called Mount Conrad at that time but the name was not officially allowed due to the earlier designation.

THE CONSERVATIVE TRAIL (115-F)

According to Hugh Bostock, the "Liberal Trail" was part of the original winter road between Dawson and Mayo and when placer mining developed on the creeks to the north, the government was urged to build a new trail that would serve more miners. In one of the elections, the Conservative candidate supported the financing of this new trail, while the Liberal advocated maintaining the trail as it was. The Conservative won, so the new trail was built. It ran from Minto Lake, along Bear Creek, across the McQuesten River and up Vancouver Creek to Clear Creek, at which point it merged with the old trail. Thus, the two trails were locally known as the "Liberal" and "Conservative" Trails.

The trails are now abandoned as mail routes but the names are still in use and the trails appear clearly in aerial photographs.

MOUNT CONSTANTINE 10,295′ 61°25′N 140°34′W (115-F). Overlooking the huge Klutan Glacier in the St. Elias Range.

This peak was named in July 1900 by J.J. McArthur, DLS, of the International Boundary Survey.

Charles CONSTANTINE was born in Bradford, Yorkshire, in 1849. A short, neat man with a piercing eye and a commanding presence, he joined the army at an early age. He took part in the Red River Expedition of 1870, became Chief of the Provincial Police of Manitoba and held a commission in the Winnipeg Light Infantry (The Little Black Devils). He saw action in the Northwest Rebellion in 1885 and then enlisted in the NWMP with the rank of inspector.

In 1894 there were no government officials of any kind in what was to become the Yukon Territory; the only law was the miners' meeting. When attended by the usual working miner and prospector it was a most democratic procedure. However, as the flow of gold and the population both increased, the settlements became filled with the usual frontier scum and parasites. When a miners' meeting was called, these people attended, while most of the miners were out at work on the creeks. The verdicts of such meetings became more and more frivolous and biased.

By early 1894 Bishop Bompas and Captain J.J. Healy (who had organized the NAT&TC and built Fort Cudahy at Fortymile) had asked the Canadian government for police to bring law, order and justice to the territory.

In June 1894 Insp. Constantine with Staff Sergeant Charles Brown of the NWMP arrived at Fortymile and, after an inspection of conditions in the region, returned to Ottawa and recommended that a force of NWMP and a

Customs Agent be established at Fortymile. S/Sg. Brown remained behind to represent the government.

Constantine returned on the *Porteous B. Weare* (the NAT&TC's riverboat) from St. Michaels on 24 July, 1895, with NCO's and constables, Insp. D'Arcy Strickland, Ass't Surgeon Willis and D.W. Davis, Collector for Customs for the Yukon. Constantine was appointed Magistrate, Mining Recorder, Coroner, Land and Timber Agent and all other necessary government posts not specified. His powers were wide and his instructions were to govern by the spirit rather than the exact letter of the law. They built Fort Constantine just below Fort Cudahy on the west bank of the Yukon, the most northerly military post of the British Empire.

In August 1896, when the Klondike gold was discovered, Constantine was the sole government official with authority, with the exception of William Ogilvie, who ably assisted him.

When the first claims were being recorded Constantine decided to use the local miners' name for the river and district and he settled on "Klondyke" as being nearest their pronunciation of the Indian name. In all the excitement and pressure on him he never lost control and his handling of such a potentially explosive situation, almost alone, still excites admiration.

In 1904, he was given command of the Athabaska District, NWT, and from 1905-07 was engaged in building a road from Fort St. John, BC, to the head of Lake Teslin, via Bear Lake, BC, and the headwaters of the Skeena River. The road was never completed.

Superintendent Charles Constantine died in Long Beach, California, while on leave, on 5 May, 1912.

CONTACT CREEK 60°00'N 127°44'W (95-D). Crosses the Yukon-BC border at mile 588.1 (K947) of the Alaska Highway.

On 24 September, 1942, bulldozers working their way south from Watson Lake met those working north from Fort Nelson, BC. This meeting of the road construction crews of the US Army Engineers marked the breakthrough of the Alaska Highway from Dawson Creek, BC, to Whitehorse and the first road access to the Yukon Territory. (See Beaver Creek.)

MOUNT CONYBEARE 2,062' 69°29'N 140°07'W (117-C). Ten miles south of the Arctic coast.

This was named by John Franklin (later Sir), in 1826, after William Daniel

CONYBEARE (1787-1857), a prominent English clergyman and noted amateur geologist.

COOK LAKE   62°09'N 130°54'W (105-J). 15 miles northwest of the Pelly Lakes.

This was named in September 1971 after Lesley "Les" COOK, who was a bush pilot and trader. He had a cabin on this lake and a trading post at Sheldon Lake. The trading post was run for a short time by his brother Jim, who was killed by a gun-trap he had set for bears.

Cook scouted the route of the Alaska Highway between Watson Lake and Teslin Lake in 1942 for the US Army Engineers, flew supplies to their survey camps and was later posthumously awarded the US Air Medal for several emergency flights he flew at that time.

He crashed in the Yukon River at Whitehorse later in 1942 and was killed.

MOUNT COOK   13,760'   60°11'N 139°58'W (115-B&C). A boundary peak in the St. Elias Range.

This was named by W.H. Dall, Assistant of the US Coast Survey in 1871 (later the USC&GS) in 1874 after Captain James COOK, RN (1728-1779), the famous English navigator and explorer who carried out much of the first mapping and exploration of the Alaska coast.

MOUNT COOK   61°55'N 132°55'W (105-F). About 15 miles southwest of Ross River.

In 1951 this mountain was named to honour the memory of J-6276 Squadron Leader Robert Geoffrey COOK, DFC, who was born in Toronto, Ontario, on 5 February, 1921. He enlisted in the RCAF at Toronto on 20 September, 1940. He served in Canada and overseas and was missing, presumed killed in action, on 4 December, 1943.

The mountain had previously been mapped and named "Priest" Mountain in the spring of the same year by a GSC party in the area. The population of the area being almost nil, they had been completely surprised one day when a priest, in clerical garb, riding a motorcycle, went by. However, the Board on Geographical Names disallowed this name the same year. Some of the local people still use it.

MOUNT COOPER   61°11'N 136°19'W (115-H). At the headwaters of the Nordenskiold River.

This was named in 1898 after George COOPER, member of GSC survey party in the area that year. He was with J.B. Tyrrell.

CORBETT HILL 2,511' 66°20'N 136°43'W (116-1). West of the Eagle River.

In 1973 this feature was named to commemorate K-73831 Sapper Herbert Logan CORBETT, 2nd Tunnelling Company, Royal Canadian Engineers. He was killed in a blasting accident while constructing underground fortifications at Gibraltar on 28 November, 1942. He had been a placer miner at Dawson and Atlin, BC, before the war.

MOUNT CORCORAN 2,514' 62°48'N 137°27'W (115-1). Two miles northwest of Fort Selkirk.

This was named in November 1971 after Reg. No. 42 Gunner J. CORCORAN, Royal Canadian Artillery. He was a member of the Yukon Field Force and died and was buried at Fort Selkirk on 27 September, 1898. (See Mount Evans.)

MOUNT CORP 65°22'N 133°13'W (106-F). East of the Snake River in the Canyon Range.

This mountain was named by Hugh S. Bostock, GSC, in 1973, after Ernest J. CORP who came to the Klondike in 1897-98, via the Mackenzie and Gravel Rivers, Bonnet Plume Pass and the Stewart River. He was a successful miner in the Klondike and later prospected for silver on Keno Hill. He was elected for several years a member of the Yukon Council for the Mayo riding.

CORWIN VALLEY 60°17'N 134°58'W (105-D). The valley of the Wheaton River from Lake Bennett north to Annie Lake.

Frank Corwin, a pioneer Yukoner and his partner, Tom Rickman, camped in this valley and prospected the area in 1893. They found several, rich-looking deposits of gold and silver-antimony ores. They returned to Juneau in the fall where both died within a few months. Although they had staked claims on their finds, others whom they had told were unable to relocate them. Some were found in 1906 by later prospectors. (See Carbon Hill and Gold Hill.)

MOUNT COUDERT 60°32'N 136°03'W (115-A). On the northeast side of Kusawa Lake.

This hill was named in 1966 in memory of Bishop John Louis COUDERT, the first Roman Catholic Bishop of Whitehorse. He had served in the north for 45 years. He died in November 1965 while attending a Vatican Council in Rome. His body was brought back and buried in Whitehorse.

COWARD CREEK   62°39′N 134°04′W (105–L). A small tributary to the Tay River.

Aleck COWARD came in the Klondike rush and remained to trap and trade. He and his partner Zimmerlee ran a trading post at Armstrong's Landing on the MacMillan River between 1905–10. Coward then set up a trading post at Fork Selkirk where he traded, trapped and prospected until the 1950's. His wife, who had been a missionary teacher at Fort Selkirk since 1916, did not care for her husband's surname and always styled herself Mrs. Cowaret after their marriage in 1929.

CRAIG CREEK 69°37′N 140°55′W (117–C). Flows into Clarence Lagoon on the Arctic coast.

This stream was named in 1912 by the International Boundary Survey party for J.D. CRAIG, DLS, who was in charge of the Canadian survey team. (See Mount Craig.)

MOUNT CRAIG   13,250   61°16′N 140°53′W (115–G&F). In the Ice-field Ranges of the St. Elias Mountains.

John Davidson CRAIG (1875–1936), BSc, DLS, a surveyor, joined the International Boundary Commission in 1905. In the following years he surveyed the Yukon-Alaska boundary from Mount St. Elias to the Beaufort Sea. From 1910 he was chief of Canadian survey parties until the task was finished in 1914. He was a member of the International Boundary Commission from 1925–31 and Director General of Surveys for the Department of the Interior from 1924–31.

CRATER CREEK   61°04′N 133°05′W (105–F). Flows into the west side of Quiet Lake.

This was probably named in 1887 by John McCormack and his three companions when they were the first men to find and prospect Quiet Lake. It was so named because of a peculiar, circular basin or valley nearby.

CRAWFORDSVILLE   61°34′N 134°52′W (105–E). On the east bank of the Yukon at the mouth of the Teslin River.

A short-lived but active settlement was built here in early 1898 and abandoned the following year. Captain Jack CRAWFORD, a famous American army scout, Indian fighter, poet and miner, was the Assistant General Manager of the Klondike, Yukon and Copper River Company. He hired large numbers of men and brought in much equipment to start a dredging operation on the Teslin River. Owing to various physical problems and a shortage of cash, the operation failed and Captain Jack went on to other ventures in Dawson City.

MOUNT CREEDEN 7,000' 61°16'N 137°15'W (115-H). On the west side of Aishihik Lake and six miles north of the Three Guardsmen Mountains.

This mountain received its name in 1966 to perpetuate the memory of J-15353 Pilot Officer James Waldron CREEDEN, DFM. He was born 4 February, 1922, at Brantford, Ontario. Enlisting in the RCAF at Hamilton, Ontario, he served in Canada and overseas. He was killed during air operations on 16 May, 1942.

CRIPPLE GULCH 64°00'N 139°22'W (116-B&C). A short brook, flowing into Bonanza Creek from the east, three miles from the Klondike River.

On 5 November, 1897, William Dugan staked the Discovery claim and named the gulch after CRIPPLE Creek, Colorado, one of the richest gold-mining camps in the USA. The hill above the gulch carried extremely rich gold in the White Channel gravels and was very productive. The stream was first named Cripple Creek.

MOUNT CRONIN 66°47'N 136°10'W (116-I). East of the Rock River in the Richardson Mountains.

In 1973 this mountain was chosen to honour the name of Lt. Alfred CRONIN, born 24 March, 1884, in Liverpool, England. He was working in the Yukon at Whitehorse and went to Victoria, BC where he enlisted in the 57th Batalion CEF on 28 October, 1915. He served in Canada and Great Britain, and was killed in action in France on 27 September, 1918.

MOUNT CRONKHITE 65°32'N 137°08'W (116-H). West of the Blackstone River.

Supt. Howard Hooper CRONKHITE, RCMP, served in the Yukon from 1921 to 35 and 1942 to 46. This peak was named in 1973.

CROSBY CREEK 62°50′N 137°06′W (115-I). A tributary to the Pelly River.

This was named in the early 1900's after George CROSBY who was a trapper and long-time prospector in this area. Crosby came to the Yukon in 1898 and was a partner of John Barr for many years. They lived in cabins 20 miles apart but worked together.

CROUCHER CREEK 60°47′N 135°04′W (105-D). Enters the Yukon River three miles below Whitehorse from the east side.

This creek was named in 1949 as a memorial to J-26857 Flight Lt. Gordon CROUCHER, MID, who was born 2 January, 1916, at Montréal, Québec. He enlisted there on 7 June, 1942 and served in Canada and overseas. He was missing, presumed to have been killed in action, on 29 July, 1944.

CUB LAKE 60°47′N 135°26′W (105-D). The smaller of two lakes, five miles south of Takhini.

This was named several years ago when the CUBS and Boy Scouts initiated their annual summer camp there.

CUESTA CREEK 68°45′N 136°54′W (117-A). A tributary of Rapid Creek.

In the summer of 1970 F.G. Young, GSC, named this creek after an uncommon geological formation found near its mouth. CUESTA is a Spanish term meaning, roughly, a hill. The term is used mostly by geologists in the American southwest to describe a hill in which the rock-bedding is normal to the gentler-sloping side of the hill rather than parallel to it as is mostly the case.

CYR CREEK 61°19′N 138°34′W (115-G&F). Flows into Gladstone Creek.

This was named about 1903 after Michael CYR of Québec, who mined here. He was a well-known trapper and prospector in the Yukon for many years.

d'ABBADIE RIVER (See Big Salmon River.)

D'ABBADIE CREEK 61°46′N 134°22′W (105-E). A tributary to the North Big Salmon River.
(See Big Salmon River.)

MOUNT D'ABBADIE 61°43′N 134°05′W (105–E). Lies at the head of D'Abbadie Creek.

This was named because of its position on the creek.

DAIL CREEK 60°16′N 135°04′W (105–D). A small tributary to the Wheaton River from Gold Hill.

In the summer of 1906 a stampede of prospectors was caused by the finding of rich lode-gold ore on Gold Hill. George DAIL, a Klondiker, was one of the first to locate claims on this creek. He was a successful prospector and miner and was widely known in the Yukon for many years.

DAIL PEAK 60°01′N 134°40′W (105–D). A prominent ridge on the southwest side of Windy Arm.

George DAIL was one of the pioneer prospectors in the area. He found and staked the first mineral claims here in 1905 when the hill received its name from the local prospectors.

DALTON CREEK 60°19′N 137°17′W (115–A). Flows into Alder Creek, ten miles southwest of Dezeadash Lake.

This was named in May or June 1898 after Jack DALTON, famous Yukon and Alaska pioneer.

Born in the Oklahoma Territory in 1855, he ran away from home at the age of 15, some say because of a shooting scrape in which he was forced to kill a man. He roamed the American west in its most lawless period until — another shooting is hinted — he reached Juneau in 1887.

In 1890 he was hired by E. Hazard Wells to accompany the Frank Leslie Illustrated Newspaper Expedition into the Yukon along the old Chilkat trade route, which he later transformed into the Dalton Trail. He and E.J. Glave, an English adventurer, explored the Alsek River country and were the first men to descend the Alsek to the sea.

The following year he travelled much the same country, he and Glave bringing in the first horses seen in the Yukon. When the expedition left, Dalton, who had seen the potential of the country, remained. He started to improve the trail and established posts on it. He proposed both to trade with the Indians in the interior and to freight supplies from Pyramid Harbour to the Yukon River for the ever-increasing mining population there. He also saw that this trail was the only feasible way to get sizeable numbers of livestock into the goldfields.

By 1895 he had found and laid out the best trail and had built posts. The first herds of cattle and sheep to enter the Yukon were taken over the trail in the summer of 1896, to the mouth of the Nordenskiold River.

The only man to control a major route into the Yukon and the Klondike, Dalton ran pack trains and drove livestock to the miners. He allowed others to use his trail on payment of a toll and backed his authority with his reputation and a gun. One group which refused to pay was accompanied for the whole journey by Dalton, who kept them well away from his route and in rough country. They lost most of their stock. No one else tried to travel without paying again. He also set up and ran a Pony Express service for a short time in 1898 to speed mail into the diggings.

After the gold fever died down Dalton continued his packing and freighting until the WP&YR. and the riverboats put him out of business. He stayed in the country for many years, engaging in mining activities in the White River and nearby Alaska country. He helped survey the routes of the Alaska and Copper River railroads.

Retiring in the late 1920's, he spent many more years in Seaside, Oregon and died in January 1945 in San Francisco.

Gold-seekers using the Dalton Trail prospected along the way and found good gold on Shorty Creek. Either Dalton himself, or men working for him, found gold on this stream immediately afterward. Over the years he prospected and invested in many mining propositions in this part of the Yukon with some success.

DALTON POST or HOUSE 60°07′N 137°02′W (115-A). About 18 miles south of Dezeadash Lake and two miles west of the Haines highway.

Jack DALTON established a trading post and base camp here in 1893 or 94 to trade with the interior Indians. The climate being good he wintered his pack horses nearby for many years. A NWMP post was built here in 1897 and closed in 1904. In 1898 Dalton brought in an additional 250 head of fine Oregon horses and started the Dalton Pony Express, to give rapid service to passengers and mail between Pyramid Harbour and Fort Selkirk. He could not compete with the riverboats and the venture soon stopped. Most of the livestock brought into the goldfields came this way.

DALTON RANGE 60°29′N 137°10′W (115-A). A short range of mountains facing the west side of Dezeadash Lake.

This was probably named by J.J. McArthur, DLS, in 1897, after Jack DALTON, one of the most colourful of the Yukon and Alaska pioneers.

DALTON TRAIL

This was a major route from the sea to the Klondike goldfields and the only one over which horses, cattle, sheep and other animals could be driven easily and quickly.

The route was originally an ancient Chilkat Indian "Grease Trail" or trade route to the interior. The Chilkats carried fish oil, or grease, along with other trade goods (except guns). The route was, like the Chilkoot Pass, jealously guarded, as it was so lucrative to the Chilkats.

In 1869 Professor George Davidson, senior officer of the USGS in Alaska, persuaded the Chilkat Chief Koh-klux to draw a map of the trail. (See Fort Selkirk.)

In 1882 Dr. Aurel Krause of the Bremen Geographical Society was the first white man known to enter the country by this route, which he mapped to the Tatshenshini river.

In 1890 the Frank Leslie Illustrated Newspaper Expedition, led by E. Hazard Wells and E.J. Glave, with A.B. Schantz and Jack DALTON, went to Kusawa Lake where the party split in two. Wells and Schantz went on to the Tanana country while Glave and Dalton returned down the Alsek River. Glave and Dalton returned the following year. This time Dalton stayed in the country and began building his trail and trading posts.

By 1896 he had his operation organized: a home and a trading post at Pyramid Harbour; a post at Pleasant Camp, (near the Yukon-Alaska border); and his main trading post at Dalton House, where he wintered most of his horses.

The trail was quickly and very roughly mapped by J.J. McArthur, DLS, in 1897. In the winter of 1897–98, following reports of starvation conditions in the Klondike, the American government gathered reindeer and Lapland herders from Scandinavia and sent a herd over this trail to relieve the miners. By the time they arrived (and less than half got there) the famine had been averted and the remainder of the herd was sent on into Alaska.

A railroad was proposed over this route in 1898 and would have provided the best and cheapest access to Dawson. It was forgotten when the WP&YR was begun the same year. The Haines Junction Highway now follows the Dalton Trail for much of its length from Haines to Dalton House.

The first recorded herd of cattle to be taken over the trail was that driven by Willis Thorpe, his two sons, "Long Shorty" Brooks, George Bounds (a butcher) and two other men in 1896. It is not certain whether they were working for Dalton or paid him toll to pass. The herd consisted of about 40 steers which carried packs of freight. They were driven to Carmacks and rafted down-river to Dawson, arriving in early September 1896.

DALZIEL CREEK 60°29'N 127°10'W (95-D). A tributary of Rock River, 60 miles northeast of Watson Lake.

This was named after George Campbell Ford DALZIEL, trapper, bushman, bush pilot and big-game guide. At 18, in 1926, he came to the Yukon from North Vancouver, BC, and spent the first winter alone, trapping on the Coal River in the southeastern Yukon. Soon acquiring an aircraft he quickly became a superb bush pilot. He scouted the location of the Alaska Highway in this area for the US Army Engineers and was instrumental in finding several downed aircraft that had been lost while being ferried from Edmonton to Alaska and Russia during the Second World War.

A pioneer in the Watson Lake and surrounding country, Dalziel is noted for his ability to survive anywhere, in any season, alone.

DANGER CREEK 62°02'N 132°39'W (105-K). Flows into the Pelly River, two miles below the Lapie River.

In the summer of 1905 Charles Sheldon, noted amateur naturalist and big-game hunter, named this stream after his horse "DANGER." The horse was the first one ever seen in the upper Pelly region. Some maps have this creek named "Old Danger" Creek.

DAN MAN CREEK 62°58'N 139°17'W (115-J). A small creek flowing into the Yukon four miles above Kirkman Creek.

This was known for many years as the home and territory of Daniel MAN, a well-known trapper and prospector.

MOUNT DAOUST 62°04'N 136°06'W (115-I). About five miles southeast of Carmacks.

This was named about 1905 after an operator on the Yukon Telegraph Line who was stationed at Carmacks.

DAUGHNEY LAKE 60°10'N 130°55'W (105-B). On the Swift River six miles north of mile 720 (K1159) on the Alaska Highway.

In 1947 this lake was given the name of an outstanding Canadian soldier, Major Ralph Herman DAUGHNEY, DSO. He was born 30 November, 1908, at Dalhousie Junction, New Brunswick and was commissioned in the Canadian army on 5 September, 1940, at Woodstock, New Brunswick.

He served in Canada, Great Britain and northwest Europe and was killed in action on 10 August, 1944.

DAVIDSON CREEK 63°47'N 135°27'W (105–M). Flows into Duncan Creek near Mayo Lake.

About 1901 Jake DAVIDSON was one of the four men who staked the first claims on Duncan Creek. Shortly afterward he found gold on this stream.

DAVIS LAKE 66°11'N 136°25'W (116–I). One half-mile south of Moose Lake.

This quiet lake was named in 1973 to honour the name of Pte. Harry Henry DAVIS, K-76942, who died a prisoner of war in Holland on 15 January, 1945. He was born in Dawson on 9 January, 1921, enlisted at Whitehorse and served in Canada, Great Britain and northwest Europe in the Lake Superior Regiment (Motor).

DAWSON (CITY) 64°04'N 139°25'W (116–B&C). At the junction of the Yukon and Klondike Rivers.

Dawson City, the "Paris of the North", was the capital of the Yukon Territory from 1897 to 1951.

This was the site of an Indian fishing camp for untold years before white men ever saw the territory, as the Klondike River was one of the best salmon streams in the country.

George Carmack camped here with Skookum Jim and Tagish Charlie, fishing for salmon in early August 1896 before they made their journey of discovery up Rabbit (Bonanza) Creek.

Joseph Ladue, who operated the trading post and small sawmill at Ogilvie (Sixtymile River), had for years been a booster of the gold-mining possibilities of the district on the east side of the Yukon River and had grubstaked Robert Henderson who was and had been, with others, prospecting the tributaries of the Indian River.

While Carmack's party found the riches of Bonanza and started the great rush, Henderson and three companions were digging on Gold Bottom Creek with indifferent results. Henderson went down the Indian River to Ogilvie for more supplies and in early August 1896 showed Ladue a small amount of gold dust from his workings. Ladue, confirmed in his belief of the value of the Klondike district, decided to move some lumber and supplies down river to the mouth of the Klondike, stake a townsite and establish a small trading post.

Seldom has a decision been more fortuitous. He arrived on the scene on 28 August to hear for the first time of the Bonanza strike and to find the area alive with excited men. He immediately staked out a 160-acre townsite on the only available ground and, on 1 September, started to build his store, the first building in Dawson. He sent some of his men back to Ogilvie to bring up the sawmill (which ran night and day for the next two years). He built a small log building and opened the Pioneer, the first saloon in town. He sold lots in his townsite and bought rich claims from the cheechako stakers who did not foresee their value. In January 1897 William Ogilvie, DLS, surveyed the townsite and Ladue and his partner, Arthur Harper, had it officially named after Dr. George Mercer DAWSON (1849–1901), Director of the Geological and Natural History Survey of Canada from 1895 to 1901, explorer, scientist and human being extraordinary.

Called the "Little Doctor" by all who knew him, he was born in Pictou, Nova Scotia on 1 August, 1849, a son of Sir John William Dawson, naturalist, geologist and the first principal of McGill University. A severe illness at the age of 12 made him a hunchback and stunted his growth, leaving him in poor health for the remainder of his life. Tutored at home, he had an abounding interest in the natural sciences and carried this into his studies at McGill and at the Royal School of Mines in London, England where he graduated at the head of his class.

In 1873 he was appointed Geologist and Botanist to the British North American International Boundary Commission. His report on the geology and mineral resources along the 49th parallel from the Lake of the Woods to the Pacific Ocean is still a Canadian classic and resulted in his appointment to the G&NHSC in 1875.

Although crippled and frail he carried out some of the most strenuous surveys ever attempted in Canada, and his yearly reports are incredible for both the quality and sheer quantity of the work accomplished. He reported exhaustively on everything and everyone he encountered. In 1887, with William Ogilvie, DLS, of the Department of the Interior, he organized and headed the first geological and lateral survey conducted in the Yukon Territory. It was typical of Dawson that he chose the hardest route for himself. He came from Wrangell up the Stikine River, the Dease River, the Liard and Frances Rivers and into Frances Lake. From there he went down the Pelly River to the Yukon, up that stream and over the Chilkoot Pass to Dyea on the Pacific. His report encompassed almost everything known about the Yukon to that time.

He was an authority on ethnology, archaeology and botany as well as geology and was later to be called "The Father of Canadian Anthropology".

His collections in these fields, made on his surveys, laid the base of the ethnological collection of the National Museum of Canada. He published dozens of technical papers, many of them still standard.

Appointed Director of the Geological Survey of Canada in 1895, he enhanced and continued the work of his towering predecessors, Logan and Selwyn. His honours included the CMG, LLD from both Queen's and McGill Universities, FRS, President and Charter Member of the RSC, the Patron's Gold Medal of the RGS and FASAS.

He died unexpectedly, after a one-day illness, of acute bronchitis, in Ottawa, on 2 March, 1901.

Dawson City's heyday was from 1897 to late 1899, and most of the literature concerning it was written about this period. The exhaustion of the richest, hand-worked, placer gold and the news of more fabulous finds in the beach sands of Nome depleted the population in 1899 and the equally rich finds at Tanana (Fairbanks) in 1903 took many people away from the Klondike. By 1900 many wives and families had arrived. The machine methods of mining attracted a more skilled and settled people and Dawson became a quieter and more stable town.

The population in late 1898 was estimated at greater than 5,000 but the town was a service and social centre for more than 30,000 in the immediate area. In January 1902, Dawson was incorporated to city status but with the drop in population a petition to rescind the charter was accepted and it was cancelled in 1904. The town then had no mayor and affairs were managed by the Office of the Commissioner of the Territory.

The town always had a rich and varied social life, the more so because of its isolation, especially during the eight winter months. However, as the placers were worked out and little new gold found, the population steadily declined. The final blow was the cessation of dredging activities by the Yukon Consolidated Gold Corporation Ltd., in 1966. Owing to the development of the Clinton Creek asbestos mine at Fortymile and to an increase in the tourist trade, Dawson now has about 800–900 persons.

In the last few years the Canadian government has finally realized the importance of the town as an historical site of major importance and is busy saving and restoring many of the old buildings.

DAWSON CHARLIE CREEK   60°14′N 135°10′W (105–D). A tributary of the Wheaton River, flowing from Gold Hill.

After August 1896, Tagish Charlie, nephew of Skookum Jim and Kate Carmack, became known as "DAWSON CHARLIE". He and Skookum Jim prospected widely in the southern Yukon and grubstaked other Indian friends and relatives. This area was close to his home at Carcross and in 1903 he staked mineral showings on this stream.

Charlie became a wealthy man from his Klondike claim on Bonanza Creek. On 2 July, 1904, a special Act of Parliament enfranchised him, "with all the rights and privileges of a white citizen." He could vote, sue and be sued, buy and drink liquor and hold office.

Returning home from a celebration on 26 January, 1908, he fell from the WP&YR bridge at Carcross and was drowned. (See Bonanza and Fourth of July Creeks.)

DAWSON RANGE 62°40′N 139°00′W (115-J&K). The range of mountains stretching for nearly 40 miles west of the Yukon River, north of its junction with the Pelly.

These hills were named well before the turn of the century after Dr. G.M. DAWSON, GSC.

The area came into prominence about 1969 with the discovery of potentially vast deposits of copper-molybdenite mineralization, which are still being studied.

(See Dawson City.)

DEADMAN'S CREEK 60°20′N 133°04′W (105-C). A small tributary to Teslin Lake, crossing the Alaska Highway at mile 816 (K1314).

Although officially named at the time of the Alaska Highway construction, the local people claim that the name is much older and was given because the stream runs off DEADMAN'S Hill. The hill, named in early times, resembles a reclining man.

DEADWOOD CREEK 64°06′N 139°28′W (116-B&C). A tributary to the Yukon River from the west at Dog Island, three miles below Dawson.

B.B.S. Phillips, who had probably mined at DEADWOOD, in the Black Hills of South Dakota, named this creek when he discovered gold here on 24 September, 1897.

MOUNT DECOELI 60°50′N 137°53′W (115-A). A prominent peak about four miles west of mile 1030 (K1658) on the Alaska Highway.

This was named in 1950 after E.J. DECOELI, a member of the International Boundary Commission Survey party in 1913.

DeCOURCY LAKE 61°29′N 137°08′W (115–H). Five miles east of central Ashihik Lake.

This three-mile-long lake was named in 1956 to honour the memory of J-17641 Squadron Leader Thomas Joseph DeCOURCY, DFC. He was born 2 August, 1921, at Mitchell, Ontario and enlisted in the RCAF on 7 October, 1940, at Windsor, Ontario. He was serving overseas when he was accidentally killed on 7 June, 1945.

DEMPSTER HIGHWAY

The Yukon's newest highway, it was begun in 1959 as Yukon Territorial Road No. 11. Later it was called the Flat Creek Road when it reached that far; then, as it lengthened, it was known as the Eagle Plain Road and lastly the Aklavik Road.

Leaving the Klondike Highway at mile 26, east of Dawson, the road follows the Klondike River valley. Then it turns north through the Ogilvie Mountains to the Blackstone River, crosses the Ogilvie River to the Eagle River, follows it, and then goes east through the Mackenzie Mountains to Fort MacPherson.

The Yukon Order of Pioneers, founded in Fortymile in 1894 and active in honouring early Yukoners, proposed that the highway be named after Inspector W.J.D. DEMPSTER, RNWMP.

The route of the highway follows roughly the track of the NWMP patrols from Dawson to Fort MacPherson, started in 1905. These patrols were always done in the winter with dog teams.

Inspector F.J. Fitzgerald, Constables G.F. Kinney, Taylor and ex-Constable Sam Carter left Fort MacPherson on 21 December, 1910, on the return journey of this annual patrol. They went astray while trying to find the trail between Little Wind River and the Hart River. Running short of food, they decided to return to MacPherson but owing to exhaustion and starvation they were unable to reach it. Kinney and Taylor died about 35 miles from Fort MacPherson while Fitzgerald and Carter died about 25 miles out.

On 20 February, 1911, when the patrol had not arrived in Dawson, Insp. Snyder, the officer in charge, being concerned, ordered Cpl. Dempster with Constable J.F. Fyfe, ex-Constable F. Turner and Charles Stewart, an Indian guide, to search for the missing party. Leaving Dawson on 28 February they covered the route in record time, despite storms and bad weather which cost them valuable time. On 12 March they found a snow-covered trail on the Little Wind River, followed it with great difficulty and found the bodies of Fitzgerald and his companions. In a country of hardy men Dempster and his party earned respect for this journey.

William John Duncan "Jack" Dempster, RNWMP Regt. No. 3193 was born in Wales in 1876. He joined the force in 1897 and went to the Yukon the same year. By 1911 he was famous as a bushman and a musher. He went on to give outstanding service to the Yukon for a total of 37 years, all in the territory. He retired in 1934, with the rank of inspector, to Vancouver, BC, where he died on 25 October, 1964.

MOUNT DEMPSTER   65°08′N 136°05′W (116–H). North of the Little Wind River.

This mountain, near where he travelled many times, was named in 1973 to further honour Inspector W.J.D. DEMPSTER, RCMP.

DENNIS GLACIER   60°53′N 140°22′W (115–C). A small tongue of the Walsh Glacier, just east of the Centennial Range in the far northwest St. Elias Range.

This glacier was named in 1920 after either of two men. T.C. DENNIS, DLS, was assistant in charge of the International Boundary Survey party in 1910 and was in command of the party in 1912.

Colonel John Stoughton DENNIS, (1820–1885), DLS, DTS, PLS was Surveyor-General of Canada 1871–78 and Deputy Minister of the Department of the Interior 1878–81.

DENNIS MOUNTAIN   67°42′N 136°37′W (116–P). On the headwaters of the Bell River near McDougall Pass.

This was named by William Ogilvie in May 1888, after Col. John S. DENNIS, who had earlier been Ogilvie's superior in the Surveys Branch of the Department of the Interior. (See above.)

DESTRUCTION BAY   61°15′N 138°48′W (115–G&F). On the west side of Kluane Lake.

The first settlement here was a US Army Engineers highway construction camp in 1942. Shortly after construction, high winds destroyed most of the buildings, hence the name.

The memorial plaque erected later to commemorate this event was the result of the efforts of Bert Cluett (of Cluett Creek), a long-time pioneer who was annoyed at the false tales told the tourists about the loss of life and boats here during the Klondike rush.

THE DETOUR 62°40′N 134°36′W (105–L). The long, 15-mile "S" bend in the Pelly River, starting just below the Earn River and ending at Harvey Creek.

This was named by miners in the early 1880's or perhaps even earlier by the HBC men in the 1850's. It was so called because this sudden change of direction seemed to take them many miles out of their way.

DEVILHOLE CREEK 60°17′N 136°19′W (115–A). Flows into the west side of Kusawa Lake.

In 1950 Dr. E.D. Kindle, GSC, reported that the creek was named by the Indians of the area. They said sheep that were shot on the mountainsides disappeared into mysterious holes in the mountain and could not be found.

MOUNT DEVILLE 65°13′N 140°24′W (116–G&F). On the headwaters of the Tatonduk River in the Ogilvie Mountains.

William Ogilvie, DLS, named this mountain in March 1888 while making the first survey of the Yukon-Alaska boundary.

Edouard Gaston DEVILLE (1849–1924), DLS, DTS, OLS, QLS, was Surveyor-General of Canada from 1885–1924.

DEWDNEY MOUNTAIN 66°03′N 139°13′W (116–J&K). On the upper Miner River in the Ogilvie Mountains.

William Ogilvie, DLS, named this mountain in March 1888 after his good friend, the Hon. Edgar DEWDNEY.

Dewdney, born 1835 in Devonshire, England, and educated as a civil engineer, came to British Columbia in 1859 as a surveyor. When rich gold placers were found in the Similkameen he was given the contract to build a road from Fort Hope, head of navigation on the Fraser River, to Similkameen. Started in 1860, it was completed in 1863 and was called the "Dewdney Trail". When new gold finds were made farther east he extended his road to Wild Horse Creek in the Big Bend country of the Columbia River in 1865. These roads opened the interior of British Columbia to the coast and lessened the American influence in the interior.

He was elected to the provincial legislature in 1868–69. He represented Yale, BC, in the House of Commons in Ottawa from 1872–79, when he was appointed Lieutenant-Governor of the North West Territories as well as retaining the Indian Commissionership. During this time he is credited with averting major Indian uprisings during the Riel Rebellion by his just treatment of the larger tribes. He served Sir John A. MacDonald as Minister of the Interior and Superintendent of Indian Affairs from 1888 to 1892. In 1892 he was appointed Lieutenant-Governor of British Columbia and served until 1897. He died 8 August, 1916, at Victoria, BC.

DEZEADASH LAKE 60°28′N 136°58′W (115–A). A beautiful, 15-mile-long lake about 25 miles south of Haines Junction.

One of the earliest known features in the Yukon, this lake was described to George Davidson, senior officer of the US Geodetic Survey in Alaska in 1869 by Kho-klux, the great Chief of the Chilkat Indians. They called it "Dasar-dee-Ash" or "Dasa-dee-Arsh", meaning "Lake of the Big Winds".

DIAMAIN LAKE 62°55′N 136°19′W (115–1). Ten miles northeast of Pelly Crossing.

In 1935 Hugh S. Bostock, GSC, was looking for the name of this lake while mapping the area. Mrs. Ira Van Bibber told him the Indian name was DIAMAIN. The generic term "main" itself means "lake", so that the presently-used name is redundant.

DICKSON CREEK 61°07′N 138°56′W (115–G&F). A tributary of the Duke River.

Thomas A. DICKSON, (1856–1952), was one of four brothers, all ex-NWMP. He was with the Tagish Lake detachment in 1898. Leaving the force, he became the first big-game guide in the Yukon. In 1916 he was the Game Warden at Kluane Lake and had his homestead on this creek. Many of his descendants are still in the Yukon.

DICKSON HILL 60°12′N 135°01′W (105–D). Just south of the Wheaton River.

Ole DICKSON staked one of the first copper discoveries in the Whitehorse area, the Rabbit's Foot claim, on 7 July, 1899. He actively prospected in these parts for many years.

MOUNT DINES 65°37′N 140°37′W (116–G&F). North of the Nation River.

John Dawson DINES was born in Dawson City. He served overseas in the Second World War and was later Mining Recorder at Dawson and Yellow-knife, NWT. He moved up to Land Administrator at Ottawa with the

Department of Indian and Northern Affairs where he died in 1973.

DION CREEK   64°02′N 139°27′W (116–B). A small creek entering the Yukon from the east about two miles above Dawson.

This creek was named after H. DION, the leader of a prospecting party from Québec. They found gold here in October 1897.

DIP CREEK   62°32′N 139°23′W (115–J&K). A tributary of the Klotassin River.

Gold was discovered here by Jens Rude and the creek named on 12 August, 1915. (See Jens and Rude Creeks.)

DISCOVERY CREEK   62°04′N 137°14′W (115–I). A tributary to Nansen Creek from the west.

Captain H.S. Back made the first discovery of gold in the area on this creek in August 1899, at the point where it joins Nansen Creek. No work was done at the time but he returned to the region in 1907 with a large prospecting party. On 13 June, 1910, his son, Frank H. Back, with Tom Bee staked the first claim on both Nansen Creek and this stream. (See Mount Nansen, and Back and Seymour Creeks.)

DIXIE CREEK   61°02′N 137°49′W (115–H). A small tributary to McKinley Creek in the Alsek district.

P. Harvey Hebb created a great deal of excitement in August 1906 when he thought he had found diamonds in the blue clays on this stream. He had not. The creek had been named in July 1903 when it was first staked for placer gold during the stampede to the Ruby Creek finds in the Shakwak valley. (See Monte Cristo Gulch.)

DOGHEAD POINT   61°21′N 138°47′W (115–G&F). A point on Kluane Lake on the west side of Talbot Arm.

In the summer of 1945 H.S. Bostock, GSC, gave this name because of the remarkable similarity to a husky's head.

DOGPACK LAKE   61°42′N 139°12′W (115–G&F). A small lake about 12 miles north of Brooks Arm, Kluane Lake.

The name has been used for many years by the local Indians who used pack-dogs to take supplies in to the lake for their winter trapping.

DOLLIS CREEK (See Squaw Creek.)

DOLLY CREEK 62°04′N 137°13′W (115-I). A short brook flowing into upper Nansen Creek.

About 1910, George Mack, one of the original discoverers of gold here, named the stream after his daughter DOLLY (Mack) Golter, who lived on the creek with him.

DOLORES CREEK 64°53′N 133°21′W (106-C). 15 miles east of Fairchild Lake, in the Bonnet Plume Range.

Louis Brown, long-time trapper and big-game guide in this area, named this creek in 1964 after his wife and partner, DOLORES Cline Brown. He had found rich copper mineralization here in 1951. Bonnet Plume Copper Mines Ltd., was organized to explore the deposit.

Mrs. Brown wrote a most interesting book about their guiding and living experiences, entitled *Yukon Trophy Trails.*

DOMINION CREEK 63°37′N 138°42′W (115-O&N). Flowing into the Indian River from the north.

One of the richest and most famous of the Klondike creeks. There is good evidence that "Hootch Albert" Fortier found gold here in late 1896 but did nothing more about it until the spring of 1897. He staked the Lower Discovery claim in late May 1897 but did not record it. Instead, he allowed John E. Brannin to stake it on 12 June while he recorded No. 1 Above. At the same time, Frank Biederman was prospecting the upper part of the stream and, thinking he was the first to find gold on it, staked a Discovery claim on 28 May. The Mining Recorder allowed both discoveries and accepted the name DOMINION, proposed by Fortier.

Albert Fortier came to the Yukon in 1887 from Québec and, as his nickname implies, was noted in the Fortymile country for being able to make alcohol out of almost anything.

This stream was the locale for many of the charges of corruption against the Yukon administration in 1898. The action of Commissioner James Walsh in reserving alternate claims on the creek as a government reserve aroused great bitterness among the miners. His action however, in opening the claims to staking shortly afterwards aroused an even greater outcry when it was found that friends and relatives of government officials had staked claims the day before the general public was informed that the creek was open to staking. These, and other complaints, soon led to Walsh's recall to Ottawa and to the appointment of William Ogilvie, whose integrity was accepted by all.

The major settlement on the creek was at its junction with Caribou Creek and was called Caribou City until 1905. From that date it was called Dominion. The village died during the First World War.

DONJEK CITY 62°40′N 140°05′W (115-J&K). On the west side of the White River, one mile below Caledonia Creek.

A roadhouse was built here in 1913 on the trail from Stewart to the Chisana goldfields. Some gold was found on creeks nearby and a smaller settlement grew here for a number of years to service the miners. The place was abandoned in the 1920's.

DONJEK RIVER 62°36′N 140°00′W (115-J&K). A major tributary to the White River.

This large river was apparently named by Charles Willard Hayes on his 1891 expedition to the district. He took the name from the Indian word "Donyak" or "Donchek", it being the name of a type of pea-vine which grows profusely in the valley. It is extremely nutritious and makes excellent winter feed for game and stock animals.

DONOVAN CREEK 63°32′N 139°56′W (115-O&N). Flows into Abraham Creek in the Sixtymile district.

This name has been used locally since 1911 after Daniel DONOVAN who found the first gold and staked the first claim at Discovery Pup in that year.

MOUNT DOOSHKA 7,156′ 61°20′N 127°10′W (95-E). Almost on the Yukon-NWT border near the head of the Coal River.

This name was submitted in 1971 under the auspices of the Commissioner of the Yukon Territory, James Smith. It was adopted in 1972.

DOOSHKA is the Kutchin Indian word for "Love"; as noted in a popular song entitled "The Squaws Along The Yukon". One line says "Dooshka, Dooshka, Dooshka, which means, I love you."

DOUGLAS CREEK 60°53′N 138°38′W (115-B&C). A tributary of Slim's River, about ten miles above Kluane Lake.

86

Gold was found and this creek named by J. Kay in March 1904 during the rush to the Kluane Lake goldfields.

DRAPEAU CREEK 63°59'N 136°53'W (115-P). A short tributary of Hobo Creek.

Gerrard "Jerry" DRAPEAU prospected in these hills and the Mayo district for many years.

DRURY SPIRE 62°22'N 134°16'W (105-L). At the south end of Drury Lake.

H.S. Bostock, GSC, proposed this name in 1954 to honour William S. DRURY of Yorkshire, England. Coming to the Yukon in early 1898, Drury met Isaac Taylor while working on the Discovery claim on Pine Creek, Atlin, BC. They became partners and over the years built a thriving merchandising business all over the Yukon. (See Tadru Lake.)

DRY CREEK 62°20'N 140°23'W (115-J&K). A tributary of the White River near Snag.

Prospectors working on this creek about 1913 gave it the name because it froze to bottom in the winter. This is not remarkable as it runs through Snag, the coldest spot in Canada.

DUBLIN GULCH 64°03'N 135°51'W (106-D). A small valley off Haggart Creek in the Mayo district.

This is one of the best known and most famous names in the Mayo area. Thomas Haggart, one of the area's first and longtime prospectors, found coarse gold here in 1889. In 1896 he built the first cabin on the gulch and gave it its name. When the influx of Klondikers invaded the country Haggart and others decided to record their claims to protect them against claim-jumpers. John J. Suttles recorded claim No. 1 and continued to work it until 1910.

DUKE RIVER 61°26'N 139°06'W (115-G&F). Flows into the Kluane River a few miles above Kluane Lake.

George DUKE was one of the first prospectors in the Kluane Lake country before 1900. This river was then named for him.

DUNCAN CREEK 63°47'N 135°31'W (105-M). A tributary of the Mayo River just above Mayo Lake.

In 1898, three Norwegians, Gustavus Gustavusen and his two sons, alone in this part of the Yukon, discovered rich placer gold in the canyon on this stream. Because they wished to keep their find secret and because the Mining Recorder was so far away, they did not record any claims on their find. They went to great lengths to prevent anyone else from finding out about it, so much so that they were known on the lower Stewart River as the "Mysterious Three." By September 1901 they had recovered more than $30,000 in gold.

A party of four Scottish Klondikers began prospecting in the area that summer and found the Gustavusen workings. The four, Duncan Patterson, Colin Hamilton, Allen McIntosh and Jake Davidson, found that the claims were not recorded and promptly jumped them while the Gustavusens were down river for supplies. They staked on 12 September, 1901, and named the creek after DUNCAN Patterson. The remainder of the creek was quickly staked by others.

The Gustavusens left the country; the creek was one of the richest ever found in the Yukon outside the Klondike.

The "Code of the North" became badly bent after the Klondike Gold Rush. (See Gustavus Range.)

EAGLE CREEK 64°47′N 141°00′W (116-B&C). A tributary of the Yukon River, north of Fortymile.

E.C. Barnard of the USGS, gave this creek its name in 1898 because the bluffs near its mouth (which is in Alaska) are a favourite nesting place for the bald eagles of the area.

EAGLES NEST BLUFF 2,445′ 62°02′N 135°49′W (105-L). On the north bank of the Yukon River, five miles below the mouth of the Little Salmon River.

This was formerly called Eagle Rock by early miners and riverboat men, from the Indian name meaning the same.

It was here that the worst riverboat disaster ever to happen in the Yukon took place. On 25 September, 1906, the riverboat *Columbian* was destroyed by an explosion and fire which killed six men and wrecked the ship. A crew member, shooting at some wild fowl, accidentally hit a shipment of gunpowder and explosives placed on the forward deck, setting it off. The efforts of the survivors to help the injured were heroic. A monument in the Whitehorse Cemetery is the only record of this disaster.

EAGLE RIVER 67°18′N 137°09′W (116–P). This large stream flows into the Porcupine River from the south, a few miles below Lapierre House.

John Bell, Chief Factor at Fort MacPherson, was probably the first white man to see this river and record the Indian name when he first crossed into the Yukon in 1839.

This lonely river was, in January and February 1932, the scene of the first aircraft-assisted man hunt in Canada. From a fort-like cabin on the Rat River, NWT, Albert Johnson, the "Mad Trapper of Rat River", for 48 days, in temperatures averaging – 40°F., fought a series of four gun battles with the RCMP. He crossed the continental divide and, but for the use of an aircraft piloted by the famous bush pilot "Wop" May, might have escaped. He killed Constable Edgar "Spike" Millen (see Mount Millen) and wounded two other constables. He was killed on 17 February in a small ravine about 15 miles upstream from the mouth of this river.

Little was ever found out about who he was, his past, or his motives.

EAR LAKE 60°40′N 135°02′W (105–D). A small lake on the south side of the Yukon River at the foot of Miles Canyon.

Originally the site of a construction camp of the WP&YR, this pleasant little lake became a favourite camping spot for the people of Whitehorse. It was the scene of the worst mass murder in Yukon history when Alexander Gagoff, a Cossack, shot and killed the section foreman and three workers of the WP&YR here on 30 September, 1915. He was executed in Whitehorse jail on 10 March, 1916.

EARN RIVER 62°45′N 134°45′W (105–L). Enters the Pelly River near the start of the Detour.

Robert Campbell of the HBC, the famous explorer of the Pelly and Yukon Rivers, named this stream after a river of the same name near his home in Perthshire, Scotland. The date was the summer of 1840 when he made his momentous journey down the Pelly to the Yukon.

EDMONTON CREEK 63°47′N 134°48′W (105–M). Flows into the southeast side of Mayo Lake.

On 13 June, 1904, gold was discovered here by P. Beliveau and his partner, Desutel. Beliveau had come to the Yukon via the Edmonton Trail. Before his discovery the creek had been known locally as "Fan" or "Old Fan" Creek.

EIKLAND MOUNTAIN 4,773′ 62°15′N 140°50′W (115-J&K). Five miles west of mile 1185 (K1908) on the Alaska Highway.

In 1967 the name of this mountain, then known as "Nigger Head" Mountain, was changed to that of Peter EIKLAND, a long-time prospector in the area. The change was made by the Board on Geographic Names, owing to complaints that the original name might offend people.

The original name was probably given by stampeders going this way to the Chisana goldfields in 1913–14. It describes the large clumps of grass growing in the muskeg swamps which make walking difficult. They are unstable and if a person trying to step from one to the other slips, he or she is precipitated into the swamp mud. The name is an old one, common across northern Canada. Earlier, they were given the name "Têtes des Femmes" by the French-Canadian voyageurs of the HBC.

EINARSON LAKE 63°52′N 131°35′W (105-O). A small lake on Einarson Creek, a tributary of the Rogue River.

This was named in 1946 to immortalize a hero, J-17276 Flight Lt. Johann Walter EINARSON, DFC, DFM, RCAF. He was born in Wynyard, Saskatchewan on 20 November, 1920, and enlisted in the RCAF on 10 February, 1941 at Saskatoon. He served in Canada and overseas and was missing, presumed killed in action, on 25 February, 1944.

ELDORADO CREEK 63°55′N 139°19′W (115-O&N). The main tributary of Bonanza Creek.

On 1 September, 1896, a party of five, Anton Stander, Frank Kellar, James Clements, Jay "Old Man" Whipple and Frank Phiscator, who had just staked Nos. 32 to 36 Above on Bonanza Creek, decided to prospect this stream on their way back to the Klondike River. Clements and Kellar had panned gravel here in late August on their way up Bonanza and had recovered some gold. A number of others had passed it up and a story persists that someone blazed a tree at the mouth of the creek and wrote "Reserved for Swedes and cheechakos."

They discovered rich gold on No. 3 claim. Whipple claimed discovery and named the creek after himself. They staked their claims on 1 September. Another party of four arrived on 5 September and found dissension among the original five over claim ownership. They reached agreement and that evening Knut Halstead, a Fortymiler, suggested the name ELDORADO. Whipple's name was overruled because he was trying to hog too many claims and had also jumped claims in the Fortymile district.

Because of a rule newly passed by Inspector Constantine, NWMP, limiting the number of Discovery claims on a creek and the number of claims to be held by any one man in a district, further claim-jumping took place. F.W. Cobb, a famous Harvard University football star, jumped Frank Phiscator's No. 2 claim on 6 September but Constantine disallowed his claim. He later claimed to have discovered and named Eldorado Creek.

It has been claimed by various authorities that Eldorado Creek was the richest placer gold stream ever found anywhere in the world. The first 40 claims (about three and one half miles) on the creek produced well over half a million dollars each, with gold then valued at $20 per ounce. Some of the claims gave up over a million and a half dollars in a length of 500 feet. Gold is still being taken from the gravels of this small stream, 80 years later.

ELLEN CREEK 66°41′N 137°55′W (116-I). A small tributary of the Porcupine River.

A local name after an Indian woman "Elentsie" who was buried near the mouth of the stream many years ago.

ELLIOTT CREEK 64°36′N 135°49′W (106-D). A tributary of the Beaver River, in the Wernecke Mountains.

This stream was named in 1945 after Frederick ELLIOTT who prospected in this area in the 1920's. He was associated with Charles Settlemier, another well-known prospector. Elliott Ridge, a mountain north of the creek, was named later.

ELSA 63°55′N 135°29′W (105-M).

This small village, on Galena Hill in the Mayo district, was established in 1929 to house miners at the newly discovered Calumet silver-lead mine; it is not known after whom the settlement was named. Production at the mine did not start until 1937. A post office was started in 1949 and a little later the first oil exploration winter road, called "The Wind River Trail", was built from here north 300 miles to drilling sites in the Bell River area.

ENGER LAKES 62°15′N 140°40′W (115-J&K). Four small lakes near mile 1185 (K1908) on the Alaska Highway.

These were named during the rush to the Chisana goldfields in 1913 as the

"Niggerhead" Lakes by those who had the misfortune to have to backpack across this country. The territorial government in 1967 requested the name be changed as it might offend people.

Harry ENGER was a long-time prospector in the area. (See Eikland Mountain.)

ENGINEER CREEK 65°21′N 138°19′W (116-G&F). A tributary to the Ogilvie River.

This name replaced Big Creek in 1971 at the request of Commissioner James Smith. It was renamed to commemorate the work of the Department of Public Works engineers in the district during the location of the Dempster Highway.

ENSLEY CREEK 63°54′N 139°43′W (115-O&N). A tributary to the Yukon River below Indian River.

The lower Discovery claim was staked on 29 November, 1897 by S. ENSLEY.

ERICKSON GULCH 63°56′N 135°20′W (105-M). A small tributary of Christal Creek on Galena Hill in the Mayo district.

L.B. ERICKSON, a pioneer miner in the Mayo area, made one of his first discoveries of silver-lead ore on this gulch.

ERVIN CREEK 64°28′N 135°15′W (106-D). Flows into Carpenter Creek in the Wernecke Mountains.

E.ERVIN found silver-lead ore on the banks of this stream in 1923 during the rush to the Grey Copper Hill finds. (See Beaver City.)

ESAU HILL 65°42′N 136°51′W (116-H). Eight miles southwest of Pothole Lake and north of the Hart River.

ESAU was an Indian guide whose report to Inspector Snyder at Dawson resulted in Cpl. Dempster being sent to search for the lost Fitzgerald patrol in 1911. (See Dempster Highway.)

ESCAPE REEF 69°00′N 137°15′W (117-A). A long, low, narrow island or reef about three miles east of Shingle Point in Mackenzie Bay on the Arctic coast.

In 1826 John Franklin, (later Sir), named this reef after a touchy meeting with a band of Eskimos at Shingle Point.

ETHEL LAKE 63°22'N 136°06'W (115-P). About 12 miles east of Stewart Crossing.

This large lake was named after his daughter by J.J. McArthur, DLS, in 1898, while he was surveying in the vicinity. He was one of the first government surveyors in the territory and was active in tracing new routes and in claim surveys in the early days of the Klondike.

ETTRAIN CREEK 65°27'N 141°00'W (116-G&F). A tributary to the Nation River.

Thomas Riggs, American member of the International Boundary Survey team, named this creek in 1910. An Indian family in this area at the time had the family name "Yetran". The word was said to mean "Mosquito" in the local dialect.

EUREKA CREEK 63°36'N 138°49'W (115-O&N). A tributary to the Indian River from the south.

Gold was found here and a Discovery claim staked on 28 August, 1897, by J.C. Brown from EUREKA, California. His discovery did not lead to payable gold until February 1905 when a newer and richer discovery led to a stampede in which the whole creek and its tributaries were staked.

EUREKA LANDING 61°15'N 134°36'W (105-E). On the Teslin River.

This was a riverboat landing and supply point for the miners of the Livingstone Creek area, to which a wagon road was built in the summer of 1902. It was abandoned when a shorter route was made from Mason's Landing.

MOUNT EVANS 4,232' 62°57'N 137°04'W (115-I). 15 miles northeast of Fort Selkirk.

Lt. Col T.D.B. EVANS was the first commander of the Yukon Field Force (1898-1900). Evans marched his 280 men and four women from Telegraph Creek on the Stikine River, to the head of Teslin Lake in the spring of 1898. They built boats and sailed to Fort Selkirk. There they built quarters and half the detachment remained here while the other half went on to Dawson to assist the NWMP.

Three of his group were buried at Fort Selkirk.

Lt. Col. Evans accepted a reduction in rank to lieutenant in order to go overseas during the First World War. This mountain was given his name in 1971. Four others, Hansen, Watson, Walters and Corcoran were named at the same time after the men of his command who died while on service in the Yukon.

EVERETT CREEK   60°51′N 130°35′W (105-B). Flows from near Wasson Lake southwest to the Liard River.

This was named after EVERETT Wasson, a pioneer bush pilot of the Yukon and northern BC. This stream was near the scene of the first air search and rescue mission attempted in the Yukon. The creek had previously carried the name Quartz Creek and is so named on many maps. (See Wasson Lake.)

EXAMINER GULCH   64°02′N 139°23′W (115-B&C). The first valley on the right side above the mouth of Bonanza Creek.

This small valley was given the name of W.R. Hearst's newspaper, the San Francisco *EXAMINER* by W.H. Campbell, a former employee. He discovered gold and staked the first claim on the gulch on 28 October, 1897.

EXCELSIOR CREEK   62°53′N 138°58′W (115-J&K). A tributary to the Yukon River just above Coffee Creek.

This was named in July 1898 by Mrs. Martha Munger Black, MP, probably the most noted woman in Yukon history. Camping here while on her way to Dawson, she met a group of New Zealand miners prospecting the stream. They had found gold and their leader, William J. Beaven, asked Mrs. Black to name the stream. They then staked claims for all, including Mrs. Black, and her claim was later profitable.

MOUNT FAIRBORN   65°06′N 139°52′W (116-G&F). 19 miles east of Sheep Mountain.

In 1973 this mountain was named after James FAIRBORN who was a pioneer transportation man and was agent for the WP&YR at several locations for many years.

FALSE TEETH CREEK   62°12′N 137°49′W (115-I). Tributary to the Klaza River.

In the summer of 1937, W.H. Miller and H.S. Bostock of the GSC were camped here. Their packer, J.V. White, a man of 43 and exceptionally athletic, left his ill-fitting false teeth here when they moved camp to a high ridge seven miles to the west. Arising early the next morning he discovered his loss. He ran back down to the camp here and returned in time for breakfast.

FANGO LAKE 63°40'N 131°42'W (115-O). A small lake which drains into Old Cabin Creek and Rogue River.

This was named by Dr. Aro Aho, President of Dynasty Exploration Co. Ltd., about 1971. It is a Spanish word meaning "Swamp".

FARO 62°14'N 133°20'W (105-K). 25 miles west of the junction of the Ross and Pelly Rivers.

The newest town in the Yukon was built in 1969 to house the people from the nearby Anvil Mine. This is a large, open-pit mine producing lead, zinc and silver. On 13 June, 1969, a forest fire destroyed most of the newly-built town but it was rebuilt in three months.

The game of FARO was an old and simple gambling game of cards, popular throughout the early west. It was probably given to the town by Dr. Aro Aho from the name of the first claims staked on the orebody.

FAT CREEK 60°11'N 132°55'W (105-C). Flows into Fat Lake and then Teslin Lake on the west side.

Arthur St. Cyr, DLS, in 1897, recorded the local name of this stream as "Hall River", probably after Hall Williams, an ex-HBC man who trapped around Teslin Lake in the 1890's and early 1900's.

By 1903 the stream was being called the "North River" on maps of the area. In 1931 the GSC, when mapping the geology, reported that the local people were calling it "Flat Creek" and they so marked it. Somehow, when their maps were issued, the name appeared as FAT Creek and so it remains. (See Hall Creek.)

FENWICK CREEK 60°11'N 135°19'W (105-D). Flows into the Wheaton River.

In 1910 one of the Yukon's early geologists, D.D. Cairnes, GSC, gave this creek his wife's maiden name while he was mapping the geology of the region.

MOUNT FERRELL 64°05'N 133°12'W (106-C). Just south of the Nadaleen River.

James E. FERRELL was a Yukon Councillor for the Dawson District in

1922–28. He also ran a trading post at Lansing from 1908–15. This hill was named for him in 1973. (See Christie Pass.)

FIDO CREEK 63°32′N 132°15′W (105-N). A tributary to the Rogue River from the north.

This was named in 1973 by Dr. Aro Aho, President of Dynasty Exploration Co., Ltd. after Norman Niddery's lead sled dog. The name is a common one for dogs and comes from the Latin *"fidus"* meaning "faithful". (See Niddery Lake.)

FIELD CREEK 63°47′N 135°42′W (105-M). A tributary to the Mayo River from the north.

Fred FIELD, of Gordon Landing, went out hunting before the close of navigation in the fall of 1902, and did not return when he was expected. In February 1903 he was reported lost and search parties went out. On 25 May, 1903, his body, surrounded by all his belongings, was found on a raft in the ice on the Stewart River near Lansing Creek. He had apparently died of exposure and starvation. He had probably got lost on land and was floating down the river, hoping to find a settlement, before the river froze. His body was perfectly preserved.

A terse and chilling report to this effect was made by the NWMP constable in the district and was the epitaph of a hardy Klondiker, one of the first men to prospect in the Mayo region. It is believed that Field found gold prospects on and staked the first claim on this creek that bears his name.

FIELD LAKE 62°40′N 131°03′W (105-J). One of the four lakes near the junction of the Ross and Prevost Rivers.

This was named in 1907 by Joseph Keele, GSC, after Poole FIELD, who kept the trading post at nearby Ross River.

Field was born at Fort Garry, Manitoba, where his father was the HBC trader. He had worked his way west, across the territories and eventually was caught up in the stampede to the Klondike. He spent some time in the NWMP. He and his partner, Clement Lewis, liked the Pelly and Ross River country and bought out Tom Smith's trading post at Ross River in 1905. They named it "Nahanni House".

A third associate, Martin Jorgenson, was one of the mystery men of the Nahanni country. In 1910 he went in to the Nahanni in search of the rich gold supposed to be there and later sent a message to Field by some wandering Indians; it said that he had found rich diggings and requested his assistance and supplies. The message had taken two years to deliver. Field made the journey and found Jorgenson's skeleton, minus the skull, his cabin burned and no gold or signs of workings. Field was convinced enough by his partner's story to return many times to the Nahanni in later years.

FINLAYSON LAKE   61°41′N 130°38′W (105–G). At the height of land between Frances Lake and the Pelly River.

This lake and river were named by Robert Campbell of the HBC in July 1840 while he was on his famous journey of exploration of the central Yukon. It was named after Chief Factor Duncan FINLAYSON, his friend and sponsor, who later became a director of the HBC. The stream and lake were on the main supply route, — Fort Liard, Fort Frances, Fort Pelly Banks — to Fort Selkirk.

Placer gold was mined from the bars at the mouth of the river in 1875, the miners taking $8–$9 per day. This was among the first gold mined in the Yukon Territory.

FIRTH RIVER   69°32′N 139°32′W (117–D). A large river which flows to the Beaufort Sea southwest of Herschel Island.

This was first named "Mountain Indian" River by John Franklin (later Sir) in July 1826. He encamped on the Arctic shore just east of the river and met a group of Eskimos who told him that once a year each spring, a band of Indians came down the river from the interior to trade with them.

J.H. Turner, USC&GS, in 1890 renamed the river after John FIRTH, HBC Agent at Rampart House, who had accompanied him to the Arctic coast that year.

Firth lived in the country as an HBC Factor for over 50 years. A Klondiker who met Firth at Fort MacPherson in 1898 was much impressed, saying that he looked like a man of granite. He was a square, quiet and powerful man with tremendous effect on the Indians and Eskimos. They felt that he could look right into their thoughts, and were careful to mind their manners. John Firth had a large family and one of his grandsons has been twice elected as Member of Parliament for the Northwest Territories.

Gold was found on High Cache Creek, a small tributary of the river, in 1908 by Jujira Wada, a famous Japanese traveller and prospector and his partner, Ben Smith. This led to a small rush to the area.

There have been several rushes to stake the stream about every ten to 15 years but no paying gold has yet been found. (See High Cache Creek.)

FISHER CREEK   61°02′N   138°38′W   (115–G&P). A small creek flowing into Sheep Creek from the west.

Two brothers, Bruce and A.C. FISHER, were early and continuing prospectors and trappers in the Kluane country. They found gold and named this creek during the stampede of 1903–04 to the Bullion Creek finds.

The grave of A.C. Fisher had to be removed from the right-of-way of the Alaska Highway in 1943 and was placed just south of the marker on Soldier's Summit.

FISHER CREEK   64°12′N   136°12′W   (116–A). A tributary to the North McQuesten River.

In September 1898 two unknown prospectors started a fake stampede to this area. So many people took part that a man named FISHER was appointed Mining Recorder for the district.

The rush died quickly and almost everyone left the creek. Fisher remained here, alone, all winter. In Dawson it was reported that he was dead and the fact was accepted officially. His relatives claimed and received his effects and life insurance. All were surprised when he arrived in Stewart in the spring of 1899 and handed in his records.

FISHING BRANCH   66°27′N   138°35′W   (116–J&K). Flows into the Porcupine River.

On 28 May, 1888, William Ogilvie, DLS, on his way to Fort MacPherson, stopped here. His report stated that at the mouth of the creek there were old racks for drying fish that had been erected by the Indians. Thus he called the stream the "Fishing Branch" of the Porcupine.

MOUNT FITTON   68°28′N   137°58′W   (117–A). In the Richardson Mountains near the Arctic coast.

This was named in 1826 by John Franklin (later Sir) after William Henry FITTON MD (1780–1861), who in 1852 was President of the Geological Society of Great Britain. It was originally named Fitton Peak.

FIVE FINGER RAPIDS   62°16′N   136°21′W   (115–1). In the Yukon River about 20 miles north of Carmacks.

Four columns of basalt rock separate the river into five channels of which only the eastern one is passable by riverboats. They were named by one of the earliest miners, W.B. Moore of Tombstone, Arizona, in 1882.

Lt. F. Schwatka, US Army, on his excursion in 1883, changed the name to

"Rink Rapids" but the name was never accepted and later Dr. G.M. Dawson gave it to the rapids a little lower down the river. (See Rink Rapids.)

FLAT CREEK 63°57′N 138°37′W (115-O&N). Flows into the Klondike River from the south.

William Ogilvie, DLS, named this creek in 1896 as it enters the Klondike in a large, flat valley. It was said that this creek was the mythical "Too Much Gold" creek of the early Indians, who told the miners that there was a creek far up the Klondike River in which the gold was so plentiful that they would have to put gravel with it in order to sluice it.

FLET CREEK 63°59′N 136°20′W (115-P). Tributary of the North McQuesten River.

Robert G. FLETT was a well-known trapper and prospector in this area in the early 1900's. He was subject to fits of insanity and frightened others in the district who complained to the authorities. In 1907, two RNWMP constables were sent in to apprehend him. He evaded them easily and they eventually returned to Dawson empty handed. (The Mounties didn't always get their man!)

In the winter of 1907–08 a group of miners captured him and he was taken to Dawson by dog-team and placed in a mental hospital. The name was misspelled by the map-makers.

MOUNT FOLLÉ 60°18′N 135°03′W (105-D). On the north side of the Wheaton River at the Big Bend.

John "Jack" A. FOLLÉ, was a Klondiker and pioneer prospector in the Wheaton River area, with his partner W.F. Schnabel. In 1905 he staked claims on this hill and worked hardrock prospects for many years.

FOREST CREEK 65°09′N 135°44′W (106-E). Tributary to the Little Wind River.

This was named about 1905 when Special Constable A.E. FORREST, RNWMP, made the Dawson to Fort MacPherson patrol most years from 1905-11. He was noted as one of the greatest travellers of the time. He once carried the mail by dog-sled from Fort MacPherson to Dawson in 19 days—a distance of over 500 miles, in January and February. The mouth of this creek is one of his overnight camping places. His name was misspelled by the map-makers.

He enlisted in Joe Boyle's Yukon Motor Machine Gun Battery in November 1914 and was made sergeant major in France in 1917.

FORT CONSTANTINE   64°26′N   140°32′W   (116–B&C). On the north side of the Fortymile River at its junction with the Yukon, north of Fort Cudahy.

This was the first NWMP post in the Yukon Territory. From 1895 to 1897 it contained all the law and government in the territory and Inspector Charles CONSTANTINE was just that.

Fort Constantine was abandoned in 1898 when the growth of Dawson City and the abandonment of the Fortymile mining district required NWMP headquarters to be at Dawson. (See Mount Constantine.)

FORT CUDAHY   64°26′N   140°32′W   (116–B&C). On the north side of the Fortymile River at its junction with the Yukon, directly across the Fortymile River from the settlement of Fortymile and adjoined by Fort Constantine on the north.

Captain John Jerome Healy was a soldier, Indian fighter, trader and early Alaskan and Yukon pioneer. Engaging in the whisky trade in Montana and what is now Alberta in the 1870's, he built and operated Fort Whoop-Up in Alberta until dispossessed by the newly formed NWMP. He had at one time been Sheriff of Cocteau County, Montana (Fort Benton). He arrived in Alaska in 1882 and operated the first trading post at Dyea.

He was a firm believer in the potential of the interior country and in 1893, with the backing of his old partners, the Cudahy meat-packing interests of Chicago, formed the North American Trading and Transportation Company and began establishing trading posts along the Yukon River. The post at Fortymile was named after John CUDAHY, a Chicago merchant and a director of the NAT&TC.

The first post office in the Yukon Territory was opened here in October 1894 and used American postage stamps.

This fort too was forced to close down in 1898 as business moved to the larger centre of Dawson.

FORT FRANCES   61°17′N   129°16′W   (105–H). On the point of the north side of Frances Lake at the junction of the East and West Arms.

In 1840 a rough building called "Glenlyon House" was built here by Robert Campbell of the HBC. Trading with the Indians did not start until

December 1842, when the post was enlarged and named Fort Frances, after Lady Frances Simpson, wife of the Governor of the HBC. It was the first trading post in the Yukon Territory. The post prospered as long as Campbell ran it but in the late 1840's, while he was establishing Fort Pelly Banks and Fort Selkirk, his assistant allowed it to deteriorate and did little trade. By 1851 the post was vacant for periods while personnel were at Pelly Banks. When Campbell came this way in October 1852 after the loss of Fort Selkirk, he found that the natives had burned and destroyed this post. After 12 years the HBC had no posts left in the Yukon.

The post was revived by the HBC for a short time in the early 1900's and rebuilt on the south side of the narrows. It was later sold and operated at various times by independent traders, and again by the HBC from the 1930's until the Alaska Highway was built. The local Indians then moved to Lower Post and Watson Lake and no business remained. In these later years the post was called simply, "Frances Lake", the name used on present day maps. (See Frances River.)

FORT NELSON **(See Stewart River.)**

FORT RELIANCE **64°09′N 139°29′W (116-B&C). Eight miles north of Dawson on the east bank of the Yukon River.**

Now obliterated, this was the first trading post built in the Yukon Territory after the HBC's withdrawal. On 20 August, 1874, Jack McQuesten and Alfred Mayo, assisted by a young man named Frank Barnfield (Clarence Andrews, the distinguished Alaska historian, insisted his name was Bernstein), arrived here on the small steamboat *Yukon* and began erecting the post. As was common in the west in those days they called it a fort. Although the intention was mainly to exploit the Indian fur trade, these men were also prospectors and were highly optimistic about the mineral potential of the country.

Their trading was successful. Mayo stayed at his regular job, running the steamboats for the ACC and, in the spring of 1875, Arthur Harper joined McQuesten at the post. The first miners to winter in the territory were here in the winter of 1882–83. Eleven in number, they were led by E.M. Carr who later became a general in the US National Guard and Commissioner at Fairbanks in 1906. This party prospected in the Klondike area that winter and camped on Eldorado Creek; they found gold showings but none rich enough to impress them or bring them back in the spring.

In 1886 many miners had invaded the territory and good gold was being mined on the Stewart River bars so, in the spring of that year, Fort Reliance was abandoned in favour of the new post at the mouth of the Stewart River.

Fort Reliance was the centre of trade on the upper Yukon between the years 1874 and 1886. It was the Mile "O" of the Yukon River; all distances along the river were calculated from this point, e.g. the Fortymile and Sixtymile Rivers.

The abandoned buildings were soon removed for boiler wood by the riverboats.

FORT SELKIRK 62°46′N 137°24′W (115-1). On the west side of the Yukon River, just above its confluence with the Pelly.

This spot was selected by Robert Campbell in 1848 to control the fur trade of the central Yukon for the HBC. On 1 June that year he built the first post on the east bank of the Yukon, on the point between it and the Pelly. He named it after Thomas Douglas, fifth Earl of SELKIRK (1771–1820) and also after the post of the HBC at Fort Selkirk in Manitoba. It was abandoned in April 1852 because of flooding problems and the next post was built across the Yukon.

Fort Selkirk broke the trade monopoly of the Chilkat Indians of the coast with the interior Indians. They determined to rectify this situation and on 19 August, 1852, led by their Chief Kho-klux, they attacked and pillaged the post. They were careful not to hurt any of the white men there but took or destroyed almost all the trade goods, supplies and furnishings. Campbell sent some of his people to Fort Yukon and took the rest to Pelly Banks while he continued on to Fort Simpson. The local natives later burned the fort buildings to get the iron fittings for tools.

Robert Campbell then made his famous journey that winter, over 3,000 miles on showshoes, on his way to Lachine, Québec seeking permission to re-establish the post. His request was denied and, except for Rampart House and sometimes Lapierre House, the HBC left the Yukon for nearly 50 years. Campbell never saw the territory again.

On 1 September, 1889, Arthur Harper, who had split up with Ladue, landed on the site of the original fort (on the east bank) with his wife and several children. He had a large stock of trade goods and started a post here, independent of the ACC. It was known locally as "Campbell's Fort". He hired "Buffalo" Pitts to assist him and Pitts was still here when the gold rush was on.

Bishop Bompas built a mission here in 1892 and put the Rev. T.H.

Canham in charge. Canham was then needed elsewhere and the mission was closed in 1895.

The place assumed some importance in late 1898 when it became the headquarters of the Yukon Field Force of the Canadian army. There was a vague intention by Sir Wilfrid Laurier's Liberal government to make Selkirk the capital of the Yukon Territory. Owing to the loss of population caused by the Nome Gold Rush in 1899 and to the Yukon Field Force being recalled because of the South African war, nothing became of the idea. The Yukon Field Force left three of its number behind, buried at the fort. Nearby mountains are named in their memory, as well as one for their commanding officer.

Independent traders and missionaries kept the place alive for many years. In 1938 the HBC returned but remained only until 1950. With the halting of riverboat traffic due to the completion of the Alaska Highway and an allweather road from Whitehorse to Dawson and Mayo, by 1950 the settlement lost all reason for being and, with the exception of one family, was abandoned. (See Mount Pitts.)

FORTYMILE RIVER   64°26′N 140°32′W (116-B&C). A large tributary to the Yukon River about 48 miles below Dawson.

Originally called the "Shitando" or "Chittondeg" by the Tena Indians, meaning "Creek of the Leaves", this is also probably the river that Robert Campbell, on his way to Fort Yukon in 1851, called "Ayonie's River" after the chief of the Indians he found there. Even before gold was found on it in 1886, the miners called it Fortymile River, from its location that distance below Fort Reliance, which was their only supply point. Lt. F. Schwatka, US Army, in 1883 named it the "Cone Hill River" from the isolated hill a short distance above its mouth but the name was not accepted.

Arthur Harper, the pioneer prospector of the central Yukon, found gold showings on the lower part of the river a short time after 1875 but did not pursue them after being told stories of dangerous canyons and rapids upstream by the local natives. Acting on his advice, George McCue and Dick Poplin, in the summer of 1886, found the first payable gold on a gravel bar (Discovery Bar) at the mouth of Moose Creek (on the Alaska side). This again was fine or flour gold and, as usual in river bars, was of limited extent. Shortly afterward Howard Franklin and Harry Madison on 7 September, 1886, found the first coarse gold in the Yukon watershed at Franklin Gulch, about 85 miles up the Fortymile River and well into American territory.

Coarse gold was the goal of all miners and this find established the credibility of the Yukon Territory as a major mining district. The real rush to the Yukon started at this time.

Michael "Mickey" O'Brien found coarse gold on a nearby creek, also a tributary of the Fortymile, a short time after Franklin and Madison, which reinforced the impact of the first discovery.

Harper, McQuesten and Mayo realized the importance of the finds. Harper immediately went from the Stewart River post to the mouth of the Fortymile and in June 1887 started the erection of a trading post there for the ACC. It quickly grew into a thriving town as more of the Fortymile creeks gave up their gold and by 1893 it was serving several thousand miners in the area.

The settlement was almost completely abandoned in weeks after 17 August, 1896, with the discovery of the Bonanza gold and never again regained any importance.

49 GULCH   63°59′N 139°21′W (115-O&N). A tributary to Bonanza Creek from the west, five miles from the Klondike River.

The Discovery claim was located on 29 May, 1897, by Louis Hansen who named it because the mouth of the gulch was on claim No. 49 Below Discovery on Bonanza.

MOUNT FOSTER 61°09′N 140°03′W (115-F). East of the Steele Glacier in the St. Elias Range.

This was named in 1970 by the Alpine Club of Canada after Col. William Wasborough FOSTER (1875-1954), a past president (1920-1924) of the club.

FOURTH OF JULY CREEK   61°07′N 138°02′W (115-G). A tributary of the Jarvis River in the Kluane region.

On 4 July, 1903, gold was found and the Discovery claim staked by "Dawson" Charlie of Carcross, (better known as "Tagish" Charlie). Dawson Charlie, with George Carmack and Skookum Jim Mason had found the rich gold of Bonanza Creek in 1896 which started the Klondike Gold Rush. The 1903 find was the first payable gold found in the Kluane district. This started a large rush to the Kluane which lasted for the next few years.

MOUNT FOWLIE 65°47′N 139°11′W (116-G&F).On the east side of the East Porcupine River.

Gavin FOWLIE was a Yukon Councillor from 1920 to 23 and this hill was named for him in 1973.

FOX CREEK   60°11'N 132°48'W (105-C). A tributary to Teslin Lake on the east side.

This creek and Fox Point were named many years ago by the Teslin Indians. A legend of theirs tells of a supernatural warning to the tribe against returning to this area. It told of a great disaster to come, on a point in the lake where they would see a fox. Disregarding the warning, the tribe returned and a fox entered their camp. Shortly afterwards, the Tahltan Indians attacked and destroyed their camp, killing everyone except one young woman who escaped to tell the story.

FOX LAKE   60°39'N 134°04'W (105-D). 12 miles northeast of Marsh Lake.

In 1943 Major FOX of the US Air Force made a forced landing on this lake and it has been the local name since.

FRANCES LAKE   61°23'N 129°30'W (105-H), and

FRANCES RIVER   60°16'N 129°10'W (105-A). The river is a tributary to the Liard River. The lake is about 90 miles north of Watson Lake, between the Campbell and Logan Mountains.

In the summer of 1840 Robert Campbell of the HBC made his famous journey of exploration from Dease Lake into the central Yukon, the first white man to do so. He ascended the Liard River to the Frances River and then to Frances Lake and on to the Pelly River.

The local Indians called the Frances River the "Too-Tsho-Tooa", meaning "Big Lake River". Campbell named both river and lake after Lady FRANCES Simpson, wife of Sir George Simpson, for nearly 40 years the Governor of the HBC.

For a number of years this river was part of the HBC's route to the central Yukon but it was finally abandoned because of the loss of life in the dangerous waters both here and on the Liard.

FRANKLIN LAKE   60°41'N 135°18'W (105-D). The southernmost of the two small Jackson Lakes.

This local name has been used since the early 1900's when a copper mining company camped and operated here.

MOUNT FRANK RAY   64°28′N 138°33′W (116–B). At the headwaters of the Tombstone River.

This was named in 1968 by Dr. Dirk Tempelman-Kluit, GSC, after FRANK RAY, a pioneer trapper and hunter in this area. It is the highest mountain in the Tombstone River area.

FRASER CREEK   60°19′N 137°20′W (115–A). A tributary to Alder Creek and Mush Lake.

Gold was found here and the Discovery claim staked by J.W. Smith and Fred Altemose in the summer of 1902. They named the creek after Assistant Surgeon S.M. FRASER of the NWMP who was Mining Recorder and Customs Officer at Dalton Post, 1901–03.

FRASER FALLS   63°31′N 135°09′W (105–M). On the Stewart River, ten miles above Gordon Landing.

The falls were named in 1885 when the first prospectors, a party of FRASER, Chapman, Thomas Boswell and others, were exploring the upper reaches of the Stewart.

Robert Levac operated a trading post here for some time in the 1920's and 30's.

FREDERICK LAKE   60°23′N 136°40′W (115–A). Between Kusawa and Dezeadash Lakes.

This was named by the English explorer Edward James Glave in 1890 when, with Jack Dalton, he made the first entry into this part of the country. He made camp at the head of the lake and named it FREDERICK in remembrance of his brother, who had died a few years earlier.

FREEGOLD   MOUNTAIN   4,772′   62°17′N 137°06′W (115–1).   30 miles northwest of Carmacks.

Lode gold was discovered here in June 1930 by P.F. "Fred" Guder on his Augusta claim. A rush immediately developed in the area, resulting in many other mineral discoveries. (See Guder Creek.)

FRENCH GULCH   63°54′N 139°18′W (115–O&N). A small tributary of Eldorado Creek.

In December 1896, George Lamarre of Québec, found rich gold on this gulch and, because of his origin, named it FRENCH Gulch. Claim No. 17 on Eldorado Creek, at the mouth of this gulch, was reported to be the richest claim ever found in the Klondike, yielding nearly 100,000 ounces of gold in a length of 500 feet.

FRENCH HILL 63°54'N 139°19'W (115-O&N). On the west side of Eldorado Creek above French Gulch.

One of the famous "Hill" or "Bench" deposits of the fabulously rich "White Channel" gravels whose existence went unsuspected for the first year and a half of the gold rush. (See Cheechako Hill.)

On 20 October, 1897, William "Cariboo Bill" Dettering, an old Cariboo miner from Illinois and his partner, Joseph Stacey, staked the first bench claim. They were acting on a theory formed by Dettering and sank a prospect shaft on the hill. It was reported that they recovered 11 ounces of gold from the first pan of gravel taken from bedrock. They took out $13,000 and sold the claim (100 feet by 100 feet square) in July 1898 for $40,000. J.N. Demers staked a bench claim on 9 September, 1897, but did not work it until Dettering and Stacey made their find. He then found rich gold on bedrock.

FRESNO CREEK 64°16'N 139°48'W (116-B&C). A tributary to the Yukon River from the west, 25 miles below Dawson.

F.R. Chandler found some gold here on 14 April, 1898. He staked a claim and probably named the stream after the city of the same name in California.

FRISCO CREEK 63°13'N 139°32'W (115-O&N). A tributary of Thistle Creek.

Gold was found and the Discovery claim staked on 10 November, 1897, by a California miner.

FRYING PAN CREEK 62°00'N 140°55'W (115-F). A tributary of Beaver Creek about 12 miles south of Dry Creek.

This was discovered and named in November 1913 during the rush to the Chisana goldfields. The prospector who found the first gold washed it from the gravels with his frying pan. (See Pan Creek.)

FULLER LAKE 62°58'N 130°15'W (105-J). At the headwaters of the South MacMillan River.

This lake was named on 1 April, 1943, by Herman Peterson, of Atlin, a northern bush pilot well-known for many years in the Yukon and northern BC. He landed Kent FULLER, surveyor who was laying out the Canol Pipeline, here on that day. To keep his log in order he asked Fuller what to call the lake. Fuller told him to choose any name he wished.

MOUNT FYFE   4,793′   65°17′N 136°52′W (116-H).On the east side of the Hart River.

Near the route of the Dawson-MacPherson Patrol, this mountain was named in 1973 after Rgt. No. 4937 Constable J.F. FYFE, RNWMP. He was one of Cpl. Dempster's party who searched for and found the lost Fitzgerald Patrol in February and March 1911.

FYSH CREEK   64°09′N 139°11′W (116-B&C). Flows into Lepine Creek, 15 miles northeast of Dawson.

This was named by miners about 1905 after a popular public official in the Gold Commissioner's Office in Dawson, Frederick A.H. FYSH, of London, Ontario.

Fysh, a young accountant, and his brother-in-law Charles Williams made one of the most incredible and least known journeys of the Klondike Gold Rush. In the fall of 1897 they were prospecting on the northwest coast of Alaska with little success. After the first snowfall their companions decided to return to St. Michaels for the winter. Fysh and Williams however, decided to go overland to Fort Yukon and Dawson.

In the dead of an Alaskan winter, with only a small toboggan to haul their supplies and a map torn from a high school atlas to guide them, this amazing pair crossed nearly 600 miles of almost unknown country, including several unmapped mountain ranges. They reached Dawson in early January 1898.

Fysh secured a position in the Gold Commissioner's Office which he kept until he moved his family to the Okanagan valley in British Columbia in September 1909. He was a modest man who was very well liked and respected, especially by the prospectors who appreciated his hardihood.

GALENA   63°47′N 139°46′W (115-O&N). On the Yukon River opposite the mouth of Indian River.

This was a trading post at the mouth of Galena Creek, owned by Wy Spees, to serve miners nearby and travellers on the river. It burned down in April 1954 and was never rebuilt.

GALENA CREEK   63°55′N 135°35′W (105-M). Flows into Flat Creek about three miles west of Elsa.

H.W. McWhorter named this creek in 1906 when he and his partner found a rich vein of silver-lead ore in a canyon on the stream. Their first shipment of high-grade ore was the start of silver-lead mining in the Mayo district.

GARDEN CREEK   60°07′N 128°22′W (105-A). Flows into the Hyland River east of Watson Lake.

A prospector-trapper kept a good garden for many years on the banks of this stream. In the early years both people and gardens were rare in this part of the Yukon.

GATES CREEK   (See Brown's Creek.)

GAUCHE LAKE   (See Big Kalzas Lake.)

GAUVIN GULCH   63°55′N 139°16′W (115-O&N). A short creek flowing into Bonanza Creek.

Alfred and Wilfred GAUVIN of St. Simon, Québec, came into the Yukon in 1895. On 20 May, 1897, they found this small, rich valley and made their fortunes.

GAY CREEK   63°14′N 139°04′W (115-C). Flows into the Stewart River from the north, about 12 miles above the mouth.

About 1886–87 Emil Meriguet (known in the Yukon as Emil GAY) prospected and named this creek. It is now known locally as "Three Kings Creek", after three partners who worked it later. (See Gay Gulch.)

GAY GULCH   63°52′N 139°13′W (115-O&N). A very short gulch off Eldorado Creek on the east, four miles from the mouth.

Emil GAY (Meriguet) discovered the wealth of this tiny valley on 4 January, 1897, when he staked the first claim and named it. An old-time Yukoner, he had come into the country in 1886 and became wealthy from this and other Klondike claims and mining ventures. He returned to France, to his birthplace, where he retired.

His Discovery claim on this gulch yielded over $3,000 to the running foot for a distance of 500 feet.

In 1962 Gay's grandson, Henri Meriguet, of Annecy, France, came to the Yukon during the Dawson Festival, hitchhiking across Canada. He wished to visit the claim that had made his grandfather wealthy and to see the wonderful country he had talked about. He was murdered and his body buried in a gravel pit at mile 693 (K1123) on the Alaska Highway. His suspected murderer, Karoli Marsi, hung himself in the Don Jail in Toronto, Ontario, in August 1967.

GEM CREEK   63°57'N 136°49'W (115-P). Tributary to Sprague Creek.

In the late 1930's George Retter, Jack Alverstone and Cecil Poli found and mined placer gold on this creek.

GEORGE CREEK   63°10'N 133°28'W (105-N). A tributary of Russell Creek.

This was named in 1901 by Major Neville A.D. Armstrong after his partner GEORGE Leith of England. They worked the Gillis, or Armstrong Concession for placer gold on Russell Creek in 1901-02. (See Mount Armstrong.)

GHECHUCK CREEK   63°27'N 136°17'W (115-P). A short creek flowing into the Stewart River, east of the Crossing.

The name was recorded in 1957. It was named after Billy "GHECHUCK" Malcolm, whose Indian name means "Porcupine."

MOUNT GIBBEN   6,500'   64°43'N 139°11'W (116-B). 45 miles north of Dawson at the head of the Fifteen Mile River.

The highest mountain in the area, it was named for the Honourable Justice J.E. GIBBEN, former Commissioner of the Yukon Territory and Judge of the Territorial Court. In 1970 the name was officially adopted.

MOUNT GIBSON   61°14'N 140°05'W (115-G&F). On the southeast side of the Steele Glacier in the St. Elias Ranges.

This was named in 1970 by the Alpine Club of Canada after a past president of the club, E. Rex GIBSON (1892-1957).

MOUNT GILLIAM   60°18'N 134°55'W (105-D). On the north end of Gray Ridge, ten miles northwest of Carcross.

This name was reported by W.E. Cockfield, GSC, about 1920. Marc H. GILLIAM was a Cornish miner and a pioneer prospector and mine superintendent locally for many years. The mountain had borne his name for a long time locally before it was made official.

GILLIS LAKES   66°26'N 134°45'W (106-L). A large group of small lakes west of the Peel River.

In 1973 these lakes were named after A.J. GILLIS, Speaker of the Yukon Council from 1912–15. He represented South Dawson in the council.

MOUNT GILLIS 5,418′ 62°51′N 133°21′W (105–K). An isolated peak east of Stokes Lake, north of the Tay River.

Duncan GILLIS of Nova Scotia came to the Yukon in 1892. While on a holiday at home he heard the news of the Klondike find. He returned to the Yukon via the Edmonton Trail and the Gravel (Keele) River. He descended the MacMillan River, mistaking it for the Hess. It was on this journey that he discovered the placer gold of Russell Creek. (See Mount Armstrong.)

GIROUARD HILL 1,672′ 68°09′N 138°17′W (117–A). Ten miles west of Bonnet Lake.

This was named in 1973 after J.E. GIROUARD, Registrar of Land Titles in the Yukon from 1898–1908 and appointed Member of the Yukon Council for the same period.

GLACIER CREEK 64°01′N 140°43′W (116–B&C). A tributary to Big Gold Creek in the Sixtymile district.

Gold found on this creek in 1891 started the rush to the Sixtymile district. The creek received its name because glacial ice had to be removed on the upper reaches of the stream to work the gold-bearing gravels.

MOUNT GLADMAN 64°43′N 140°49′W (116–B&C). Near the International Boundary and the Yukon River.

William Ogilvie, DLS, had four assistants with him in 1887–88 when he established the first part of the Yukon-Alaska boundary, from the Yukon River south to the Sixtymile River country.

In March 1888 he named this mountain after one of them, Charles GLADMAN, of Peterborough, Ontario. It was first called Gladman Peak. Gladman accompanied Ogilvie on many other surveys in other parts of Canada. He died in Peterborough in July 1947.

He had also accompanied Warburton Pike, the English explorer of the Frances Lake country, to Lower Post in 1893 but had to leave him there as Ogilvie wanted him for another task.

GLADSTONE CREEK (See Bertha Creek.)

GLADSTONE CREEK 61°19′N 138°40′W (115–G&F). Flows into Kluane Lake.

Although this creek was named during the original stampede to the Silver Creek country of the Kluane in 1903, it was not until 1911 that T.T. Murray and Axel Swanson found the first payable gold on it.

GLENLYON HOUSE   61°17′N   129°18′W   (105–H).   On a point on the north side of the channel between the east and west arms of Frances Lake.

The first trading post in the Yukon Territory was built here. Robert Campbell of the HBC, in the summer of 1840 left some of his crew here to construct a small building while he continued his exploration to the Pelly River.

He decided to make this a permanent trading post and named it after GLENLYON HOUSE, the seat of the Campbell clan in Scotland. In 1842 he changed the name of the post to Fort Frances.

The post was destroyed by fire in the spring of 1852. (See Fort Frances.)

GLENLYON   PEAK   7,184′   62°32′N   134°28′W   (105–L).   The northernmost peak in the Glenlyon Range.

A.C. Tuttle, topographer, in 1946–47 gave this peak the name Mount Hodder, from the creek flowing at its base. This was soon changed to honour Robert Campbell but the name Hodder appears on some old maps.

GODDARD POINT   61°21′N   135°14′W   (105–E).   A point on the northeast side of Lake Laberge.

This was named in 1899 after the little steamboat *A.J. GODDARD* in turn named after her builder, owner and captain. The hull was built in San Francisco and, with the engine, was hauled over the White Pass in the winter of 1897–98 and assembled at Lake Bennett. It was 40 feet long and displaced 15 tons. The *A.J. Goddard* was the first steamboat to make the run from Lake Bennett to Dawson; she left Lake Bennett on 29 May, 1898, ran Miles Canyon and the Whitehorse Rapids and arrived in Dawson on 21 June.

The boat was wrecked in a storm near this point in September 1899 with the loss of the captain (not Captain Goddard), the fireman, cook and a waiter. Their bodies were not recovered until 3 May, 1902. The boat was never raised; its remains may still be seen in calm weather.

GOLD BOTTOM CREEK   63°58′N   138°58′W   (115–O&N).   The west branch of Hunker Creek.

Robert Douglas Henderson, born in 1857 in Pictou County, Nova Scotia, came to the Yukon over Chilkoot Pass in June 1894. Grubstaked by Joe Ladue, the trader at Ogilvie (Sixtymile), and by some small earnings gained on Quartz Creek, he spent the next two years prospecting the tributaries of the Indian River.

In April 1896 he crossed the divide between Quartz Creek and the west branch of what was later Hunker Creek. On this branch he found low gold values but better than any others he had seen. In his imagination he saw the bedrock of this stream paved with gold nuggets and named it GOLD BOTTOM. Needing supplies and wishing to explore a little more of the country, he went down Hunker to the Klondike River where, at its mouth, he met George Carmack and his party who were fishing for salmon.

He extolled his new find to Carmack and invited him to visit his creek. However, he stipulated that he did not wish Carmack's Indian relatives and friends to stake claims. (The Indians of the Yukon had always had the same right to stake mineral claims as the whites.)

Henderson continued on to Ogilvie and obtained supplies. He returned to Gold Bottom by way of Quartz Creek where he induced 18 miners working there to accompany him to his new find. Arriving at Gold Bottom 14 of the men, after investigating the gravel, immediately returned to Quartz, unimpressed with Henderson's find. Henderson, with the remaining three (one man had turned back), set to work on his claim. In a period of about three months they recovered $720 worth of gold. This was not enough to buy food at that time.

In early August, George Carmack, Skookum Jim and Tagish Charlie travelled up Rabbit Creek (later Bonanza) to visit Henderson. On the way they found encouraging showings of gold.

On Gold Bottom they examined Henderson's showings and were not greatly impressed. Carmack staked a claim beside Henderson's. They then returned to the mouth of the Klondike along Rabbit Creek. It was on this journey that they found rich, coarse gold on the stream that Carmack now renamed Bonanza. Skookum Jim remained on the claim, Tagish Charlie stayed at the fishing camp at the mouth of the Klondike and Carmack went to Fortymile to obtain more supplies. (Some accounts claim that he and Tagish Charlie took saw-logs to Fortymile to sell for supplies). No one went back to Gold Bottom to tell Henderson.

The rush started and Andrew Hunker, after staking on upper Bonanza, looked east. With his partner, Charles M. Johnson, he went up Hunker Creek from the Klondike River. Panning as they went, they soon discovered rich gold showings and staked a Discovery claim and two others, on 6 September, 1896. They went back down to Fortymile and recorded their claims and named the creek Hunker. On their return Hunker went farther up the creek and found Henderson and his three companions at work. They had heard nothing. He persuaded them to come downstream to his discovery. When Henderson saw Hunker's showings he and his companions immediately staked beside Hunker's claims. Henderson staked No. 3 Above Discovery. Henderson then set out for Fortymile where he tried to record a Discovery claim on Gold Bottom. This was disallowed by Constantine as being part of Hunker Creek. Faced with a choice he recorded No. 3 Above rather than his original claim. On his way down he had also staked No. 12 on Bear Creek. This also was not allowed as rules had been made allowing only one claim per man in a mining district. In September 1897 Henderson sold No 3 A to Big Alex McDonald for $3,000, a very respectable sum in those days. McDonald recovered over $800,000 from the claim. Timothy Crowley staked Henderson's original claim on Gold Bottom on 18 September, 1896. There is no record of any appreciable amount of gold being taken from it or any other claim on Gold Bottom. Crowley sold his claim to Big Alex in December 1897.

GOLD HILL   63°55′N 139°22′W (115-O&N). The hill on the west side of Bonanza Creek at its junction with Eldorado Creek.

On 3 July, 1897, according to O. Finnie, the government historian, G.A. Lancaster located a bench claim at claim No. 2 on Eldorado Creek. (A bench claim is the first claim uphill from a creek claim — the bottom of the hillside.) The claim was part of what later was called Gold Hill. A Dr. P.D. Carper, who had possibly grubstaked Lancaster, gave the hill its name. Lancaster's was the first claim on, and produced the first gold mined from the White Channel gravels.

On 23 July, 1897, Nathan Kresky (he later changed it to Kresge) and Nils Peterson staked the Discovery hill claim. (A hill claim was one hundred feet square and was not connected to any creek claim). In ten days, using a rocker and re-circulated water, they won $6,375 from a piece of ground 11 feet by 17 and three feet deep. This is a little better than $300 per cubic yard — rich indeed! Nils Peterson moved a little farther up the hill, sank a shaft 63 feet deep to bedrock and found far richer gold at the bottom. The hill was well named.

By 14 September every possible claim on the hill had been staked. This find led to the discovery of similar deposits on the Hunker Creek hills a few days later. (See Cheechako Hill.)

GOLD HILL 60°17'N 135°08'W (105-D). On the north side of the Wheaton River, 17 miles northwest of Carcross.

In 1893 Frank Corwin and Thomas Rickman of Juneau prospected this area and found extremely rich gold in a quartz vein on this hill. Both men died shortly after their return to Juneau and as the area was unmapped at the time, the exact location of their find was lost.

Many others searched for the vein and although some of their claim posts were found, it was not until 25 June, 1906, that David Hodnett and Jack Stagar found and staked the Gold Reef claim, believing that they had found the lost lode. Within 90 days over 700 claims had been staked surrounding them. (See Mt. Hodnett, Carbon Hill and Corwin Valley.)

GOLDEN HORN MOUNTAIN 5,610' 60°34'N 135°03'W (105-D). The solitary peak 12 miles south of Whitehorse.

Used as a landmark by the miners boating down the Yukon River, this beautiful hill was named by the earliest white men to see it, about 1881–82.

MOUNT GOOD 6,556' 64°20'N 134°26'W (106-D). In the Wernecke Mountains north of the Beaver River.

In 1973 this peak was named to honour the memory of J-88030 Pilot Officer Ralph Edward GOOD who was born at Carcross on 1 May, 1919. He enlisted in the RCAF at Vancouver, BC on 24 August 1942 and served in Canada and overseas. He was killed during air operations over Germany on 19 August, 1944.

GOODE CREEK 60°33'N 133°52'W (105-C). Flows northeast into Jackfish Lake.

Bob GOODE and his two brothers trapped in this area for many years.

GOOD NEIGHBOUR PEAK 15,700' 60°22'N 139°42'W (115-B&C). Two miles north of Mount Vancouver.

This peak is supposed to be the second highest in the Yukon, Mount St. Elias being the highest. It was climbed as part of the Canadian Centennial Celebration in 1967 by eight members of the Yukon Alpine Centennial Expedition, four American and four Canadian climbers. Monty Alford, of the Water Resources Branch, Department of Northern Affairs, Whitehorse, was Canadian co-leader and Vin Hoeman the American co-leader of the climbing party. They made the ascent on 25 June, 1967. (See Centennial Range.)

GORDON LANDING 63°37′N 135°27′W (105-M). A former settlement on the Stewart River above Mayo, near the mouth of Janet Creek.

This little settlement was established about 1902 to serve the new placer goldfields on Duncan Creek. A trader by this name built the post. Roads were pushed out to Duncan, Highet and Haggart Creeks. The place was abandoned as Mayo and Keno assumed importance.

GRAND FORKS 63°55′N 139°18′W (115-O&N).

This was the largest settlement in the Klondike after Dawson City. Forming naturally at the junction of Bonanza and Eldorado Creeks, one day's journey from Dawson, the settlement began to grow in early 1897. Belinda Mulroney built the first roadhouse, the Magnet, in September 1897. Surrounded by the richest gravels in the world, the town expanded; hotels, stores and services of all kinds flourished. By 1903 the population was over 3,000 and the town was incorporated with Peter Coutts, of Grey North, Ontario, the first mayor. As long as the gravels were rich enough to sustain hand work the town prospered but as these dwindled so did the people and business died down. By 1921 dredging operations encompassing the whole valley had destroyed the town and dug up the ground underneath.

It was the last remaining chartered town in the Yukon Territory until that was revoked on 9 December, 1905.

MOUNT GRANGER 6,675′ 60°32′N 135°15′W (105-D). 16 miles southwest of Whitehorse.

William P. GRANGER came from Kentucky to the Yukon in 1895. He was one of the first to find and develop the copper deposits at Whitehorse and the gold-quartz ores of the Wheaton Valley country.

He was killed by carbon monoxide poisoning in a prospect shaft at the Copper King Mine at Whitehorse on 10 May, 1907. This hill was named shortly after.

GRANVILLE 63°40′N 138°37′W (115-O&N). On Sulphur Creek just above its junction with Dominion Creek.

The Granville Mining Company was established in 1911. It was the first large attempt by English capital to consolidate the Klondike placer deposits and mine them by large-scale, mechanical means. A.N.C. Treadgold, an Oxford don and one of the most colourful figures of the Klondike for many years, was the leading figure in this enterprise.

The company was named after Lord GRANVILLE, a backer and the British Secretary of State for the Colonies in the late 19th century. This settlement, started by Treadgold and named by him, was the headquarters of his operations from 1903 for many years and was later used by the Yukon Consolidated Gold Corporation Ltd. It was abandoned about 1965.

MOUNT GRAY 6,085′ 60°09′N 134°51′W (105–D). Six miles west of Carcross on the north shore of Lake Bennett.

This was named by William Ogilvie, DLS, in 1887 or possibly by miners a few years earlier. The name was much later applied to the whole ridge north to Needle Mountain.

GREAVES CREEK 66°29′N 137°39′W (116–1). A tributary to Canoe Creek.

Robert Bruce GREAVES was a well-known figure in early Dawson as the proprietor of the Red Feather Saloon. He later was in business in Mayo. This creek was named in 1973.

GREEN CREEK 63°04′N 139°25′W (115–O&N). A tributary of Thistle Creek.

Gold was first found and the creek named in October 1898. The finder named the stream after the Mining Recorder at Stewart River, a man named GREEN. It is now called Green Gulch.

MOUNT GREEN 6,669′ 61°44′N 132°26′W (105–F). In the St. Cyr Range.

In 1951 this mountain was named to honour the memory of Lt. A.D. GREEN, MID, of the Canadian army, who was killed in action during World War Two.

GREW CREEK 62°04′N 132°56′W (105–K). Flows into the Peel River from the south.

This name was known before 1905. James "Jim" GREW was an old HBC man who lived and trapped this area for a long time. He was about 70 years of age when he died here, alone in 1906.

GREY COPPER HILL 5,254 64°26′N 135°15′W (106–D). East of Carpenter Creek in the Wernecke Mountains.

This was named by Robert Fisher, a pioneer prospector who found rich tetrahedrite (a silver-copper mineral of a rich, grey colour) float here in the autumn of 1923, which led to a stampede to the area in the winter of 1923–24. Several hundred men took part in this rush.

GREY HUNTER PEAK 7,265' 63°10'N 135°40'W (105-M). In the McArthur Group of mountains.

This was named by H.S. Bostock, GSC, in 1940, from its dark, grey, forbidding appearance.

GROUSE CREEK 60°03'N 132°51'W (105-C). A tributary to Fat Creek from the west.

This was named McCleary Creek by the GSC in 1946–47 after the trader and Justice of the Peace at Teslin, Robert McCleery. The Forest Warden at Teslin protested in 1955 that the common name for this stream was GROUSE Creek, that no one used McCleary, that the spelling was wrong and that McCleery should be commemorated by a mountain north of Teslin. (See Mount McCleery.)

GUDER CREEK 62°19'N 137°12'W (115-I). A tributary to Seymour Creek in the Mt. Freegold area.

Paul Fritz "Fred" GUDER was born in June 1895 in Middle Waldenburgh, Silesia, Germany. As a young man he took ship to Panama and walked across the isthmus. Working his way north by ship he arrived in the Yukon in 1912, walking from Skagway to Whitehorse. He worked for a number of years for the noted Captain H.S. Back in the Mount Nansen area and independently for many more years in the Mount Freegold district which he pioneered and named.

This creek was named in 1929 by his friend, "Happy" Lepage of Carmacks. Fred had found lead ore and was living on the creek at the time.

Among other exploits, Fred once spent a winter alone, trapping in the Nahanni Valley. In the winter of 1918–19 he came and went, hauling supplies from Ross River with a hand-sled up the Pelly River and across the mountains. Still actively prospecting in his late 70's, this quiet, hardworking man is liked and respected by all who know him. (See Mount Freegold.)

GULL LAKE 62°15'N 129°52'W (105-I). Northeast of the Pelly Lakes and near Mt. Pike.

This small lake was named in 1893 by Warburton Pike, the English sportsman, explorer and later, trader at Dease Lake, 1898–99. He found enormous numbers of black-headed gulls (Arctic tern) breeding here. (See Narchilla Brook.)

GUSTAVUS RANGE 63°52′N 135°15′W (105-M). The range of hills lying north of Mayo Lake.

This was named in 1904 by Joseph Keele, GSC, while he was mapping the geology of the district. Known as the "Mysterious Three", GUSTAVUS Gustavusen, a Norwegian, and his two sons found the first gold in the district on Duncan Creek in 1898.

The name has been variously reported as Gustavus, Gustavessen, Gustavuson and Gustavusen, which seems to be the correct spelling from most contemporary accounts. (See Duncan Creek.)

HAECKEL HILL 60°47′N 135°16′W (105-D). Eight miles northwest of Whitehorse.

This hill was named Haeckel Butte by Lt. F. Schwatka, US Army, on his excursion down the Yukon River in the summer of 1883, after Professor Ernst Heinrich HAECKEL, a distinguished German naturalist of Jena.

Because Haeckel was a noted scientist and also because the mountain had no previous name, Dr. G.M. Dawson, GSC, allowed his name to stand in 1887.

HAGGART CREEK 63°54′N 136°01′W (115-P). A tributary to the South McQuesten River.

Thomas Nelson prospected this stream in 1895 and in 1896 found good gold in the canyon about four miles upstream from the mouth. At that time it was locally called "Nelson" Creek. At the same time Thomas Haggart built a cabin on the creek and one on Dublin Gulch. No claims were recorded in the area at that time.

Taking part unsuccessfully in the Klondike rush, they returned to the creek in 1898. Thomas Haggart and his brother, Peter, Thomas Nelson and Warren Hiatt left Dawson but *en route* they quarrelled and split into two parties. Peter HAGGART and Warren Hiatt reached Nelson Creek first and staked a Discovery claim. When they recorded their claims they renamed the stream after Peter Haggart.
(See Highet Creek.)

HAINES JUNCTION 60°45′N 137°30′W (115–A). **Situated at the junction of the Haines Highway and the Alaska Highway.**

Begun in late 1942 and starting at mile 1016 on the Alaska Highway, a road was built south to Haines, Alaska on the Pacific coast. It was a wartime measure to increase the shipment of materials and supplies from the US to Alaska. It was constructed by the US Army Engineers and follows quite closely the old Dalton Trail.

The first buildings at the junction were US Army Engineers barracks and shops. Because of its position the settlement has continued to grow.

It was named after Haines, Alaska, a town which was originally located in 1879 by the famous pioneer missionary, S. Hall Young, as the site of a Presbyterian mission. It was given the name of the first Secretary of the Committee of Home Missions, Mrs. Francine E. HAINES.

MOUNT HALDANE 6,015′ 63°55′N 135°55′W (105–M). **About 15 miles west of Mayo Lake.**

This was named about 1920 for an early prospector of that name who lived and mined on HALDANE Creek at the foot of the mountain. Up to that time and to most of the local people since, it was "Lookout" Mountain.

HALL CREEK 60°30′N 133°41′W (105–C). **Flows into the west end of Squanga Lake.**

This name seems to have been applied for no particular reason in the 1940's. HALL Williams was an old HBC man who lived on Teslin Lake about the turn of the century, trapping for a living. Fat Creek, on the west side of Teslin Lake was called the Hall River for a time in the 1900's. Also, just south of Fat Creek in BC, there is a Hall Lake named after the same man about 1898.

HANCOCK HILLS 61°10′N 135°00′W (105–E). **On the east side of Lake Laberge.**

This was named by Lt. F. Schwatka, US Army, in 1883, after one of his superiors, General Winfield Scott HANCOCK (1824–1886).

MOUNT HANSEN 3,127′ 62°47′N 137°15′W (115–I). **A low hill two miles east of Fort Selkirk.**

This hill was named in 1971 after Corporal G. HANSEN, Rgt. No. 63 of the Royal Regiment of Canada, a member of the Yukon Field Force. He died while serving at Fort Selkirk, on 18 February, 1899.

HAPPY VALLEY   60°00′N   133°30′W   (105–C). A large valley crossing the Yukon-BC border between Atlin and Teslin Lakes.

On 12 May, 1899, George White-Fraser, DTS, was setting survey monuments on the Yukon-BC boundary between Teslin and Bennett Lakes. This valley, with its chain of small lakes, was so pleasant after the rugged, mountainous terrain he had just encountered that he rested his crew and horses here and gave the valley its name.

MOUNT HARBOTTLE   65°48′N   138°20′W   (116–G&F). South of the Whitestone River.

This was named in 1973 after Francis E. HARBOTTLE. He was a member of the NWMP in the Yukon from 1901–05 and was afterward with the Canadian Customs Service.

HARDLUCK CREEK   65°05′N   141°00′W   (116–G&F). A tributary to Harrington Creek in Alaska.

An International Boundary Survey party lost some of its supplies here in 1910. The name originally applied to the whole creek, including Harrington.

MOUNT HARE   4,073′   66°38′N   136°11′W   (116–I). In the Richardson Mountains.

This was named in honour of a soldier named HARE who was killed in action in the Second World War.

MOUNT HARPER   6,149′   64°41′N   139°52′W   (116–B&C). A high peak in the Ogilvie Mountains, north of Dawson.

This was named by William Ogilvie, DLS, while he was surveying the International Boundary in 1887–88, after one of the Yukon's earliest pioneers and the first recorded prospector.

Arthur "Cariboo" HARPER was born in County Antrim, Ireland, in 1835. As a young man he mined in California and moved north in the search for gold, always in the advance guard. From the Fraser River goldfields he went on to the Cariboo and then opened the Omineca diggings of northern BC. In 1872 with Frederick Hart and others he went down the Liard River and up the Mackenzie, crossed the Rocky Mountains to the Porcupine River and arrived at Fort Yukon on 15 August, 1873, about the same time as McQuesten, Mayo and their party.

In the fall and winter of 1873–74 Harper, Fred Hart and George Fitch went up to the headwaters of the White River, following an Indian tale of gold. They found prospects of placer gold and also of copper deposits but nothing they could mine at a profit. They were the first white men to explore the stream and the first to prospect what is now the Yukon Territory.

Harper alternated prospecting with trading and for many years, in a loose association, ran the ACC's posts at Fort Reliance, Sixtymile (Ogilvie), Stewart River, Fort Selkirk and other locations. He married an Indian woman and had several children.

Although he pioneered most of the major goldfields that were found in the Yukon and his experience and advice led other men to fortune, he never found the riches he sought. He left the Yukon in 1897, a poor man, broken in health from his privations and hardships, and died of tuberculosis in Yuma, Arizona, in November 1898.

HARRISON CREEK 60°55′N 136°14′W (115–A). A small creek, tributary to Cranberry Creek, which in turn flows into the Mendenhall River.

This was named in 1951 to perpetuate the memory of Cpl. E. HARRISON MID, killed in action with the Canadian army in the Second World War.

HART RIVER 65°51′N 136°23′W (116–H). Flows north to the Peel River from the Wernecke Mountains.

This was named very early, after Howard Hamilton HART of Montana, who came to the Yukon in 1884 over the Chilkoot Pass, one of the earliest prospectors in the Yukon. He was an active man and was constantly pushing farther afield than most. He prospected and mined gold on most of the tributaries of the Yukon. In the fall of 1886, acting on advice from Arthur Harper, he discovered and mined gold on "Hamilton Bar" on the Fortymile River.

From 1896 to 98 he had a lay (lease) on Tagish Charlie's No. 1 Above claim on Bonanza Creek, from which he took a fortune. Most of it was lost when the steamer *Islander* was wrecked near Juneau, Alaska in 1905. He died in Dawson in 1908 after falling into the freezing waters of Bonanza Creek. He sometimes called himself Howard Hamilton.

HARVEY GULCH 63°46′N 136°13′W (115–P). A short creek, flowing into Highet Creek from Scheelite Dome.

This was locally named for HARVEY Ray, a prospector-trapper who lived here in the 1930's.

HASSELBERG CREEK   60°38'N 129°56'W (105-A). A tributary to the upper Liard River.

This stream was named in 1959 after Frederick HASSELBERG who mined and trapped in the upper Liard country for many years from 1910. His cabin is at the mouth of the creek.

When first mapped it was wrongly spelled Heigelberg.

HASSELL CREEK   60°18'N 132°16'W (105-C). A small lake and creek ten miles north of Morley Lake.

This creek and lake were named in the summer of 1951 to honour the name of Sgt. D.B.L. HASSELL, MID, of the Canadian army who was killed in action in the Second World War.

HATCH'S ISLAND   64°02'N 139°27'W (116-B&C). A large island a mile long and a half mile wide, in the Yukon River, a mile and a half above Dawson.

George A. HATCH bought this island in 1901. He cut off the cottonwood trees and sold them for firewood in Dawson. In 1902 he planted potatoes on the ground he had cleared and by 1909 he was producing more than 60 tons per year as well as large crops of oats and other grains and vegetables. He also raised hogs and chickens. He was probably the most successful farmer in the Yukon. He died at his home in Morrill, Maine, in 1917.

HAUNKA CREEK   60°14'N 133°54'W (105-C). Flows into Little Atlin Lake from the east side.

This is a very old name probably dating back to the 1880's. Locally it is said to be the Tagish Indian pronunciation of the name of an old HBC trapper, Hall Williams, who roamed this region in those days. (See Hall Creek.)

HAYDEN LAKE   61°02'N 138°08'W (115-G&F). Ten miles east of the south end of Kluane Lake.

Named after Jack HAYDEN, Klondiker, trapper and noted guide who lived and worked in this area from the earliest years. An American, Hayden was a colourful character who had driven stage coaches in Colorado, punched cattle in Texas and mined in the Klondike. He married a native woman and lived here for many years.

HAYES CREEK   62°43'N 138°15'W (115-J&K). A tributary to the Selwyn River.

This was named for Dr. Charles Willard HAYES who made the first map of this area in his exploration report for the American Geographical Society in 1891. Hayes was later made Director of the United States Geological Survey. (See Hayes Peak.)

HAYES PEAK   6,067′   60°24′N 133°18′W (105–C). On the west side of Teslin Lake, seven miles south of Johnson's Crossing.

This beautiful, lone hill was named by Arthur St. Cyr, DLS, in 1897, when he was searching for and surveying a possible route from Telegraph Creek to the head of Teslin Lake and on to the goldfields. It was named after Dr. Charles Willard HAYES, USC&GS. Hayes, together with Mark Russell and Lt. F. Schwatka, US Army, in 1891 came this way while travelling from the Taku River to the upper White River country. Hayes later published the first notes on the geology and topography of this region. St. Cyr also named a river entering Teslin Lake at the southwest end for Hayes.

HAYSTACK MOUNTAIN   3,751′   63°39′N 139°10′W (115–O&N). On the headwaters of Ruby Creek, south of the Indian River.

The mountain was named about 1897 by the first miners in the Klondike because of its shape. It is notable as the site of one of the most unusual funerals in the Klondike.

In one June in the early 1920's Carl Hafstead died. He had mined on Quartz Creek and had looked at this mountain from his claim for all the years he was there. He had expressed the desire to be buried on the summit of this hill and left instructions in his will to that end, including money for a barrel of beer for his pall-bearers and mourners.

Upon his death a simple service was held in a roadhouse at the base of the mountain, conducted by one of his fellow miners. A party of 30 miners then set off carrying the coffin and a barrel of beer. It was a 12-mile journey and a climb of 1000 feet by wagon and foot, on a hot day. An advance party of miners went ahead and dug and blasted a grave on the top of the hill overlooking the Indian River valley. By late evening the burial party had arrived and Carl was laid to rest in his favourite place.

HAZARD CREEK   61°16′N 140°12′W (115–G). A small creek flowing into the Steele Glacier from the north side.

I. Peace HAZARD was a sponsor and member of the American Geographical Society Expedition of 1935 which was the first to explore the upper reaches of the phenomenal Steele Glacier. This stream was given his name in 1966.

HEADLESS CREEK   61°48′N 134°41′W (105-E). A tributary to the Big Salmon River immediately above Illusion Creek.

Not a murder mystery! This was named by H.S. Bostock, GSC, in the summer of 1934. Glaciation had turned the headwaters of this stream into nearby Lokken Creek, leaving this stream headless, or shorter.

HEIGELBERG CREEK   (See Hasselberg Creek.)

HELL CREEK   64°12′N 133°46′W (106-C). A tributary of the east Rackla River.

This creek got its name in 1898 from the men who tried to travel its rough course on the way from Edmonton to the Klondike. The name was originally given to the whole Rackla River.

HENDERSON CREEK   63°21′N 139°29′W (115-O&N). A large creek entering the Yukon River about two and a half miles below the Stewart River.

Robert HENDERSON of Klondike fame, with John Collins and Underwood, found gold and staked the Discovery claim on 9 June, 1897. They wrote on their No. 1 Post "This creek shall be known as Henderson Creek."

A stampede of considerable proportions took place but little payable gold was found. Henderson was so convinced of the stream's potential that he staked a 160-acre townsite on the west side of the Yukon River, opposite the mouth of the creek. Nothing came of it.

HERSCHEL ISLAND   69°35′N 139°05′W (117-D). The only major island on the Arctic coast of the Yukon.

The most northerly place in the Yukon, this historic island was first sighted and named by John Franklin, RN, (later Sir), in 1826 but he did not land there. He gave it the name of Sir William HERSCHEL (1738–1822), the famous English astronomer.

The USS *Thetis* surveyed the island in 1889 and named many of its features. This was also the year the first whaler wintered at the island. It was the only safe winter anchorage from Point Barrow to the Mackenzie delta. As the riches of the Beaufort Sea whaling grounds became known, more whalers wintered here. Being remote from authority of any kind, they began a period of unlicensed debauchery and murder. As many as 100 ships lay here at one time and took full advantage of the unsophisticated Eskimo population. It was the only time and place in western Canada's history that complete and unbridled lawlessness ran amok.

In 1896 the Canadian Church Missionary Society learned of conditions on the island and Isaac O. Stringer (later Bishop of the Yukon), a fearless and indomitable man, was sent to erect a mission and attempt to alleviate the lot of the natives. He pressed Ottawa for help but it was not until 1903 that the RNWMP set up a detachment here. By that time the whaling industry had recessed and conditions on the island had bettered.

The island continued to be a trading centre and a little whaling by both natives and whites was carried on. In 1925 a post office (run by the RCMP) was opened. As population lessened and trade decreased, the settlement dwindled. In September 1938 the post office was closed. By 1968 all had ceased and no one remained.

HESS RIVER 63°33′N 133°56′W (105–N). A major tributary of the Stewart River.

Michael HESS was one of the earliest miners in both the Canadian and Alaskan Yukon. He entered the country over the Chilkoot Pass in 1884 and prospected most of the major Yukon River tributaries. He was one of the discoverers of Cassiar Bar in the Yukon River, the first rich diggings found on the Yukon. It is probable that he prospected and named this stream before 1886. Although well known and prominent in the literature of the time, little is known of the man himself. He died and was buried at Fortymile in 1892.

The range of mountains between the Rogue and Hess Rivers was later given his name.

HESTER CREEK 63°59′N 139°02′W (115–O&N). Flows into Hunker Creek from the southwest, two miles above Last Chance Creek.

John Huntington staked the Discovery claim on this stream on 28 October, 1897 and probably named it after someone in his family.

MOUNT   HICKSON   61°11′N 140°04′W (115–F).   Beside   Mount Gibson in the St. Elias Range.

This was named in 1970 by the Alpine Club of Canada after J.W.A. HICKSON (1873–1956), a past president (1924–1926) of the club.

MOUNT HIGGINS 2,973' 66°09'N 136°33'W (116-1). At the head of Eagle River.

In 1973 this hill was named in remembrance of K-49920 Trooper Struan Alexander HIGGINS who was born on 12 July, 1918, in Vancouver, BC. He enlisted at Dawson and served in Canada, Great Britain and northwest Europe. He was reported missing in action and presumed killed on 9 August, 1944, in France.

HIGH CACHE CREEK 69°09'N 140°09'W (117-C). A tributary of the Firth River about 75 miles from the mouth.

Jujira Wada found placer gold on the Firth River at this point on 1 March, 1908, and named this stream. A cache is a small, log building, usually built on high posts, used to store dry supplies out of the reach of animals.

Wada was an exceptional musher (dog team driver) and made many extraordinary journeys to the far corners of the Yukon and Alaska. He took part in all major and many minor gold rushes and stampedes in both countries from 1898 to 1925. He went from Fairbanks (before it had that name) to Dawson with the news of a new, rich (and mainly imaginary) gold strike. About 1,000 men followed him back and, when they assessed the new camp, held a miners' meeting in which they discussed hanging him. As it happened, they really did not mean it and by summer gold had been found in large amounts. He once mushed, in 1923, from central northern Alaska to Herschel Island, down the Mackenzie and on to Winnipeg, Manitoba, a distance of 2,500 miles.

His find here sparked a stampede but results were uneconomic. Every ten or 15 years another rush takes place to the same prospects. (See Firth River.)

HIGHET CREEK 63°43'N 136°04'W (115-P). Flows into the Minto River.

Warren HIATT discovered the first gold here in May 1903. When he was recording the Discovery claim, his name was spelled phonetically by the Mining Recorder. It was the richest creek in the Mayo area; by 1915 over $500,000 in gold had been won from it. Native bismuth, a mineralogical rarity, was common in its gravels.

William Ogilvie, DLS, when connected with the Stewart River dredging operations of the Yukon Basin Gold Dredging Company in 1908, called it Hyatt Creek.

MOUNT HINTON 6,755′ 63°54′N 135°08′W (105-M). Six miles north of Mayo Lake in the Gustavus Range.

This was named in 1904 after Thomas HINTON, a well-liked Mining Recorder at Dawson and Mayo in the early 1900's.

HOBO CREEK 63°56′N 136°57′W (115-P). Flows into the Little Klondike River.

This was named by the famous Captain H.S. Back on 13 November, 1897, when he prospected this creek. (See Back and Nansen Creeks.)

HODDER CREEK 62°34′N 134°26′W (105-L). Flows into the Pelly River from the Glenlyon Range.

HODDER, a Swede, was a ne'er-do-well who existed on a little trapping and the charity of the local Indians. He died on the Pelly River in the winter of 1940 when he drunkenly locked himself outside his cabin in sub-zero weather and froze to death. Mount Hodder is now Glenlyon Peak.

HODGSON GLACIER 61°11′N 140°19′W (115-G). A western branch of the Steele Glacier.

In 1966 Walter Wood named this feature in memory of Forest A. HODGSON Wood, a member of four scientific expeditions (1935, 39, 1941, 47) to the area of the Steele Glacier.

Wood on 27 July, 1957, left the Seward Glacier in a Norseman aircraft with the pilot and his daughter, Valerie. They were never seen again. In 1957, Mount Forest in Alaska was given his name.

MOUNT HODNETT 6,540′ 60°19′N 135°12′W (105-D). Between the Watson and Wheaton Rivers.

This was named in 1906 after David HODNETT, the discoverer of lode gold in this area that same year. Hodnett Lakes were also named for him at a later date. (See Gold Hill.)

MOUNT HOFFMAN 64°28′N 136°20′W (116-A). In the south Wernecke Mountains.

Fred HOFFMAN was a pioneer prospector and trapper in this area and a partner of Frank Rae.

HOGAN LAKE 66°21′N 134°03′W (106-L). Between the Caribou and Peel Rivers.

This was named in 1973 for Eugene A. HOGAN who was a Yukon Councillor for the Klondike District, 1912–15.

MOUNT HOGE 61°14'N 139°23'W (115-G&F). In the Donjek Range, west of Kluane Lake.

This peak was named in 1945 by Allan Jeckell, Comptroller of the Yukon Territory and H.S. Bostock, GSC, after Brigadier General William A. HOGE, US Army. Hoge was the Officer Commanding the Northern Command of the Army Engineers during the construction of the Yukon section of the Alaska Highway, March to August 1942. It was his drive and leadership which led to this section of the highway being built in so short a time.

A native of Booneville, Missouri, and a career soldier, he was awarded the DSM in the First World War.

A creek flowing from the mountain was also given his name at a later date.

MOUNT HOGG 6,774' 61°20'N 132°14'W (105-F). East of the McConnell River.

This mountain was named in 1951 to perpetuate the name of another Canadian hero, Squadron Leader J.E. HOGG, DFC, of the RCAF who was killed in action during the Second World War.

HOIDAL MOUNTAIN 2,969' 68°17'N 137°49'W (117-A). Seven miles north of Bonnet Lake.

Anker HOIDAL was a noted northern prospector who headquartered in Dawson and Aklavik. He spent many years from 1920 to 60 prospecting the Arctic slope of the Yukon Territory. This mountain was named for him in 1973. (See Anker Creek.)

HOLMANS LAKE 60°21'N 134°20'W (105-D). A small lake three miles northwest of Tagish.

Although not officially named until after his death in 1952, this lake was the home of HOLMON Good. He settled here shortly after the Klondike rush and remained, trapping and prospecting, for many years. Holmon is the correct spelling.

HOMESTAKE GULCH 63°55'N 139°15'W (115-O&N). Flows into upper Bonanza Creek, two miles from Grand Forks.

James H. Sullivan staked the Discovery claim here on 28 June, 1897, and

129

was working the claim when it was "jumped" (staked illegally by another person) on 13 July. He was able to confirm his ownership and carried on earning a homestake.

A "homestake" is the term used among miners to denote enough money to go home, as opposed to a "grubstake" which is enough money to go prospecting.

HOOLE RIVER   61°45′N 131°42′W (105–G). A tributary to the Pelly River.

Francis HOOLE, half Iroquois and half French-Canadian, was a lifelong employee of the HBC and for a number of years interpreter for Robert Campbell and his companions on their journeys of exploration in northern BC and the Yukon.

This river and the major rapids on the Pelly River, Hoole Canyon, were named for him by Campbell in the summer of 1843 when they made their first trip down the Pelly.

HOOTALINQUA   61°35′N 134°54′W (105–E).

This spot was from ancient times an Indian fishing camp. Situated at the junction of the Teslin (earlier called the HOOTALINQUA) River and the Yukon it soon became in early days, a steamboat landing and supply point for the miners in the Teslin River country. A roadhouse here catered to the travellers on the river. The settlement, except for a telegraph operator, was nearly abandoned by 1910.

The name was sometimes spelled "Hootalinka."

HOPE GULCH   63°55′N 135°12′W (105–M). A tributary to Lightning Creek from Keno Hill.

The Rev. George Pringle, the noted Klondike minister and active prospector, staked the first claim and named this small stream on 3 March, 1902.

There is a Faith Gulch next to the west and a Charity Gulch immediately to the east.

HORNET CREEK   68°45′N 136°35′W (117–A). Flows into Rapid Creek, a tributary of the Blow River, near the Arctic coast.

In 1972 F.G. Young, GSC, was working on this stream when his party ran into trouble due to the excessive numbers of these pesky insects.

HORSFALL CREEK 62°55′N 135°00′W (105-L). A tributary to the MacMillan River.

Joseph S. HOSFALL (to give his correct name) was an Englishman who came into the country during the Klondike stampede, overland from Edmonton. The country and the life suited him so well that he married one of Jack McQuesten's daughters and stayed. He earned a living trapping and prospecting. He accompanied F.C. Selous, Charles Sheldon and other noted big-game hunters into the MacMillan River country and, in their writings, was well-spoken-of by them. He spent a good deal of his time searching for the Lost McHenry Gold Mine, a legendary stream supposedly located in the headwaters of the Pelly River. Remarkably, he was a poor bushman and was often lost. The Hosfalls started a farm on the east bank of the Yukon about five miles below Fort Selkirk and grew good crops of vegetables for several years. He died on or near this stream about 1935.

No account of Hosfall would be complete without particular mention of his wife. In almost every written account which mentions her, she is invariably spoken of in superlatives. She was educated at the mission school at Fort MacPherson and at 20 she married Hosfall. She evidently inherited the best characteristics of both her Indian mother and her New Englander father. She could hunt and shoot, handle boats and canoes, trap, and build cabins as well as most men; in addition, she was as well educated, well-spoken, modest and graceful as any woman might aspire to be. Her knowledge of woodcraft and animal life was superior to that of most people. She did all the traditional tasks of Indian women — tanning skins, catching and drying fish, making clothes, doing beadwork — and she was an excellent cook. The Hosfalls had four daughters, the two youngest of whom were born in the middle of winters, when Mrs. Hosfall was alone with her other children in their cabin on the Pelly. Her husband was away on his trapline, so Mrs. Hosfall kept the house warm, looked after her little daughters and gave birth, entirely unaided, with the temperature outside far below zero. She was liked and respected by everyone who knew her.

HORTON CREEK 61°49′N 132°01′W (105-F). A small creek joining the Pelly River from the south above Hoole Canyon.

This was named in 1909 after an early prospector of this name who lived here.

HOTSPRING CREEK 63°02′N 135°52′W (105-M). A tributary to Woodburn Creek in the McArthur Mountains.

One of the few, true, hot springs located in the Yukon is on the headwaters of this creek.

HOUGHTON LAKE   61°22′N 137°20′W (115-H). A small lake about six miles west of Aishihik Lake.

In 1956 this lake was chosen to honour the memory of Pte. Donald HOUGHTON of the Canadian army, who was killed in action during the Second World War.

HOWARD LAKE   60°14′N 136°49′W (115-A). At the head of the Takhanne River.

In March 1898 ex-Lt. Adair, US Cavalry, came from Haines, Alaska, and arrived at the new gold finds on Shorty Creek, just north of Dalton Post, with 36 men and large amounts of equipment and supplies. His party, run on military lines, was sworn to secrecy, so much so that the other prospectors and the NWMP called them the "Mysterious 36". It was thought that Adair was backed by the Standard Oil Company and eastern Canadian capital. They built large camps on Shorty Creek and prospected widely in the area for both placer gold and lode minerals. HOWARD S. Scott was Adair's second-in-command and highly regarded by the local NWMP. It is thought that this lake was named after him by his prospectors.

MOUNT HUBBARD   15,015′   60°19′N 139°04′W (115-B&C). In the St. Elias Range.

In 1890 Professor Israel C. Russell, USGS named this high peak in honour of Gardiner Green HUBBARD (1822–1897), Massachusetts lawyer and educator, regent of the Smithsonian Institution, founder and first president of the National Geographic Society, which office he held from 1888 to his death. Interested in the exploration of Alaska, he helped to organize Russell's 1890 and 1891 expeditions, which were sponsored jointly by the National Geographic Society and the USGS.

In 1960, because of continued support of exploration in the St. Elias region by the National Geographic Society, the Canadian government also gave his name to a large glacier on the northwest side of the mountain.

MOUNT HULEY   65°54′N 138°40′W (116-G). On the east side of the East Porcupine River.

In 1973 this mountain was named after Peter HULEY who spent 50 years in the Dawson area. Known as the "Charlie Chaplin" of the Yukon, he had been a silent film comedian who was exact in his imitation of Charlie Chaplin.

HULSE LAKE   60°31′N 127°52′W (95–D). West of the Coal River.

In 1969 James A. Harquail, president of Fort Reliance Minerals Ltd., requested that the name of this small lake be changed to perpetuate the name of John HULSE. He was a geophysicist who spent the last three months of his life in this area and was killed in an aircraft crash on 2 September, 1968. The name was formerly Quartz Lake.

HUNGRY CREEK   65°35′N 135°27′W (106–E). A tributary to the Wind River from the west.

This was named in the winter of 1897–98 by stampeders from Edmonton who were caught here by winter with short supplies of food.

HUNKER CREEK   64°02′N 139°13′W (116–B&C). Flows into the Klondike River from King Solomon's Dome.

Andrew "Old Man" HUNKER, a native of Wittenberg, Germany, and an old Cariboo miner who had come into the Yukon in 1886 or 87, was on the upper Fortymile diggings when he heard the news of Carmack's find. When he and his partner, Charles Mathew Johnson, a Swedish farmer and logger from Ohio, reached Bonanza they were in time to find ground open for staking. Hunker staked No. 31 Below Discovery and Johnson No. 43 Below, a few days after the discovery. Not bothering to record these claims immediately (miners had 60 days in which to record their claims after staking) they decided to prospect some of the creeks farther up the Klondike River.

They reached this stream about 1 September and spent four days prospecting upstream, finding better colours (fine gold) as they went. About 12 miles from the mouth they found a location which gave them $22.75 in gold in two hours panning. This was extremely rich. Hunker and Johnson staked the Discovery claim, Hunker staked No. 1 Below and Johnson No. 1 Above. They then went up to Henderson's workings on Gold Bottom and informed the men there of their find. Henderson and his three men came down immediately and staked claims above Hunker's. It is doubtful that they knew of the finds on Bonanza or Eldorado until told by Hunker. Henderson, Swanson and Munson soon sold their claims to Big Alex McDonald or his agents, without testing the ground. They got about $3000 each. Dalton kept and worked his claim and became fairly wealthy. None of them recorded a claim on Gold Bottom.

Hunker married a Swedish woman whom he had financed to operate a roadhouse near his claim. A man of sober habits, he was never ostentatious and remained active in mining and prospecting. In 1907 he was in Fort MacPherson, NWT, after spending some time investigating reports of gold-quartz deposits on the upper Peel River discovered by H.F. Waugh, whom he had backed.

Hunker Creek was one of the richest placer gold creeks in the world. In the Klondike it ranked next to Eldorado and Bonanza.

MOUNT HUNT 61°29′N 129°12′W (105-H). On the east side of Frances Lake in the Logan Range.

This mountain was originally named Mount Logan by Dr. G.M. Dawson, GSC, in 1887, after Sir William Edmond Logan (1798-1875), founder and director of the Geological and Natural History Survey of Canada.

In 1916 the name was changed as it was in conflict with the later-named Mount Logan in the St. Elias Range, (a more appropriate mountain, being the highest in Canada and the second highest in North America).

This mountain was then renamed after Thomas Sterry HUNT (1826-1892), a chemist with the Geological and Natural History Survey of Canada.

HUOT GULCH 63°59′N 140°29′W (115-O&N). A short stream running into Boucher Creek in the Sixtymile district.

On 12 August, 1902, W.M. Richardson, I.A. Jackson and James HUOT filed locations on the Discovery claim and others on what they named Huot Gulch, a tributary of Boucher on which they had just previously also made the discovery. James Huot was a son of Napoleon Huot of Québec, an early staker in the Klondike.

HYLAND RIVER 59°52′N 128°12′W (105-A). A major tributary of the Liard River at Lower Post, BC.

Robert HYLAND, an Englishman, shipped around Cape Horn in the 1860's and was one of the first men in the rush to the Stikine River and Dease Lake (or Cassiar) goldfields. He was always in the vanguard and though primarily a trader was an adventurous prospector. He was the first man to ascend the river which bears his name, in the summer of 1874 or perhaps as early as 1873. Near Stewart Lake he staked the first lode mineral claim in the territory on a deposit of silver-lead ore which he discovered there. He lived the remainder of his life in this area, owning and operating trading posts at Spatzi River, Dease Lake, Cassiar and Lower Post. He was always in competition with the HBC and other traders and at one time printed and circulated his own money, which was accepted by natives and miners.

In 1834 Peter McLeod of the HBC was the first white man to see this stream which he named the "MacPherson" but by 1873 this name had been forgotten.

The Indians in this region were afraid to go to the headwaters of the Hyland as they believed that something evil lived there. One of their legends tells of a party of hunters who ascended the river and, while passing through a canyon, met with a sudden darkness during which an evil monster rose from the depths of the river and dragged the unlucky hunters into a whirlpool. Since then the Indians dislike the rivers in the district and turn back whenever they see the bones of huge animals (fossil remains) on the bars.

ICE CHEST MOUNTAIN 3,895′ 63°30′N 137°35′W (115-P). Five miles southwest of McQuesten.

H.S. Bostock, GSC, named this mountain in the summer of 1949 to preserve the name of ICE CHEST Reef, a bad rock in the channel of the Stewart River just to the west. Named by the early steamboat captains and pilots, the rock had caused a number of accidents.

ILLES BROOK (See Money Creek.)

ILLUSION CREEK 61°49′N 134°40′W (105-E). A tributary of the Big Salmon River.

This was named in the summer of 1934 by H.S. Bostock, GSC, when some of his party missed a rendezvous, mistaking this stream for Lokken Creek.

MOUNT INA 5,261′ 64°25′N 139°34′W (116-B&C). 30 miles north of Dawson.

This was named in 1970 after the wife of the Hon. Justice H.E. Gibben, a long-time Yukoner, Justice of the Territorial Court and one-time Commissioner of the Yukon Territory.

INDEPENDENCE CREEK 63°31′N 137°49′W (115-P). A tributary to the Stewart River.

Fine gold was found here about 4 July, 1893, by Hugh and A.H. Day. They were among the first miners to enter the Yukon, coming over the Chilkoot Pass in the spring of 1884. They were successful miners on the Stewart River bars.

Later, in the summer of 1896, Jack McQuesten and Dick Poplin (another old-timer who had been here since 1883) found coarse gold on this creek but the find was over-shadowed by the Klondike discoveries.

INDEPENDENCE CREEK 63°59′N 139°01′W (116–O&N). Flows into Hunker Creek between Hester and Colorado Creeks.

Sam Abramson was optimistic when he found enough gold here to stake a Discovery claim and name the stream on 6 December, 1897.

INDIAN RIVER 63°47′N 139°44′W (116–O&N). Flows into the Yukon River.

This river and the Klondike River enclose what is now called the Klondike area. All the rich placer creeks are between these two streams.

The earliest travellers on the Yukon River noted an Indian community at the mouth of the stream from which it received its name. As was the case in those times, the Indians moved from here and settled closer to the trading posts as they were established.

When Robert Campbell, HBC, made his first journey from Fort Selkirk to Fort Yukon in 1851 it was probably this river that he named "Forcier" River, after one of his French-Canadian voyageurs, Baptiste Forcier.

INGERSOLL ISLANDS 62°41′N 137°11′W (115–I). Ten miles above Fort Selkirk in the Yukon River.

This group of small islands was named by Lt. F. Schwatka, US Army, in 1883 after Col. INGERSOLL, US Army, of Washington, DC.

MOUNT INGRAM 7,080′ 60°44′N 135°37′W (105–D). 20 miles west of Whitehorse and south of the Ibex River.

This peak was named in August 1897 by J.J. McArthur, DLS. He was making a hurried trip over the Dalton Trail for the Department of the Interior and mapped it roughly as he went.

On the bank of the Takhini he had found a grave, with a headboard saying INGRAM. Ingram and his partner had come up the Yukon from its mouth, and, after a few years of prospecting, they headed upstream for the coast. They were told to take the righthand stream at the first fork above the Pelly but mistakenly ended up on the Takhini. The ten miles of rapids were evidently too much for them. Ingram's body was buried by William Dickenson, a half-breed Tlinkit trader.

INGS RIVER   61°04′N   131°00′W   (105-G). Joins the upper Liard River from the north, in the St. Cyr Range.

It was named in 1947 in memory of Wing Commander R.R. INGS, RCAF, who was killed in action in the Second World War.

INNISSIAG HILL   69°22′N   139°31′W   (117-D).On the bank of the Firth River, near the Arctic coast.

This is an Eskimo word meaning "the useful flintstone." In earlier years the Eskimos gathered flint rock from here to make stone tools and weapons.

In the summer of 1956 Dr. R.S. McNeish, an archaeologist with the National Museum of Canada, found the remnants of nine prehistoric cultures near this place. The lower remains may be some of the oldest found on the continent, up to 10,000 years old. This find filled in several gaps in the knowledge of Canadian prehistory. Dr. McNeish noted the old Eskimo name for the hill at that time.

IRON CREEK   60°51′N   133°19′W   (105-C). A tributary of Sydney Creek, about ten miles west of the Canol Road.

Gold was found here and the creek staked and named in June 1905 by W. Mooreside, Joe Brewer, Jim Thompson and Charles Anderson. The Mining Recorder, R.C. Miller, gave it the name IRON Creek, because he claimed that there were too many Willow Creeks in the country already. Many attempts were made to mine the creek profitably up to 1936 but with little success, as the values were too erratic.

IRVINE CREEK   60°35′N   131°35′W   (105-B). A large stream which flows into the east side of Wolf Lake.

Formerly known as Murray Creek, this name was changed in 1947. W.T. IRVINE lived here in the 1920's and 30's, trapping and prospecting. His cabin was near the mouth of the stream. He made the first sketch map of the area to assist the GSC.

ISAAC CREEK   61°27′N   137°35′W   (115-H). Flows into the west side of Sekulmun Lake.

This was named many years ago after Chief ISAAC of the Aishihik band of Tutchone Indians. Chief Isaac guided the first white men, Jack Dalton and E.J. Glave when they entered this part of the country in 1890 and 1891.

A small, short-lived settlement was established at the mouth of this creek in 1913 during the stampede to the Chisana goldfields in Alaska. The settlement was on the winter trail and catered to the miners passing through.

ITSI LAKES   62°48′N 130°15′W (105-J). On the headwaters of the Ross River.

This is an old Indian name meaning "wind". Some years ago the small range of mountains north of the lakes was given the same name.

IYON RIVER   (See Big Salmon River.)

JACKSON POINT   61°03′N 138°30′W (115-G&F). On the shore of Kluane Lake about mile 1063 (K1722) of the Alaska Highway.

This point was named in 1960 after Rex JACKSON, the first Forestry Engineer in the Yukon Territory.

JACQUOT ISLAND 61°20′N 138°46′W (115-G&F). The largest island in Kluane Lake, opposite mile 1086 (K1759) of the Alaska Highway.

This was named in 1945 by H.S. Bostock, GSC, after two brothers, Eugene and Louis JACQUOT of Alsace-Lorraine. They came over the Chilkoot Pass in 1898. They were not successful in the Klondike but decided to stay and trap in the Yukon.

Taking part in the rush to the Burwash Creek gold finds, they instead established a trading post and a settlement at Burwash Landing in 1903. Here they remained, trading, homesteading, guiding and successfully mining on Burwash Creek in 1909.

JAKE'S CORNER   60°20′N 133°58′W (105-C). At mile 865.5 (K1402) on the Alaska Highway.

In 1942 the US Army Engineers set up a construction camp here under the command of Captain Jacoby (or Jackobsen) to build this section of the Alaska Highway and a cut-off to Tagish and Carcross for the Canol Pipeline. In 1949–50 a highway south to Atlin, BC, was built from here.

138

JAMES TRAIL 62°20′N 140°32′W (115-J&K). **The road from Snag Junction to Snag.**

William JAMES was one of the first prospectors in this area and laid out the trail which the government later followed to make this road. He spent most of his life in the district. (See Beaver Creek.)

JANET LAKE 63°40′N 135°30′W (105-M). **12 miles northeast of Mayo Landing.**

In 1898, J.J. McArthur, DLS, was surveying in the area and named this lake after his daughter.

JARVIS CREEK 63°42′N 136°08′W (115-P). **A tributary to Minto Creek at its mouth.**

Archie McIntyre staked the Discovery claim and named this creek when he found placer gold here on 14 May, 1903.

JARVIS RIVER 60°46′N 138°08′W (115-B&C). **A tributary to the Kaskawulsh River.**

The river was named by the first prospectors in the area about 1899–1900, after Major Arthur Murray JARVIS, Inspector in the NWMP, who established the police post and Customs on the Dalton Trail in the first days of the gold rush.

MOUNT JECKELL 6,400′ 64°19′N 138°50′W (116-B&C). **25 miles northeast of Dawson.**

This mountain was named about 1957 to commemorate George Allan JECKELL, a school teacher who was appointed Comptroller of the Yukon Territory from 30 June, 1932 to 18 September, 1947. During the Depression, the federal government did away with the office of Commissioner of the Yukon Territory in an attempt to reduce expenses in the territorial government. Jeckell proved to be an outstanding administrator and performed an exceptional job.

JENS CREEK 62°40′N 138°40′W (115-J&K). **A small brook or valley on Rude Creek.**

When JENS Rude discovered the gold of Rude Creek in March 1915, he and his partner built their cabin at the mouth of this small stream. The other miners called it Jens Creek. However, the gold on it was found by Otto F.

Kastner and John A. Ross, who staked and officially named it on 16 September, 1915. (See Rude and Dip Creeks.)

JESSICA CREEK   63°08'N   133°25'W   (105-N). Enters Russell Creek from the east, one mile above Limestone Creek.

Major Neville A.D. Armstrong, who worked for many years in this area, named this stream after the wife of his partner, Mrs. George Leith of England. The Leiths spent 18 months on Russell Creek with Armstrong and his wife in 1904–05.

MOUNT JESUS   64°02'N   132°59'W   (106-C). Three miles southwest of Ortell Lake.

A landmark on the Stewart River from the time of the earliest miners, it was named and known about 1885. It is a beautiful, solitary peak; William Ogilvie, DLS, described it as a very high peak that resembled Mount Hood in Oregon. Somehow, about 1900, it disappeared from all maps, – a curious happening, as it had been so well known up to that time.

MOUNT JETTÉ   8,460'   60°00'N   139°03'W   (115-B&C). On the corner of the International boundary where the Yukon, Alaska and British Columbia meet.

It was named in 1905 after Sir Louis JETTÉ, KCMG, Lt. Governor of Québec and Member of the Canadian-Alaskan Boundary Tribunal in 1903.

JOHN LAKE   62°49'N   130°23'W   (105-J). On the upper Ross River.

In 1909 when Joseph Keele, GSC, was mapping the geology of this area, he named this little lake after his favourite sled dog, JOHN.

JOHNSON CREEK   66°58'N   138°09'W   (116-J&K). A small stream flowing into Pine Creek.

This was named by Otto Heist in 1958 after Andrew JOHNSON, a trapper from Fort Yukon who married a woman from Old Crow and settled in this extremely isolated country for many years. He died at Fort Yukon about 1955.

JOHNSON CREEK   63°49'N   136°27'W   (115-P). Enters the Mc-Questen River just below Ortell's Crossing.

In 1894 the two Garrison brothers found gold on this creek but did not mine it. In the autumn of 1898, F. JOHNSON, who had been unlucky in the Klondike and had prospected this stream previously, returned and staked a Discovery claim, naming the creek.

JOHNSONS CROSSING 60°29'N 133°18'W (105-C). On the Alaska Highway where it crosses the Teslin River.

During 1942 the Teslin River was bridged here to carry the Alaska Highway and the Canol Pipeline. An army construction camp first occupied the site. The US Army Engineers, building the bridge and the highway, named the camp after their Commanding Officer, Col. Frank M.S. JOHNSON, 93rd Engineers.

Local people claim that the crossing was named after George JOHNSTON, a Teslin Indian who ferried the army men and their supplies across the Teslin River at this point, when the bridge was being built.

JONES RIDGE 65°06'N 140°59'W (116-G&F). Crosses the Yukon-Alaska boundary.

About 1914 D.D. Cairnes, GSC, named this ridge after Charles JONES who had been a member of his geological survey parties in this area for a number of years.

MOUNT JOY 7,333' 63°45'N 132°55'W (105-N). The highest peak in the Lansing Range.

While mapping the geology of this region in 1909, Joseph Keele, GSC, named this peak after Sergeant G.B. JOY, Rgt.No. 3045, of the RNWMP.

MOUNT JOYAL 3,055' 66°37'N 136°48'W (116-I). East of the Eagle River.

This mountain was chosen in 1973 to honour 2140278 Pte. Eli Felix JOYAL who was born in Merril, Wisconsin on 13 January, 1887. He enlisted in Victoria, BC on 2 July, 1918, and succumbed to the dreaded "Spanish Flu", which was epidemic around the world at that time, on 19 October, 1918, before leaving Canada.

JUBILEE MOUNTAIN 5,950' 60°12'N 134°07'W (105-D). On the east side of Tagish Lake.

Dr. G.M. Dawson, GSC, named this prominent hill in 1887 in honour of Queen Victoria's Jubilee. In that year she had reigned on the throne of the British Empire for 50 years.

JUDAS CREEK   60°25′N 134°14′W (105-D). Flows into the east side of Marsh Lake.

A stampede took place here from Whitehorse in August 1911, to stake claims near a find made earlier in the month by Benjamin Miller. Some of the stampeders wanted to call it "All-In" Creek because they were exhausted when they reached it. When they found there was almost no gold whatsoever on the stream they gave it this name.

This is wrongly attributed by some to a name given by highway construction crews in 1942.

JUNGLE CREEK   65°29′N 141°00′W (116-G&F). Flows across the Yukon-Alaska boundary to the Nation River in Alaska.

The International Boundary Survey party of 1910 named this creek because of the exceptionally luxuriant growth of vegetation in its valley, which made travel exceedingly difficult.

JUNKERS LAKE   61°02′N 131°21′W (105-G). At the headwaters of the Liard River.

This lake was named in the summer of 1930 by bush pilot Captain E.J.A. "Paddy" Burke and mechanic Emil Kading. They set up a food and fuel cache here to service prospecting activity in the area, from Atlin, BC. They were flying a low-wing JUNKERS aircraft, serial CF-AMX.

On 11 October, 1930, Burke, Kading and prospector Robert Martin left Lower Post, BC, to return to Atlin. Blinded by a blizzard, they were forced down on the ice of the Liard River a short distance north of the present upper Liard River bridge, damaging the aircraft on the second landing. They set out on foot, without snowshoes, to reach this lake and its store of food and fuel. Burke died of exhaustion and exposure after 27 days. Martin and Kading were rescued on 6 December by Everett Wasson and one of the Yukon's best bushmen, Joe Walsh.

This was the first air search and rescue mission ever carried out in the Yukon, and perhaps BC.
(See Wasson Lake and Burke Creek.)

KALZAS LAKE   62°56′N 135°35′W (105-L). On the Little Kalzas River.

This lake was named by Robert Campbell of the HBC, or one of his men, about 1849–52 while establishing Fort Selkirk. It was named after one of his Indian employees. Fish, needed for the fort, were plentiful here. The lake is noted on the earliest map of the territory. It is sometimes called Little Kalzas Lake. (See Big Kalzas Lake.)

KANDIK RIVER 65°51'N 141°00'W (116–G&F). Crosses the Yukon-Alaska boundary and flows to the Yukon River.

This is an Indian name recorded by Lt. F. Schwatka, US Army, on his 1883 excursion. He did not report the translation. It was called "Charlie's River" by the miners and traders of that time, after the chief of the Indian band who had a village at the mouth of the river.

KASKAWULSH RIVER 60°39'N 137°49'W (115–A). The east fork of the Alsek River.

The river names in this area have been much confused and mistaken since the first exploration. This name was first recorded by E.J. Glave in 1891. Later it was applied to what is now the Dezeadash River and at one time was applied to the whole upper Alsek River. For many years this stream was locally called the "O'Connor" River, after a rather mysterious Captain M.J. O'Connor, who prospected and mined in this part of the country, it was said, even before Glave and Dalton explored it. A river in Alaska, farther west, is also named for him.

KATHLEEN LAKES 64°14'N 134°11'W (106–D). Empty into the Rackla River.

This was named on 4 July, 1945, by Bernard J. Woodruff, DTS, of the Geodetic Survey of Canada, after KATHLEEN Emery, the wife of the CPA pilot with their survey party. The name was originally applied only to the largest of the three lakes.

(These are not to be confused with the Kathleen Lakes west of the Haines Highway.)

KATRINA CREEK 62°53'N 140°13'W (115–J&K). Tributary to the White River.

Although the origin of the name has been lost, this creek was known by this name to the miners long before the Klondike Gold Rush.

KAY POINT 69°18'N 138°22'W (117–D). At Phillips Bay on the Arctic coast.

This was named by John Franklin, (later Sir), in 1826, while on his second expedition, after an esteemed nephew.

MOUNT KEARNEY   3,923′ 66°22′N 135°49′W (106–L). On the headwaters of the Trail River in the Richardson Mountains.

This was named in 1973 after Thomas J. KEARNEY who was a Yukon Councillor for the Bonanza District, 1907–09.

KEELE PEAK   63°26′N 130°19′W (105–O). In the Hess Mountains north of the Canol Road.

Joseph KEELE was a noted northern explorer-geologist who was hired in 1898 by the GSC as a topographical surveyor. He spent much of his time from 1901 on in the Yukon and NWT. He mapped much previously unexplored country and added greatly to the knowledge of these areas. He was an expert bushman, canoeman and above all, a scientist. His traverse from the Pelly and up the Ross River, over Christie Pass and down the Gravel River to the Mackenzie in the winter of 1907–08 is among the great Canadian explorations.

He died of throat cancer in 1923, at the height of his career. This large mountain was named in his honour in 1909 by R.G. McConnell, GSC, whose assistant he was that season. Keele Creek and Lake were named much later.

KEELE RANGE   66°55′N 140°20′W (116–J&K). The range of mountains crossing the Yukon-Alaska boundary south of the Porcupine River.

D.D. Cairnes, GSC, named this range in 1911 in honour of his compatriot, Joseph KEELE. (See Keele Peak.)

KELLY CREEK   62°15′N 136°00′W (105–L). A tributary to the Tatchun River.

This was probably named after Gerry KELLY, a trapper and prospector for many years in this area. He married Rose Hosfall, a granddaughter of Jack McQuesten. He was for a number of years an operator of the Yukon Telegraph at the Stewart River station.

MOUNT KELVIN   60°40′N 136°32′W (115–A). Eight miles south of Champagne.

This was named before 1909 after William Thomson, Lord KELVIN, the celebrated British mathematician and physicist.

KENNEBEC CREEK   62°47′N 140°06′W (115–J&K). A tributary to the White River.

The KENNEBEC is a river in the state of Maine and the name was an Indian one, known long before the Revolutionary War. The river was noted during much of the 19th century for its immense stands of white pine and the evolution of modern lumbering methods.

The name was carried by lumberjacks and used again in Québec and Ontario in the late 1880–90's. This stream was probably named by one of these lumberjacks turned miner during the rush to the upper White River copper deposits in 1903.

MOUNT KENNEDY 13,905' 60°20'N 138°58'W (115-B&C). Four miles east of Mount Alverstone in the St. Elias Range.

This was named for the late President of the United States of America, John Fitzgerald KENNEDY at the request of Prime Minister Lester B. Pearson of Canada, on the anniversary of the assassination of President Kennedy. The feature was chosen by Dr. Bradford Washburn, a world-famous mountaineer and a friend of the president.

It was first climbed on 24 March, 1965, and Senator Robert Kennedy, the president's brother, was one of the three to attain the summit.

KENO HILL 6,065' 63°57'N 135°10'W (105-M). 12 miles north of Mayo Lake.

KENO is a gambling game that was popular for many years in western mining camps. Originally this mountain was known as "Sheep Hill" by the first miners; the name was changed in 1919. In July of that year Louis Bouvette (or Beauvette) found the first of the very rich silver-lead ore deposits which started this enormously productive camp. Beauvette had named his claim "The Keno."

KENO LADUE RIVER 63°54'N 134°03'W (105-M). Flows north of Keno Hill to the Stewart River.

Before 1897 this stream was known as Ladue Creek, after Joseph Ladue, a pioneer Yukoner, who had prospected its lower reaches in the 1880's. Later, it was given its present name to avoid confusion with the river and creek of the same name in the Sixtymile district.

KENTUCKY CREEK 64°18'N 139°21'W (116-B&C). A tributary to Twelve Mile Creek.

A stampede from Dawson to this creek took place in early October 1898 and the first man to stake a claim named it after his home state.

KETZA RIVER 61°53′N 132°15′W (105–F). **Enters the Pelly River about ten miles upstream from Ross River.**

This river was named by Robert Campbell of the HBC on his initial journey down the Pelly River in 1843, after his Iroquois canoeman and companion, KITZA. The name was subsequently misspelled by map-makers.

KILLERMUN LAKE 61°10′N 137°41′W (115–H). **In the Ruby Range, this lake empties into the West Aishihik River.**

Recorded in 1962, this name is an old Indian word meaning "flint rock". It is believed that the ancient Indians obtained a type of chert (flint) here to make tools and weapons. .

KIMBERLEY CREEK 60°52′N 138°04′W (115–B&C). **Tributary to the Jarvis River.**

During the rush to the Alsek goldfields in January 1904, Tom Laird discovered gold on this creek and named it.

MOUNT KING 65°13′N 140°18′W (116–G&F). **At the head of the Tatonduc River near Mount Deville.**

In March 1888 William Ogilvie, DLS, named this peak after William Frederick KING (1854–1916), DLS, DTS, Chief Astronomer of Canada from 1890–1905, Director of the Dominion Observatory from 1905–1916, and member of the International Boundary Commission (Canada-U.S.) 1892–1916. (See King Peak.)

MOUNT KING GEORGE 12,250′ 60°32′N 139°44′W (115–B&C). **25 miles north of Mount Vancouver in the St. Elias Range.**

In February-May 1935 a National Geographic Society Yukon Expedition explored the central part of the St. Elias Range. They named this peak in honour of the Silver Jubilee year of KING GEORGE V of Great Britain. The twin peak about 12 miles to the north they named after Queen Mary. The two peaks they called the Jubilee Peaks.

The party, led by Bradford Washburn, was the first to cross the St. Elias Range on foot from the Yukon to Alaska. They were assisted by Jack Haydon of Carcross whose dog-team moved most of their supplies.

KING PEAK 16,971′ 60°35′N 140°39′W (115–B&C). **Ten miles west of Mount Logan.**

This was named about 1918 after Dr. W.F. KING, one-time International

Boundary Commissioner. The peak was first climbed on 6 July 1966. (See Mount King.)

KING POINT 69°07′N 137°52′W (117–D). 15 miles southeast of Phillips Bay on the Arctic coast.

This was named by John Franklin, (later Sir), in 1826 after Captain Phillip P. KING RN (1793–1856), who made the first survey of the coast of Australia.

Roald Amundsen, the famous Arctic explorer, wintered here in 1905–06 in the *Gjoa*, studying and collecting Arctic bird life.

KING SOLOMON'S DOME 4,048′ 63°52′N 138°57′W (115–O&N). The highest and most central hill in the Klondike District.

From it radiate the six richest creeks in one of the richest placer goldfields ever found in the world. Before 1896 miners in the area called it simply, the "Dome", because of its shape. When the riches of the surrounding ground became apparent the present fanciful name was applied, in reference to KING SOLOMON'S riches and to his mythical lost gold mines. From the summit the whole Klondike country, and more, are visible.

MOUNT KINNEY 5,674′ 65°02′N 137°04′W (116–H). East of the Hart River.

Constable G.F. KINNEY, RNWMP, died on the Peel River 35 miles from Fort MacPherson, a member of the lost Fitzgerald Patrol in 1911. This mountain lies just east of their route to Dawson and was named in his memory in May 1973.

KIRKLAND CREEK 61°45′N 136°02′W (115–H). The west branch of the Nordenskiold River.

J.B. Tyrrell, GSC, named this creek in 1898 while mapping the geology of the area, after Professor R. Ramsay Wright of the University of Toronto. The creek was abandoned and the name forgotten. In 1915 a new discovery was made here and the first staker renamed it.

KIRKMAN CREEK 62°59′N 139°25′W (115–J&K). Flows into the Yukon about 15 miles above the White River.

On 13 October, 1898, Grant and Albert KIRKMAN of Tulare, California, discovered the first gold here. Their claim did not pay and the creek was soon abandoned. However, in April 1914 a new discovery was staked by

Joseph C. Britton and William Heas. They found the pay streak and prospered. The creek was a good producer for many years and a small settlement grew up at its mouth.

(See Touleary Creek and Britton Ridge.)

KLETSAN HILL 4,698′ 61°43′N 140°58′W (115–G&F). An isolated hill south of the White River and near the boundary.

The hill takes its name from the creek on the Alaska side, a Tanana Indian name "Klet-San-Dek", meaning Copper Creek or stream. The name of the creek was first reported by C.Willard Hayes, USGS, in 1891 and D.D. Cairnes GSC, applied the name to the hill in 1913–14 when he was mapping the geology of the international boundary.

It was sometimes locally called "Klutson" or Copper Creek because from ancient times the Yukon Indians came here to obtain nuggets of native (pure) copper for tools, weapons and ornaments.

KLINES GULCH 62°38′N 137°59′W (115–I). Tributary to Hayes Creek which flows into the Selwyn River.

About 1904 a prospector of this name found coarse gold, some nuggets up to two ounces, on this stream. It was said to be the only place where gold was found on the Selwyn River or its tributaries.

KLINE later committed suicide in a most efficient manner. Using dynamite, he arranged two charges so that the first blast killed him inside his cabin while the second blast destroyed the cabin walls, allowing the three feet of soil on the roof to effectively bury him.

KLONDIKE RIVER 64°03′N 139°26′W (116–B&C). A large stream entering the Yukon River from the east.

The earliest reports of this river were given by Frank E. Ketchum and Michael Laberge of the Western Union Telegraph Company in 1867, although this may also be the "Deer River" noted by Robert Campbell in 1851. Ketchum and Laberge were exploring a route for an overland telegraph line through BC, the Yukon and Alaska to the Bering Sea near Nome. They reported its name as the "Deer River", from the Indian word "Chandik". In 1883 Schwatka called it the "Reindeer River". These names were not used by the early miners who were trying to twist their tongues around the then-Indian name "Thron-Duick" or "Tron-Deg", these words meaning, as far as can be determined, "Hammer-water". It derived from the Indian practice of driving stakes in the bed of the stream to form fish traps to catch the salmon migrating upstream. The miners finally settled on the pronunciation, "Clunedik", "Clundyke" or "Clondyke". Insp. Charles Constantine NWMP, and Mining Recorder at Fortymile, on the discovery of Bonanza Creek, made the name "Klondyke" official. Most of the miners were Americans and their usage substituted an "i" for the "y". British and some Canadian publications continued to use the word Klondyke for some time afterward but with the issue of the first report of the Canadian Board on Geographical Names, the name Klondike was made official in 1898.

It was one of the finest salmon streams in the Yukon and the local Indians maintained drying racks at the mouth of the river. George Carmack and his party were here to catch salmon in early August 1896. It was only because of the poor run of fish that they decided to prospect up Bonanza.

KLOO LAKE CITY   60°58′N 137°52′W (115-A). On the north side of Kloo Lake.

A small sawmill settlement was built here in 1905 to supply lumber for the Alsek diggings. It was abandoned a few years later.

MOUNT KLOTZ   5,903′   65°23′N 134°06′W (116-G&F). In the Ogilvie Mountains.

This was named by the Board on Geographical Names in 1945 after Dr. Otto Julius KLOTZ (1852–1923), Assistant Chief Astronomer of Canada, who carried out several geodetic surveys in western Canada. He had earlier named a mountain in southern BC after himself but his superiors had disallowed it.

KLUANE   61°02′N 138°23′W (115-G&F). On the south end of Kluane Lake, near mile 1054 (K1707) of the Alaska Highway.

This old settlement started in 1903 with the discovery of good placer gold in the streams nearby. The name at first was "Silver City" but the next year was changed to Kluane as there was another Silver City in the White River country. This was the main supply point for the area for many years but it was gradually abandoned as the Burwash Creek placer fields assumed importance and the local creeks were worked out. The wagon road from Whitehorse was extended to the west in later years, which did away with steamboat landings here.

The first post office was opened in October 1904 with the name "Bullion Creek", altered four months later to Kluane. It was finally closed in 1921.

Originally an Indian fishing village, its name was Tlinkit Indian, meaning, "Whitefish Place" or "Big Fish Place."

The lake name was first reported by Professor Aurel Krause of the Bremen Geographical Society on his expedition in 1882. Kluane Lake is the largest in the Yukon with an area of about 154 square miles. The name Kluane has since been given to a glacier, river, hills, ranges and a plateau.

KLUKSHU LAKE   60°19′N 136°59′W (115–A). Three miles south of Dezeadash Lake.

This name was recorded by E.J. Glave on 22 November, 1890, on his first expedition into the region. He did not find out the meaning of the word. Later reports say the word is Tlinkit Indian, meaning "Last Lake".

KLUTLAN GLACIER   61°27′N 140°37′W (115–G&F). In the St. Elias Range.

This large glacier is the source of the Generc River, and a major source of the White River. The native name was recorded without translation by C. Willard Hayes, USGS, in 1891.

KNORR CREEK   65°22′N 134°40′W (106–E). A tributary to the Bonnet Plume River.

A.N. KNORR came into the Klondike in 1898. He later married a woman from Old Crow and raised sums of money in Dawson to prospect the Bonnet Plume River country. He and his wife lived here for a number of years between 1905–10 in complete isolation and seem to have disappeared without trace after that time. (See Margaret Lake.)

KOIDERN   RIVER   62°03′N 140°27′W (115–J&K). Flows into the White River.

This is from an Indian word meaning "Water Lily". Miners in the area before 1915 called it "Lake Creek" because of the number of ponds along its valley but the name was not adopted. The name was first noted by C. Willard Hayes, USGS, in 1890, on his expedition to the White and Copper Rivers.

KOHSE CREEK   64°32′N 133°26′W (106–C). A tributary of the Bonnet Plume River.

In the sumer of 1952 E. and F. KOHSE were packers for the GSC party surveying the region, led by J.O. Wheeler. He named this creek to show his high regard for their work.

KUSAWA LAKE 60°20′N 136°22′W (115-A). Empties into the Takhini River.

This lake was known and described to Dr. George Davidson in 1869 by the Chilkat chief, Kho-klux. (He led the raid on Fort Selkirk in 1852). In June 1882 the lake was visited by Dr. Arthur Krause, the first white man to see the lake. He was a geographer of the Bremen Geographical Society and brother of Aurel Krause. In 1890 it was again seen by E. Hazard Wells, Chief of the Frank Leslie Illustrated Newspaper Expedition, who renamed it "Arkell Lake" after W.J. Arkell, sponsor of the expedition.

In 1898 the Board on Geographical Names restored the original name. (See Arkell Creek.)

LAKE LABERGE 61°11′N 135°12′W (105-E). On the Yukon River about 15 miles north of Whitehorse.

In the summer of 1867 Frank E. Ketchum of Saint John, New Brunswick and Michael LABERGE of Chateaugay, Québec, explorers for the Western Union Telegraph Company, came up the Yukon River from Fort Yukon to Fort Selkirk. They were looking for a possible route for the Collins Overland Telegraph line being built from New York to Paris. It was never clear if Laberge did visit the lake but he had it described to him by the local Indians. Returning to Fort Yukon they found the project had been stopped. William H. Dall, Director of the Scientific Corps of the Western Union Telegraph Expedition, wrote a massive report on Alaska in 1870 and gave Laberge's name to the lake.

In 1883 Schwatka reported the Tagish Indian named "Kluk-tas-si" and in 1882 Dr. Aurel Krause had recorded the Tlinkit name "Tahini-wud", both without translation.

LACELLE LAKE 61°23′N 137°01′W (115-H). A small lake just east of central Aishihik Lake.

In 1956 this lake was named to perpetuate the memory of Pte. Henri LACELLE, Canadian army, who was killed in action in the Second World War.

LADUE RIVER 63°10′N 140°20′W (115-O&N). A tributary to the White River.

This river was prospected and named in the early 1880's by Joseph LADUE who found some gold on it, as well as on the small creek of the same name which enters the river near its mouth.

Ladue, who came from New York State, was one of the first prospector-entrepreneurs to come to the Yukon, arriving over the Chilkoot Pass in the spring of 1882. Combining prospecting with trading and other enterprises, he was early convinced that a major goldfield would be found in the general area of the Indian and Klondike Rivers. This belief led him to encourage and grubstake prospectors to work there. He grubstaked Robert Henderson in 1894–95 and sent him up Quartz Creek to visit William Redford who was successfully mining there. He himself was one of the first to prospect the Sixtymile and Fortymile districts, although with limited success. He and Jack McQuesten prospected Bonanza Creek in early 1886 but missed the rich gold there. Loosely associated with the ACC, he and Arthur Harper opened a trading post and brought in the first sawmill to the Yukon, at the mouth of the Sixtymile River in 1894. At first called Sixtymile Post, they soon changed the name to that of their friend, William Ogilvie.

In early August 1896 Ladue had, by a remarkable coincidence, decided to remove his sawmill from Ogilvie to the flat at the mouth of the Klondike River, where he intended to set up a small trading post. He arrived there on 28 August and realizing the potential of the new finds, staked the flat land, 160 acres, as a townsite. He set up his sawmill and trading post and quickly built a fortune, becoming a millionaire in the next two years.

He returned to Schuyler Falls, New York in 1897 and married his childhood sweetheart. On 27 June, 1901, suffering from tuberculosis, he died at his home there.

(See Dawson City.)

LAFORCE LAKE   62°41′N 132°18′W (105–K). This lake drains to the Riddell River.

In 1946 this lake received the name of a brave man, Pte. Alphonse LAFORCE MM, of the Canadian army. He was killed in action on 12 May, 1945.

LAHCHAH MOUNTAIN   67°36′N 140°56′W (116–O&N). A long, low ridge 20 miles west of Old Crow.

This is an old name, a Vanta Kutchin Indian word meaning "Low Hill".

LAKE CREEK   62°26′N   140°05′W   (115-J&K). A tributary to the White River.

Alyre Morin and Wilfred Grenier prospected this stream and in the summer of 1913 had found enough gold to warrant staking the Discovery claim. They named the stream, "Lake Creek" for the number of ponds and small lakes along its course in the wide valley. On 2 March, 1914, the Gold Commissioner changed the name to "Pond Creek" as the miners in the White River area were already calling the Koidern River and the Tchawsahmon Creek by that name. A number of years later, when names were being sorted out in the area, the name reverted to the original Lake Creek.

LAKE CREEK   64°38′N   137°10′W   (116-A). The west fork of Rae Creek.

This is the only "Lake" feature in the Yukon in which it is not a descriptive name. In 1956 this creek was named after Frederick LAKE who, with his partners Frank Rae and Afe Brown, trapped and prospected in the Hart River region during World War One and did a little mining on this stream.

MOUNT LAMBART   10,725′   61°31′N   140°59′W   (115-G&F). In the St. Elias Range, just north of the Klutlan Glacier.

This was named after Howard Frederick John LAMBART, DLS, (1880-1946), one of Canada's best mountaineers. He was born and died in Ottawa, Ontario. He graduated in Civil Engineering from McGill University in 1904. He spent most of his working life with the Geodetic Survey of Canada. He was a pioneer of the development and use of aerial photography for mapping. He was the Canadian leader of the joint Canadian-American Expedition which made the first ascent of Mount Logan in 1925.

He surveyed the Yukon-Alaska boundary from 1906–17, including the position and altitude of this mountain.

MOUNT LANDREVILLE   65°09′N   132°52′W   (106-F). East of the Snake River in the Backbone Range.

Max LANDREVILLE was a journalist who came to the Yukon in 1898. He was active politically and was chosen as one of the group to carry the miners' complaints of government inefficiency and corruption to Ottawa that same year. He was also a Yukon Councillor for the Klondike District in 1903. This hill was given his name in 1973.

MOUNT LANSDOWNE   5,875′ 60°22′N 134°31′W (105-D).   15 miles northeast of Carcross on the west side of Marsh Lake.

William Ogilvie, DLS, in 1887 named this feature after Henry Charles K. Petty Fitz-Maurice, fifth Marquis of LANSDOWNE, who was Governor-General of Canada from 1883–1888.

LANSING   63°45′N 133°32′W (105-N).

This was named because of its location at the confluence of the Stewart and Lansing Rivers. In 1897–98 Frank Braine, who had been a trader in northern Saskatchewan, and Percival Nash travelled through this country on their way to the Klondike from Edmonton. Disappointed in their search for gold, they returned to the vicinity of Fort Norman in the NWT to trap and trade. In 1902 they decided to return to this area to reap the fur harvest. They brought several families of Mackenzie River Indians with them and built a trading post here. James Mervyn took over the post in 1912. The post prospered until many of the Indians died during an epidemic of influenza in the late 1920′s. The post gradually lost its importance and with the coming of roads and the cessation of riverboat travel, it faded into oblivion in the 1950′s.

LANSING RIVER   63°45′N 133°28′W (105-N). A tributary of the Stewart River.

Samuel LANSING was one of the first prospectors in the Yukon Territory and mined the bars of the Stewart River in 1883. He prospected this stream that year, when it received his name. He prospected widely in the Yukon and was one of the first at the Fortymile finds in 1886. He was moderately successful in the Klondike and was, for a number of years, the manager of the Harper and Ladue Co.'s mining operations there. He retired in 1926 to Sumner, Washington.

LAPIE RIVER   62°02′N 132°36′W (105-K). A tributary of the Pelly River, west of Ross River.

Dr. G.M. Dawson, GSC, named this river in 1887 after one of Robert Campbell's Iroquois Indian canoemen, who had accompanied him on his explorations on the Pelly in 1843.

LAPIERRE HOUSE   67°24′N 137°00′W (116-P). On the Bell River near the mouth of the Rat River.

Lapierre House was established in 1843–44 by Chief Factor John Bell,

HBC, of Fort MacPherson, as an outlier of that place, to facilitate trade with the tribes west of the Richardson Mountains.

LAPIERRE, the man who built and ran the post for the first few years, was half Iroquois and half French-Canadian. The first post was probably at the junction of what is now the Little Bell and the Bell Rivers, about 35 miles upstream from the present site.

After Alexander Hunter Murray built Fort Yukon in 1847, the post became a way point between there and Fort MacPherson, used to transfer goods and furs. After the building of the second Rampart House on the Porcupine and the supply of that place by steamboat up the Yukon, at much lower cost, Lapierre House fell into disuse and was abandoned by 1890.

For many years the post supplied much of the meat and fish consumed at Forts MacPherson and Yukon. Caribou were killed by the thousands and fantastic numbers of fish were caught and dried.

In the fall of 1847 Anne Murray, wife of A.H. Murray, gave birth to a daughter, Helen, while staying here. Helen Murray was the first white child born in the Yukon Territory. Robert Kennicott, the brilliant young American naturalist and explorer, at that time Director of the Scientific Corps of the Collins Overland Telegraph, spent about a month here in the winter of 1862, studying the natural history of the region.

Sometimes spelled LaPierre's, Lapierre's, or Lapiers, it was also known to HBC employees as "The Small House", and to the Indians as "Koahze" meaning "Little House".

MOUNT LAPORTE 7,050′ 61°13′N 127°42′W (95–E). In the southeast corner of the Yukon Territory.

In 1972 at the request of the Commissioner of the Yukon, James Smith, this mountain was named after the Hon. Pierre LAPORTE, journalist and Minister of Labour in the Québec government. He was kidnapped and murdered by FLQ terrorists in Montréal in 1971.

LARSEN CREEK 60°10′N 125°01′W (95–C). Flows into the Beaver River.

In 1958 the long-known local name was officially adopted for this creek and lake, where L. LARSEN, the first white trapper in the area, lived and died in his cabin at the head of the lake.

LASKA GULCH 63°49′N 136°19′W (115–P). A small stream off Johnson Creek.

Joe Laska placer mined on Johnson Creek for many years in the 1930's and 40's. George Ortell lived about a mile and a half away and though the two men had frequent disputes and times when they hardly spoke, they were partners in a way. When one saw no smoke from the other's chimney, he investigated. Ortell admitted that Laska was a great help in time of trouble. (See Ortell's Crossing.)

LAST CHANCE CREEK 64°01′N 139°06′W (116–B&C). A tributary to Hunker Creek two miles from its mouth.

The Discovery claim was staked on 2 October, 1896, by Fred Belanger who may have named it, although a miner on the creek later wrote that a native, "Indian Sam" first found gold on the creek and staked a claim.

LAST MOUNTAIN 4,407′ 60°46′N 126°37′W (95–D). On the Yukon-NWT boundary.

This was named in the 1940's by G.C.F. Dalziel, big-game guide of Watson Lake, and at one time owner-operator of Northern British Columbia Air Services. The hill was used by bush pilots as a landmark. (See Dalziel Creek.)

LAST PEAK 6,062′ 61°36′N 134°14′W (105–E). East of the Big Salmon River and south of Teraktu Creek.

In 1898 Arthur St. Cyr, DLS, surveyed the Quiet Lake-Big Salmon country. He occupied ten triangulation stations on various mountain peaks within the area. This was the last one he used.

MOUNT LAURIER 5,838′ 61°02′N 134°52′W (105–E). Ten miles east of the head of Lake Laberge.

Originally named Mount Dawson by William Ogilvie in 1888, the name was changed in 1890 by Dr. G.M. Dawson, GSC, to honour the then Prime Minister of Canada, Sir Wilfrid LAURIER.

MOUNT LEACOCK 10,200′ 60°38′N 138°43′W (115–C). In the St. Elias Range, five miles east of Kaskawulsh Mountain.

This beautiful peak was named in 1970 in remembrance of Stephen LEA-COCK (1876–1944), Professor of Economics at McGill University and Canada's beloved humourist and author.

LECKIE LAKE 61°33′N 129°38′W (105–H). Located between the arms of Frances lake, at the north end.

In 1962 this lake was named to honour another of Canada's war dead, Sergeant J.C. LECKIE, Canadian Infantry Corps, who was killed in action in the Second World War.

LEDGE CREEK 63°40′N 134°52′W (105–M). Flows into Mayo Lake.

Gold was first discovered here and in several nearby creeks about August 1903 by a party of four Australian prospectors. They named the creeks when they were recording their claims in Dawson. The creeks were rich, for the discoverers brought with them 175 ounces of coarse gold.

LEGAR LAKE 62°39′N 136°33′W (115–I). About ten miles northeast of Minto.

In 1936 Dan Van Bibber reported that this name had been in local use for many years. Because of the number of pike in the lake, the name may have been given by a French-Canadian prospector or trapper who fished them.

MOUNT LEOTTA 3,156′ 63°58′N 138°50′W (115–O&N). Between Hunker Creek and the Klondike River.

John Scott named this hill during the Klondike rush in 1897, after his sister. He had been in the Yukon for many years.

LEPINE CREEK 64°05′N 139°05′W (116–B&C). The west fork of Rock Creek, ten miles east of Dawson.

W. LEPINE was working for the HBC when R.G. McConnell GSC, met him on the Liard River in 1887. He had spent many years in the Yukon and NWT. Before the '98 rush he went to Fortymile and it is believed that he prospected and lived on this stream in 1897–98.

LESLIE RIDGE 62°38′N 138°45′W (115–J&K). Between Dip Creek and the Klotassin River, northeast of Stevenson Ridge.

H.S. Bostock, GSC, gave this name in 1941 after the junior partner of a mining company on Rude Creek. They were successful miners and prospectors for many years in the district. At the start of the Second World War in 1939, LESLIE and his partner Stevenson bought an expensive radio in Dawson. They laboriously packed it and the heavy batteries used at the time into their camp and set up an elaborate aerial. Switching on the set, the first station they received was a German short-wave propaganda station. They instantly chopped the radio to bits and threw it outside the cabin, their patriotism outraged. They never bought another. (See Stevenson Ridge.)

LEWES RIVER   The old name for the Yukon River above its junction with the Pelly River.

On 16 June, 1843, Robert Campbell of the HBC arrived at this junction. He called the river below this point the Pelly and considered the river above it to be a tributary of the Pelly and named it after John Lee LEWES, Chief Factor of the HBC. The local Indians told him that the headwaters of this stream formed a trade route to the coast, which undoubtedly influenced his selection of this place as the site of Fort Selkirk. By the 1880's the miners were using this name for the river as far as Lake Laberge.

In 1883, Lt. F. Schwatka, US Army, ignoring Campbell and the miners, named it the Yukon River. It was not until May 1945 that the Canadian government officially changed the name Lewes to the Yukon River.

In the early years the section of the Yukon from Lake Laberge to Marsh Lake was called the Thirtymile River. This was later dropped and included in the Lewes and then, the Yukon.

LEWIS LAKE   60°22′N 134°50′W (105-D). On the west side of the WP&YR tracks, about 15 miles north of Carcross.

Although often misspelled Lewes (after the old name for the Yukon River at this point), this lake received its name in the summer of 1898 from an engineering error during the construction of the railway. A.B. LEWIS, the locating and construction engineer, while carrying out his grade survey, found that the surface of this lake was somewhat above the railway grade. A ditch was dug from the south end of the lake to drain away the excess water. The plug was removed in the evening and during the night the force of the out-flow washed the ditch much deeper in the loose gravel than was anticipated and the lake was quickly drained by a depth of 50 or more feet. The flood washed out a considerable length of newly constructed roadbed below the lake, holding up construction and embarrassing the engineer. The name was early mistaken with that of the Lewes River and has been so printed on maps since then.

LEWIS LAKE   62°35′N 131°05′W (105-J). Part of the upper Ross River.

Joseph Keele, GSC, named this lake in 1907 during his explorations, after Clement S. LEWIS, son of Archbishop Lewis of Ottawa. Lewis came into the Yukon in 1898. After various prospecting and mining ventures of limited success, he and Poole Field bought the trading post at the mouth of Ross River in 1902. Tom Smith, the owner, had built it a few years earlier. They named it "Nahanni House." About 1906 or later they sold out to

Taylor and Drury, Whitehorse merchants, and Lewis managed it for them for a number of years, until about 1910. He was Justice of the Peace for the area and collected specimens of the local flora and fauna for the National Museum of Canada at Ottawa.

He then managed the Taylor and Drury post at Teslin until about 1915 and during this time he accumulated an important collection of birds of the area which was purchased by the museum.

LIARD RIVER   60°00′N 128°35′W (105-A).

The headwaters of the mighty Liard River are in the St. Cyr Range of mountains of the south central Yukon. The river flows southeast to cross the Yukon-BC border a few miles below Watson Lake. From there it flows east and north to join the Mackenzie River at Fort Simpson.

The early HBC traders on the Mackenzie called this stream the "West Branch", the "Mountain River" and the "Great Current River". The Mackenzie Indians called it the "Erett-Chichie" and "Thattadesse" and the Yukon Indians, the "Too-Ti", words expressing its size and force.

The Liard was first explored by John McLeod of the HBC when the company began expanding its empire across the Rocky Mountains and westward. He traversed the river at least as far as what is now Lower Post in 1834. It was his French-Canadian voyageurs who gave it the name "Rivière aux Liards", "liard" being the French name for the cottonwood (poplar) trees which still line the banks of the lower river in profusion.

The next white man on the river was Robert Campbell, also of the HBC who, from 1838 to 1852, opened up the route from the Mackenzie to the central Yukon. Campbell explored the Yukon Territory by way of the Liard and its tributary, the Frances River, leading to the Pelly River and the Yukon proper. While travelling the Liard in 1838 Campbell did not realize that it was the same river McLeod had explored, and named it the "Bell River" after Chief Trader John Bell. The name was used on some maps but when its course was determined the old name "Liard" was kept.

In 1874 a party of Cassiar miners ascended the headwaters of the river where they found and mined placer gold on a number of its tributaries. This was the first production of gold in what is now the Yukon Territory. These miners corrupted the name of the river to "Deloire" and for at least the next 15 years they prospected its upper reaches with indifferent results.

The river is dangerous and in 1852 the HBC abandoned the route because of the number of men lost while trying to supply the posts at Frances Lake and Pelly Banks from Fort Simpson on the Mackenzie. Numerous prospectors were drowned in the river, especially in the Great Canyon, below Watson Lake. A number of Klondikers tried to reach the goldfields in 1897–98 by this route but few were successful, the recorded tragedies of that time only emphasizing those of earlier years.

Of scholarly interest is the number of variations of the names used for the river. Deloire, Deliore, Delyare, d'Eloir, D'Liard, Delaird, Del'Liard, Liard, Rivière des Liards, Lizzard and the Ure. Confusion in the early history also arises from the fact that the Fort Nelson River (not Nelson River) and the Dease River, both tributaries of the Liard, were sometimes called the Deloire River and that Delure Creek, a tributary of the Dease River, was sometimes called Deloire Creek. (See Cabin and Sayyea Creeks.)

LIBERTY CREEK   62°19′N 137°06′W (115-I). A tributary of Stoddard Creek in the Mount Freegold area.

This has been a local name since 1929 when Fred Guder staked his Liberty claim on the creek, the first mineral find there.

LIBERAL TRAIL   (See Conservative Trail.)

LIGHTNING CREEK   63°53′N 135°21′W (105-M). Tributary to Duncan Creek in the Mayo district.

In 1907, the discoverers of gold on the creek gave it the name of the riverboat *LIGHTNING*, which brought miners and supplies up the Stewart River to Duncan Creek in the early 1900's.

LISTER CREEK   61°27′N 137°12′W (115-H). Flows from Houghton Lake into the west centre of Aishihik Lake.

In 1956 this stream was selected to honour the name of Flying Officer J.E. LISTER, RCAF, who was killed in action during the Second World War.

LITTLE   BLANCHE   CREEK   63°49′N 139°04′W (115-O&N).   A tributary to Quartz Creek from the west.

Bob Ensley staked and named this creek in October 1897. He was in love with a Dawson dance-hall girl and named the stream after her. Later in 1898 when his claim proved to be rich he induced LITTLE BLANCHE to marry him, by giving her her weight in raw gold.

This little creek is notable as the scene of one of the tantalizing stories of gold found in the Klondike before 1896. It is claimed that in the spring of 1894, Andrew Hart and his partner Hansen prospected the creek and found payable gold. They mined it for a couple of months before running short of supplies and recovered over $2,000 in gold. They went out to Fortymile and, because no one had seen them all summer, decided to keep their find a secret. For unknown reasons they did not return and Ensley and Little Blanche profited from the gold they left.

LITTLE GEM CREEK 63°48′N 138°55′W (116-B&C).   A tributary to Hunker Creek.

In October 1898 Frank Criderman was so pleased with his initial find of gold that he applied this name. The Little Gem Mining Company was later formed and operated in several localities in the Yukon.

LITTLE JIMMY LAKE 60°54′N 129°43′W (105-A). About 20 miles northwest of Simpson Lake.

In 1949 LITTLE JIMMY, a local Indian, had erected a sign at his cabin here proclaiming his ownership. He had trapped from here to the east arm of Frances Lake for many years. Named by the trader at Lower Post, Jimmy was something of a prospector. In 1937 he brought samples of high grade silver-lead ore to Anton Money at McDame Creek in the Cassiar. The samples came from the east side of Frances Lake. Money made arrangements with a Vancouver, BC, firm to finance the search for the vein and others like it. The search was carried out over the next few years with some success. (The property has not yet made a mine but it has been investigated several times again in the past few years.) (See Money Creek.)

LITTLE RIDGE 4,482′ 61°03′N 135°54′W (105-E). On the east side of Thirty Seven Mile Creek.

H.S. Bostock, GSC, named this small hill after the old LITTLE River Roadhouse, on the old Dawson Trail five miles to the southeast.

LITTLE SALMON RIVER 62°03′N 135°40′W (105-L). A tributary of the Yukon above Carmacks.

Miners in 1882 translated the Indian name for the stream and used it. In 1883 Schwatka ignored both the Indians and miners and named it after the Hon. Charles P. Daly, President of the American Geographical Society. Dr. G.M. Dawson, GSC, disallowed the name and it was forgotten.

LITTLE VIOLET CREEK   61°25′N   134°23′W   (105–E). A tributary to the South Big Salmon River.

The prospector who first found gold here about 1903 was a widower who had his small daughter with him. A mining company was later formed using the same name.

LIVINGSTONE   61°20′N   134°21′W   (105–E).

A small settlement near the mouth of Livingstone Creek came into being in the summer of 1898 to serve the miners in the newly found goldfields of the area. It was connected to Lake Laberge by a 40-mile-long winter trail and a little later by a 16-mile wagon road to Mason's Landing on the Teslin River. The settlement flourished for many years. It contained a dance hall and a red light section in addition to roadhouses and stores. It decayed with the goldfields as they were worked out and died in the 1930′s.

LIVINGSTONE CREEK   61°22′N   134°23′W   (105–E). A tributary of the South Big Salmon River.

Joseph E. Peters prospected this area before the gold rush and, it is claimed, sank a prospect shaft on this creek in 1894. In any event he and George Black (later to be the Member of Parliament and Commissioner of the Yukon Territory), were partners when they discovered the rich, coarse gold of this stream. They named it after Black's friend and fellow lawyer, M.D. LIVINGSTONE of Whitehorse and Dawson. He may have contributed to their grubstake. In the four weeks preceding freeze-up the two took out $3,600 in gold.

Peters worked in this area until the First World War. It is claimed that over a million dollars in gold was taken from the creek by 1920. Placer mining is still carried on sporadically in the area.

MOUNT LOGAN   19,850′   60°34′N   140°24′W   (115–B&C). In the St. Elias Range.

This is the highest mountain in Canada and the second highest in North America. It was named by Professor Israel Cook Russell, USGS, in 1890. He first saw it when he was on a National Geographic Society Expedition in southeast Alaska and southwest Yukon, in the foothills of the St. Elias Range.

He named it in honour of Sir William E. LOGAN, founder and for many years director of the Geological Survey of Canada.

Sir William Edmond Logan, KB, LLD, FGS, FRS, was born in Montréal, Québec, on 20 April, 1798. Taken to Scotland at 14 by his father, he attended Edinburgh High School. His work in geology in Wales (a spare time project) was so good that it was accepted *in toto* by the Geological Survey of Great Britain. When the Canadian government decided to set up such a department in Canada Logan was so highly recommended that he was chosen over others more academically qualified. He served 27 years and, mostly by his own work in the field, laid the basis of eastern Canadian geology. He received most of the scientific honours of his day. He died in Llechryd, Wales, in 1875. His monument, erected in Ottawa reads:

The Father of Canadian Geology
Founder and First Director of the Geological
Survey of Canada. 1841-1869.

His name is on several other features in Canada.

This mountain was first climbed on 23 June, 1925, by a joint Canadian-American Expedition, led by H.F. Lambart, Canadian, and A.H. McCarthy, American. (See Mount Hunt.)

LOGAN MOUNTAINS 61°30′N 120°00′W (105-H). The mountain range on the east side of Frances Lake.

In 1887 Dr. G.M. Dawson, GSC, gave this range the local name "Too-Tsho", which is their name for Frances Lake, meaning "Big Lake". This was changed in 1929 to the Logan Mountains. (See Mount Logan.)

LOKKEN CREEK 61°50′N 134°38′W (105-E). Flows into Walsh Creek.

This was named in 1936 after H.O. LOKKEN, a long-time pioneer from gold rush days. He was for many years the head linesman on the Yukon Telegraph. He was always an active prospector, especially in this area.

The mountain at the headwaters of the creek was given the name first by W.H. Miller, GSC, while he was mapping the area, and the creek was named later.

LOMBARD GULCH 63°52′N 138°53′W (115-O&N). The last small stream entering the headwaters of Dominion Creek from the north.

L.H. LOMBARD found the first gold and staked the Discovery claim here on 13 July, 1897. It was never very productive.

LONELY DOME 63°35'N 134°28'W (105-M). Ten miles east of the south end of Mayo Lake.

H.S. Bostock, GSC, named this isolated hill while mapping the area in 1940.

LONER MOUNTAIN 63°32'N 131°58'W (105-O). Between the Rogue and Hess Rivers on the west end of the Rogue Range.

This was named in 1973 by Dr. Aro Aho of the Dynasty Exploration Company, while he was working in the area.

LONG'S CREEK 61°54'N 140°14'W (115-G&F). Flows into the Koidern River.

This brook was given its name in 1953 to perpetuate the name of Pilot Officer R.W. LONG, RCAF, who was killed in action in the Second World War.

LOOTZ LAKE 60°11'N 126°53'W (95-D). Lootz Lake and Creek flow into the Rock River.

Clem LOOTZ, a trapper, lived on the north shore of the lake for a number of years and both the lake and the creek were officially given his name in 1949. His family still resides at Lower Post, BC.

LORD CREEK 67°33'N 139°09'W (116-O&N). A tributary to the Porcupine River near Old Crow.

David LORD, a French-Canadian, was a grand old man in his 80's when he died in Dawson in 1954. A Klondiker, he had lived and trapped with his family in this region for many years. He had lived at New Rampart House and Old Crow since 1900. He was respected and well-liked by all who knew him.

MOUNT LORNE 60°28'N 134°42'W (105-D). On the west side of Marsh Lake.

In 1887 William Ogilvie, DLS, named this landmark after the Right Honourable Sir John Douglas Sutherland Campbell, Marquis of LORNE, who had been Governor-General of Canada from 1878-1883.

The section stop on the WP&YR was named from its proximity to the mountain in 1899.

LOST HORSES CREEK 63°56'N 137°08'W (115-P). A tributary to the Little South Klondike River.

In 1947 H.S. Bostock's GSC party lost half their pack horses here. The search time for the animals upset their schedule.

LOUISE LAKE   60°32'N 137°27'W (115-A). The westernmost of the Kathleen Lakes.

In 1938 George Chambers named this beautiful lake after LOUISE Davis, (Mrs. Alex Dickson) who lived alone in this area for some years. The lake tends to be calm and serene and reminded Chambers of Mrs. Davis' disposition. In 1959 she was living in Champagne and had 12 living children, 45 grandchildren and 17 great grandchildren.

LOVETT GULCH   64°01'N 139°22'W (116-B&C). The first small tributary from the east on Bonanza Creek, a mile above the mouth.

B.F. LOVETT was very active in the Klondike and had many mining interests. He probably staked this gulch in late 1896. He accumulated much ground on the hill between this short stream and the Klondike River. It was known as Lovett Hill and proved very rich, with wide stretches of the White Channel gravels. (See Mint Gulch.)

LOWELL GLACIER   60°17'N 138°30'W (115-B&C). Just north of Mount Kennedy.

Bradford Washburn named this feature in 1908 for a former and famous president of Harvard University, Abbott Lawrence LOWELL.

MOUNT LUCANIA   17,150' 61°01'N 140°28'W (115-G&F). In the Icefield Ranges of the St. Elias Mountains.

On 31 July, 1897, the Duke of Abruzzi saw this huge mountain and named it after the Cunard liner in which he and his party had crossed the Atlantic Ocean. It was first climbed on 9 July, 1937, by Bradford Washburn and Robert H. Bates.

LUCKY LAKE   60°02'N 128°35'W (105-A). A small lake at mile 626 (K1014) of the Alaska Highway, just south of Watson Lake.

This pond was named by American Army Engineer troops in 1942 during the construction of the highway and is still so called. At that time a young woman set up a tent business and clients there referred to transactions as "a change of luck". The lake is shallow and protected and warms quickly in the summer. It is one of the few lakes in the area where swimming is possible and comfortable.

LUCKY LAKE 61°30'N 127°22'W (95-E). A narrow lake almost on the Yukon-NWT border, on the headwaters of the Coal River.

On 20 August, 1968, Dr. E.J. Roots GSC, was in a small float plane when the engine failed. Their glide barely reached this lake where they made a safe landing.

LUSK LAKE 66°21'N 135°15'W (106-L). At the headwaters of the Caribou River.

Isaac LUSK was a freighter who carried the mail between Dawson and Minto Bridge for many years. He was also a Yukon Councillor for South Dawson from 1912-15. This lake was given his name in 1973.

LYNX CREEK 63°59'N 135°52'W (105-M). Flows into Haggart Creek.

Originally named "Lick Creek" after a salt lick nearby, the name was corrupted to "Link" and finally to Lynx. H.S. Bostock, GSC, was told of this by old miners in the area.

MOUNT MACAULAY 61°13'N 135°15'W (115-F). Just south of Mount Wood in the Icefield Ranges of the St. Elias Range.

In 1958 this mountain was named after Judge Charles Daniel MACAULAY who served for many years with distinction on the Territorial Bench.

MacAULEY CREEK 60°03'N 135°15'W (105-D). Flows into the west end of the west arm of Lake Bennett.

A good gold prospect was found here in the spring of 1900 by Dr. L.S. Sugden and "Red" Rogers. They were grubstaked by Norman MacAULEY and Thomas O'Brien. MacAuley was the builder and owner of the Miles Canyon Tramway and the proprietor of the Whitehorse Hotel as well as many mining interests.

The mountain at the headwaters of the creek, on the Yukon-BC border, was given his name at a later date.

MOUNT MacDONALD 6,750' 63°09'N 135°50'W (105-M). In the McArthur Group of mountains.

James MacDonald, a pioneer prospector, spent his later years (he was in his 70's and 80's) searching for a lost copper mine in this area. The mountain received his name in 1972.

MOUNT MacDONALD 64°43'N 132°47'W (106-C). On the head-waters of Corn Creek, west of the Snake River.

This was named officially in 1973 after a well-known prospector, Allan John "Hardrock" MacDONALD, who explored much of the northern territory from 1920 to 1960.

"Hardrock John" was noted as a musher, and once travelled alone in the dead of winter from Mayo to Aklavik in 17 days, a journey seldom equalled. In 1961, while he was still alive, there were requests to give his name to a tributary of the Boswell River where he had prospected. (See McDonald Creek.)

MACK'S FORK 63°49'N 139°03'W (115-O&N). A small tributary of Quartz Creek from the east, above Little Blanche Creek.

On 20 August, 1897, A. MACK staked a normal-sized claim on Quartz Creek at the mouth of this stream. The stream received his name but for some reason his claim was known afterward as Mack's Discovery. It was not, for he gave Stewart's discovery higher up Quartz Creek as a reference point when recording his own claim. (See Quartz Creek.)

MacKINNON CREEK 62°05'N 139°50'W (115-J). A tributary to the Donjek River south of Wellesley Lake.

Andrew MacKINNON was a prospector who lived here while he mined and trapped in the area. The name was locally used for many years and was made official in 1953.

MACKINTOSH CREEK 61°57'N 137°17'W (115-H). Flows into the Nisling River.

In 1965 G.W. Rowley requested this name after George Whitfield Cameron MACKINTOSH. He joined the NWMP in 1900 and served until 1902 when he took his discharge in Whitehorse. He lived for many years at the Bear Creek trading post and died 29 November, 1939, a respected man.

MacMILLAN RIVER 62°50'N 135°56'W (105-L). A major tributary of the Pelly River.

Robert Campbell of the HBC, while on his first journey down the Pelly River in June 1843, named this stream after Chief Factor James McMILLAN, who had sponsored his employment with the HBC.

Correct spelling is McMillan; sometimes spelled Macmillan, M'Millan.

McARTHUR PEAK   14,253'   60°37'N 140°11'W (115-B&C). About seven miles northeast of Mount Logan.

This was named in 1918 after James Joseph McARTHUR DLS, (1856–1925). He was in charge of survey parties of the International Boundary Commission from 1901-24 and in 1917 was appointed a commissioner and served until 1924.

McArthur was one of the surveyors sent to the Yukon by the Department of the Interior in May 1897 to survey the routes to the Klondike. He travelled the Dalton Trail from Pyramid Harbor to the Yukon River and with a minimum of instrument work produced a very rough map. He approved the route as being suitable for either a wagon road or a railroad. It is probable that a railway would have been built on this easier route if the WP&YR had not been begun first.

He did further work in the Yukon of a much better quality. Some years after his death a small range of mountains, in the south Mayo area where he had also worked, was named the McArthur Group.

McCABE CREEK   62°32'N 136°46'W (115-I). Five miles south of Minto.

After the business establishments and other services in Fort Selkirk had closed their doors, the post office closed in December 1952. The few remaining people moved up the river to where the old Whitehorse-Dawson winter stage road leaves the river near Minto. Here, near the mouth of McCabe Creek, they settled and another post office was opened on 5 December, 1953, by Mrs. Alec Cowaret under the name McCabe Creek. In October 1970 this too was closed as the last remaining people had left.

McCABE had been a trader here in the 1920's and 30's and was noted for his highly successful potato crops.

McCANN HILL   64°55'N 141°00'W (116-B&C). A boundary peak, south of the Tatonduc River.

Named by D.D. Cairnes, GSC, after his assistant, W.S. McCANN while they were mapping the geology of the boundary country in 1912.

MOUNT McCLEERY   60°19'N 132°02'W (105-C). At the south end of Englishman's Range.

F.S. Bailey, Forest Warden at Teslin, requested this name in 1954 after Robert McCLEERY, his late admired friend. McLeery came in with the

Klondike rush, was a veteran of the First World War and, in 1926, built a trading post at Teslin which he operated until 1951. He was also a Justice of the Peace and postmaster at the same time. A creek, tributary to Fat Creek across Teslin Lake, carried his name for a few years in the 1920's but was changed to Grouse Creek. This is a better monument to a fine man.

M'CLINTOCK LAKES 60°55'N 134°31'W (105-D). A series of small lakes on the headwaters of M'Clintock River.

These were named by Arthur St. Cyr, DLS, in November 1897 while he was surveying a route to the Klondike from Telegraph Creek in BC to the south end of Teslin Lake. He had finished his survey and had decided to cross overland from Teslin to Marsh Lake and determine if a trail this way would be feasible. (See M'Clintock River.)

M'CLINTOCK RIVER 60°33'N 134°29'W (105-D). This stream flows into the northeast end of Marsh Lake.

Lt. F. Schwatka, US Army, named this river in 1883 after one of the most famous of the early Arctic explorers, Admiral Sir Francis Leopold M'CLINTOCK, RN, (1819-1907). It is one of Schwatka's names that Dr. G.M. Dawson, GSC, allowed to stand.

McCONNELL LAKE 60°27'N 134°55'W (105-D). About 25 miles north of Carcross.

This was the last feature to be named after this famous explorer and geologist. In 1956 the Geographical Board gave this lake his name as he had based some of his surveys from here. (See McConnell Peak.)

McCONNELL PEAK 6,182' 61°18'N 132°21'W (105-F). At the mouth of the McConnell River.

This was named about 1945 after one of Canada's foremost geological explorers, Richard George McCONNELL (1857–1942). Born in Chatham, Québec, he graduated with a B.A. from McGill University. He joined the Geological Survey of Canada in 1880. He made an exploratory circuit of the Yukon Territory in 1887–88 which, while more difficult, was over-shadowed by that of Dawson at the same time. He spent ten years mapping the geology of the Yukon, especially making the first authorita-tive study (1901) of the Klondike goldfields and the Whitehorse copper belt. His great work was the solution of the foundation of the Rocky Mountain system. He was the author of many geological reports and maps, many still in use. In 1914 he became Deputy Minister of Mines in the federal government and filled the post with distinction throughout the war years and until 1920. He died in Ottawa on 1 April, 1942.

McCONNELL RIVER   61°16'N   132°30'W   (105–F). A tributary of the Nisutlin River.

This was the first feature to be named after R.G. McCONNELL, GSC, and was probably designated by Morley Ogilvie, son of William Ogilvie and at the time assistant to Arthur St. Cyr, while they were surveying the east side of Teslin Lake in 1897.

MOUNT McCOUBREY   10,250'   61°13'N   140°04'W   (115–G&F). To the east of the Steele Glacier.

This was named in 1970 after Alexander Addison McCOUBREY (1885–1942), surveyor and past president of the Alpine Club of Canada (1932–1934).

MOUNT McCULLUM   5,559'   65°28'N   137°34'W   (116–H). West of the Blackstone River.

In 1973 this peak was named after the Rev. Creighton McCULLUM, Anglican Minister at Mayo and Dawson in the 1920 and 30's. He served as a private soldier in the First World War and as a chaplain in the Second World War.

MOUNT McDADE   4,918'   62°07'N   136°58'W   (115–I). About 23 miles west of Carmacks.

This was first called McDade Hill in 1931 when George McDADE discovered rich silver-lead ore and precipitated a staking rush which uncovered many more potential ore bodies. He and Afe Brown made the first finds on Victoria Creek. The hill was officially named Mount McDade in 1958.

McDONALD CREEK   61°02'N   133°47'W   (105–F). A tributary to the Boswell River.

This creek has been known locally by this name for a number of years. On it was the home of Allan John "Hardrock" MacDONALD, an old-time prospector in this area who was noted for his stamina and hardihood.

In 1961 G.W. Rowley, Forest Warden, suggested the name be made official. As "Hardrock" was still alive the request was denied. (See Mount MacDonald.)

McDOUGALL PASS 67°43′N 136°27′W (116-P). Through the Continental Divide between the Bell and Rat Rivers.

In May 1888 William Ogilvie, DLS, named this pass after Junior Chief Trader James McDOUGALL of the HBC. Travelling out of Fort Mac-Pherson in 1872, McDougall was the first white man to discover and map the pass, although his clerk Thomas Scott was the first white man to actually cross it. It was used by a number of Klondike stampeders in 1897–98 on their way from Edmonton to Dawson.

McEVOY LAKE 61°48′N 130°14′W (105-G). Northwest of Frances Lake.

Dr. G.M. Dawson, GSC, while on his survey up Frances Lake and on to the Pelly, explored the area at the head of the lake and named this lake after his assistant, James McEVOY, BS, ME.

MOUNT McGUIRE 5,116′ 67°56′N 137°22′W (116-P). West of the Bell River.

Mr. Justice T.H. McGUIRE, the first Judge of the Court of the Provisional District of the Yukon in 1897 and for a number of years after, was commemorated by this designation in 1973.

McINNES HILL 64°07′N 139°24′W (115-B&C). The hill between Examiner Gulch and Klondike City (South Dawson).

William Oscar Smith, on 16 September, 1906, found gold enough to stake a Discovery hill claim here. He named the hill after the then Commissioner of the Yukon Territory, William Wallace Burns McINNES, who was born in Dresden, Ontario, on 10 April, 1871, the son of the Hon. T.B. McInnes, Lt. Governor of British Columbia. Graduating in law, he was appointed Commissioner of the Yukon on 27 May, 1905, and served till 31 December, 1906. He instituted an unpopular regime of government economies, cutting down the number of both civil servants and the RNWMP in the territory. His short term was noted for controversy.

He served eight years as a County Court Judge in Vancouver, BC; he unsuccessfully tried for political office but died in obscurity.

McINTYRE CREEK 60°46′N 135°05′W (105-D). A tributary to the Yukon River, northwest of Whitehorse.

On 6 July, 1898, John McINTYRE of San Bernardino, California, found the first of the high grade copper ore bodies of the Whitehorse Copper Belt on this creek, which received his name at that time. His first claim was named the "Copper King". The first shipment of ore from the claim was made in 1900 and contained nine tons of bornite grading 46.40% copper.

In the winter of 1902–03 McIntyre was in Atlin, BC and had contracted to carry the mail from there to Log Cabin on the WP&YR. He and Joseph Abbey left Atlin with the mail carried by dog sled, on 25 November, 1902. They never arrived at Log Cabin. A long search was made and the dogs, sled and mail were found beneath the ice of Windy Arm by George Coutts and John Fountain. Abbey's body was found in the lake on the 28 April and that of McIntyre was recovered on 14 May, 1903.

McINTYRE MOUNTAIN 5,200' 60°37′N 135°08′W (105–D). Seven miles southwest of Whitehorse.

Shortly after his death in 1902, this mountain was named after John McINTYRE. (See McIntyre Creek.)

MOUNT McINTYRE 64°21′N 138°41′W (116–B). 27 miles northeast of Dawson and south of Tombstone Mountain.

This was after Angus McINTYRE who came to the Yukon in 1898 and remained until 1942. He was "Foreman of the Ditch" during the construction of the immense 70-mile-long flume and ditch built to bring large quantities of water to the hydraulic workings in the Klondike before the First World War. He died in Kelowna, BC, in 1950 at the age of 90.

McKAY HILL 64°21′N 135°25′W (106–D). In the eastern Ogilvie Mountains.

This was named after Thomas McKAY who prospected in this area in the 1920's. He was a Yukon Councillor for the Mayo District about 1929–30.

McKINNON CREEK 63°44′N 139°05′W (115–O&N). Flows into the Indian River from the south.

Donald and Archibald McKINNON were brothers who found and tried for many years to develop a huge gold deposit they had found in widespread conglomerate rocks here in 1910–15. They had earlier, in 1898–1900, worked a placer gold claim on the same creek.

McKINNON LAKE 60°02′N 129°19′W (105–A). On Albert Creek, 25 miles west of Watson Lake.

Dan McKINNON trapped and prospected for many years in a wide area around here. He died near Toobally Lakes.

McLAGAN CREEK   63°41'N 136°12'W (115-P). Tributary to Minto Lake.

Miners on this creek in 1902 named it after Jack McLAGAN who was Mining Recorder for the Mayo district at that time.

McLEAN   CREEK   64°25'N 135°19'W (106-D).   A   tributary   of Carpenter Creek.

John McLEAN was one of a group who first prospected and found silver-lead ore on Silver Hill, part of Settlemier Ridge, in late 1923.

McLEOD   CREEK   63°55'N 135°20'W (105-M).   A   tributary   to Lightning Creek, off Galena Hill in the Mayo district.

About 1915 A. McLEOD found a vein of silver-lead ore on the banks of this creek.

McMILLAN LAKE   60°31'N 127°55'W (95-D). A mile west of Hulse (Quartz) Lake.

This was named by James Harquail, president of Fort Reliance Minerals Ltd., after a trapper named McMILLAN of Lower Post, whose cabin still stands at the west end of the lake.

MOUNT McNEIL   60°08'N 135°27'W (105-D). Two miles northeast of Mount Skookum, north of the Wheaton River.

This was named in 1911 after Hector McNEIL, a prospector well-known in this district for many years.

McPARLAND CREEK   66°05'N 137°56'W (116-I). A tributary of the East Porcupine River.

This stream was chosen in 1973 to commemorate K-98595 Cpl. George Lynn McPARLON, MM, who was killed in action at the storming of Ortona, Italy, on 23 December, 1943. Lynn McParlon was born at Waldo, BC, on 29 June, 1912. He enlisted in and served with the Seaforth Highlanders of Canada at Vancouver, BC, on 18, July, 1940.

Through some error his name was written as McParland.

McPARLON CREEK   (See McParland Creek.)

McPHERSON LAKE   61°53'N 129°32'W (105-H). 20 miles north of Frances Lake.

In August 1840 Robert Campbell of the HBC, while exploring the Frances

173

Lake country and upper Pelly River region, named this lake after Murdoch McPHERSON, Chief Factor of the Mackenzie District at that time.

McQUESTEN RIVER   63°33′N 137°27′W (115–P). A major tributary of the Stewart River.

Leroy Napoleon "Jack" McQUESTEN, was born in 1836 at Litchfield, New Hampshire, USA. As a young man attracted to life in the wilds, he entered the employ of the HBC at Fort Garry in what is now Manitoba. For about two years he worked in the area between Minnesota and Hudson Bay. Although he was six feet tall and weighed 200 pounds he was disappointed that he could not handle the standard, 200-pound packs over the portages as easily as could the much smaller French-Canadian voyageurs.

Leaving, he went on to California in the early years of that gold rush and found prospecting for gold attractive. Working north, he was on the Fraser River in BC when gold was first found there in 1858. He worked at the Gamble Lumber Mill near what is now Vancouver for a short period. Always moving north, he next mined in the Cariboo country. In 1863 he left Quesnel, BC, for the Peace River basin and for the next ten years prospected and traded with the Indians in northeastern BC and into Hay River and Lake Athabaska.

In 1871, while wintering with Alfred Mayo at the mouth of the Nelson River, he met Arthur Harper and Frederick Hart. There they learned from the Hudson's Bay men of the American purchase of Alaska and decided to go there.

The parties split up in the spring of 1873 and McQuesten and Mayo went down the Mackenzie to the Peel, which they followed to its headwaters, and traversed McDougall Pass to the Rat River and the Porcupine to Fort Yukon. They arrived there on 15 August, 1873. Arthur Harper and Hart arrived shortly afterwards.

After spending the winter on the lower Yukon River and at St. Michaels, they came to a loose working arrangement with the ACC and purchased a trading outfit from that company. On 20 August, 1874 McQuesten, Mayo and Barnfield (Bernstein) landed at the site of Fort Reliance (six miles down river from Dawson) on the little steamboat *Arctic*. Here they built their first trading post.

McQuesten and Mayo spent the next eight years setting up and operating trading posts along the Yukon River for the ACC, but always prospecting when the opportunity arose. In the winter of 1882–83 11 miners wintered at Fort Reliance, the first to do so in the territory. The first miners' meeting to be held in the territory took place and McQuesten was elected the first Mining Recorder.

He alternated trading and prospecting and was up the Stewart River in 1885 shortly after the first rich bar gold was found. The miners there at the time gave his name to the first north branch of the river.

Although he was running his trading post at Circle City when the Klondike goldfields were found, he grubstaked others and purchased interests in claims on Eldorado and Bonanza and so participated in the new-found wealth.

He left the Yukon in late 1898 with over $200,000, and built a large home in Berkeley, California, for his wife and children. He invested widely in mining interests in California and the west without losing his fortune. When the Alaska-Yukon Pacific Exposition was held in Seattle, in 1909, he was appointed the official representing the Yukon. While in that city he underwent an operation for bunions, contracted blood poisoning and in a few days the "Father of the Yukon" was dead.

That title had been bestowed on him by the miners in the Yukon while he was still alive and in business in the territory. His name was a byword for integrity and honesty. His trust in his fellow man was unbounded and seldom wrong. Nowhere in the literature of the Yukon is it possible to find a critical or unkind word about him. It is rare anywhere to find a man as highly regarded during his own lifetime as was Jack McQuesten.

McQUESTEN   63°33′N 137°25′W (115–P).

Shortly after the discovery of gold on the Stewart River bars the miners chose this spot to winter over and a small settlement sprang up. It later became a roadhouse on the winter trail from Whitehorse to Dawson. It was abandoned in the 1950's.

McRAE CREEK   63°46′N 136°11′W (115–P). A small tributary to Highet Creek.

J.D. McRAE found placer gold and staked the Discovery claim on this little stream on 24 June, 1903, during the rush to the Mayo and Minto finds.

McTAVISH LAKE   60°00′N 128°24′W (105–A). A small lake crossing the Yukon-BC border, 17 miles southeast of Watson Lake.

It was officially named in 1943 to confirm a long-established local name after the trapper from Lower Post whose base camp was here for many years.

MAGNET HILL   63°57'N 139°21'W (115–O&N). The hill on the west side of Bonanza Creek, one mile below Adams Gulch.

This was one of the early high level diggings. Gold was discovered here in the White Channel gravels by J.E. McKenzie in early 1897. He named the hill because of its resemblance to a horseshoe magnet.

Magnet City, a small community of dwellings, stores, shops and a roadhouse was begun here in early 1897. Mrs. M.P Rothweiler started for the Klondike by herself in the spring of 1897 but was caught by weather and spent the winter of 1897–98 in the ice at the mouth of the Stewart River. Arriving in Dawson in the spring, she bought a dug-out called "Mary's Place" near No. 17 Below Discovery on Bonanza Creek, rebuilt it and called it the Magnet Hotel. Magnet City was the largest settlement between Dawson and Grand Forks.

The gulch below the hill was discovered and staked on 10 July, 1897, by Peter Erussard de Ville.

MAGUNDY RIVER   62°12'N 134°26'W (105–L). Flowing into the east end of Little Salmon Lake.

This area has been the trapping grounds of the MAGUNDY family for many years.

MAIDEN CREEK   64°23'N 140°38'W (116–B&C). A tributary to the Fortymile River.

Andrew Jackson MAIDEN was one of the hardy prospectors who followed the trail of gold up the west coast of North America from California to the Yukon. He crossed the Chilkoot Pass in 1884 and in 1886–87 found gold on this creek during the rush to the new, coarse gold finds on the Fortymile River.

Being middle-aged in a country where young men were the rule, he was nick-named "Old Maiden". He carried a stack of about 50 old newspapers with him on his travels, claiming that they not only improved his mind but were useful in settling arguments. His good character and open heartedness were remarked upon by his peers in a country where these qualities were taken for granted.

George Carmack claimed that Andrew Maiden had prospected in the Klondike in 1889 and that he had reported this to the YOOP in Fortymile.

He had found gold but not in what was then considered paying quantities. He returned here in 1896 and being too late to stake on Bonanza or Eldorado creeks, found good ground elsewhere. He mined here until 1906-07 when he went to Fairbanks. He died there, a respected pioneer, in 1913, at the age of 76.

MAISY MAY CREEK   63°14′N   138°48′W   (115–O&N). Flows into the Stewart River from the north.

In 1897 Samuel Henry took up a homestead at the mouth of this stream and started the MAISIE MAE ranch. He grew 26 tons of hay that year and successfully continued farming for a number of years afterward. He specialized in feed for the horses in Dawson and the mines. In 1906 he had over 100 acres under cultivation.

The name was first spelled Maisie Mae, then Maizy May.

MOUNT MALASPINA   60°19′N   140°34′W   (115–B&C). 11 miles east of Mount St. Elias.

A peak in this range was given this name in 1874 by W.H. Dall, USC&GS, after Captain Don Alessandro MALASPINA, Italian navigator and explorer who, while in the service of Spain, explored the northwest coast of North America in 1791.

Professor Israel C. Russell, who led an expedition to Mount St. Elias in 1890, wrote that it was impossible to decide to which peak Dall had applied the name of the great navigator, so they gave his name to a peak about 11 miles east of Mount St. Elias.

MALCOLM   RIVER   69°33′N   139°37′W   (117–D).   Flows   into   the Beaufort Sea about five miles west of Herschel Island.

John Franklin (later Sir) during his exploration of the Arctic coast in 1826, named this river after Admiral Sir Pulteney MALCOLM (1768-1838), on 23 July.

MOUNT MALONEY   6,375′   61°41′N   137°44′W   (115–H). 30 miles northwest of Aishihik Lake in the Nisling Range.

This was named in 1897 after J.F. MALONEY who was one of Jack Dalton's freighters between Pyramid Harbour and the Yukon River during the gold rush years.

MOUNT   MANITOBA   11,150′   60°58′N   140°48′W   (115–B&C).   In the Centennial Range of the St. Elias Mountains.

This was one of the 13 previously un-named and unclimbed peaks in this locality chosen to celebrate Canada's centennial year of 1967. (See Centennial Range.)

MARGARET LAKE   65°21′N 134°30′W (106–E). Near the junction of Knorr Creek and the Bonnet Plume River.

It is believed that the cabin on this lake was built by A.N. Knorr and his wife MARGARET about 1907. (See Knorr Creek.)

MARION CREEK   63°10′N 133°28′W (105–N). A tributary to Russell Creek.

In 1901 N.A.B. Armstrong named this stream after his wife. (He spelled her name Marian and sometimes, MARION). She spent 18 months here in 1905–06 with her husband and their friends George and Jessica Leith. Neither woman had ever spent any time outside England; they were completely isolated here for most of the time. (See Jessica Creek and Mount Armstrong.)

MARSH LAKE   60°25′N 134°18′W (105–D). Part of the Yukon River system, this 20-mile-long lake is about 25 miles southeast of Whitehorse.

Originally called "Mud Lake" by the first miners, this lake was renamed by Lt. F. Schwatka, US Army, in 1883 after Professor Othniel Charles MARSH (1831–1899), palaeontologist at Yale University from 1866 to 99. He was a founder and first president of the National Academy of Sciences for 12 years and was the Chief of Vertebrate Palaeontology for the USGS from 1881 to 99. A wealthy man, he served Yale with no salary and left his entire estate to the university after his death.

This is one of Schwatka's names that Dawson did not consider changing.

MARSHALL CREEK   60°48′N 137°20′W (115–A). A tributary to the Dezeadash River from the north.

Antoine and Mac Cyr were on their way to the newly found Ruby Creek goldfield in the Shakwak valley when they stopped to examine this stream. On 6 August they found enough gold to stake a Discovery claim. It is thought that they named the creek after one of their party.

MOUNT MARTHA BLACK   60°40′N 137°37′W (115–A). In the Auriol Range about seven miles south of Haines Junction.

This was named about 1945 by H.S. Bostock, GSC, for Martha Munger

BLACK, wife of George Black, MP and one-time Commissioner of the Yukon Territory. When her husband was forced to retire from politics for a period, due to ill health, Martha Black ran for Parliament and was elected. She was a pioneer Klondiker, who came to the Yukon in 1898, and was a leading personality there for the rest of her life. She was probably the most outstanding woman in the history of the Yukon.

MOUNT MARTIN 4,460′ 60°08′N 124°09′W (95–C). In the extreme southeast corner of the territory, just west of the Labiche River.

In 1963 this mountain was given the name of Major Ivan Harold MARTIN, MID. He was born at Sterling, Ontario on 2 August, 1912 and enlisted in the Canadian army at Chatham, Ontario on 7 December, 1949. He served in Canada, Great Britain and Northwest Europe and died of wounds sustained in action on 21 August, 1944.

MASCOT CREEK 62°47′N 138°25′W (115–J&K). A tributary to the Yukon River, six miles below the Selwyn River.

Gold was found on this stream in the late fall of 1900 by two French-Canadian prospectors, Archill Massicotte and Albert Leboeuf. When they came to Dawson on 16 February, 1901, and recorded their claims it was a Monday. The news got out and the whole creek was staked from end to end by Tuesday night. Massicotte's name was shortened by the recorder.

MASON HILL 67°19′N 137°40′W (116–P). West of Lapierre House.

This was named in 1973 after the brothers, Willoughby and Reuben MASON. (See Mason Lake.)

MASON LAKE 66°24′N 138°59′W (116–J&K). Near the junction of the Fishing and Miners Rivers.

This was named by Professor Otto W. Geist of the University of Alaska on 27 November, 1958, after the MASON brothers, Willoughby "Bill" and Reuben. The Masons trapped and prospected in this general area from 1900 to the 1930's.

Due to a vague location the name was given to the central of the three small lakes shown. The creek beside the lakes and a few hundred yards to the south is probably Mason Creek.

MASON LANDING 61°26′N 134°39′W (105–E). On the Teslin River about 20 miles south of Hootalinqua.

This now-abandoned settlement was a steamboat landing and stopping place for miners on their way to and from the Livingstone Creek goldfields from 1901 to 14. A wagon road led from here to Livingstone.

MOUNT MATHESON 7,515′ 60°02′N 134°43′W (105–D). One and one half miles south of Montana Mountain.

This peak is the highest point in the Conrad district. It was named by D.D. Cairnes, GSC, in 1907 after H. MATHESON, who was his assistant and topographer in the area in 1907–08.

MATSON CREEK 63°43′N 140°12′W (115–O&N). A tributary to the Sixtymile River.

John MATSON, a Swedish prospector, came into the Yukon in 1898. Discovering gold on this creek in the early years, he remained to mine it until he died and was buried on the claim in 1947.

Matson's one claim to fame was his marriage on 14 July, 1933, to "Klondike Kate" Rockwell, a dance-hall entertainer in Dawson in 1898 – 99 and self-styled "Queen of the Klondike".

The *Whitehorse Star* of 19 January, 1912, stated "The Gold Commissioner has changed the name of the South Fork of the Sixtymile River on which the discovery was made, to Matson Creek, after John Matson, who first prospected it and discovered gold on it fourteen years ago."

MAUNOIR BUTTE 61°31′N 135°04′W (105–E). A prominent hill on the east bank of the Yukon (Thirty Mile River), about ten miles below Lake Laberge.

This landmark was named in 1883 by Lt. F. Schwatka, US Army, after M. Charles MAUNOIR, secretary of the Geographical Society of France.

MAY CREEK 61°16′N 134°11′W (105–E). A tributary to the South Big Salmon River in the Livingstone area.

This is a long-known local name after Samuel MAY who prospected this area for many years after 1903.

MAYO 63°35′N 135°54′W (105–M).

This village at the mouth of the Mayo River was started in the winter of 1902–03 after gold was discovered on Duncan, Minto and Hyatt Creeks. As steamboats could navigate the Stewart from the Yukon, this was a close supply point for the miners. It grew fast enough to have the townsite surveyed in March 1903. The Keno Hill silver mines increased the traffic by their large ore shipments and the town was an important centre for many years. A road was opened in 1949 to connect the town with the Dawson road. In a few years the riverboats stopped and the population dwindled to its present small size.

It was also called Mayo Landing.

MAYO LAKE 63°43'N 135°04'W (105-M). The largest lake in the Mayo District.

Alexander MacDonald of New Brunswick was the first man to prospect the Mayo region. In 1887 he found this lake and named it after Captain Alfred S. MAYO, a partner of Harper and McQuesten. Together with Frederick Hart, these men were the first to realize the prospecting potential of the upper Yukon. The first three utilized trading as a means to support themselves while prospecting and, because the region was rich in fur, they prospered. They built every trading post from Rampart (Alaska) to Fort Selkirk. McQuesten and Harper were the traders; Mayo captained the small steamboat *New Racket* which they had bought from Ed Scheiffelin in 1883.

Mayo was born in Maine and in his younger days had been a circus acrobat. He often astounded the natives with displays of his agility. Marrying a native woman, he alone of all the partners spent the rest of his life in the country, dying at Rampart on 17 July, 1924.

MacDonald, the first explorer of this country, left his name nowhere. A solitary traveller, he was the first man to ascend the Beaver (McQuesten) River and enter the watersheds of the Wind and Peel Rivers from the south. He was found dead of natural causes in his lone camp on the banks of the Yukon in 1894.

MAYO RIVER 63°36'N 135°57'W (105-M). A tributary of the Stewart River.

This was named by William Ogilvie, DLS, after talking to Alex MacDonald in 1887. He also knew Alfred MAYO well as he was in charge of the trading post at the mouth of the Stewart at the time.

MEANDER CREEK (See Miller Creek.)

MEISTER RIVER 60°19'N 129°28'W (105-A). A tributary to the upper Liard River from the west.

This stream was known in the 1880's and later as the "Rondeau" River. After 1898 the name was forgotten and in 1947 it was renamed. The name of Pte. L. MEISTER, MM, was perpetuated here. He was from Nova Scotia and was killed in action during the Second World War.

MELOY CREEK 62°42′N 138°48′W (115-J&K). Flows into Casino Creek in the Dawson Range.

In 1970, C.D.N. "Red" Taylor, P. Eng. named this creek after Jack MELOY, a Yukon prospector for nearly 50 years and discoverer, among other things, of the porphyry-copper deposits in the Dawson Range. He was born in 1894 in the state of Washington and lived in Dawson most of his life.

MENDENHALL RIVER 60°45′N 136°03′W (115-A). A tributary to the Takhini River.

This stream was probably named in 1890 by E.J. Glave, the English explorer and member of the Frank Leslie Illustrated Newspaper Expedition. The name honours Professor Thomas Corwin MENDENHALL, (1841–1924) Superintendent of the USC&GS.

MERRICE CREEK 62°23′N 136°35′W (115-I). A tributary to the Yukon River below Yukon Crossing.

This creek was named in 1898 after Homer MERRICE, who first discovered gold on the stream. In 1908 the name was changed, by mistake, to "Merritt Creek" which it remained for a number of years until corrected by the Geographical Board.

MERRITT CREEK   (See Merrice Creek.)

MICHELLE CREEK 64°59′N 137°09′W (116-A). A tributary of the Hart River.

This was named on 29 June, 1956, by Forest Warden C.J. Shattuck, after a half-breed Indian who had trapped and prospected on this creek about 1910. Not much is known about him.

MOUNT MICHIE 5,830′ 60°30′N 134°06′W (105-D). About eight miles east of Marsh Lake.

Lt. F. Schwatka, US Army, named this hill in 1883 during his excursion down the Yukon, after one of his teachers, Professor MICHIE of West Point.

Michie Creek, named many years later, flows from the mountain to the M'Clintock River.

MICKEY CREEK 64°24'N 140°37'W (116-B&C). Flows into the Fortymile River, just above its mouth.

This was named in late 1886 by or after "MICKEY" O'Brien who was said to be one of the first discoverers of gold on the upper Fortymile River that year, supposedly on Franklin Bar. He is credited by others with finding O'Brien Creek on the Alaska side, the first find of coarse gold in that region.

MIDNIGHT DOME 64°04'N 139°24'W (116-B). The mountain behind Dawson.

From the earliest days this was called "Moosehide Hill" or Dome and sometimes "Mooseskin Mountain," from the peculiar shape and colour of a rock slide on the slope facing the Yukon River. About 1900 the custom began of picnicking on the summit on the evening and night of 21 June to observe the sun barely setting before it arose again. The event became a yearly custom and people began to call the hill "The Midnight Dome".

MILES CANYON 60°40'N 135°02'W (105-D). On the Yukon River two miles south of Whitehorse.

First called the "Grand Canyon" by the early miners, this constriction was renamed by Lt. F. Schwatka, US Army, after his superior officer, Brigadier General Nelson A. MILES, Commander of the Department of the Columbia (which included Alaska) of the US Army, on 1 July, 1883.

Although Miles Canyon was most awesome in appearance, and was approached with apprehension by miners and stampeders, it was the Whitehorse Rapids immediately below which were the more dangerous. Such records as there are show only a dozen deaths by drowning up to 1896 and about the same in the following three years. Most of these were in the rapids.

John McKenzie in 1883 is the first man known to have run a boat through Miles Canyon and the Whitehorse Rapids. The narrowness of the channel and the velocity of the current together with the whirlpool halfway through the canyon gave a real spice of danger which made this the highlight of the whole journey to the stampeders.

The canyon and rapids were the one major obstruction to navigation on the whole Yukon River, from the head of Lake Bennett to the Bering Sea. Without them, the largest steamboats could have run freely from Carcross to St. Michaels. The WP&YR would have ended at Carcross, making it the main freight terminal of the region and obviously making the city of Whitehorse unnecessary.

Several small to medium riverboats ran the canyon and rapids both ways; in July 1907 Fred R. Alley took a raft 132 feet long through safely.

Since the building of the power dam below, the rapids have disappeared and Miles Canyon can be navigated in safety by the smallest craft.

MILES CREEK   61°57′N 140°33′W   (115-G&F). A tributary of the White River.

Frank R. MILES came into the Yukon in 1898. In 1900 he found native copper on this stream and gave it his name. He died in Kalispell, Montana, in 1912. The ridge along the north side of the creek was given this name many years later.

MOUNT MILLEN   67°28′N 136°25′W   (116-P). Northeast of Lapierre House.

Constable Edgar "Spike" MILLEN RCMP, was born in Belfast, Ireland in 1901 and joined the force in 1920, volunteering for northern service. He was stationed at Aklavik and in the Mackenzie valley, where he was well liked.

He was killed in a gun battle with Albert Johnson, the "Mad Trapper of Rat River" on 30 January, 1932, during the greatest man-hunt in the history of the northwest. This mountain was named for him in 1973.

MILLER CREEK   61°22′N 134°40′W   (105-E). A tributary to the Teslin River below Mason's Landing.

Henry "Hank" Summers came from California to the Yukon country in 1885, one of the first miners here. He mined on the Stewart, the Fortymile and the Sixtymile, and made a fortune in the Klondike.

In 1913 he found gold on this creek and when he recorded his claim he named the stream, "Meander Creek". The Mining Recorder, who was Assistant Gold Commissioner R.C. MILLER, changed it to his own name.

Summers died in Whitehorse on 6 December that year.

MILLER CREEK   63°57′N 135°21′W   (105-M). Flows from Galena Hill to Cristal Creek.

In 1924–25 Oscar MILLER found silver-lead ore at the head of this stream, on Galena Hill and staked the Dragon claim.

MILLER CREEK 63°59′N 140°48′W (115–N). Tributary to the Sixty-mile River.

Oliver C. "Three Fingered Jack" MILLER came into the Yukon in 1883 among the very first prospectors. He travelled far and wide and was the first, or among the first, in three of the most important goldfields to be found here. In late 1891 he found the first payable gold on this creek, which has, together with nearby creeks, produced for many years. He was also among the first to find the Birch Creek goldfields (in Alaska) in 1893, which established Circle City. In the Minook District another creek was given his name and he was elected the first Mining Recorder there. Like many since, he seemed more interested in looking for than in mining the gold he found. He was noted for his long and arduous journeys in the Yukon and Alaska.

MOUNT MILLER 4,047′ 62°11′N 136°25′W (115–I). Ten miles above Carmacks.

This was named in 1911 for the pioneer coal miner and prospector, Captain Charles E. MILLER, who first developed and mined the coal deposits near Carmacks. Miller, who was a coal miner from Mauchunk, Pennsylvania, came to the Klondike in 1897. Although G.W. Carmack of Bonanza fame had first found coal here about 1893, Miller was the first to locate on the deposits and mine them. (Carmack, with Arthur Harper as a silent partner, had made limited attempts to mine coal at Five Finger Rapids about 1893–95 but without success.)

Between 1897 and 1900 Miller built and operated the riverboats *Clara*, *Reindeer*, and *Eldorado* as well as building and running the Yukon Saw-mill at Dawson City.

He located and mined the Five Fingers Mine in 1900 and the Tantalus Mine in 1903 and in two years produced 40,000 tons of coal for the river-boats. In 1905 he located the Tantulus Butte Coal Mine and estimated 5,000,000 tons of coal reserves. This is the mine which is now being worked for the Anvil Mining Corporation at Faro.

MILLER'S RIDGE 5,021′ 62°06′N 136°30′W (115–I). About 15 miles west of Carmacks.

In 1960 H.S. Bostock, GSC, and Col. Cyril H. Smith, RCE, named this ridge after the late W.H. MILLER, a former Director of the Surveys and Mapping Branch of the Department of Mines and Technical Surveys.

Miller organized and started the topographical mapping of Canada by Canadians, a task formerly performed by the US Army Engineers. It was

185

on this ridge that he laid out his baseline for the mapping of the Carmacks and Laberge areas.

MILLHAVEN BAY   60°06'N 134°55'W (105-D). The bay on the north shore of Lake Bennett, ten miles west of Carcross.

Here, in the winter and spring of 1897–98, Otto H. Partridge, general manager of the Bennett Lake and Klondyke Navigation Company, erected a sawmill and shipyard on the west side of the bay. They built the riverboats *Ora*, *Flora* and *Nora*. These were all taken through Miles Canyon and the Whitehorse Rapids and worked the Whitehorse-Dawson run until 1903. The mill continued to turn out timbers and railroad ties for the WP&YR as well as lumber to build Whitehorse.

MILLS CREEK   63°26'N 138°49'W (115-O&N). A tributary to Blackhills Creek from the west, seven miles from the mouth.

Joseph Victor MILLS found placer gold here and staked the Discovery claim on 26 January, 1907.

MOUNT MILTON   62°12'N 136°15'W (115-I). Five miles north of Tantalus Butte.

This small hill was named in 1968, probably by H.S. Bostock, GSC, after George H. MILTON, who organized and was general manager of the Five Fingers Coal Company, which owned all the coal deposits known in the district.

MINERS RANGE   61°09'N 135°41'W (105-E). The range of hills ten miles west of and parallel to, Lake Laberge.

Dr. G.M. Dawson, GSC, on his 1887 journey back to the coast, named these hills after the miners in the Yukon whom he admired and who aided him in his work.

MINT GULCH   63°56'N 138°53'W (115-O). A short, half-mile-long stream flowing into the south side of Hunker Creek.

Gold was discovered here, Discovery claim staked and the stream named on 7 August, 1897, by B.F. Lovett.

This gulch is remarkable because of the enormous number of fossil bison and mastodon bones found in the gravels of its bed. The numbers were so great as to suggest that whole herds of these animals had perished here in some prehistoric disaster.

MINTO   62°35′N 136°52′W (115-I). On the east bank of the Yukon River, 15 miles southwest of Pelly Crossing.

Originally an Indian settlement called "Kitl-ah-gon", meaning "The Place Between The High Hills", this village, now almost totally destroyed, was a riverboat stop and a roadhouse on the Whitehorse-Dawson stage road for many years.

Lord MINTO, when Governor General of Canada, visited the Yukon with Lady Minto in 1900 and it was in his honour that the settlement was given its name.

MINTO CREEK   63°43′N 135°55′W (105-M). Empties Minto Lake into Mayo River.

Many discoveries of gold were made in this general area after the finding of rich gold on Duncan Creek. J.G. Scrivener and P.F. Haggart were two of the most active prospectors of the time. This was one of the gold-bearing streams they found, staking the Discovery claim on 19 May, 1903. They named the creek after Lord MINTO, Governor General of Canada, who had visited Dawson in 1900. (See Haggart, Highet and Paradise Creeks.)

MINTON CREEK   63°47′N 136°21′W (115-P). Tributary to Johnson Creek.

This was named in 1957 by H.S. Bostock, GSC, after Peter MINTON who relocated No. 9 Below on 21 May, 1916, and remained here working the claim for many years. The original discovery of gold had been made by Mike Sed in February 1915.

MIRROR CREEK   62°28′N 140°54′W (115-J&K). Flows into the Snag River near mile 1206 on the Alaska Highway.

This creek got its name in 1898 from W.J. Peters and A.H. Brooks of the USGS because of its exceptionally clear water, which is unusual for the region.

MIST LAKE   63°12′N 134°21′W (105-M). Southwest of Big Kalzas Lake.

In 1939, H.S. Bostock, GSC, and his party were on pack horses crossing the country to this location. The topographer had missed this lake when he was mapping and the geological crew had to make a long trip around the lake in a snow storm to get to their camp site. When they suggested the name "Missed Lake", the topographer did not appreciate the irony and compromised on the present name.

MOUNT MOFFAT 61°12′N 140°02′W (115–F). In the Icefield Ranges of the St. Elias Mountains.

This undistinguished peak was named in 1970 by the Alpine Club of Canada after Thomas Black MOFFAT (1870–1939), an engraver and past president (1928–30) of the group (which seems to have named everything in the St. Elias Range that any member has ever seen).

MONEY CREEK 61°24′N 129°36′W (105–H). Flowing into the West Arm of Frances Lake.

This was noted by Dr. G.M. Dawson, GSC, in 1887 as "Illes Brook" and by others as "Il-es-too-a", meaning "Salt Lick". These names were forgotten in time and about 1930 Anton MONEY, an English prospector, found gold on the stream and worked it. The name was given by local people at the time.

One of the few men living who have features in the Yukon bearing their names, Money was born in Albury, Surrey, England on 16 September, 1900. Educated at Cranleigh he served for two years in the British forces in the First World War and then tutored privately as a mining engineer. He engaged with the HBC in 1923 and was sent to their post at Telegraph Creek on the Stikine River. He soon left their employ and started his life of successful prospecting. From 1929 to 46 most of his work was in the Frances Lake region. He was most successful in mining placer gold in "Half Moon Canyon" in the Finlayson River. He recently published an interesting account of his experiences entitled *This Was The North*.

MONITOR CREEK 63°18′N 138°44′W (115–O&N). A tributary of Black Hills Creek.

This was named in July 1898 by a group of Scandinavians from Minnesota who called themselves the "MONITOR Gold Mining and Trading Company". They staked claims here and named the stream but found no payable gold. (See Blueberry Creek.)

MOUNT MONSON 62°08′N 136°24′W (115–I). Six miles northwest of Carmacks.

This was named in April 1911 after Constable MONSON of the NWMP, a long-time Yukoner.

MONSTER RIVER 64°59′N 140°56′W (116–B&C). A tributary of the Tatonduc River.

Although not an official name, this stream has been known by this name locally since 1952, instead of the previous Sheep Creek. Intending to haul supplies northward for the construction of the Distant Early Warning (DEW) Line from Eagle, Alaska, the contractors bought a Letourneau "Snow-Freighter". This immense machine was a 24-wheeled vehicle with five trailer units, capable of hauling 125 tons of freight across country. The machine caught fire on the upper reaches of the river and was abandoned. However, the company managed to salvage it about three years later. In the interval, passing trappers and prospectors had renamed the river after the "MONSTER" lying at its headwaters.

MONTANA CREEK   63°41′N 138°58′W (115-O&N). A tributary to the Indian River.

There was a stampede to this creek in January 1897. The original stakers were working for Captain John Jerome Healy, an old Indian fighter, Montana law officer and manager of the NAT&TC, of Fort Cudahy. Because Captain Healy and most of his men were from MONTANA, they were called "The Montana Boys", and so the creek got its name.

MONTE CRISTO GULCH   63°59′N 139°22′W (115-O&N).   A tributary to Bonanza Creek, one half-mile above Boulder Creek.

P.H. Hebb and Edward Monahan had worked at the small, rich MONTE CRISTO Gold Mine west of Everett, Washington, before they came to the Klondike. Too late to stake claims on the main streams they turned to this small feeder. Here they found good gold showings and staked their first claims on 6 July, 1897.

The hill above the gulch was much richer in gold, as the White Channel gravels lay there.

Hebb later prospected many parts of the Yukon and gained the nickname "The Diamond King". (See Dixie Creek.)

MONTREAL CREEK   63°47′N 139°25′W (115-O&N). A tributary to the Indian River.

Robert Picotte (whose father staked and mined No. 17 on Eldorado Creek) found the first gold here and staked the Discovery claim on 3 July, 1901. He named it after his home town in Québec.

MONUMENT ISLAND   60°01′N 134°54′W (105-D). A small island on the east side of Bennett Lake, near the BC border.

Inspector Constantine and Staff Sergeant Charles Brown of the NWMP, the first of the force to enter the Yukon, are said to have built their boat here in 1894. Stories of the time claim that when the first rough survey of the Yukon-BC boundary was made, a temporary boundary marker, or monument, was set on this little island.

MOONEY CREEK   60°10′N 125°03′W (95–C). A tributary to Larsen Creek.

In 1963 this creek was chosen to commemorate the name of Honorary Captain Thomas Edmund MOONEY, MID. He was born on 21 January, 1906, at Westport, Ontario, and was appointed to the Canadian army as a chaplain on 10 January, 1942. He served in Canada, Great Britain and northwest Europe and was killed in action on 14 September, 1944.

MOOSEHORN RANGE   63°06′N 140°58′W (115–O&N). A 14-mile-long ridge extending across the Yukon-Alaska border, south of the Ladue River.

This ridge was originally named "Moosehorn Mountain" by A.H. Brooks and W.J. Peters, USGS, while they were on their expedition up the White River to the Tanana in 1898.

MORLEY RIVER   60°06′N 132°30′W (105–C). Flows into the southeast corner of Teslin Lake.

In the spring of 1897 Arthur St. Cyr, DLS, of the Department of the Interior was given the task of finding and surveying a feasible wagon road or railway route from Telegraph Creek, BC, on the Stikine River, to the head of Teslin Lake. He was also placed in charge of other surveyors engaged in defining the boundary between the Yukon Territory and British Columbia. His assistant on the Telegraph Creek-Lake Teslin survey was W. MORLEY Ogilvie, DLS, the son of William Ogilvie, DLS.

They quickly found and surveyed a trail to the foot of Teslin Lake. St. Cyr then set out for Tagish Lake and Bennett to oversee the boundary survey. Morley Ogilvie was instructed to survey the east shore of Teslin Lake and continue down the Teslin River to its junction with the Yukon (Lewes) River. Ogilvie carried out this task successfully and St. Cyr afterward named this river, near his starting point, after him.

Ogilvie went on to spend some years as a government surveyor in and around Dawson. By 1908 he was associated with his father as field superintendent of the Yukon Basin Gold Dredging Co. on the Stewart River. His father was the president of the company.

The names Morley Bay, Lake and Mount were added in the 1930 to 50's. The settlement, lodge, restaurant and gasoline station were started about 1943–44 by Clyde Wann, one of the first bush pilots in the Yukon. (See Mount Wann.)

MORRIS LAKE 60°27′N 131°40′W (105–B). At the head of Morley River.

Jake MORRIS, an Indian trapper, had his cabin on this lake before 1900 and for many years after.

MORRISON CREEK 63°50′N 136°06′W (115–P). A tributary to Seattle Creek.

This was named in the early 1900's by Hector MORRISON. Born in Zorra, Ontario, in 1856, he came to the Yukon in 1894. In 1911 he found a rich deposit of silver-lead ore in Gambler's Gulch on Keno Hill. He later sold his holdings to Keno Mines and retired to Vancouver, BC, where he died in 1930.

MOUNT MORRISON 64°44′N 140°56′W (116–B&C). Two miles north of the Yukon River, just east of the Alaska border.

This was called Morison Peak by William Ogilvie, DLS, in 1887 after a member of his boundary survey party. William T. MORISON of Ormiston, Québec, worked for Ogilvie for five or six years in the Yukon and BC, all on exploratory surveys. After leaving Ogilvie's employ he entered theological school and became a Presbyterian minister, serving for many years in Montréal. He died in May 1951, aged 87. The name was later misspelled.

MOSES HILL 67°19′N 136°48′W (116–P). South of Rat River.

This hill was named in 1973 after John MOSES. He was the Indian special constable who drove dog teams for the RCMP in their hunt for Albert Johnson, the "Mad Trapper", in 1932. (See Mount Sittichinli.)

MOSQUITO GULCH 63°58′N 139°21′W (116–B&C). Flows into Bonanza Creek, opposite Boulder Creek.

A Discovery claim was staked here on 1 September, 1897 by L.W. Steele. It had been staked earlier but the claim had been abandoned and never worked.

MOUNTAIN INDIAN RIVER (See Firth River.)

MUNROE LAKE   60°02′N   135°01′W   (105–D). South of the West Arm of Lake Bennett.

Alexander MUNROE was the best axeman on Arthur St. Cyr's boundary survey crew in 1899–1900. He broke his leg near here and St. Cyr named this lake after him in 1901. He named the peak on the east side of the lake Munroe Peak (6,735′) at the same time.

MURRAY   CREEK   62°09′N   136°22′W   (115–I). A tributary to the Yukon River from the west.

Although named before the turn of the century, this stream has been known locally for many years as "Meyer's Creek". Myers was a woodcutter who provided fuel for the WP&YR riverboats for many years. His cabin is at the mouth of the stream. He came into the country from Cordova, Alaska, during the Chisana rush of 1913.

The name MURRAY probably came from the first man to stake a claim on the creek; he found no gold and quickly left.

MURRAY   CREEK   63°46′N   133°22′W   (105–N). A tributary to the Stewart River above Lansing.

"Mike" MURRAY prospected this area and the Rogue River country for many years in the early 1900′s. For a number of those years he was the only white man in the region, with the exception of Frank Braine and Percy Nash, the traders at Lansing.

MURRAY CREEK   61°36′N   139°40′W   (115–G&F). A tributary to the Donjek River.

This was named about 1903–04 after T.T. MURRAY who was a long-time prospector in the area and who worked on this creek.

MOUNT   MURRAY   7,093′   60°53′N   128°49′W   (105–A). 20 miles northeast of Simpson Lake, in the Logan Mountains.

The old name was "Tent Peak", given by Dr. G.M. Dawson, GSC, in 1887 because of its shape. The name was regarded as redundant by the Geographical Board in 1949. They then changed it to the name of Alexander MURRAY (1810–1884), assistant to Sir William E. Logan, the first director of the Geological and Natural History Survey of Canada.

MUSH CREEK   60°18′N   137°29′W   (115–A). Flows into Mush Lake.

The discovery of coarse gold in the summer of 1902 by M.I. Christner led to a staking rush in this area and the naming of this and other nearby streams. Christner had been prospecting this area since early 1900.

MUSSELL GLACIER   60°43′N 140°54′W (115–C). A branch of the Ogilvie Glacier in the St. Elias Range.

This was named in 1966 after H.S. MUSSELL, DLS, who was in charge of the International Boundary Survey party for Canada 1910 to 12.

MOUNT MYE   6,763′   62°20′N 133°08′W (105–K). 12 miles northeast of Faro.

J.R. Johnson, GSC, named this peak in 1935 after his fiancée Myrtle "MYE" Hay. He used her nickname as it resembled that of an old trapper and prospector in the area, years before.

NADALEEN RIVER   63°58′N 133°39′W (105–N). A major tributary to the Stewart River.

In 1885 this stream was named by the first miners to see it, Thomas Boswell and perhaps his brother George, who were from Peterborough, Ontario. About 1905, perhaps because the name had been forgotten or because there was another Boswell River in the Big Salmon country, the name NADALEEN was adopted. It is supposedly a local Indian name. (See Boswell River.)

NAHONI MOUNTAINS   65°30′N 139°30′W (116–G&F). At the headwaters of the Porcupine River.

In April 1888 William Ogilvie, DLS, named these mountains because he believed them to be the home of the NAHONI (Nahanni) Indians.

NANSEN CREEK   61°59′N 137°12′W (115–H). A tributary of the Nisling River.

Captain Henry Seymour Back and his party discovered gold on this creek in July 1899 but did not work it. He returned to the region with a large prospecting party in 1907. Re-examining the creek they found prospects worth working and the Discovery claim was staked by his son, Frank H. Back and Tom E. Bee on 13 June, 1910.

Captain Back named the stream in honour of the famous Norwegian Arctic explorer, Fridtjof NANSEN. (See Mount Nansen.)

MOUNT NANSEN   5,593′   62°06′N 137°18′W (115–I). At the headwaters of Nansen Creek.

Mount Nansen overlooks a richly mineralized area which was discovered by Captain Henry Seymour Back, an outstanding pioneer. He gained his rank in the American Civil War and, moving west, became an Army scout and Indian fighter, later a trader and prospector. He came to the Klondike in 1897 where he was successful. This area came to his attention in 1899. Attracted by stories of richer finds he went on to Alaska. In 1907 he returned with a party of seven or eight men, including his son Frank and prospected the area intensively until about 1920. He was then in his 80's. He and his men found gold and named many of the streams in this area; this mountain is named after Fridtjof NANSEN, the Norwegian explorer.

His son, Frank H. Back, remained in the country after his father died. He continued prospecting and in 1917, owned and operated a black fox fur farm at Carmacks. (See Back, Hobo, Discovery and Seymour Creeks.)

NARCHILLA BROOK   61°52′N 129°45′W (105-H). Flows into the foot of McPherson Lake.

Warburton Pike, the English sportsman and explorer, named this stream in 1893 after his guide and companion, a Frances Lake Indian.

NARES LAKE   60°10′N 134°39′W (105-D). A small lake joining Bennett and Tagish Lakes.

Called "Moose Lake" by the early miners, this lake was renamed by Lt. F. Schwatka, US Army, in 1883, after Vice Admiral Sir George Strong NARES, RN, a famous English Arctic explorer. The mountain immediately to the northeast of the lake was later also named for Nares.

NASH CREEK   64°39′N 134°37′W (106-D). A tributary to the Wind River.

Percival NASH, prospector and trader in this area, was a partner of Frank Braine when they operated the trading post at Lansing on the Stewart River in the early 1900's.

NATAZHAT GLACIER   61°34′N 140°55′W (115-G&F). A small glacier on the northwest of the St. Elias Range.

This was reported in 1912 by Thomas Riggs, Jr., of the US International Boundary Survey. The Indian name was recorded by C.W. Hayes, USGS, in 1890 but no translation was given.

NATION RIVER   65°31′N 141°00′W (116-G&F). A tributary to the Yukon River in Alaska.

This was first mapped in 1883 by Lt. F. Schwatka, US Army, who called it "Tahkandik". J.E. Spurr, USGS, in 1896 reported "Tahkandit". At the same time F.C. Schrader, USGS, noted that the early miners had already named it the "Nation River". The stream had some prominence in 1897–98 because of a coal seam found near its mouth.

NELSON CREEK   63°39′N 134°48′W (115-M). A tributary of Mayo Lake at the east end.

Rich placer gold was found here in 1916 by two prospectors known only as "Big Steve" and "Little Steve". One of them was surnamed NELSON.

NESHAM GLACIER   61°23′N 140°50′W (115-F). A branch of the huge Klutlan Glacier.

In 1916 this name was given after E.W. NESHAM, DLS, a British member of the International Boundary Survey party of 1915.

NESKATEHEEN LAKE   60°10′N 137°04′W (115-A). Three miles north of Dalton Post.

It was near here that the old Indian village of the same name was occupied long before any white man recorded it. It was an important meeting place where the coast tribes came to trade with the interior Indians.

The first white men known to have visited the lake and village were E.J. Glave and Jack Dalton of the Frank Leslie Illustrated Newspaper Expedition in 1891. Dalton later established his headquarters a short distance below here. Klondikers called the place "Neskatahin" and J.J. McArthur, DLS, while travelling the Dalton Trail, called it "Weskatahin". No one gave a translation. (See Weskatahin.)

MOUNT NEVIN   60°00′N 136°10′W (115-A). Marks the boundary between the Yukon and British Columbia.

James NEVIN Wallace, DLS (1870-1941), surveyed this mountain in 1908. It was the highest peak he had crossed in two survey seasons and he had personally made more ascents than any other boundary surveyor up to that time. He was engaged in such surveys from 1907 to 24.

NEWBAUER CREEK   62°02′N 137°12′W (115-I). A small tributary of Nansen Creek.

A long-known local name after the prospector who worked here and in the general area from about 1910–15, it was made official in 1968.

MOUNT NEW BRUNSWICK 11,115' 60°55'N 140°38'W (115-B-&C). In the Centennial Range of the St. Elias Mountains.

This mountain was named to celebrate Canada's Centennial Year. (See Centennial Range.)

MOUNT NEWFOUNDLAND 12,040' 60°57'N 140°33'W (115-B&C). In the Centennial Range of the St. Elias Mountains.

This mountain was named in 1967 to celebrate Canada's Centennial Year. (See Centennial Range.)

MOUNT NEWTON 13,811' 60°19'N 140°53'W (115-B&C). In the southwest corner of the St. Elias Range.

Professor I.C. Russell named this mountain when he mapped it with the National Geographic Society and USGS Expedition in 1890, after Professor Henry NEWTON of the Columbia School of Mines and the USGS.

Until 1964 this was the highest unclimbed peak in North America. In that year it was climbed by the Blanchard-Eichorn party.

NEW ZEALAND CREEK (See Printers Creek.)

NIDDERY LAKE 63°18'N 131°20'W (105-O). A small lake south of the Hess River.

Norman NIDDERY was a trapper and prospector in this area for many years. In 1946 Bernard J. Woodruff of the Geodetic Survey of Canada proposed this name in gratitude for Niddery's help and information about the region. (See Fido Creek.)

NIGGERHEAD LAKES (See Enger Lakes.)

NIGGERHEAD MOUNTAIN (See Eikland Mountain.)

NIGGER JIM'S GULCH 63°55'N 139°15'W (115-O&N). A tributary to Bonanza Creek, two miles above Grand Forks.

James "Nigger Jim" Daugherty was from Virginia and gained his nickname from his accent. He was a famous figure in the Klondike and many stories were written about him. He was especially noted as a stampeder. He discovered gold on and staked this little stream on 4 December, 1897.

NISUTLIN RIVER 60°14'N 132°34'W (105-C). **The major tributary to Teslin Lake from the northeast.**

This name was known from the earliest times. It is a Tlinkit Indian word meaning "Quiet Water" and was probably first applied to the large and beautiful Nisutlin Bay.

NOBLE CREEK 64°10'N 139°15'W (116-B). **Tributary to Lepine Creek, ten miles northeast of Dawson.**

George NOBLE, an early Yukoner, staked the first claim on this creek about 1897. His brother, who worked in the Gold Office in Dawson, was known as "Colonel Bill".

NOGOLD CREEK 63°27'N 135°05'W (105-M). **Tributary to the Stewart River at Horseshoe Slough.**

This was named by miners in 1895 who found gold colours here but no payable gold.

MOUNT NOLAN 4,566' 63°59'N 140°36'W (115-O&N). **South of the Sixtymile River.**

This was called "Dog Tooth Mountain" by the early miners on the Sixtymile creeks in the 1890's. The name was changed by the GSC in 1920. They named it after the manager of the NAT&TC at the time.

NORDENSKIOLD RIVER 62°06'N 136°18'W (115-I). **Flows into the Yukon River at Carmacks.**

This was called "Thuch-en-Dituh" meaning "Meeting Place" by the Indians who lived there. The Chilkat Indians met the interior Indians here to trade every year. The route the Chilkats used from the coast became the Dalton Trail and Carmacks was one of its terminals.

In 1883 Lt. F. Schwatka, US Army, named this river after Baron Nils Adolf Erik NORDENSKIOLD, 1832-1901, the famous Swedish Arctic explorer and geologist. Nordenskiold made the first passage northeast of the European and Asian continent in his ship, the *Vega*, in 1878-79.

NORTH CROOKED CREEK 63°16'N 136°30'W (115-P). **Crooked Creek flows into the Stewart at Stewart Crossing.**

Named by the Geographical Board in 1941, the only claim to distinction held by this stream is that neither of the local names was officially adopted. "Hardrock" MacDonald and "Hotstove" Douglas lived and worked here and no one called the creek Crooked. Both of these old-timers were alive when it was proposed to make the name(s) official. (See Mount MacDonald.)

NORTHERN LAKE   61°45'N 133°45'W (105–F). Between the Big Salmon and Salmon Rivers.

Although this appears to be a descriptive name, in fact it is the name of a brave Canadian, J-14566 Flight Lt. Edward NORTHERN, DFC, who was born 7 December, 1917, in Sheffield, England and enlisted in the RCAF at Toronto, Ontario, on 10 September, 1941. He was missing on air operations on 1 May, 1944, and was presumed killed in action.

MOUNT NORTHWEST   10,550'   60°59'N 140°58'W (115–B&C). In the Centennial Range of the St. Elias Mountains.

This was named in 1967 after the NORTHWEST Territories to celebrate Canada's Centennial Year. (See Centennial Range.)

MOUNT NOVA SCOTIA   10,800'   60°56'N 140°29'W (115–B&C). In the Centennial Range of the St. Elias Mountains.

This was named during Canada's Centennial Year of 1967. (See Centennial Range.)

NUTZOTIN MOUNTAINS 62°00'N 140°45'W (115–J&K). Straddling the Yukon-Alaska boundary in the north Kluane district.

In 1898 W.J. Peters and A.H. Brooks, USGS, first mapped this area and named these mountains after the NUTZOTIN Indians of the region. A.H. Brooks later became Alaska's foremost geologist and Chief Alaskan Geologist of the USGS. The huge Brooks Range in northern Alaska was named for him.

O'BRIEN CREEK   62°38'N 140°04'W (115–J&K). A tributary of the White River, four miles above Donjek City.

This creek was named when Antoine Boulay staked the Discovery claim on 1 November, 1913. He was working for, or grubstaked by, Thomas O'BRIEN, the old Fortymiler and Klondike millionaire. Boulay found the gold on this stream when he prospected it on his way to the new gold finds in the Chisana District in Alaska. (See Brewery Creek.)

OBSERVATION MOUNTAIN   60°49′N 138°42′W (115–B&C). At the junction of Slim's River and the Kaskawulsh Glacier.

In June 1952, J.O. Wheeler, GSC, mapped this area using bearings from this hill to place other features nearby. A. Cameron Ogilvy, of Whitehorse, a student engineer assisting Wheeler at the time, carried the transit to the summit and suggested the name.

O'CONNOR RIVER   (See Kaskawulsh River.)

OGILVIE   63°34′N 139°44′W (115–O&N).

In the summer of 1894 Arthur Harper and Joseph Ladue set up a trading post on this large island in the Yukon River, opposite the mouth of the Sixtymile River. They were taking advantage of the increased activity in the Sixtymile gold fields.

At first it was called the Sixtymile Post but Harper and Ladue shortly renamed it after William OGILVIE, DLS, of the Department of the Interior, who had surveyed the Yukon-Alaska boundary line in the Fortymile district, settled the miners' disputes and was the only government official visible at the time.

Ladue built and ran the first sawmill in the Yukon at this place. It was abandoned shortly after the discovery of gold in the Klondike. (See Ogilvie Mountains.)

OGILVIE MOUNTAINS   65°21′N 138°15′W (116–G). North of Dawson and encompassing the headwaters of the Ogilvie and Porcupine Rivers.

In 1966 this range of mountains was named by the Government of Canada to honour one of Canada's outstanding men.

William OGILVIE was born in Ottawa, Upper Canada, on 7 April, 1846, the son of James Ogilvie and Margaret Halliday. He was educated in Ottawa and in 1869 was admitted to practice as a Provincial and Dominion Land Surveyor. He later became a Dominion Topographical Surveyor, passing one of the most exacting survey examinations in the world.

Between 1875 and 1898 he carried out many surveys and explorations in the Canadian west, the most notable of these being the first survey of the Yukon-Alaska boundary in the Fortymile area in 1887–88, and his initial surveys in the Klondike goldfields and the Dawson townsite in 1896. At this time he was the only representative of the Canadian government, with the exception of Insp. Constantine, in the territory and his reputation for honesty, integrity and impartiality was such that his unofficial decisions were accepted by all.

In September 1898 he was made Commissioner of the Yukon Territory, replacing Major James Walsh and in April 1901 he resigned. He was later made a Fellow of the Royal Geographical Society for his survey explorations in the Yukon.

Ogilvie, in June 1901, after his resignation, went up the Yukon in the riverboat *Susie*. Leaving Skagway, Alaska, he visited Nome on his way home and while he was there, he rescued a young lady, a Miss Richardson, from drowning. A short time later he married her at her home in Paris, Texas. She was his second wife.

Ogilvie died on 13 November, 1912, in Winnipeg, Manitoba.

OGILVIE RIVER   65°52′N 137°15′W (116–H). The north branch of the Peel River.

This river was named by the Dominion Geographer, J. Johnston, in 1888 to honour William OGILVIE'S great exploratory work.

OGILVIE VALLEY   61°25′N 135°16′W (105–E). The valley extending northwest from the foot of Lake Laberge to Coghlan Lake.

In 1887 Dr. G.M. Dawson, GSC, named this feature after William OGILVIE, DLS, of the Department of the Interior who carried the first accurate survey from the Lynn Canal into the interior of the Yukon Territory and gave the GSC its accurate base for geological mapping.

O.K. CREEK   64°02′N 139°31′W (116–B&C). Flows into the Yukon from the northeast, five miles above the town of Dawson.

Joseph Pellerin found the first gold and staked a Discovery claim here on 19 January, 1898. He renamed it "O.K.;" it had formerly been called Six Mile Creek.

OLD CROW   67°34′N 139°50′W (116–O&N). On the Porcupine River.

This settlement of Loucheaux Indians has been in existence since 1911. Their forebears had lived around old Fort Yukon, established in 1847 by Alexander Hunter Murray of the HBC, at the confluence of the Porcupine and Yukon Rivers. When the HBC was driven from American territory in 1869 the Indians, priding themselves on being "King George Men" and not

"Boston Men", moved with the company to Old Rampart House, farther up the Porcupine River and thought to be on Canadian soil. Again the post was found to be in American territory and again it was moved. The new site was called New Rampart House. In 1911 the population was devastated by an epidemic of smallpox. The survivors burned the post and moved again, this time to the junction of the Porcupine with the Crow River.

The new settlement took its name from a noted chief of the old days, "Te-Tshim-Gevtik", meaning "Walking Crow". He died in the 1870's, leaving his people a legacy of high standards and moral principles which have persisted to the present time. The settlement is in the centre of the most prolific muskrat-breeding grounds in the entire northwest, if not in all of Canada. In 1955 Father J.M. Mouchet, of the Oblate Fathers, introduced skiing to the native people and in 20 years, some of Canada's finest young cross-country skiers have developed here.

Edith Josie has for many years, as a reporter for the *Whitehorse Star*, contributed one of the most colourful newspaper columns written in Canada.

The Old Crow Mountains north of the town and the river, were all named after the same chief, "Walking Crow". The word "crow" here refers to the northern raven, as true crows are unknown this far north.

OLD DANGER CREEK   (See Danger Creek.)

OLD TRAIL CREEK   63°26'N 137°49'W (115-P). A tributary to Lake Creek.

This name was suggested by the GSC in 1949 as the old trail from Stevens Roadhouse to Stewart Crossing followed this stream.

OLD WOMAN ROCK   64°31'N 140°29'W (116-B&C). On the Yukon River, 15 miles below Fortymile.

This is an Indian name known to the early miners. Old Woman Rock is on the east side of the river and Old Man Rock is on the west side. The names are from an old Indian legend.

Lt. F. Schwatka, US Army, on his raft voyage down the Yukon in 1883, renamed these the "Rocquette Rocks" after M. Alexandre de la Rocquette of the Paris Geographical Society. The name was never accepted or used.

MOUNT OLIVER WHEELER   61°12'N 140°09'W (115-F). East of the Steele Glacier in the St. Elias Range.

In November 1970, the Alpine Club of Canada named this mountain after Sir Edward OLIVER WHEELER, KB, MC, Leg. H., RE (1890–1962), engineer and surveyor. He was president of the club from 1950 to 54.

O'NEIL'S GULCH 63°55′N 139°14′W (115–O&N). A tributary to Bonanza Creek about three miles above Grand Forks.

John King staked the first claim here and recorded it on 7 July, 1897. It had previously been staked by a prospector named O'NEIL but he did not regard it highly enough to record his claim; however, his name stuck to the creek.

MOUNT ONTARIO 12,200 60°58′N 140°44′W (115–B&C). In the Centennial Range of the St. Elias Mountains.

This mountain was named in honour of the province of ONTARIO during Canada's Centennial Year, 1967. (See Centennial Range.)

OPHIR CREEK 63°47′N 139°20′W (115–O&N). A small stream flowing into the Indian River from the north.

Alexander MacDonald, Scottish mining engineer and author, named this creek in the winter of 1897 when he found good prospects of gold on it. The name "Ophir" is that of the legendary place in Africa where the Queen of Sheba got her gold and is synonymous with the idea of untold wealth.

MacDonald (not to be confused with "Big Alex" McDonald) returned to Scotland in early 1898 and wrote some vivid and highly coloured accounts of his adventures in the Klondike, including gun fights and battles with the Indians, for various newspapers. He prospected in Africa and Australia and wrote several fictionalized accounts of his travels and adventures.

ORA GRANDE GULCH 63°53′N 139°17′W (115–O&N). A short stream entering Eldorado from the northeast, opposite Nugget Gulch.

Ransom Noblett named this gulch in Spanish for "Big Gold", on 27 September, 1897. It did not live up to its name.

ORCA COVE 69°34′N 139°15′W (117–D). On the west side of Herschel Island.

This bay was named by Lt. Commander Stockton of the USS *Thetis*, when he surveyed the coast of Herschel Island in 1889. He named it after the whaler *ORCA* which was in the bay at the time.

ORCHAY RIVER 62°08'N 132°58'W (105-K). A tributary of the Pelly River.

In June 1843 this stream was named by Robert Campbell of the HBC, during his major journey of exploration down the Pelly River. It was named after a river of the same name in his native Perthshire, Scotland.

ORTELL'S CROSSING 63°49'N 136°23'W (115-P). On the Stewart River at Johnson Creek.

Ortell's Crossing was on the trail from the Stewart River, along Johnson Creek and down Highet Creek to Minto Creek and Mayo. It was used by miners in the early 1900's to carry supplies to the new diggings on Highet and surrounding creeks. It was so named because George L. ORTELL had lived for many years near the head of Johnson Creek, at one time the only person in this area.

He came into this part of the country shortly after 1900 and spent the rest of his life near here. Well known and highly respected for his abilities as a bushman and trapper, he assisted Joseph Keele, GSC, with his exploration and mapping of the upper Stewart country.

He died 3 April, 1943 in St. Mary's Hospital in Dawson. The manner of his death was a display of stark courage and endurance. About the end of February 1943 he froze his hands on a trip to Highet Creek, the temperature at the time being –61°F. He stopped at the cabin of a friend, Joe Laska, who persuaded him to remain there while Laska went to Mayo for help. Laska, himself in his early 70's, was persuaded when he reached Minto Bridge to rest while the roadhouse keeper arranged for someone else to go for Ortell. Contacting the RCMP it was found that every dog team in Mayo was out on a job for the US Army. On the third day a dog team was found and the rescue mission began.

In the meantime, Ortell had begun to worry about Laska and his safety in the intense cold. He decided to walk to Mayo to see if Laska was alive.

Twelve miles down the trail a snowshoe strap broke. With his frozen hands he was unable to repair it so he discarded the snowshoes and struggled on in the deep snow. Fatigue and the Arctic night overtook him. He was unable to light a fire. His only hope was to remain erect and to keep moving, in the hope that someone would happen by.

Too tired to walk, he stood beside the trail and banked snow around his legs up to his knees and steeled his mind to keep standing. He knew that if he sat or lay down he would die. All through the night and into the following afternoon he stood, slowly freezing to death, only his indomitable will keeping him erect.

Dick Kimbel and Corporal d'Easum were stunned when they found him. They lifted him from the snow and rushed him to the nurse at Mayo who did everything possible to relieve his suffering. A plane took him to Dawson the next day.

Both feet had to be amputated and he appealed to the doctor to save as much as he could: "I got to hobble around some way. Figure to get me a fine catch of beaver on the McQuesten River this spring."

When he realized that he could never return to his beloved wilderness he lost heart. He gave up, for the first and last time in his life.

MOUNT ORTELL 6,769' 63°58′N 132°49′W (105–N). In the Tasin Range, south of the Stewart River.

Joseph Keele, GSC, named this peak in 1907 after George L. ORTELL, whose help and knowledge of the region greatly aided him in his geological mapping of the area.

MOUNT OSBORNE 65°46′N 140°50′W (116–F). South of the Kandik River.

Harriet C. OSBORNE, OBE, wife of Franklin Osborne of Dawson, was active in the Anglican Church, IODE and St. John's Ambulance. She organized the first Girl Guides in the Yukon in 1914 at Dawson. She was made an Officer of the Order of the British Empire for public service and in 1973 this mountain was named for her.

OSCAR CREEK 60°39′N 128°51′W (105–A). Flows south to False Canyon Creek, a few miles north of Stewart Lake.

The creek and lake were named in 1943 after OSCAR Stewart, a trapper and the son of a trapper, both of whom had spent many years in this area. The name had been in local use for a long time.

MOUNT OSGOODE 63°02′N 132°29′W (105–N). North of Mount Selous.

This mountain was named in 1909 after Wilfred Hudson OSGOODE (1875–1947), a member of the US Biological Survey. Osgoode came into the Yukon in 1899 on an expedition for the US Department of Agriculture, over the White Pass and down the Yukon. He was with F.C. Selous, the famed African white hunter and naturalist, in this area in 1904 and camped on the mountain while he studied the local flora and fauna.

OTTER FALLS   61°05′N 137°00′W (115–H). On the Aishihik River at the foot of Canyon Lake.

This falls is sometimes called "Five Dollar" Falls because its picture appeared for many years on the reverse side of the five-dollar Canadian banknotes.

PACKARD POINT   60°58′N 133°04′W (105–C). The large point at the southeast end of Quiet Lake.

During the 1920 and 30's a wealthy American construction man by this name came yearly to hunt in this area. His companies had built many of the New York City docks. A large, impressive and friendly man, he claimed that he could build anything. He died here and his body was sent to the northeastern United States for burial.

PACKERS MOUNTAIN   4,743′   61°50′N 135°32′W (105–E). On the east side of the Chain Lakes.

A.E. Pattison was head packer for D.D. Cairnes, GSC, from 1905 to 17. He was a master horseman and an exceptional bushman. Possessed of a fine singing voice, he and Cairnes often gave impromptu concerts when they came to town. In 1930 he died and W.D. Cockfield, GSC, who had also worked with him, named this mountain to commemorate him and the other packers who had served the GSC in the Yukon. (See Mount Pattison.)

MOUNT PAGE   4,198   69°20′N 140°53′W (117–C). On the headwaters of the Malcolm River, 25 miles south of the Arctic coast.

In June 1958 this mountain was chosen to perpetuate the memory of Lt. Pierre Roger Joseph PAGE, MID. He was born on 2 February, 1918, at Knowlton, Québec and enlisted in the Canadian army on 10 September, 1940, at Sherbrooke, Québec, He served in Canada, Great Britain, Newfoundland and northwest Europe and died of wounds received in action on 13 August, 1944.

PAN CREEK   62°00′N 140°55′W (115–J&K). A tributary of Tchawsahmon Creek, which flows into the White River.

In the winter of 1912–13, William E. James, Peter Nelson and Frederick Best discovered good placer gold on this stream. One of them used a frying pan to wash the first colours (gold) from the gravel. They claimed to have good values but an inrush of water to their workings forced them to stop.

In the spring of 1913 James and Nelson prospected farther west over the Alaska border. There they found the rich and famous Chisana goldfields.

On 23 August, 1913, Paul Jacobs recorded a new Discovery claim on the creek and at this time the Gold Commissioner for some reason changed the name from the original "Frying Pan" Creek to Pan Creek. In 1915 it was again changed to Frying Pan Creek.

PARADISE CREEK 63°42'N 136°08'W (115-P). A tributary to the southeast corner of Minto Lake.

On 19 May, 1903, J.G. Scrivener staked the Discovery claim on this stream and named it for its beautiful setting.

PARENT CREEK 63°50'N 135°27'W (105-M). A tributary to Duncan Creek from the east.

During the rush to this area Dennis PARENT and G. Beaudet prospected this stream and found placer gold. They staked the Discovery claim and named the creek on 20 June, 1902.

PARIS 63°49'N 138°40'W (115-O).

This was a small mining camp and settlement at the junction of Dominion and Portland Creeks in the southwest Klondike district. It had a post office from 1904 to 43 but was abandoned after that date.

PARTRIDGE CREEK 60°14'N 135°08'W (105-D). Flows into the Wheaton River.

Officially named in May 1911 but locally known for at least ten years before that, this creek bears the name of Otto H. PARTRIDGE, a prominent but lesser known figure of the Klondike Gold Rush.

In 1897 Partridge, as general manager of the Bennett Lake and Klondyke Navigation Company, brought the boilers and fittings for three small steamboats over the White Pass. That winter he built a sawmill and ship-yard at Millhaven Bay on the west arm of Bennett Lake. Early in the spring of 1898 the three boats went down to Whitehorse. Although there is some argument, it is likely that one of these boats was the first to navigate through Miles Canyon and the Whitehorse Rapids.

His mill and shipyard prospered and he cut timber on this and other near-by creeks. Partridge was early interested in the development of the

Engineer Gold Mine (hard rock) on Windy Arm of Tagish Lake. The locale suited him and he and his wife settled on the west side of the arm. Their home "Ben-My Chree", (Manx for "Girl of my Heart") was a showplace for tourists on the WP&YR until the early 1930's.

PAT LAKE   65°06′N   136°40′W   (116-H). About 15 miles east of the Hart River.

This lake was named by bush pilot I.A. Reid for the convenience of himself and other pilots assisting mining exploration in the area. It was probably named after E.P. "PAT" Callison, noted pioneer Yukon bush pilot who landed the first aircraft on the lake. It is the only lake within a very large area that is large enough on which to land a fixed-wing aircraft.

MOUNT PATTERSON   11,300′   61°09′N   140°07′W   (115-F). On the east side of the Steele Glacier in the St. Elias Range.

It was named in November 1970 after John Duncan PATTERSON (1864-1940), business man and past president of the Alpine Club of Canada.

MOUNT PATTERSON   6,819′   61°56′N   133°51′W   (105-F). North of the North Big Salmon River in the Pelly Mountains.

This beautiful mountain was chosen in November 1951 to honour the memory of a Canadian hero, Lt. William Clark PATTERSON, MID. He was born on 22 August, 1915, in Toronto, Ontario and enlisted in the Canadian army on 27 May, 1940, at Toronto. He served in Canada and Great Britain and was killed in action during the attack on Dieppe in France on 19 August, 1942.

MOUNT PATTISON   62°28′N   138°34′W   (115-J&K). East of the Klotassin River in the southeast Dawson Range.

A.E. PATTISON trapped and prospected this country for many years. He worked as a packer for GSC parties from 1905 to 30. An excellent horseman and packer, he was liked for his cheerful disposition and ability as a bushman.

In the summer of 1930 he was as usual packing for the GSC. It was a bad year for flies and Pattison, worried about his horses, stayed up at night and kept smudge fires burning to protect them from the insects. He carried on with his normal work during the day but it was too much for his health and he suffered a stroke. He was taken to Vancouver where he died shortly afterward at the age of 64.

D.D. Cairnes, GSC, had named this peak for him about 1916. (See Packers Mountain.)

PATTON GULCH   62°45′N   138°51′W   (115-J&K). On the north side of Patton Hill at the head of Canadian Creek.

This gulch and the mountain above it were named in 1911 by Jack Meloy, a well-known Yukon prospector. His old friend James "Jim" PATTON had found and worked the first placer gold in the area at a much earlier date. Patton spent many years prospecting in the Dawson Range. The name was made official in 1970. (See Meloy Creek.)

PATULLO LAKE   68°03′N   139°20′W   (117-A). A small lake east of Old Crow Flats.

This name was proposed by Gordon McIntyre in June 1973 as a sheet designation for the new series of topographical maps.

Dufferin PATULLO was a lawyer, prominent in Dawson and Yukon politics during the gold rush era. He later became premier of British Columbia.

PAULINE COVE   69°34′N   138°55′W   (117-D). On the east side of Herschel Island.

It was named by Lt. Commander Stockton of the USS *Thetis*, when he surveyed the coast of Herschel Island in 1889. He used the name of a whaling ship that was in the bay at the time.

PEASOUP   CREEK   64°17′N   138°29′W   (116-B&C).   Crosses   the Dempster Highway and flows into the North Klondike River.

This was named in 1969 by highway construction crews when one of their number, a French Canadian, fell into the stream. The blunt sense of humour of his companions supplied the name.

PEEL RIVER   67°00′N   134°59′W   (106-L). A tributary of the Mackenzie River.

In 1826, John Franklin (later Sir) on his second overland expedition to the Arctic, named this large river after Sir Robert PEEL (1788-1850), Home Secretary and later, Prime Minister of Great Britain. Peel organized and established the first police force of the modern type. (Hence, British police were and are called "peelers" or "bobbies").

The Peel River was first explored by Chief Factor John Bell of the HBC in

1839, when he ascended it as far as the Snake River. He explored the Snake thinking it was the Peel. In 1840–41 it was explored farther by Alexander Kennedy Isbister, also of the HBC, and still farther in 1893 by Count V.E. de Sainville. Charles Camsell, GSC, made the first complete survey of the river in 1905.

The river was most important for many years as the only route to the lucrative fur trade of the upper Yukon Territory and the Yukon River.

PELLY BANKS   61°46′N 131°07′W (105–G). On the north side of the Pelly River opposite the mouth of Big Campbell Creek.

On 25 July, 1840, Robert Campbell of the HBC arrived here, while establishing the true course and location of the Yukon River. That day he named the Pelly River and the high bluffs across the stream after Sir John Henry PELLY (1777–1852), Governor of the HBC. Later, when Campbell wrote his report informing Pelly of his discoveries, Pelly replied calling the river and banks, "Campbell" River and Banks. Campbell declined the honour but regretted his decision in later life.

In 1846 he built a trading post here, on the east bank of Campbell Creek on the Pelly, supplied from Fort Frances. It never did well. In the early winter of 1849, while Campbell was at Fort Selkirk, the post burned down, leaving the staff destitute. Two of his men died of starvation that winter and some of the Indians resorted to cannibalism to save themselves.

The post was never re-established by the HBC. Independent traders operated here for many years after 1900.

PELLY CROSSING   62°49′N 136°34′W (115–I). About 25 miles east of Fort Selkirk on the Pelly River.

Situated on the Whitehorse-Dawson road, this small settlement had two roadhouses and a trading post run by Ira Van Bibber and his partner Woolen. In 1958 the ferry across the Pelly River was replaced by a modern bridge but the settlement still persists and grows.

PELLY LAKES   62°05′N 130°17′W (105–J). Two long narrow lakes at the head of the Pelly River.

These lakes were named about 1840 by Robert Campbell of the HBC, while he was exploring the country, after the Governor of the company, Sir John Henry PELLY (1777–1852).

PELLY MOUNTAINS   61°40′N 132°30′W (105–F). The huge range of mountains that lies south of nearly the total length of the Pelly River.

These hills were named in 1887 by Dr. G.M. Dawson, GSC, while he was mapping this country for the first time.

In 1947 his nomenclature was expanded so that the Pelly Mountains now include the Big Salmon, the St. Cyr, the Glenlyon, Campbell and Simpson Ranges. (See Pelly Banks.)

PELLY POST OFFICE   62°47′N 137°24′W (115–I). At the junction of the Pelly and Yukon Rivers.

Although the settlement here was always called Fort Selkirk, the government established a post office in September 1899 and named it Pelly Post Office. It was closed in 1939.

PELLY RIVER   62°47′N 137°20′W (115–I). A major tributary of the Yukon River and one of the longest.

The early Indian name for this river was the "Ayan" or "Iyon", after the native tribes who lived near its mouth. The latter name was used on the USC&GS maps of the late 1880's.

Robert Campbell named the river in 1840 after Sir John Henry PELLY, Governor of the HBC.

The Pelly was one of the first streams to be prospected in the Yukon; men panned its gravels as early as 1883.

MOUNT PERKINS   6,665′   60°20′N 135°06′W (105–D). In the upper Corwin Valley.

In 1905 J. PERKINS found and staked the first gold-quartz lode claims found on the mountain.

PERTHES POINT   60°09′N 134°27′W (105–D). On the north side of Tagish Lake, at the foot of Nares Mountain.

In 1883 Lt. F. Schwatka, as he was passing, named this point after Justus PERTHES of Gotha, Germany, a famous geographer.

MOUNT PHELPS   65°03′N 133°56′W (106–F). South of Rapitan Creek.

This is a map designation name given in 1973 for Willard PHELPS, a long-time Whitehorse lawyer and a Yukon Councillor for the Whitehorse District for many years in the 1930's.

PHILLIPS BAY   69°17′N 138°30′W (117–D). At the mouth of the Babbage River on the Arctic coast.

John Franklin, (later Sir) on his second Arctic expedition in 1826, named this bay after Thomas PHILLIPS (1770–1845), professor of painting at the Royal Academy in London.

PILLAGE POINT 68°52′N 136°43′W (117-A). The point of land immediately south of Tent Island in Shoalwater Bay.

On Friday, 7 July, 1826, John Franklin and his two small boats *Lion* and *Reliance* were seized in the shallow waters of this point and forced to land. The Eskimos robbed the boats of stores and supplies and owing only to the coolness of Franklin and Lt. Back, there was no loss of life. The Eskimos, after listening to another chief from Hudson Bay who was accompanying Franklin, restored the goods and thereafter traded.

PILOT MOUNTAIN 6,739′ 61°01′N 135°33′W (105-E). West of Lake Laberge in the Miners Range.

This peak was named in honour of the first riverboat pilots who ran the Lewes (Yukon) River, by H.S. Bostock, GSC, in 1935. The pilots used it as a landmark.

PINGUICULA LAKE 64°41′N 133°24′W (106-C). East of the Bonnet Plume River.

In the summer of 1940, Mr. and Mrs. George Black, accompanied by Livingstone Wernecke, flew into this lake on a camping trip to the area. The large number of butterwort plants (*Pinguicula vulgaris*) growing around the shores of the lake suggested the name to Mrs. Black. She was an acknowledged authority on the wildflowers of the Yukon. (See Mount Black.)

PIRATE CREEK 60°04′N 137°08′W (115-A). A tributary of the Tatshenshini River just south of Dalton Post.

In 1949 H.S. Bostock, GSC, mapped this area. He gave this name because the stream features had altered in the area. This creek had captured the headwaters of Robbed Creek and other small streams in the neighbourhood.

MOUNT PITTS 5,214′ 62°35′N 137°35′W (115-J). 25 miles west of Minto.

In June 1899, J.J. McArthur, DLS, named this after Harold PITTS, a member of his boundary survey party in the area that year. He was nick-named "Buffalo" Pitts.

Pitts came into the Yukon over the Chilkoot Pass in 1895. He lived at Fort Selkirk almost continously till late 1909 when he went outside and saw Whitehorse for the first time. He made his living trading with the Indians.

In a letter to E.G. DeVille, Surveyor General of Canada, on 24 September, 1909, at Fort Selkirk, Pitts asked that this peak be officially named for him, giving as a reason that he was "somewhat like a mule, without pride of ancestry or hope of posterity."

Pitts was on the riverboat which made the first successful trip up the White and Donjek Rivers in 1909. (See Fort Selkirk.)

PLATINUM GULCH   64°01′N 135°51′W (106-D). A small tributary to Haggart Creek.

This small stream was named by early miners because of the amount of platinum found with the gold in the 1920's.

POLICE CREEK   64°25′N 135°22′W (106-D). The north fork of the Beaver River.

This stream was probably named about 1905 or a little later. One of the trails used by the RNWMP MacPherson Patrol ran along it. This route was from Dawson to Fort MacPherson via the Little Wind River.

POLLEY HILL   66°51′N 136°40′W (116-I). West of Rock River.

43176 Bombardier Frank POLLEY was born on 31 July, 1874, at Benson, Oxfordshire, England. He enlisted in the Royal Canadian Artillery at Valcartier, Québec on 24 September, 1914, one of the first Canadians. He served in Canada, Great Britain and France and was discharged as medically unfit, from wounds received, on 30 November, 1917.

He died later from the effects of his wounds. In June 1973 this mountain was named in his memory.

POOLY CANYON   60°02′N 134°37′W (105-D). On the south side of Montana Mountain on the west side of Windy Arm.

The canyon below the forks of Pooly Creek was named in 1905 after the existing Pooly Creek.

POOLY CREEK   60°02′N 134°37′W (105-D). Flows into Windy Arm from the south side of Montana Mountain.

This was named in early 1905 after John M. POOLY, one of the first hardrock prospectors in the Windy Arm district. Pooly gave the creek the name Uranus Creek, after the first claim he staked there but the GSC soon changed it to the present one.

PORCUPINE RIVER 67°25′N 141°00′W (116-O&N). A major tributary to the Yukon River, which leaves Canada at this point.

This river was explored by John Bell, Chief Trader for the HBC at Fort MacPherson in 1842 and 44. Bell first saw the Yukon River on his second trip in 1844. Shortly afterward, in 1847, he sent Alexander Hunter Murray to establish Fort Yukon at the junction of the two streams. The Porcupine remained a regular trade route until the transfer of Alaska to the United States in 1867, when Fort Yukon was abandoned. It remained in limited use until 1894 when the HBC abandoned the territory.

The river was first surveyed and mapped by R.G. McConnell, GSC, in 1888. F.F. Sparks, a member of William Ogilvie's party in 1888, travelling from Fortymile to Fort MacPherson, found the source of the Porcupine to be a small hot spring.

PORTER CREEK 60°47′N 135°09′W (105-D). A tributary to the Lewes (Yukon) River.

This creek was named by H.E. PORTER in July 1899 when he found a rich copper ore body on the seventh of the month, which he called the "Pueblo" claim. Porter lived and prospected in the district for many years. He died while prospecting on the headwaters of the Stewart River in early June 1907. Porter Creek subdivision of the City of Whitehorse was given this name.

PORTLAND CREEK 63°49′N 138°41′W (115-O&N). A tributary to Dominion Creek, four miles above Jensen Creek.

John Salme named this stream after his home town in Oregon when he discovered gold and staked the first claim on 27 December, 1897.

POTATO CREEK 68°09′N 140°23′W (117-B). A tributary to Surprise Creek and the Old Crow River.

This name was reported by Cpl. E.A. Kirk, RCMP, in 1949. The name "Schaefer Creek" had been applied mistakenly by the International Boundary survey crew of 1911 and was shown as such on maps until 1950.

POVOAS MOUNTAIN 61°22′N 135°06′W (105-E). At the northeast corner of Lake Laberge.

This was named about 1908 by D.D. Cairnes, GSC, after an early prospector and miner of this name who lived in the area.

PREJEVALSKY POINT   60°05′N 134°53′W (105–D). The point on the south side between Lake Bennett and the West Arm.

This was named by Lt. F. Schwatka, US Army, in 1883 after a well-known Russian explorer of the time.

PREVOST RIVER   62°36′N 131°10′W (105–J). A tributary of Ross River.

PREVOST, a French Canadian, was probably the first white man to travel this river. He and a partner trapped and prospected here in 1900 and at Prevost Canyon on the Ross River in the early 1900's.

PRIMROSE LAKE   60°06′N 135°41′W (105–D). A long (12 miles) narrow lake east of the Takhini River.

This was probably named by George White-Fraser, DLS, of the Department of the Interior, while setting out monuments on the Yukon-BC boundary in 1900. He named it after Captain, later Inspector, P.C.H. PRIMROSE, NWMP, who was in charge of the Tagish Post and this district that year. The river was named later. Rose Lake, farther up the river was derived from this name. The mountain was named last of all.

MOUNT PRINCE EDWARD ISLAND   12,260′   60°57′N 140°39′W (115–B&C). In the Centennial Range of the St. Elias Mountains.

This peak was named in honour of the province during Canada's Centennial Year, 1967. (See Centennial Range.)

PRINGLE LAKE   60°08′N 136°59′W (115–A). On the west side of the Haines Junction Road near Dalton Post.

Sgt. J.A. PRINGLE, NWMP, served at Dalton Post in the early 1900's and after being discharged, continued to live here for many years. He was a brother of John and George Pringle, the famous Presbyterian ministers of the Klondike and Atlin goldfields and the First World War.

PRINTERS CREEK   61°10′N 138°24′W (115–G&F). Flows into Cultus Creek on the east side of Kluane Lake.

Named "New Zealand Creek" by the first men to find gold and stake claims during the rush to the Kluane goldfields in 1903–04, by 1914 the creek was abandoned. A new find was made and another stampede to stake claims took place. The new stakers named it Printers Creek. To many of the local people it was known as "Buck-Off Creek", after an incident concerning pack horses.

MOUNT PROFIET   64°47′N 133°04′W (106–C). West of the Snare River.

This was named in January 1973 by Gordon McIntyre, Territorial Land Titles Agent, for the Topographical Branch's new series of 1:50,000 maps, after Alexander PROFIET, the first school teacher in the Mayo district, in 1914.

PROSPECTOR MOUNTAIN   62°27′N 137°48′W (115–I). In the Dawson Range.

This was proposed by H.S. Bostock, GSC, in 1934, to commemorate the prospectors of the Yukon whom he admired and respected. His liking for the working prospectors was only equalled by their respect and liking for him.

PTARMIGAN CREEK   62°07′N 130°07′W (105–J). Flows into the east end of Pelly Lake.

In 1893 Warburton Pike, an English gentleman-explorer, travelled the Liard River, Frances River and Frances Lake and examined this area. He named this creek because of the numbers of these birds he found upon it. (See Narchilla Brook.)

QUARTZ CREEK   63°45′N 139°07′W (115–O&N). Flows from King Solomon's Dome to the Indian River in the Klondike district.

Although the mouth of Quartz Creek was seen by prospectors working on the Indian River as early as 1887, it was probably named by William "Billy" Redford who found and mined the first gold in 1894. The creek gained its name as about 80% of the gravels are composed of quartz pebbles.

William Redford was born in Devon, England in 1861 and became a sailor. While on a whaling voyage, he reached the mouth of the Mackenzie River in 1891. The following year he went to southwestern Alaska and in 1893 crossed the Chilkoot Pass and went down to Fortymile.

In late 1893 or early 1894 he was the first to find and mine the gold of this stream, first on the bars and then in the deeper gravels. He staked a

Discovery claim near the mouth of Calder Creek (unnamed at the time). This was the first payable gold recorded on the east side of the Yukon River below the Stewart. Previous to this it had been the consensus of opinion among the miners of the region that none would be found in this part of the territory.

Joe Ladue, who had a trading post at the mouth of the Sixtymile River (Ogilvie), used Redford's find to encourage others, including Robert Henderson, to prospect in the area the following year. Thus, in the summer of 1896 about 20 men worked for Redford and others mining on the stream. A number of pre-1896 miners claimed that Henderson worked for Redford in the winter of 1895–96. The men who accompanied Henderson to Gold Bottom Creek that spring all came from Quartz Creek.

Because he obtained his supplies at Sixtymile Post which was only 45 miles away and the Mining Recorder was at Fortymile, 85 miles downstream, Redford did not bother to record his claim. It was safe in those days as long as he was working it. When Bonanza and Eldorado Creeks were discovered, Quartz was deserted except for Redford. The overflow of men from the Klondike in the summer of 1897 threatened his claim and he went to Dawson and recorded it in September. He was not allowed a Discovery claim as one had been filed on 11 August by D.D. Stewart, evidently on Redford's own claim. Also, another Discovery claim had been allowed to A. Mack, higher up the stream, on 20 August. However, the recorder seems to have reversed his decision sometime later and evidently returned Redford's claim to him.

Redford also found when recording his claim that the district had been divided into two mining divisions; the Klondike comprised all streams entering the Klondike River and the new Indian River division contained those streams running into the Indian River. This new partition was later used effectively to ignore Redford's claim to being the first to find payable gold in the Klondike, which enhanced Henderson's claims to that honour.

His priority was acknowledged by most of the pre-1896 miners and by R.G. McConnell, GSC, the noted explorer-geologist who made the first study of the Klondike goldfields and who included the south-flowing tributaries of the Indian River as part of the Klondike district.

Redford was a shy, self-effacing man who made few public claims. He mined on his Discovery claim continuously every year from 1894 to 1937, never making better than good wages. He died in St. Mary's Hospital in Dawson on 18 October, 1944, sadly neglected by history. A settlement grew up on his claim and lasted until the 1940's. (See Readford).

QUARTZ LAKE (See Hulse Lake.)

QUEBEC CREEK 64°10′N 139°33′W (116-B&C). **A tributary to the Yukon from the west, about two miles below Fort Reliance.**

S. Villeneuve, of Québec, named this stream when he and his partners first found gold and staked the creek.

MOUNT QUEBEC 12,300′ 60°56′N 140°42′W (115-B&C). **In the Centennial Range of the St. Elias Mountains.**

This was named in honour of the province of Québec during Canada's Centennial Year of 1967. (See Centennial Range.)

MOUNT QUEEN MARY 12,750′ 60°39′N 139°42′W (115-B&C). **In the centre of the St. Elias Icefield Ranges.**

This peak was named in 1935 by Bradford Washburn in honour of King George V and QUEEN MARY's Silver Jubilee Year. (See Mount King George.)

QUIET LAKE 61°05′N 133°05′W (105-F). **About 40 miles north of Johnson's Crossing, west of the Canol Road.**

John McCormack and three companions prospected up the Big Salmon River in the summer of 1887, as far as this lake. They named the lake, which almost always lives up to its name, when they prospected and named many of the streams which flow into it. McCormack gave Dr. G.M. Dawson, GSC, a good description of the river, the lake and the surrounding country when he met him later in the year.

QUILL CREEK 61°32′N 139°19′W (115-G&F). **A tributary of the Kluane River at mile 1112 (K1801) on the Alaska Highway.**

The creek probably received its name in the stampede to the Burwash Creek diggings in late 1904.

About 1952 Wellington Green, who had come into the Yukon in 1944 after prospecting in eastern Canada, California and BC, discovered a deposit of nickel-cobalt ore. The Hudson Bay Mining and Smelting Company developed the mine, naming it the Wellgreen, and brought it into production in June 1972. However, costs were high and the ore body proved limited, so they were forced to close in August 1973.

QUINN GULCH 63°46′N 138°53′W (115-O&N). **A small tributary**

to Sulphur Creek, one mile below the settlement of Sulphur.

William QUINN found the first gold here and named the stream on 28 August, 1897.

QUINTINO SELLA GLACIER 60°35′N 140°53′W (115–B&C). North of the Columbia Glacier in the St. Elias Range.

This was named by His Royal Highness, Prince Luigi Amadeo of Savoy, Duke of the Abruzzi, on his expedition to Mount St. Elias in 1887, after an illustrious pioneer of Italian mountain climbing.

RAABE'S HILLS 62°10′N 136°09′W (115–I). A low range of hills a few miles northeast of Tantalus Butte.

These hills were named in 1968 after Captain George RAABE of Portland, Oregon. He had piloted riverboats between Whitehorse and Dawson from 1900 to 20. Raabe's Slough, three miles above Tantalus Butte, although misspelled on some maps, is the backwater of the Yukon River in which he laid up his boats in the winter.

RACKLA RIVER 64°07′N 134°23′W (106–D). Tributary to the Beaver River. (North branch of the McQuesten River).

From 1897 this stream was called "Hell River" by the stampeders who came this way from Edmonton. The GSC, however, applied the local Indian name, without translation. It is swift and shallow, making for extremely difficult boating.

RADER LAKE 62°20′N 130°45′W (105–J). 20 miles northwest of Traffic Mountain.

Louis Thomas "Slim" RADER in his earlier years was an employee of the HBC in the NWT. It is said that he accompanied Peary's North Pole Expedition in 1909 as far as the Arctic coast. In the 1920 and 30's he trapped on the Mackenzie and Liard Rivers and moved into this part of the Yukon. He once spent a winter in the Nahanni Valley without supplies, living by his rifle. He managed the T&D trading post at Pelly Lakes from 1938 to 50. In the early 1960's he was caretaker of the Hudson Bay Quill Creek Mine after its closure.

Retiring to Haney, BC, he died on 31 July, 1967, liked and respected.

RAE CREEK 64°53′N 137°01′W (116–A). Flows north into the Hart River.

Frank RAE was an old-time trapper and prospector in this region. He had his cabin on Rae Lake (Worm Lake). He and his partner, Fred Hoffman, worked here in the 1930 and 40's.

RAILWAY SURVEY CREEK 62°10′N 134°00′W (105–L). A small creek flowing north into the Magundy River.

In 1942 Col. James J. Truitt, US Corps of Engineers, headed a survey group on a proposed railway location through this country, naming this creek on the way. (See Truitt Creek and Truitt Peak.)

RAMPART HOUSE 67°25′N 140°59′W (116–O&N). Just east of the Yukon-Alaska boundary, on the Porcupine River.

When Fort Yukon, the HBC post at the confluence of the Porcupine and Yukon Rivers, was closed after the American purchase of Alaska in 1867, it was moved to a site up the Porcupine River thought to be in Canadian territory. The new location was called "Rampart House" because of the steep banks of the river at that place. Turner's survey of 1889 showed that this post was also on American soil. They burned the post and moved farther upstream to this location where they were sure of being on Canadian ground.

For a time it was called "New Rampart House." The HBC abandoned this post and all others in the territory in 1894.

Dan Cadzow, a Scot and early Klondiker, opened a new trading post in the summer of 1905 and traded until 1911. In that year the settlement was again abandoned and burned, due to an outbreak of smallpox in the community. The people moved to a new community farther up the river at Old Crow.

RANCHERIA RIVER 60°13′N 129°07′W (105–A). A tributary to the Liard River, west of Watson Lake.

This is an old Californian or Mexican miners' term from the Spanish, meaning a native village or settlement.

When Dr. G.M. Dawson, GSC, passed this river in 1887 he found that the Cassiar miners had named the creek during the Sayyea Creek excitement in 1875–76.

RANKIN CREEK 64°01′N 134°55′W (106–D). Flows into the Keno Ladue River in the Mayo district.

This stream was named on 21 April, 1945, to honour the memory of

Captain Robert Lowe James RANKIN who was born on 29 May, 1910, in London, England. He enlisted in Toronto, Ontario on 3 June, 1941, and served in the Canadian army in Canada, Great Britain and northwest Europe. He was killed in action in France on 18 July, 1944.

RAY CREEK 62°40′N 138°38′W (115-J&K). A tributary to Rude Creek.

During the rush to the new placer gold finds on Dip and Rude Creeks in the fall of 1915, Peter Anderson and David RAY found the first gold on this stream and named it on 16 September, 1915.

RAY LAKE 60°21′N 137°11′W (115-A). West of Dezeadash Lake.

Irvine RAY was a well-known miner in the Whitehorse and Mayo districts. He mined on Shorty Creek in 1946. This creek was known locally by his name for many years and the name was made official in September 1973.

MOUNT RAYMOND 66°24′N 136°10′W (116-I). In the Richardson Mountains.

Born in Digby, Nova Scotia on 22 February, 1896, George Vail RAYMOND enlisted in the Canadian army at Dawson, YT, as a private in the Yukon Infantry Company on 2 October, 1916. He was appointed a second lieutenant in the RAF on 20 December, 1917 and was killed in action on 24 July, 1918. This mountain was named in his memory in 1973.

READFORD 63°47′N 139°07′W (115-O&N).

The postal department opened an office on Redford's Discovery claim on Quartz Creek on 19 August, 1905. There was a small settlement here at the time. The authorities called this first post office "Radford". It was closed from April 1934 to September 1934. On 16 November they changed the name to "Readford" when they re-opened. The office was closed permanently on 31 December, 1952; two tries in 47 years and the name was misspelled both times. (See Quartz Creek.)

READY BULLION CREEK 63°53′N 139°08′W (115-O&N). A tributary to Bonanza Creek.

This was named on 6 November, 1897, by the first staker, Peter Farrell, after the READY BULLION Mine at Juneau, Alaska in which he had been employed. This small stream produced good gold, almost the only stream on upper Bonanza Creek to do so.

REID HOUSE 63°32′N 137°25′W (115-P). Supposedly on the south bank of the Stewart River, near the mouth of the creek emptying the Reid Lakes.

All the above is supposition. The existence and location of Reid House is a genuine Yukon mystery. The first map to show any of the interior features of the Yukon Territory was John Arrowsmith's map, drawn in 1854 in London, England. Arrowsmith gained all his information about the central Yukon from Robert Campbell of the HBC, the first explorer, in 1853. This place was shown on Arrowsmith's map. Campbell, when interviewed later by Dr. G.M. Dawson, GSC, stated that no such place existed although he had had a John REID with him at Pelly Banks and Fort Selkirk in the years 1846 to 51. John Reid was also questioned by Dawson and denied any knowledge of such a settlement although he did state that there were a number of small lakes near this location where they obtained good numbers of fish and that a small hut or shelter had been built there while fishing.

Both Reid House and Reid Lakes were shown on almost every map of the territory until 1899. Reid Lakes are still there, sometimes spelled Reed.

MOUNT REID 60°10′N 135°28′W (105-D). On the north side of the Wheaton River between Skukum and Barney Creeks.

This feature was named in May 1911 after Percy REID, the Mining Recorder of the Conrad Mining Division which included this area. He was well regarded by the miners of that day.

REMINGTON PUP 63°52′N 138°51′W (115-O & N). A very short stream entering Dominion Creek one half-mile below Upper Discovery.

On 13 August, 1897, Edward REMINGTON found gold in this little gulch and staked the first claim.

REVENUE CREEK 62°21′N 137°17′W (115-I). Flows into Big Creek three miles above Seymour Creek, from the south.

This creek was named about 1940 by Fred Guder, who has sporadically worked placer gold here since then, because he said he could always win enough gold from the creek to get a grubstake. The present Yukon Revenue Mining Company bases its name on mineral deposits owned near the stream.

REVERSE CREEK 63°33′N 136°48′W (115-P). Tributary to Moose Creek.

Because this stream turns 180° to reverse its flow, H.S. Bostock, GSC, gave it the name in 1949 while mapping the geology of the area.

RICE CREEK 63°15′N 140°51′W (115-N). A tributary to the Ladue River from the north.

This stream was named in May 1920 by a GSC party after an old trapper of the name who was living here.

MOUNT RICHARDS 66°04′N 136°05′W (116-I). East of Canyon Creek.

This hill was named on 22 June, 1973 to honour the name and memory of R-252 612 Flight Sgt. Edward Gordon Coke RICHARDS. Born 10 October, 1916, at Strathmore, Alberta, he enlisted in the RCAF on 25 March, 1943. He was missing, presumed killed in action on 14 March, 1945.

RICHARDSON MOUNTAINS 67°55′N 136°40′W (116-P). This range parallels the Yukon-NWT boundary.

In 1825 John Franklin, RN, (later Sir,) named these mountains after Sir John RICHARDSON (1787-1865). An Arctic explorer in his own right, Richardson was the surgeon and naturalist on Franklin's land expeditions of 1819-20 and 1825-27 and later commanded a boat expedition in search of Franklin in 1848.

RICHTHOFEN ISLAND 61°06′N 135°10′W (105-E). On the west side of Lake Laberge.

In 1883 Lt. F. Schwatka, US Army, thought this was a peninsula and gave it the name "Richthofen Rocks". Dr. G. M. Dawson, GSC, corrected the error in 1887 but allowed the name to stand in honour of Freiherr von RICHTHOFEN of Leipzig, Germany, a famous geographer of the time.

The stream behind this island was called the "Red River" by the early miners because of the red rocks along its banks but the name was changed about 1930 or 40 to Richthofen Creek.

MOUNT RIDDELL 6,101′ 62°43′N 131°18′W (105-J). South of the MacMillan River.

In 1907 Joseph Keele, GSC, hired Robert B. RIDDELL to accompany him while he mapped the geology of the headwaters of the Pelly, Ross and Gravel Rivers, the first exploration of much of this area. Riddell had been the first white man to explore and trap in a great part of this region from about 1898 on.

Keele named this mountain in recognition of Riddell's character and services.

RIDDELL RIVER   62°50'N 132°24'W (105-K). A tributary of the upper MacMillan River.

In 1904 Captain Frederick C. Selous, the famed African white hunter and naturalist was assisted by Robert B. RIDDELL to obtain big game specimens for various museums. He admired Riddell for his hardihood in exploring this great tract of wilderness by himself, following no other white man. He noted the name of the river, which was the site of Riddell's home.

RIGHTHOOK CREEK   63°41'N 137°03'W (115-P). Flows into Vancouver Creek.

The outline of this creek when it was mapped suggested this boxing term to H.S. Bostock, GSC and his men in 1949.

RIGHT ON MOUNTAIN   61°06'N 138°47'W (115-G). Near the head of Congdon Creek.

This was named in October 1973 by junior members of the Yukon Scenic and Wilderness Study Project, from a then-current slang expression, "Right on . . . wow", which is intended to express approval.

RINK RAPIDS   62°19'N 136°23'W (115-I). Five miles downstream from Five Finger Rapids.

This name, after Dr. Henry RINK of Christiana, Denmark, an authority on Greenland and Director of the Royal Greenland Trade at Copenhagen, was originally applied to what is now Five Finger Rapids by Lt. F. Schwatka, US Army, in 1883. It was never used by travellers on the river and the name was transferred to this minor obstruction by Dr. G.M. Dawson, GSC, in 1887.

In the winter of 1902–03 most of the dangerous rocks were blasted from the channel by P.E. Mercier, Territorial Engineer.

ROAL CREEK   64°19'N 140°00'W (116-B&C). Enters the Yukon River from the west about five miles above Cassiar Creek.

This creek was named after Louis ROAL who prospected this area and found lead-zinc ore near here in the 1920's.

ROBBED CREEK   60°07′N 137°02′W (115–A). A tributary to the Tatshenshini River at Dalton Post.

H.S. Bostock, GSC, named this creek in 1949 while mapping the area. The headwaters of this stream were diverted by glacial action and now flow into Pirate Creek.

ROBERT SERVICE CREEK   64°27′N 138°13′W (116–B&C). A tributary to the North Klondike River. (See below.)

MOUNT ROBERT SERVICE   62°25′N 138°11′W (116–B&C). At the headwaters of the North Klondike River.

These names were proposed in 1968 by Dr. Dirk Tempelman-Kluit, GSC, to commemorate the Bard of the Yukon, author of "The Cremation of Sam McGee" and other verses.

ROBINSON   60°27′N 134°51′W (105–D). A way station on the WP&YR about 22 miles south of Whitehorse.

In late 1899 the WP&YR built a way station here while constructing the railway. It was given the name of their labour foreman and construction man *extraordinare*, "Stikine Bill" ROBINSON.

William C. ROBINSON was from North Anson, Maine. He had followed railroad construction across the continent. In early 1898 he was general foreman during the short-lived MacKenzie and Mann attempt to build a railroad from Glenora, on the Stikine River, to the foot of Teslin Lake. He acquired his nickname on that job.

Mike Heney, the contractor who built the WP&YR, hired him in the same capacity. In addition, he was put in charge of the early freighting from the Summit to Bennett and Whitehorse, using both horse-teams and boats.

From 1908 to 12 he assisted Heney in building the 136-mile-long Copper River and Northwestern Railway from Cordova to Chitina and on to the enormously rich Kennecott Copper Mines. He continued to engage in prospecting and mining ventures in Alaska until he died on 29 September, 1926.

W.P. Grainger and H.W. Vance, prominent miners of Whitehorse, surveyed a townsite here in 1906 when the mineral wealth of the Wheaton River area to the west appeared capable of major production. A post office was open here from 1909 to 15.

ROCK RIVER 67°17′N 137°06′W (116–P). **A tributary to the Bell River.**

On 19 June, 1847, Alexander Hunter Murray of the HBC found and named this stream the "Blue Fish River". This name was later changed to avoid redundancy with the "Blue Fish River" near Ramparts on the Porcupine, in Alaska.

ROCQUETTE ROCKS (See Old Woman Rock.)

RODIN CREEK 63°51′N 136°18′W (115–P). **A tributary of the South McQuesten River.**

A prospector named RODIN (or Roden) found and mined gold on this creek in 1907.

ROLAND CREEK 69°22′N 138°57′W (117–D). **Flows into the Spring River on the Arctic coast.**

Anker Hoidal, who spent his lifetime trapping and prospecting in the Arctic Yukon, said that this stream had been known by this name after an Eskimo who lived on it for more than 30 years, beginning in the 1920's. (See Anker and Hoidal Creeks.)

ROSE CREEK 62°25′N 132°41′W (105–K). **A tributary of Anvil Creek on the north side of Rose Mountain.**

Oliver ROSE came into the Yukon over the Edmonton Trail in 1897–98. He came up the Pelly to prospect and settled here for the remainder of his life. The RNWMP reports of the time indicate that his name was probably Olivier LaRose and that his birthplace was in Québec. They also note that he was a solitary, hard-working and well-regarded man.

On 17 September, 1905, Charles Sheldon, noted big-game hunter and naturalist, while collecting specimens for American museums in the region, met Rose and named this stream where he lived. (See below.)

ROSE MOUNTAIN 6,513′ 62°20′N 133°35′W (105–K). **On the north side of the Pelly River about 12 miles west of Faro.**

Oliver ROSE had his home and a small trading post at the foot of this mountain on the Pelly River. It was known as Rose's Cabin. Charles Sheldon, the American naturalist, gave the mountain its name on 13 September, 1905. (See above.)

ROSE RIVER 61°10′N 132°59′W (105–F). **A tributary of the Nisutlin River near the foot of Quiet Lake.**

In the early 1900's Oliver ROSE prospected extensively in the area between here and the Pelly. Lapie Creek and Rose River give an almost complete waterway from the Pelly to Quiet Lake. (See Rose Creek and Mountain.)

ROSEBUD CREEK   63°17′N 138°26′W (115-O&N). A tributary of the Stewart River.

Alexander MacDonald (not "Big Alex") from New Brunswick, explored and prospected the Stewart River in 1887 or even earlier. He found some gold showings on this stream and named it, probably after the Battle of the ROSEBUD River in the Sioux Wars in the American west during the 1870's, in which it was thought he took part. (It is believed that he also named Black Hills Creek in the same vicinity.)

ROSS CREEK   63°53′N 136°02′W (115-P). A tributary of the South McQuesten River.

An early prospector named ROSS found placer gold here and named the creek about 1898–99. He remained in the country for many years. (See the other Ross Creek.)

ROSS CREEK   64°00′N 137°33′W (115-P). A tributary to the Little South Klondike River.

ROSS came into the country during the gold rush. He prospected and lived in the area until the 1930's. He was the first to find gold on this stream but there was not enough to pay. (See the other Ross Creek; both were named by or for the same man.)

ROSS RIVER   61°59′N 132°26′W (105-F). At the junction of the Ross and Pelly Rivers.

This settlement was first established by Tom Smith about 1903 but was soon sold to Poole Field and Clement Lewis who named it "Nahanni House", because a number of Indians from the Nahanni country in the NWT had followed them to this area to trap and trade.
The post was later taken over by the Whitehorse firm of Taylor and Drury. It continued under various owners until 1945.

ROSS RIVER   61°59′N 132°26′W (105-F). A major tributary of the Pelly River.

In 1843 Robert Campbell of the HBC made his famous first journey down the Pelly River to its junction with the Yukon. During this journey he named most of the tributaries of the Pelly. This was named after Chief Factor Donald ROSS of the HBC.

ROWLINSON CREEK 62°03′N 136°17′W (115-I). Flows into the Nordenskiold River three miles south of Carmacks.

D.D. Cairnes, GSC, while mapping this part of the country in 1911, recorded this name from Seymour ROWLINSON who was living and mining on the stream. He had been the first to find the gold and had then been here for a number of years.

ROY LAKE 60°32′N 127°49′W (95-D). A small lake immediately east of Hulse (Quartz) Lake.

In February 1970 this lake was named by James Harquail, President of Fort Reliance Minerals Ltd., to commemorate Andrew ROY. In the summer of 1968 Roy had been camp cook for the company's exploration crew and had lost his life in an aircraft crash on the lake on 2 September, 1968.

ROYAL MOUNTAIN 6,567′ 65°02′N 135°04′W (106-E). East of Wind River in the Wernecke Mountains.

In September 1897 George Mitchell of Montréal and his party were trapped here by winter. They were on their way to the Klondike via Edmonton, the Mackenzie, Peel and Wind Rivers. They established a small community near the mouth of the Wind River called "Wind City". Mitchell named this peak that winter because it reminded him of the shape of MOUNT ROYAL.

He later published an account of his experiences under the title, *The Golden Grindstone.*

RUBE CREEK 66°36′N 138°14′W (116-J&K). Tributary to the Porcupine River.

This name was officially proposed on 27 November, 1958, by Professor Otto William Geist of the University of Alaska after RUBE Mason. Geist stated in the application that Rube and his brother Bill were noted trappers and "highly esteemed individuals". This area was their trapping grounds and this stream was locally known as "Mason" and "Rube Mason" Creek. (See Mason Lake.)

RUBY CREEK 61°05′N 137°56′W (115-H). A small stream joining Lake Creek to flow south into Jarvis River.

The Discovery claim on this stream was staked and the creek named by

W.H. Weisdepp on 6 July, 1903, and the stampede to the Shakwak Valley goldfields was on.

The *Whitehorse Star*, on July 27, 1903, reported, "The arrival of an Indian in the town of Whitehorse in July last, with a small quantity of gold, which he said he obtained near the surface on a creek in the Shakwak district, brought this part of the Yukon into greater prominence. The Indian who made the discovery informed several other Indians who immediately started for that part. They returned after ten days and several claims were recorded on a creek they called 'Ruby'. A general stampede then took place, close upon five hundred persons went out and staked, returned and recorded. (Skookum Jim Mason and Dawson Charlie were among the first)."

The creek was worked out within a few years. During this period a small settlement of the same name grew up at the mouth of the stream, with a post office, roadhouse and stores. It died with the decline of the stream.

RUDE CREEK 62°40'N 138°43'W (115-J&K). A tributary to Dip Creek in the Dawson Range.

Jens RUDE and his partner were extremely active prospectors in this area. They found good gold on this stream and staked the Discovery claim on it on 12 March, 1915. They worked the gravels here for several years.

RUNT CREEK 66°16'N 141°00'W (116-J&K). A small tributary to the Salmon Fork, across the Yukon-Alaska boundary.

This little stream got its name from surveyors of the International Boundary Commission, in 1908.

RUSSELL COL 60°19'N 140°55'W (115-B&C). The connecting ridge between Mount St. Elias and Mount Newton.

This feature was named to honour Professor Israel C. RUSSELL, USGS, who first mapped this area and named Mount Logan. He made three expeditions to the Yukon. On the first, in 1889, he went by boat from St. Michaels to Fort Selkirk, continued up the Yukon River with a group of miners and emerged at Dyea, after exploring in the White River area. In 1890 and '91 he crossed the Chilkoot Pass and again ascended the White River to the Mount St. Elias region where he continued his mapping and explorations. He added greatly to the knowledge of this part of the territory. It was probably named in 1891 by the USGS.

RUSSELL CREEK 63°03'N 133°26'W (105-N). Tributary to the Mac-Millan River, just below the forks.

Thomas Duncan Gillies (or Gillis) prospected in the Yukon from 1892. In the winter of 1896–97 he was at his home in Nova Scotia when he received news of the Klondike discovery. He returned via Edmonton and the Mac-kenzie River, thence up the Gravel (Keele) River, across the continental divide and down the MacMillan River, mistaking it for the Hess. Pros-pecting along the way, he panned good gold at the mouth of this creek, which he named "Slate Creek" from the rocks thereon. He spent several weeks prospecting the stream and was caught by winter. Having few sup-plies and being unable to raft because of the ice, he was forced to walk overland to Fort Selkirk. He suffered great hardships and privations but arrived safely.

Returning the next year with partners he was encouraged to obtain a con-cession which was granted to him in 1900, when he changed the name of the stream to Russell Creek. The reason for the change is not known.

N.A.D. Armstrong, acting for an English company, bought out the con-cession and worked it unprofitably for many years. (See Mount Arm-strong.)

MOUNT RUSSELL 67°44'N 136°30'W (116-P). On the north side of MacDougall Pass on the Yukon-NWT border.

This peak was named by William Ogilvie, DLS, on his journey from Fortymile to Fort MacPherson in May 1888.

RUSSELL RANGE 63°13'N 133°10'W (105-N). North of the upper MacMillan River near the forks.

This was named about the turn of the century, or slightly earlier, after Mark RUSSELL, a noted pioneer Yukon prospector. He ranged far and wide in Alaska and the Yukon. He accompanied Dr. C.W. Hayes, USGS, and Lt. F. Schwatka, US Army, in 1891 from Juneau up the Taku to Teslin Lake and on into the White River country, probably the first to make the journey.

SABBATH CREEK 63°47'N 136°21'W (115-P). A tributary to Johnson Creek from the west.

Rudolph Rasmussen found the first gold on this stream on a Sunday and staked the Discovery claim on 8 August, 1909.

SABINE POINT 69°04′N 137°44′W (117-D). On the Arctic coast.

John Franklin, RN, named this in 1825 after Major General Sir Edward SABINE, RA, (1788–1883), a celebrated British astronomer and physicist. He was astronomer to the first John Ross expedition of 1818 and to the Parry expedition of 1819–20. He was President of the British Association in 1853 and of the Royal Society from 1861 to 71.

MOUNT ST. CYR 6,725′ 61°21′N 133°10′W (105-F). Ten miles north of Quiet Lake.

This mountain was named about 1901 after Arthur ST. CYR, DLS, QLS. He was sent by the Department of the Interior of the Dominion government in May 1897 to find and survey a possible wagon or railway route from Telegraph Creek on the Stikine River to the head of Teslin Lake for the expected hordes of gold-seekers. The government wished it to be an all-Canadian route. This task he accomplished that summer, exploring several alternate routes and carrying his surveys not only to Teslin Lake but also along the lake and up the Teslin River to the Lewes.

He continued this work through 1898, and in 1899 to 1901 he was engaged in surveying the boundary between the Yukon and BC.

The St. Cyr Range was named later.

MOUNT ST. ELIAS 18,008′ 60°17′N 140°56′W (115-B&C). At the southwest corner of the Yukon Territory.

This mountain, sometimes called "the corner post of Alaska", was first seen by Vitus Bering on ST. ELIAS Day, 16 July, 1741. Bering, a Dane employed by the Russian government to explore the coast of Alaska, commanded the ship *St. Peter.* This mountain was the first feature in the Yukon Territory to be named by white men.

The first attempt to climb it was made by Lt.F. Schwatka, US Army, in 1886. His expedition was a fiasco which barely got off the beach and turned back in a few days. The peak was first climbed by Prince Luigi Amadeo of Savoy, nephew of King Humbert of Italy, and his party in the summer of 1897.

ST. GERMAIN CREEK 61°25′N 134°24′W (105-E). A tributary to the Big Salmon River.

Joseph ST. GERMAIN of Québec, discovered payable gold and named this stream in the fall of 1900.

SALTER HILL 66°09′N 134°49′W (106–L). West of Peel River.

A map-designation name, this peak was given the name of Maxwell Charles SALTER, a Yukon Councillor for South Dawson from 1917 to 20.

SAMBO CREEK 60°25′N 129°33′W (105–A). Flows into the upper Liard River, east of Frances Lake.

"Old SAMBO" or "Old Sam" lived and trapped on this creek, and the lake of the same name at its head, for many years. Interviewed in 1942 shortly before he died, he could remember white men and former black slaves (from the underground railway between the southern United States and Canada) searching for gold along the Dease River in the 1870's.

MOUNT SAMPSON 11,000′ 61°12′N 140°03′W (115–F). East of the Steele Glacier in the St. Elias Range.

This was named in 1970 by the Alpine Club of Canada after Herbert E. SAMPSON (1871–1962), a lawyer and past president of the club (1930–32).

SAMUELSON HILL 2,057′ 66°19′N 137°11′W (116–I). East of the Canoe River.

In June 1973 this hill was named in memory of Helmer SAMUELSON. Born in Dawson, he served in the Second World War. He was owner, editor and printer of the *Dawson News* and, later, of the *Whitehorse Star.*

SANPETE CREEK 62°14′N 140°24′W (115–J&K). Crosses the Alaska Highway at mile 1175 (K1903).

This stream was named about the turn of the century by a prospector from SANPETE County, Utah.

SAPPER HILL 65°21′N 138°16′W (116–G). On the east side of the Ogilvie River.

James Smith, Commissioner of the Yukon Territory, in 1971 requested this name to honour the Royal Canadian Engineers for their work. In the summer of that year they had built the George Allan Jeckell Bridge over the Ogilvie River near here.

The name "Sapper" is a nickname given to all army engineers and dates from medieval days when they were employed mostly to dig "saps" or tunnels under enemy fortifications.

**MOUNT SASKATCHEWAN   11,390′ 60°57′N 140°51′W (115–B&C).
In the Centennial Range of the St. Elias Mountains.**

This peak was named for the province of Saskatchewan in Canada's Centennial Year of 1967. (See Centennial Range.)

SATAH RIVER   67°00′N 134°34′W (106–L). A tributary to the Peel River.

The Compte V.E. de Sainville, French sportsman and explorer, named this river in 1893. He was exploring this portion of the North West Territories and the Yukon and met here a band of Indians whose chief was SATAH.

SAVAGE GULCH 63°47′N 136°19′W (115–P). A small stream flowing into Johnson Creek from Scheelite Dome.

A prospector of this name found and worked a placer gold deposit here in the early 1900's.

SAYYEA CREEK   60°45′N 130°21′W (105–B). A tributary of the upper Liard River.

This small, little-known creek is the location of the first gold mined in the Yukon Territory.

Historical writings on the Yukon usually concentrate on the miners who entered the territory by way of the Chilkoot Pass and up the Yukon River. They begin with Harper and Mayo unsuccessfully prospecting the upper reaches of the White River in the fall and winter of 1873–74 from the lower Yukon, and with George Holt who was the first known white man to cross the Chilkoot Pass, finding little but prospects in the summer of 1875.

The first known payable gold mined in the watershed of the Yukon River was obtained by a miner named Cummins and his three partners from a small stream about 15 miles above Miles Canyon, in 1880.

However, in 1874 John SAYYEA and three companions came from Dease Lake up the Liard River, discovered gold on this stream and remained to mine it during the winter of 1874–75. From 115 days work they recovered 77 ³/₁₆ ounces of coarse gold, including nuggets of over an ounce in weight. Their find started a rush from the Cassiar goldfields in the spring of 1875 and gold was found on several nearby creeks. After Sayyea's first find no other payable deposits were worked, due mostly to problems of water in the deeper gravels. There was enough encouragement to keep prospectors active in this part of the Yukon until the time of the Klondike rush. The drawback to prospecting the Yukon Territory from this direction was the extreme difficulty of the route from either the Cassiar country or the Mackenzie valley. Either way was much more difficult and longer than by way of the Chilkoot Pass and the upper Liard Canyon was itself a much greater hazard than Miles Canyon. In fact, it was mainly the dangers of this route that had influenced the HBC to abandon its posts in the region in 1852. (See Cabin, Scurvy and Squaw Creeks, also Finlayson and Hyland Rivers.)

SCHAEFFER CREEK   67°50′N 139°51′W (116-O&N). A tributary of the Old Crow River.

Albert E. SCHAEFFER, a German trapper, married into the Old Crow Band. With his family he trapped the numerous muskrats in this part of the Old Crow Flats and the creek has been known locally by this name for many years. Schaeffer died of scurvy in Dawson in 1940.

The mountain in the bend of the river was named much later.

MOUNT SCHELLINGER 65°29′N 132°39′W (106-F). East of the Snake River.

In February 1973 this mountain was named after Arthur K. SCHELLINGER who was a mining engineer with the Yukon Consolidated Gold Co. of Dawson for many years, and then from 1920 to 30 worked for Keno Hill Mines Ltd., and the Treadwell Yukon Mining Company at Mayo. He was a well-known and well-regarded man.

SCHNABEL CREEK   60°19′N 134°59′W (105-D). Flows into Annie Lake at the big bend of the Wheaton River.

William F. SCHNABEL came into the Yukon in 1897. In 1898 he was the first man known to prospect Gray Ridge and that summer he found a coal seam on this creek. His wife was the first white woman in this part of the country; they lived in the district until they moved to Oregon in 1914.

Schnabel was nicknamed "Cowboy", as he never walked anywhere that he could ride a horse.

SCHWATKA LAKE 60°41′N 135°02′W (105-D). Above the power dam on the Yukon River at Whitehorse.

This lake was formed behind the hydro-electric power plant and dam on the Yukon River at Whitehorse. The lake covers the dreaded Whitehorse Rapids and Squaw Rapids and has eliminated the swift currents through Miles Canyon. This was accomplished and the plant put into operation in 1959.

Lt. Frederick SCHWATKA was born 29 September, 1849, in Galena, Illinois. His family moved west and he attended Willamette University in Oregon until he was accepted at West Point Military Academy from which he was graduated in 1871. Studying while serving at various western army posts, he acquired degrees in law and medicine.

In 1879–80 he led an expedition to the Canadian Arctic in search of the lost Franklin Expedition, which established his reputation as an Arctic explorer.

In 1883, under orders from General Nelson A. Miles, Commander of the Department of the Columbia (which included Alaska) and without notice to the Canadian authorities, he crossed the Chilkoot Pass and rafted down the Yukon River. Pte. Charles A. Homan, his topographer, made a rough but fairly accurate survey of the course of the river, the first to that time. Schwatka ignored all previous and contemporary nomenclature of the region. He seems to have assumed that no one had given names to any feature in the country before him so he named most of the rivers and lakes and some prominent hills along his route after his superior officers and prominent academicians of his day. He discarded Robert Campbell's "Lewes" River and changed it to the Yukon and named Lake Lindeman as the source of the Yukon River without investigating the Teslin or the Pelly. Dr. G.M. Dawson, GSC, disallowed most of Schwatka's names but allowed others to stand because of the international figures they honoured. Another reason was that Schwatka's work was incorporated into a map issued in 1885 by the USCGS. This was the best map of the region until the GSC issued those made by Dawson and Ogilvie in 1888.

Schwatka led an expedition in 1886 to climb Mount St. Elias, sponsored by George Jones of *The New York Times*. Schwatka was accompanied by William Libby of the College of New Jersey and by the only member of the party with any Alpine experience, Heywood W. Seton-Karr, an English sportsman and naturalist. It was remarked that for Seton-Karr to try to guide the 250-pound Schwatka up a 19,000 foot mountain would be a "quixotic enterprise". The party was away from the beach only nine or ten days and Mount St. Elias remained unclimbed.

In 1891, with C. Willard Hayes, USGS, and Mark Russell (a noted pioneer prospector who had made the trip previously), he went from Juneau via the Taku and Teslin Lake to Fort Selkirk and into the basin of the White River.

Schwatka early realized the value of publicity and rapidly published many glowing accounts of his travels, always emphasizing the hardships and dangers encountered. He became a member of many prestigious scientific societies and died in Portland, Oregon, on 2 November, 1892.

SCOTCH CREEK   63°05′N   139°19′W   (115–O&N).   The first tributary on the left up Thistle Creek.

This was named in late 1898 by someone of the party of eight Scots who first discovered the gold of Thistle Creek.

SCOTTIE CREEK   62°38′N   141°00′W   (115–J&K).   A tributary to the Chisana River in Alaska.

W.J. Peters and A.H. Brooks, USGS, named this stream for a member of their 1898 geological survey party. Gold was found in the gravels of the creek during the Chisana gold rush of 1913. It was sometimes called "Scotty" or "Big Scotty" Creek.

SCOUGALE CREEK   64°12′N   134°43′W   (106–D).   A tributary of the Beaver River.

This was named in the early 1900's by James A. SCOUGALE, a pioneer prospector in the Mayo district, who lived and mined here.

SCOUT LAKE   60°47′N   135°25′W   (105–D).   South of the Takhini River.

This lake was officially named in November 1973. A Boy Scout summer camp has been located here for a number of years.

SCOUTCAR CREEK   64°19′N   138°26′W   (116–B&C).   Crosses the Dempster Highway into the North Klondike River.

This was probably named in 1969 when highway construction workers bogged down such a vehicle in the stream.

SCROGGIE CREEK   63°12′N   138°51′W   (115–O&N). A tributary of the Stewart River.

Ernest R. SCROGGIE of Rawdon, Québec, led a party of nine prospectors into this area in the summer of 1898. On 27 August two of the men, J.G. Stephens of Deadwood, North Dakota and H. LeDuke of Québec, found the first gold and staked the Discovery claim. The remainder of the party staked claims and the creek was named by Wealthy T. SCROGGIE, a brother of Ernest.

The creek has produced gold sporadically up to the present time.

SCURVY CREEK   60°49'N 130°32'W (105-B). A tributary of the upper Liard River.

Gold was found here in the summer of 1874 by Cassiar miners working north from the Dease Lake country. The journey was arduous and some miners wintered on this and neighbouring creeks rather than face the difficult trip back to the Dease Lake country.

In the following winter at least four of these men died of scurvy and were buried near the mouth of the creek, on the banks of the Liard. The remaining men were saved by three of their number who walked to Laketon (on Dease Lake) in March 1875, for help. The Victoria *Colonist* of 21 July, 1875, carried a letter from McDame Creek;

"I think it my duty to notify you of the great suffering of the Deloire (Liard) pioneers from the scurvy. Four have died from the said disease and ten others had a narrow escape. The only thing that saved them was three of their number coming out on the ice and getting to Laketown on 12 March, to report the suffering that four of their number endured at the time of their leaving them, I may mention the date, 12 February. We all subscribed at Laketown, and in two days we dispatched one white man and an Indian with medicine, rum, vegetables, potatoes, lime-juice, vinegar, etc. which the sick men received in sixteen days. Those who got here on the 19th inst. state that only for what was sent from here more than half of the sick men would have perished. The four who died were ailing all winter and were too far gone by the time they received the medicines . . . . The unfortunate men have died easy deaths. They got frozen in with their boats on 25 October 1874."

SEAFORTH CREEK   60°27'N 133°34'W (105-C). Flows north across the Alaska Highway into Squanga Lake.

This is an early name thought to have been given by a trapper who had seen service in the famous Seaforth Highlanders Regiment. During the construction of the highway the name was changed to "John Creek" by US Army Engineers but the name soon reverted to the original.

SEAGULL CREEK   60°00'N 131°11'W (105-B). Tributary to Swift River at mile 734 (K1189) on the Alaska Highway.

This was named by US Army Engineer troops during highway construction in 1942 because of the vast numbers of these birds that visited the camp's garbage dumps nearby.

On the mountainside east of this creek about 1960, Jack Shields found the only gem quality topaz ever found in the Yukon.

SECRET CREEK   63°57′N 135°58′W (105-M). A tributary of Haggart Creek.

Narcisse A. Lefebvre and Isaac Mallette found gold and named this stream on 7 September, 1911, giving the name because the stream enters Haggart Creek in such a way as to be nearly hidden from view. They mined their claims until August 1914.

MOUNT SEDGEWICK   2,956′ 68°53′N 139°09′W (117-A). In the Buckland Mountains near the Arctic coast.

John Franklin, (later Sir) on his second expedition in 1826, named this mountain after Adam SEDGEWICK (1785-1873), the famous British geologist.

SEGUIN LAKES   66°43′N 134°22′W (106-L). East of the Peel River.

In April 1973 this map-designation name was given to commemorate Alavie J. SEGUIN, who was a Yukon Councillor for North Dawson from 1912 to 15.

MOUNT SELOUS   7,138′ 62°58′N 132°28′W (105-K). North of the South MacMillan River.

This mountain, the highest peak in the Russell Range, was named about 1907 after Frederick Courtenay SELOUS by Joseph Keele, GSC. Selous had hunted here in 1904 and 1906 for specimens of big game. He was a noted naturalist as well as a famous African white hunter. Most of his hunting was for trophy specimens which were carefully preserved for various museums. From 1870 to 90 he hunted areas in Africa in which no other white man had ever set foot, finding and procuring new species of animals for museums at his own expense.

He died as a captain in the 25th Royal Fusiliers of the British army, decorated for bravery with the DSO, leading his troops in battle against the German army in East Africa. He was 65 years old when he was killed.

The peak had previously been known as "Chang Mountain", a name given it by N.A.D. Armstrong who mined on nearby Russell Creek for many years.

SELWYN MOUNTAINS   65°00′N 135°00′W (105-O). Paralleling the Yukon-NWT boundary.

The Selwyn Mountains comprise three ranges: the Logan, Hess and Wernecke Mountains. They were named in 1901 by Joseph Keele, GSC, after Dr. Alfred Richard Cecil SELWYN (1824-1902). Born in Somerset,

England, he was one of the most distinguished geologists of his time. He was with the Geographical Survey of Great Britain from 1845 to 52. From then until 1869 he was Director of the Geological Survey of Australia and from that date until his retirement in 1895 he was the Director of the Geological Survey of Canada. His contribution to the science was immense in all three countries. In Canada alone, he organized, expanded and directed the Geological and Natural History Survey after Confederation.

SELWYN RIVER   62°48′N 138°17′W (115-J&K). A small tributary to the Yukon River.

Lt. F. Schwatka, US Army, named this stream in 1883 after Dr. A.R.C. SELWYN, Director of the Geological and Natural History Survey of Canada. The name was allowed by Dawson. There was a small settlement at the mouth of the stream from 1900 to about 1950, as a telegraph post and a wood point for riverboats.

The river was prospected in 1885 by a man named Duval, an ex-jailer from Tacoma, Washington. In August 1898 he returned and staked a Discovery claim which he soon sold. Little gold was found on the stream and it was afterwards claimed that he had salted his claim, — i.e. that he had sprinkled gold dust in the gravels to make the claim appear richer than it actually was.

SEMINOF HILLS   61°27′N 134°35′W (105-E). The range of hills on the east side of the Yukon and Teslin Rivers.

Lt. F. Schwatka gave this low range of hills the name of von SEMINOF, President of the Imperial Geographical Society of Russia, in 1883. Sometimes spelled Semenof, or Semenov.

SERGERENT CREEK   61°44′N 140°12′W (115-F). A tributary of the Koidern River.

This was named about 1923 (officially in 1949) after a French big game hunter of this name who hunted here in 1913 and again in 1923. He was outfitted and guided by Gene Jacquot of Burwash. Buck Dixon, a well-known guide in the area, supplied the name to the GSC.

SERPENTHEAD LAKE   61°40′N 138°45′W (115-G&F). At the north end of Talbot Arm of Kluane Lake.

From the hills above, the lake resembles a striking snake head. H.S. Bostock, GSC, thought so in 1945 when he and his men were mapping the geology of the district.

MOUNT SETHER 5,296' 63°20'N 136°13'W (115-P). On the south side of Ethel Lake.

Although this mountain was named in June 1967, the creek which flows from it to Ethel Lake was prospected many years before by Ole SETHER, who found and worked on a gold-quartz vein nearby.

SETTLEMIER CREEK 64°28'N 135°14'W (106-D). A tributary to the Beaver River in the Wernecke Mountains.

Charles SETTLEMIER was an editor of the Dawson *Daily News* in the 1920's. He prospected widely in the Mayo area then and in the 1930's. This creek was named when he found silver-lead ore near it in 1923. The hill on the east side of the creek was later given the name Settlemier Ridge.

SEVENTEEN MILE 63°28'N 136°18'W (115-P). On the south bank of the Stewart River.

This was the location of an old riverboat wood camp. Louis Brown's roadhouse on the old Mayo winter trail was nearby. It has been long abandoned.

SEYMOUR CREEK 62°21'N 137°10'W (115-I). A tributary to Big Creek in the Mount Freegold area.

In 1899 Captain Henry SEYMOUR Back prospected in this area. He returned in 1910 with a party of men to re-prospect the region. In 1916 he developed gold prospects on this creek and gave it his name. His party found gold not only here but on many nearby streams. Back originally named the main stream after the famous British First World War Commander in Chief, Field Marshall Lord Kitchener of Sudan. The east fork he named Seymour. The name Kitchener was never adopted. (See Back Creek.)

SHATLAH MOUNTAIN 4,166' 67°37'N 140°05'W (116-O&N). Eight miles northwest of Old Crow village.

Named in 1973 to confirm a long-known local name, the Vanta Kutchin Indian word means "Long Hair."

SHAW CREEK 64°02'N 139°33'W (116-B&C). A very short creek on the south side of the Yukon River about five miles above Dawson.

This creek, really a gulch about one quarter-mile long, saw an exciting stampede in September 1903. Fred SHAW and Fred Jorgenson found good coarse gold and half the town of Dawson ran all the way to stake claims. The Mining Recorder named the creek.

SHEEP CREEK   60°58′N 138°34′W (115–B&C). A tributary of Slim's River.

The creek was named when placer gold was discovered and staked in October 1903 by the well known prospectors, Ater, Altemose, Smith and Bones.

SHELDON LAKE   62°42′N 131°03′W (105–J). On the Ross River near the south MacMillan, east of the Canol Road.

This lake was named "Rudyard Lake" in 1900 by Poole Field and Clement Lewis, early traders and sometime prospectors in the area. The name was common locally until Joseph Keele, GSC, mapped the region in 1907. He named it for Charles SHELDON, wealthy American sportsman and amateur naturalist who had hunted and camped in the area in 1905.

MOUNT SHELDON   6,937′ 62°44′N 131°05′W (105–J). Three miles north of Sheldon Lake.

In 1900 Poole Field and Clement Lewis of the Ross River trading post "Nahanni House", named this peak "Kipling Mountain" in conjunction with Rudyard Lake at its base. Joseph Keele, GSC, however, renamed them both after Charles SHELDON in 1907.

SHELL CREEK   64°31′N 140°26′W (116–B&C). Flows into the Yukon River about five miles below Fortymile, from the east.

William Ogilvie, DLS, named this stream in the summer of 1896 when he found fossil shells in the rocks along its banks.

SHOALWATER BAY   68°53′N 136°43′W (117–A). An arm of Mackenzie Bay on the Arctic coast.

John Franklin sailed into this bay in 1826 and named it after running aground several times. (See Pillage Point.)

SHOOTAMOOK CREEK   60°49′N 131°00′W (105–B). A tributary to Scurvy Creek.

Billy Smith, Chief of the Tagish Band and a trapper and prospector, found gold on this creek in 1936 and named it "Shomdenook" which means "Rising Up" and probably relates to an Indian legend of a mythical golden man.

240

SHORTY CREEK 60°24'N 137°10'W (115–A). Flows to Alder Creek.

The man who found gold here in May or June 1896 and named the stream was an extraordinary character. "Long SHORTY" Bigelow was a pioneer in the Haines-Kluane country before 1894. He helped drive the first herd of cattle over the Dalton Trail in 1895. In 1903 he was sentenced to 15 years at hard labour in San Quentin Penitentiary in California by a St. Michaels judge after committing armed robbery on the Lower Yukon River. In 1909 he was granted a pardon when friends brought to the attention of the government the fact that he had once, in the dead of winter, hauled a crippled woman in a hand sled from the Big Salmon River to Skagway.

Returning to the country he married an Indian woman and afterward lived a quieter life.

SHUTDUNMUN LAKE 61°07'N 137°45'W (115–H). On upper Lake Creek.

This small lake which lies on the old Indian trail between Sekulmun Lake and the Jarvis River is called, in the local Indian dialect, "The Rest Place." The name was officially adopted in July 1962.

MOUNT SIBBALD 10,050' 61°14'N 140°01'W (115–G&F). On the east side of the Steele Glacier.

This was named in November 1970 after Andrew S. SIBBALD (1888-1945), lawyer and past president of the Alpine Club of Canada (1934-1938). The name was proposed by the club.

SIDNEY CREEK 60°46'N 132°57'W (105–C). A tributary to the Nisutlin River below Quiet Lake.

Gold was discovered on this stream in 1902 by Jim Thompson. News of the find started a rush to the district in June and July 1905 when he first thought he had found payable gold. He also found the first gold prospects and named Willow and Marble Creeks in the same area.

SIFTON RANGE 60°58'N 136°15'W (115–A). Small range of hills about 15 miles northeast of Champagne.

These hills were named before 1898 after the Hon. Clifford SIFTON, Minister of the Interior, 1896-1906, who had the unprecedented task of setting up the government apparatus of the Yukon Territory in 1897–98 under the most difficult conditions. This he did with outstanding ability and competence.

SIMPSON LAKE   60°44′N   129°15′W   (105–A). On the west side of the Frances River, 50 miles north of Watson Lake.

In the summer of 1834, Chief Factor John McLeod of the HBC ascended the Liard River from the Mackenzie to the Frances River (which he called the Liard). He travelled the Frances as far north as this lake which he named after Sir George SIMPSON, the Governor of the HBC. This was the first lake in the Yukon Territory to be named by a white man.

SIMPSON RANGE   60°46′N   129°33′W   (105–A). The mountains on the west side of Simpson Lake.

These were named about 1956 when the Campbell Highway (the Cantung Road at that time) was laid out.

SIMPSON TOWER   61°24′N   129°22′W   (105–H). The lone peak sitting midway between the arms of Frances Lake.

On 19 July, 1840, Robert Campbell of the HBC first saw this peak and named it after Sir George SIMPSON, the Governor of the company. He named the lake the same day after Sir George's wife, Frances. (See Frances Lake.)

MOUNT SITTICHINLI   67°11′N   136°15′W   (116–P). South of the Rat River.

Lazarus SITTICHINLI was a Special Constable of the RCMP. He drove dog teams for the RCMP patrol in the famous search for Albert Johnson, the "Mad Trapper of Rat River", in 1932. (See Moses Hill.)

SIXTYMILE RIVER   63°34′N   139°46′W   (115–O&N). A tributary of the Yukon River, 50 miles above Dawson.

In 1876 Arthur Harper, sometime partner of McQuesten and Mayo, found good showings of gold on this river. Returning to Fort Reliance which had just been established and was the only trading post in the territory, he gave this river its name because it was 60 miles upriver from the fort. Although Harper made little from his prospects, others followed him and in 1891 rich placer gold was found on tributaries of this river. (See Ogilvie.)

SKOOKUM GULCH   63°56′N   139°20′W   (115–O&N). A tributary to Bonanza Creek, just below its junction with Eldorado Creek.

Joseph Goldsmith had been in the Yukon for several years and was mining on American Creek, in Alaska, when he heard the news of the Klondike

242

find. Too late to stake a claim on one of the major creeks he prospected the feeders and found extremely rich gold on this one. He staked the first claim and named the stream on 22 March, 1897. He and his partner panned $2,800 in four days and sluiced $40,000 in four months from claims 1 and 2.

SKOOKUM is a Chinook or coast trade word meaning "Strong".

MOUNT SKOOKUM JIM 65°11'N 139°03'W (116-G&F). South of the Ogilvie River.

In September 1973, the 75th anniversary of the Klondike Gold Rush, this mountain was named to commemorate one of the discoverers, SKOOKUM JIM Mason.

He and George Carmack assisted William Ogilvie over the Chilkoot Pass in 1887. In 1896, with Tagish (later Dawson) Charlie, they discovered not the first but the richest gold in the Klondike and on the east side of the Yukon River. Although there were many arguments as to which of the three actually panned the first gold on Bonanza Creek, Jim took little or no part in them. He worked and handled his claim wisely and remained a dedicated prospector until he died. He was instrumental in finding other placer goldfields in the Yukon, such as the Kluane fields.

He died in Carcross on 23 July, 1916. He left his estate not only to his family but also to help his people. He was always generous and respected by all who knew him.

SKULL RIDGE 3,106' 68°32'N 137°26'W (117-A). 15 miles west of Mount Gilbert Davies.

This is a very old native name and was given because of the numerous animal bones and skulls they found there many years ago.

MOUNT SLAGGARD 61°11'N 140°34'W (115-G&F). In the St. Elias Mountains.

In July 1958 this mountain was given the name of Joseph R. SLAGGARD, a pioneer prospector in this area of the Yukon from the early 1900's. With his partners M.C. Harris and Solomon Albert (who made the original discovery) he staked the first claims containing significant amounts of copper ore at the headwaters of the White River near here in May 1905. Slaggard himself found the largest slab of pure native copper ever found in the territory. This specimen now stands at the McBride Museum in Whitehorse. They tried for many years to develop a mine on their discoveries but never found enough ore to be of economic value.

SLAGGARD RIDGE   61°45′N 140°45′W   (115-G&F). At the headwaters of the White River.

This name was given by prospectors about 1906 after Joseph R. SLAGGARD, who was instrumental in locating copper deposits in this area. (See above.)

SLEEP CREEK   61°24′N 132°32′W   (105-F). Flows into Seagull Creek and then into the McConnell River.

This was named in May 1962 to honour the memory of a gallant man, J-9483 Flight Lt. Kenneth Stephen SLEEP, MID. Born on 19 November, 1922, at Lindsay, Ontario, he enlisted at Toronto in the RCAF on 10 April, 1941. He served in Canada and overseas and was killed during air operations on 1 December, 1945.

SLEEPY MOUNTAIN   68°41′N 138°20′W   (117-A). In the Barn Mountains.

Anker Hoidal, a long-time prospector and trapper on the North Slope, reported in 1961, according to the CPCGN records, that the name originated from an old Eskimo legend about a woman who took refuge on this mountain from a group of men. The woman had supernatural powers and put the men to sleep, thus eluding them.

MOUNT SLIM   60°56′N 134°52′W   (105-D). South of Joe Creek.

Frank SLIM, an old-time riverboat pilot, died in 1973. This mountain was very shortly afterward named in his memory.

SLIM'S RIVER   60°59′N 138°33′W   (115-B&C). Flows into the southwest end of Kluane Lake.

In the early part of 1903, during the rush to the Bullion Creek (or Kluane) goldfields, SLIM was drowned while crossing this river. He was a prospector's packhorse and his owner honoured him in this way.

MOUNT SLIPPER   5,583′   65°16′N 140°55′W   (116-F). On the Yukon -Alaska border.

On 4 July, 1914, D.D. Cairnes, GSC, named this point after his assistant, E.S. SLIPPER. He had aided Cairnes in 1912 in mapping the geology along the boundary. This is the highest point on the boundary between the Yukon and Porcupine Rivers.

SMARCH RIVER (See Smart River.)

SMART RIVER   60°00′N 131°45′W (105-B). Flows south into British Columbia in the Cassiar Mountains.

This name is misspelled. The river was originally and for many years the homesite and trapping area of the SMARCH family, a well-known Indian family in the southern Yukon. They lived near where the river crosses the Alaska Highway.

SNAFU CREEK   60°08′N 133°53′W (105-C). A tributary to the Lubbock River.

In 1949-50 the Canadian Army Engineers located and built the road from Jake's Corner to Atlin, BC, a distance of 61 miles.

The name they gave this creek (the lake at its head was named later) was a catch-word widely used in the British and Commonwealth Armed Forces during the Second World War. It originated before the war, probably in the RAF. The term means "Situation Normal — All Fouled Up". Anyone who served in the armed forces will recognize this. (See Tarfu Creek.)

SNAG   62°24′N 140°22′W (115-J&K). A tributary to the White River.

In 1899 A.H. Brooks and W.J. Peters, USGS, named this river because of the obstacles they met while travelling along it.

The Dominion Department of Transport established a weather station and an emergency flight strip near the mouth of the stream in 1942, in conjunction with the air-lift to Russia. The coldest temperature ever officially recorded in Canada was measured here on 3 February, 1947. It was –81°F. The station was closed in September 1966.

SNAKE RIVER   65°58′N 134°12′W (106-E). A tributary to the Peel River.

When John Bell, Chief Trader of the HBC at Fort MacPherson, explored the lower part of this river in 1839 he named it the "Good Hope" River, after Fort Good Hope on the Mackenzie River. Charles Camsell, GSC, noted in 1905 that although the name had long been changed some of the local people still referred to it as the "Good Hope".

The name was probably changed by A.K. Isbister of the HBC in the winter of 1840-41 when he explored farther up the river. The stream is an unending series of bends and oxbows, which could account for the name. Oddly enough, although there are no snakes in the Yukon, the Loucheaux

Indian name for the river translates as "Hairy Worm River", perhaps in memory of an infestation of some sort of caterpillars.

SOLDIER'S SUMMIT   61°02′N 138°31′W (115–G&F). On the south-west shore of Kluane Lake at the foot of Sheep Mountain.

At this spot on 20 November, 1942, the Alaska Military Highway was offi-cially opened by E.L. Bartlett of Alaska and Ian MacKenzie of Canada, eight months after the start of construction. A monument marks the spot.

SOMME CREEK   62°24′N 138°40′W (115–J&K). Flows into the Klotas-sin River.

D.D. Cairnes, GSC, named this creek in 1916 after the Battle of the Somme in France in which he lost some of his friends.

SONORA GULCH   62°40′N 138°02′W (115–J&K). A tributary to Hayes Creek.

George Beal found gold and staked the Discovery claim on this creek in September 1898. He named the creek after the Mexican state of SONORA, where he had previously prospected.

SOUCH CREEK   61°37′N 133°45′W (105–F). A tributary to the Big Salmon River.

On 1 November this stream was honoured by the name of a Canadian hero, J-16825 Flying Officer George Allan SOUCH, DFC. He was born in Toronto, Ontario on 13 August, 1916, and enlisted in the RCAF there on 7 March, 1941. While serving overseas he was killed during air operations on 29 July, 1943.

SOURDOUGH GULCH   63°59′N 139°22′W (115–O&N). A tributary to Bonanza Creek from the west, four miles above the mouth.

Fred E. Envoldsen and his partner, John P. Hering, found the first payable gold on this stream on 5 June, 1901, and renamed it. It had been staked by others in 1897 who had named it 67 Pup, from its location, but were unable to find enough gold and abandoned it. (See Strathcona Creek.)

SPRAGUE CREEK   63°55′N 136°28′W (115–P). Flows into the North McQuesten River.

Gold was found and the creek named by a miner-prospector of this name. He continued to live here for many years.

SQUANGA LAKE 60°29′N 133°38′W (105-C). At mile 850 (K1377) on the Alaska Highway.

This small, pleasant lake received its name from the Indians long ago. The name is that of a small, rounded type of whitefish of superior flavour, which abounds in the lake.

SQUAW CREEK 60°02′N 137°10′W (115-A). Flows into the Tatshenshini River below Dalton Post.

In 1927 Paddy Duncan of Champagne and Klukshu found the gold of this stream and named the creek. In 1936 he was sentenced to life imprisonment for murder.

The creek had been called "Dollis" Creek by miners around 1898 but had been long abandoned when Duncan renamed it. The name "Dollis" is still found on some maps.

SQUAW CREEK 63°47′N 137°28′W (115-P). A tributary of Clear Creek.

About 5 May, 1901, this creek was staked and named by W.A. MacDonald, Dan MacDonald, Edward Carroll and George Kennedy. They were too late to stake claims in the stampede to the Clear Creek gold finds but found enough on this stream to stake it and name it.

THE SQUAW TITS 5,900′ 60°29′N 136°44′W (115-A). On the northeast side of Dezeadash Lake.

These rounded twin buttes beside the Dalton Trail were named by Dalton or his men before the Klondike Gold Rush and were used as landmarks by those travelling the trail. They were first reported and mapped by J.J. McArthur, DLS, who examined the trail for the Department of the Interior in 1897.

STAN LAKE 65°10′N 140°05′W (116-G&F). Southwest of Mount Deville.

This was named in September 1973 after STANLEY Rivers, a long-time prospector in the area.

STARR CREEK 61°47′N 131°51′W (105-G). A tributary to the Pelly River.

Gilmore and Elsie STARR came into the Yukon in May 1898. They had arrived in Skagway in 1897 but Gilmore contracted spinal meningitis while packing supplies over the White Pass. They had financed their journey to the Klondike by the sale of their North Dakota homestead after it had been laid waste by a cyclone.

Arriving in Dawson in the spring of 1898, they prospected up the Klondike River and then on Eureka Creek. Elsie owned and ran the Hillside roadhouse on Hunker Creek in 1899. They later prospected up the Pelly River and it is believed that they lived here about 1905 to 10, after finding some gold in the stream.

STEAMBOAT BAR 63°36′N 137°33′W (115–P). A large gravel island in the Stewart River about 14 miles below the mouth of the McQuesten River.

This is the richest bar ever found on the Stewart River and was reported in 1885 to have yielded for some time at the rate of 8½ ounces of gold per day per man. The deposits, being shallow and about two feet in thickness, were quickly exhausted.

In 1885 a group of miners hired the ACC's small steamboat the *New Racket*. It had been brought up the river from St. Michaels by the Schieffelin brothers of Arizona and was the second steam vessel on the Yukon. The boat was hauled up on the bar and her engines were detached from the paddlewheel. They were made to drive a set of pumps manufactured on the spot, which supplied water for the set of sluice boxes. With this crude machinery, the miners cleared $1,000 each and paid an equal amount to the owners of the boat. This was the first use of powered machinery to mine in the Yukon.

STEAMBOAT MOUNTAIN 6,376′ 64°15′N 135°38′W (106–D). In the Ogilvie Mountains.

This was named by Tony Hollenback, an early prospector in the region, because of its appearance. The name was confirmed in 1955.

MOUNT STEELE 16,640′ 61°06′N 140°19′W (115–G&F). In the Ice-field Ranges of the St. Elias Mountains.

J.J. McArthur, DLS, while surveying the international boundary in July 1909, named this peak after one of the most outstanding men in the history of the Yukon.

Major General Sir Samuel Benfield STEELE, KCMG, CB, MVO, was born in Purbrook, county of Simcoe, Ontario, in Upper Canada, on 5 January, 1849. His father was Captain Elmes Steele, RN, and an uncle, Colonel Samuel Steele, had served at the capture of Québec.

He was commissioned an ensign in the 35th Simcoe Foresters at the age of 15, after serving as a private. He took part in the repulse of the Fenian Raids in 1866. To see action, he reverted to corporal in the Ontario Rifles during the Red River Rebellion of 1870.

He and his two brothers enlisted at the formation of the North-West Mounted Police in August 1874, when he was immediately appointed Sergeant Major of "A" Division. He took part in the Great March of 1874 and by 1878 he had reached the rank of inspector. During the Northwest Rebellion of 1885 he commanded the cavalry composed of the NWMP and Steele's Scouts of the Alberta Field Force.

1887 saw him in command of the NWMP expedition to the Kootenays in eastern BC, the establishment of Fort Steele and the settling of the Indian troubles in that country. During this period he maintained law and order during the construction of the Canadian Pacific Railway through the Rocky Mountains.

He commanded the NWMP posts on the White and the Chilkoot Passes from February to July 1898, the height of the Klondike Gold Rush. At this time he was also magistrate and in charge of Canada Customs for the area. In July 1898 he was prompted to lieutenant-colonel, made a Member of the Council of the Yukon Territory and commander of all NWMP forces in the territory. He held all these positions with honour, distinction and efficiency until September 1899. The tradition of NWMP efficiency and incorruptibility was upheld and strongly reinforced by him and his men during this time.

He raised and commanded the Lord Strathcona's Horse and again served with more than ordinary ability and distinction in the South African War from 1899 to 1901, winning many honours and decorations. He commanded the Transvaal Division of the South African Constabulary, 1901–1906. On 1 March, 1903, he resigned from the NWMP.

In 1907 he returned to Canada and, promoted to colonel, was placed in command of Military District No. 13 (Calgary) until 1909, and of Military District No. 10 (Winnipeg) until 1914. During this period he greatly increased and developed the Canadian militia on the prairies.

In 1914 at the outbreak of the First World War, he was promoted to major general and made Inspector General of Western Canada. At this time he published his autobiography, *Forty Years in Canada*. He organized, commanded and trained the 2nd Canadian Division from May to August 1915 and from then to July 1918 commanded Shornecliff Military District which contained nearly all the Canadian troops in England. At the same time he was Chairman of the Canadian Militia Council in Great Britain, 1915–16, which made him nearly equivalent to commander-in-chief of the Canadian forces in the United Kingdom. Again he won high honours, finally being made Knight Commander of the Order of St. Michael and St. George, one of the most distinguished honours of the British Empire.

Owing to failing health he retired in July 1918. He died on 30 January, 1919, at Putney, England and was buried at Winnipeg.

STEEP CREEK 63°42′N 134°57′W (105–M). Flows into the south arm of Mayo Lake.

This was one of several rich, gold-bearing creeks found by a party of four Australian prospectors in August 1903. They named the creeks and brought 15 ounces of coarse gold from this stream into Dawson where it assayed a value of $19.57 to the ounce, probably the purest placer gold ever found in the Yukon.

MOUNT STENBRATEN 6,466′ 64°05′N 132°08′W (106–C). Near the headwaters of the Stewart River.

In May 1973 this mountain was named after John O. "Stampede John" STENBRATEN, a noted Yukon prospector from 1904 to 1960. It is said that Stampede John took part in nearly every mining rush in the Yukon, Alaska and into Siberia in these years.

STEVENS CREEK 60°15′N 134°58′W (105–D). A tributary to the Wheaton River.

In 1905 George STEVENS found the first quartz-gold lode on the hill above this creek. Later, about 1908, it was named after him. He lived beside the creek here which already had his name.

STEVENSON RIDGE 4,493′ 62°34′N 138°50′W (115–J&K). Between Dip Creek and the Klotassin River.

Hugh S. Bostock, GSC, named this ridge in 1941 after a man named STEVENSON, who was a senior partner in a placer mining company on Rude Creek for many years and an active prospector in the area at the same time. (See Leslie Ridge.)

STEWART GULCH 64°02′N 135°49′W (106–D). A small valley on the left side of Dublin Gulch.

This was named after J.S. STEWART who found and worked on a lode quartz gold vein here in 1917.

STEWART LAKE   60°38′N 128°42′W (105–A). 40 miles north of Watson Lake.

An old trapper, half-Indian, half-black, of that name, lived here and trapped in the general area toward the Frances River for many years. He and his family were still here in 1941 and some of them are buried here.

STEWART RIVER   63°19′N 139°26′W (115–O&N). A major tributary of the Yukon River from the east.

In the winter of 1849 Robert Campbell of the HBC at Fort Selkirk, sent his "dear and gallant friend" James G. STEWART, who was also his assistant clerk, northeast of the fort to find some Indians believed to be hunting in that area. Stewart travelled farther than anyone had before and crossed this stream on the ice. He reported it to Campbell on his return and Campbell named it after him. Stewart was the son of the Hon. James Stewart of Montréal.

The Indians of the district reported in 1883 to Lt. F. Schwatka, US Army, that the river's native name was "Na-Chon-De" which was also the name of the tribe living upon it. Schwatka did not change the name of this large river.

Prospecting started on the Stewart in 1884 with a few men who found encouraging signs of good, payable, fine gold on the river bars. In the spring of 1885 Frank Moffatt recovered the first of this rich bar gold. In the late summer of the same year "Slim Jim" Wynn, who had first come over the Chilkoot Pass in 1879, found a rich bar 100 miles upstream. Called "Wynn's Bar" it paid at $6,000 to the man for less than 50 days work. In 1886 fully 100 men were working on the bars of the Stewart and some had prospected nearly to its headwaters.

One group of miners made a deal with Mayo and McQuesten to rent the little steamer *New Racket* and used its engines to mine the gravels of Steamboat Bar. (See Steamboat Bar.)

Some of the bars worked were Wynn's (Winn's), Dutch John's, Lac de Bar, Halfmoon, Chapman's, Joe Jay Bar, Low Water and Black Mike's Bar. These and other bars were worked until the Klondike Gold Rush, although they were deserted for a time after the discovery of the Fortymile goldfields in late 1886. The miners in the Yukon referred to the Stewart as the "Grubstake River", because enough gold could always be won on it to provide money for supplies for another season of prospecting.

In the summer of 1886 Frederick Harper, of Harper, McQuesten and Mayo, established a trading post at the mouth of the river to serve the miners upstream. Some of the miners called the post "Fort Nelson" after Pte. Edward William Nelson of the Signal Service of the US Army, who was said to have been there at the time, collecting specimens of the flora and fauna of the region. (He went on to make invaluable collections of the Yukon and Alaska and later became one of America's most famous naturalists.) In late 1886, coarse gold was found on the Fortymile River and the miners abandoned the Stewart for a few years. Harper moved his trading post to Fortymile in June 1887.

In Klondike days the settlement of the same name at the mouth of the river was revived as a wood point for riverboats, a NWMP post and a wintering place for miners unable to reach Dawson before winter. Many of these men prospected the tributaries of the river in 1897–98 and later. In July 1897 Robert Henderson staked a 40-acre townsite on the banks of the Yukon opposite the mouth of the Stewart but it never succeeded.

William Ogilvie, who had been Commissioner of the Yukon from 1898–1901, became the President of the Yukon Basin Gold Dredging Co. Ltd., of Missouri, which held extensive leases on the Stewart and operated with limited success, 1908–12.

David and Mary Shand ran the Hotel Stewart, a roadhouse here, from 1900 until it burned in 1918. They rebuilt it and operated it as Johnson's Roadhouse until 1930. They wrote a book about their experiences there entitled *The Summit and Beyond.*

STOKES POINT   69°21′N 138°42′W (117–D). Southeast of Herschel Island on the Arctic coast.

On 16 July, 1826, John Franklin named this feature after his friend Capt. John L. STOKES RN, commander of the *Acheron.*

STONY CREEK   60°47′N 135°59′W (105–D). A tributary to the Takhini River.

This is notable only because an American Army Engineers maintenance camp was established here in 1942–43 during the construction of the Alaska Highway.

STOWE CREEK   63°37′N 138°59′W (115–O&N). A tributary to Montana Creek from the west.

Gold was discovered and the creek named by A.F. STOWE in May 1901. The lower part of this creek was originally called Conglomerate Creek.

STRATHCONA CREEK   63°47'N 139°32'W (115-O&N). A tributary to Indian River from the north.

On 5 January, 1902, Fred Eugene Envoldsen and C.W. Williams found gold, staked and named this stream, probably in honour of the Lord Strathcona's Horse, a Canadian cavalry regiment raised and first commanded by Col. Sam B. Steele of the NWMP. The regiment served with great distinction in the South African War from 1899–1902.

Envoldsen was one of the most active prospectors in the country for many years. He was a participant in the stampede to the Firth River placer gold finds in 1948. (See Sourdough Gulch, Bertha Creek and Firth River.)

MOUNT STRICKLAND   13,818'   61°14'N 140°40'W (115-G&F). In the Icefield Ranges of the St. Elias Mountains.

This was named about 1918 after Inspector D'Arcy STRICKLAND of the NWMP. He had enlisted in 1891 and was one of the first of the force in the Yukon, arriving at Fortymile in July 1895 with Inspector Charles Constantine. He was the first officer in command of the detachment on the White Pass in February 1898 and later at the important Tagish Lake Post where every gold-seeker was registered and passed through Customs.

He died in the service in 1908 in the midst of a distinguished career.

MOUNT STUTZER   4,165'   61°58'N 136°06'W (115-H). On the east side of the Nordenskiold River about ten miles south of Carmacks.

D.D. Cairnes, GSC, named this peak sometime in 1908 after Dr. Otto STUTZER, Assistant Professor of Geology at the Royal School of Mines in Freiberg, Germany. Stutzer had assisted Cairnes in 1908 when he mapped the geology of this area.

SUGDEN CREEK   60°41'N 137°54'W (115-A). A tributary to the Kaskawulsh River from the north. (See Ferguson Creek.)

SUGDEN PUP 61°01'N 138°44'W (115-G&F). A very short tributary of Bullion Creek from the south.

Dr. L.S. SUGDEN, an American physician, was prominent in early Dawson and Yukon politics. He was also an active prospector and mining promoter, in which he was fairly successful. He took part in the first prospecting of the Bullion Creek goldfields and was the first to find gold on this small gulch in the winter of 1907–08.

Dr. Sugden, in the early years of the Klondike, went to Lake Laberge one winter to attend a sick man. Upon arrival he found the man dead. He was unable to bury him, owing to the depth of frost in the ground. The wreck of the riverboat *Olive May* was nearby so Sugden cremated the body in the boiler of the boat. This incident was the basis of Robert W. Service's famous poem "The Cremation of Sam McGee".

SULLIVAN HILL 64°21'N 135°26'W (106-D). At the headwaters of the Beaver River.

This was named after John SULLIVAN, a prospector who was one of the first men into the area during the rush to the silver-lead finds on nearby Carpenter Creek in the early 1920's. He prospected in the Mayo district from 1920-50.

This map location is shown as McKay Hill, which is a few miles farther east.

SULLIVAN ISLAND 63°12'N 139°34'W (115-O&N). A small island at the mouth of the White River.

It was named after an early woodcutter who supplied the riverboats about 1897 and later. David and Mary Shand built and operated a small sawmill here in May 1898 and ran it till 1900.

SULPHUR   CREEK   63°38'N 138°40'W (115-O&N).   Flows   into Dominion Creek in the Klondike.

This creek was named about 1896 or early 1897 for the suphur-bearing mineral water springs found near the headwaters on King Solomon's Dome, claim No. 73 Above Discovery.

There were two Discovery claims filed on this creek; the first was found by a prospector named Stafford on 22 July, 1897. He was mining on nearby Quartz Creek and one night had a dream of finding gold on Sulphur. He told his partner the next morning, set out for Sulphur and did find gold! For some reason this claim was not recorded. However, on 24 August, 1897, W.A. Miller and his partner W.C. "Swiftwater Bill" Gates staked another Discovery claim much lower downstream and found gold in large enough amounts to start a stampede from Dawson in which the whole creek and its tributaries were all staked. Gates' claim been staked by another man in late July but he also did not record it.

Although not nearly as rich in gold as Eldorado, Bonanza or Hunker Creeks, Sulphur Creek paid steadily and well. The pay streak for much of the creek was the widest of any of the Klondike, up to 500 feet of gold-bearing gravels. Andrew Baird, a young Australian farmer, came over the White Pass in the spring of 1898 and staked No. 11 Above Discovery. Later in 1899, when the news of the Nome finds depopulated Dawson, he cannily purchased ten more claims on the creek for a standing price of $1,000 each, from gold won from No. 11. After mining for a number of years he sold out to a large company which wished to set up dredging operations, becoming their accountant at the same time. He eventually became the manager of the Yukon Consolidated Gold Co. from which he retired, a wealthy man, in his late 70's. He had mined for 60 years on the Klondike, the title he gave to his autobiography. He died in Vancouver, BC in April 1975 at the age of 99.

SULPHUR SPRINGS 63°52′N 138°58′W (115-O&N). At the head-waters of Sulphur Creek.

These mineral springs gave Sulphur Creek its name. In the fall of 1906 a 30-mile-long railroad, the Klondike Mines Railway, was completed from Dawson to this spot. Sulphur Springs was the terminus, with waiting rooms, offices, freight sheds and other conveniences.

SUMMIT CREEK 61°23′N 134°22′W (105-E). A tributary of the Big Salmon River near Livingstone Creek.

Gold was discovered here and the stream named by a prospector named Meany in 1901. In August 1905 a nugget of gold weighing 39 ounces, the largest found in the area to that time, was found on the stream.

SUNAGHUN CREEK 67°31′N 141°00′W (116-O&N). Flows into the Porcupine River near Rampart House.

This is a Kutcha-Kutchin Indian name reported by the International Boundary Survey party of 1914. According to Professor O.W. Geist of the University of Alaska, this word means "old woman". The creek was so named because, according to Orth's *Dictionary of Alaska Place Names*, "An old woman at Rampart House could not climb the steep river bank so she used this creek as a route to obtain her firewood. Hence, Old Woman Creek".

SUPER CUB CREEK 60°02′N 137°57′W (115-A). A small tributary to the Alsek River.

In August 1963 Dr. Alex Smith, GSC, named it after a small lake just over

255

the border in BC. The lake was named because a mining company working in the area found that a Piper Super Cub aircraft was the largest that could use the lake.

SURPRISE LAKE   60°33′N   133°20′W   (105–C). A very small lake about four miles north of Johnson's Crossing.

This little lake was named by the Chief of the Teslin Indian Band in 1952 while he was guiding a party of the Canadian Army Topographical Survey.

SURVEYS RANGE   63°35′N   132°12′W   (105–N). Between Fido Creek and the Rogue River.

Hugh S. Bostock, GSC, named these hills in November 1970 to honour the topographical and geodetic surveyors of Canada who had prepared the maps of the Yukon. They had been uncommemorated to this time. He had originally proposed the name "Surveyors Range."

SWANSON   CREEK   61°19′N   138°18′W   (115–G&F). A tributary to Gladstone Creek near Kluane Lake.

This was named by Axel SWANSON who, with T.T. Murray, was the discoverer of gold on this stream and on Gladstone Creek in 1911.

SWEDE CREEK   60°58′N   131°18′W   (105–B). A tributary of the upper Liard River.

An old prospector, known only as "The SWEDE", lived here between 1900 and 1930. He travelled the Liard River in a beautifully built dug-out canoe, 32 feet long, which he had constructed himself. It would travel lightly through the most dangerous waters and he propelled it with a minimum of effort, the envy of all the Indians and prospectors who saw it.

SWEDE CREEK   64°01′N   139°34′W   (116–B&C). A long tributary to the Yukon River, five miles above Dawson.

When C.A. Olafson and his group found gold and staked the Discovery and other claims here on 2 February, 1898, the Mining Recorder at Dawson named the stream after the nationality of the men. A stampede from Dawson resulted in over 600 claims being staked on the creek and its tributaries in the following three weeks. In spite of these efforts little gold was ever mined. For a number of years at the time a small settlement existed at the mouth of the creek. A steamboat wood point, it was also a favourite vacation camping place for Dawson people.

SWEDE JOHNSON CREEK   61°36'N 139°24'W (115–G&F). A tributary to the Kluane River, near the highway.

Ernest "SWEDE" JOHNSON prospected and trapped in this area for many years. He was the discoverer of the first gold found on Tatamagouche Creek.

SWIM LAKES   62°11'N 132°52'W (105–K). A group of small lakes 15 miles east of Faro.

These lakes were given their name in the summer of 1935 by J.R. Johnston, GSC, and his survey party. They were the only lakes found that season which were warm enough for swimming.

TABOR LAKES   66°58'N 134°46'W (106–L). East of the Peel River.

These small lakes were named after Charles William TABOR as a map-designation name in 1973. He had been a Yukon Councillor representing North Dawson from 1912 to 15 and a pioneer lawyer in the territory.

TADRU LAKE   62°28'N 135°42'W (105–L). Ten miles southeast of Tatlmain Lake.

This was named in 1950 by R.B. Campbell, GSC. The word is a contraction of the name Taylor and Drury, a firm of Whitehorse merchants. They operated trading posts in many of the most isolated parts of the Yukon from 1899 on.

Isaac Taylor was born in Thirsk, Yorkshire, England and came to the Yukon with the Klondike rush in 1898 via Australia. He met William S. Drury, from Kirme, Lincolnshire, while working on the Discovery claim on Pine Creek in Atlin, BC. Here they decided to go into business supplying the needs of the miners.

They then opened a tent store in Bennett on 14 August, 1899. They moved their store to Whitehorse when the railroad was completed in July 1900. Their venture succeeded and they expanded by opening posts in various parts of the territory: Pelly Banks in 1905; Teslin in 1906; Mayo, Carmacks and Fort Selkirk in 1919. They built a small riverboat, the *Kluane*, to service these posts. In 1912 they amalgamated with Whitney and Pedlar, Whitehorse merchants who were instrumental in developing the first copper ore bodies at Whitehorse, and built the present large store. They had stores in 18 locations at one time and even had company coins minted in Ottawa which were in use from 1912 to 1950. The business was finally sold by the family in 1974.

TAGISH   60°19'N   134°16'W   (105-D). On the narrows between Tagish Lake and Marsh Lake.

The road from Carcross to Jake's Corner on the Alaska Highway was built in late 1942 to lay the gasoline pipeline from Skagway to Watson Lake. The present settlement of Tagish grew up around the bridge built then. The old location during the gold rush years was a TAGISH Indian village about three miles south and on the east side. The NWMP built one of their most important posts in the Yukon at this place, calling it Fort Sifton after the then Minister of the Interior. Every traveller passing this point was required to register his party and his boat was given a registration number. Customs officers, sometimes police, examined all outfits. Opened in early 1897, it brought some order to the mad rush down the river. Inspector D'Arcy Strickland, who had come in with Inspector Constantine in 1895, was in charge. A post office was open from 20 August, 1897, to 1 October, 1901.

TAGISH LAKE   60°10'N   134°20'W   (105-D). A large, many-armed lake straddling the Yukon-BC border east of Carcross.

The name is ancient and from the Indian "Ta-Gish-Ai", which is also the name of the native people who lived there. Schwatka ignored the Indian name and designated it Lake Bove after a Lt. Bove of the Italian navy. Dr. G.M. Dawson, GSC, disallowed the name, relegating it to a small island at the entrance of Windy Arm. Dawson retained the old Indian name for the lake.

The early miners called it "Tako" or "Tahko" Lake. Part of the main route to the lower Yukon River and the goldfields, two places on the lake were approached with trepidation by the miners sailing down; the mouths of Windy Arm and Taku Arm were given to sudden and furious winds and these locations were the scenes of many wrecks and drownings.

MOUNT TAGISH CHARLIE   65°53'N   139°48'W   (115-G&F). West of the Porcupine River.

This northern peak was named in the Klondike Jubilee year of 1973 to commemorate TAGISH CHARLIE. He, with George Carmack and Skookum Jim Mason, found the fabulous gold of Bonanza Creek on 16 August, 1896, which sparked the greatest gold rush in history. He was afterwards known as "Dawson Charlie."

At and before the gold rush, Indians usually took English Christian names from white associates, with the tribal or band designation added, i.e. "Tagish Charlie", "Tahu Jack", "Stick Jim", etc.

Charlie was the first Indian (and perhaps the only one) of the Yukon Territory to be given the full rights of a Canadian citizen by an Act of Parliament; he was allowed to vote, hold public office, sue and be sued and to buy and drink spirituous liquors.

On 26 January, 1908, he fell from the railway bridge at Carcross and was drowned.

TAHTE CREEK 61°59'N 137°11'W (115-H). A small tributary to the Nisling River from the south.

When J.J. McArthur, DLS, made his rough survey through this country in 1897 he thought that the Nisling River was the "Tahte" of the local Indians and so mapped it. After the error was corrected this name was given to this small stream. No translation was given.

TAKHINI 60°51'N 135°27'W (105-D).

This old settlement lay at the crossing of the Takhini River on the old Dawson road. It was the first stop out from Whitehorse and had a NWMP post as well as a roadhouse. The roadhouse was owned and operated by W.A. Puckett. Both it and the police post were closed in May 1907.

TAKHINI HOT SPRINGS 60°53'N 135°22'W (105-D). About five miles up the present Dawson Highway.

These hot mineral springs were discovered and staked by W. A. Puckett, who owned the nearby Takhini roadhouse, and Stephen Simmons in late April 1907.

The water flow then and now is about 86 gallons per minute at a temperature of 118°F (47°C). The water is sweet and odourless, containing no sulphur. It is said to be beneficial to sufferers of arthritis and rheumatism.

TAKHINI RIVER 60°51'N 135°11'W (105-D). A large tributary to the Yukon River about 12 miles north of Whitehorse.

This river was first noted by Dr. Aurel Krause of the Bremen Geographical Society in 1882, the first white man to explore the southwestern part of the territory. The name, recorded by Krause, is from the Tagish Indian "Tahk-Heena", "Tahk" meaning "mosquito" and "Heena" meaning "river."

TAKIAH CREEK 67°51'N 137°58'W (116-P). Flows into Driftwood Creek.

This is a local name which in the Vanta Kutchin language means "Little".

TALBOT ARM 61°30′N 138°37′W (115–G&F). The large bay at the southeast end of Kluane Lake.

This bay was named in the summer of 1945 by H.S. Bostock, GSC, after Albert Charles TALBOT, DLS, who made the first good map of Kluane Lake and the area in 1898 while with the Department of the Interior. He liked this calm bay. He was a member of the International Boundary Commission, 1893–95. The bay had been previously known as "Little Arm".

TALLY-HO MOUNTAIN 60°14′N 135°03′W (105–D). In the big bend of the Wheaton River.

About the year 1906 there was much prospecting activity and a number of promising mineral finds were made in this area. Among the more successful was a group of young English prospectors who worked energetically in this vicinity. In a gulch on the west end of this hill they found good lode showings of gold-silver-lead ore which they called the "TALLY-HO" claims. They explored this ground until about 1916 and were known locally as the Tally-Ho boys. The mountain, which had been known as Big Bend Mountain, was soon given the name of the group. Most of them went to England in 1915–16 to enlist in the British forces for the First World War and it is supposed that most of them were killed in the fighting as they did not return to the Yukon.

TANTALUS BUTTE 2,568′ 62°08′N 136°16′W (115–I). Five miles north of Carmacks.

This lone hill was named in 1883 by Lt. F. Schwatka, US Army. Because of the convolutions of the Yukon River in this area, anyone approaching the place became confused; at one point approaching the hill, and at another going away, repeatedly.

George Carmack, the discoverer of Bonanza Creek, found a seam of coal on this hill in 1893 and made sporadic attempts to develop it. He was backed by Arthur Harper who had a 50% interest in the venture. In 1903, Captain Charles E. Miller, who had been a coal miner in Mauchunk, Pennsylvania, located a claim on this coal and mined 40,000 tons in the next two years to supply the riverboats. He came into the Yukon in 1897 and built the Yukon Sawmill in Dawson, then ran the riverboats *Clara* and *Reindeer*. After the *Reindeer* burned in 1900 he turned to coal mining. In 1905 he located the Tantalus Butte Coal Mine which had an estimated reserve of five million tons of coal. He sold out his holdings soon afterward to the WP&YR.

TARFU CREEK   60°06′N 133°53′W (105–C). A tributary to the Lubbock River, northeast of Atlin Lake.

In 1949–50 the Canadian Army Engineers located and built the road from Jake's Corner to Atlin, BC. While surveying the route they gave this stream a name derived from a common World War Two slang expression. The word TARFU was an extension of the word Snafu: "Situation Normal, All Fouled Up". Tarfu means "Things Are Really Fouled Up". (See Snafu Creek.)

TASIN RANGE   63°55′N 132°45′W (105–N). Between the Stewart and Lansing Rivers.

This was mapped in 1907 by Joseph Keele, GSC, who retained the local name which in the Indian language means "Black" or "Dark". Mount Ortell is the highest peak in the range.

TATAMAGOUCHE CREEK   61°22′N 139°18′W (115–G&F). A tributary to Burwash Creek.

Ernest "Swede" Johnson, a pioneer prospector, discovered gold here and named the creek after the river of the same name in New Brunswick in 1904 during the rush to the Kluane goldfields. It is also spelled Taddemagooch. (See Swede Johnson Creek.)

TATCHUN RIVER   62°17′N 136°19′W (115–I). A tributary to the Yukon River at Five Finger Rapids.

Dr. G.M. Dawson, GSC, retained this Indian name on his survey of 1887 but did not obtain the translation.

TATLMAIN LAKE   62°37′N 135°59′W (105–L). South of the Pelly River.

In the winter of 1848–49 Robert Campbell, while at Fort Selkirk, obtained large quantities of fish for the fort from this lake. The whitefish here are particularly succulent and plentiful. The name is the original Indian one of that time and no translation was given.

TATONDUK RIVER   65°00′N 141°00′W (116–G&F). A tributary to the Yukon River from the Ogilvie Mountains.

It was variously called Tatondu, Tatonduc, Totondu and, by the early miners, Sheep Creek. TATONDUC is an Indian name reported by Lt. F. Schwatka, US Army, in 1883 as "Tatondu" and by J.E. Spurr, USGS, in 1896 as "Tatonduc." The name means "Broken Rock" River because of the numerous rocks in the channel. William Ogilvie, DLS, was the first white man known to traverse this stream when he and his party travelled its length in the spring of 1888, on their way from Fortymile to Fort Mac-Pherson.

TAY RIVER   62°34'N 134°22'W (105-L). A tributary of the Pelly River from the north.

In 1848, Robert Campbell of the HBC, while making his epic journey down the Pelly to the Yukon River, named this stream after the River TAY which flows through the city of Perth in Scotland, near his ancestral home.

Tay Lake was named much later and Tay Mountain, 6,991', near the mouth of the stream was named because of its proximity.

TAYLOR CREEK   62°44'N 138°48'W (115-J&K). A small tributary to Casino Creek in the Dawson Range.

This creek was named by R.J. Cathro of Whitehorse in May 1970 after C.D.N. "Red" TAYLOR, BSc., P. Eng., a veteran mining engineer for 30 years in the Yukon. He explored this area and its copper deposits very extensively.

TELFORD CREEK   63°11'N 138°58'W (115-O&N). Flows into the Stewart River from the south.

It is likely that this creek was named after Captain TELFORD of the RNWMP, who was officer in charge at Mayo about 1917.

TELLURIDE CREEK   60°52'N 138°05'W (115-B&C). A tributary to the Jarvis River.

Tom Laird found placer gold here and named the stream in January 1904 during the stampede to the newly-found Alsek goldfields.

TELLURIDES are a group of rare minerals formed from tellurium, gold and sometimes sulphur, iron or other elements. None have ever been found in this area and it is likely that Laird named the creek after the gold-mining camp of Telluride, Colorado, where he may have worked earlier.

TEMPEST MOUNTAIN 61°17′N 140°11′W (115–G&F). On the north side of the Steele Glacier in the St. Elias Range.

This peak was officially named in November 1970 by the Alpine Club of Canada. It was first climbed on 26 August, 1941, by Anderson Bakewell. The name describes the weather conditions met on the climb.

TENT ISLAND 68°55′N 136°35′W (117–A). On the Yukon-NWT border of Shoalwater Bay.

On Friday 7 July, 1826, John Franklin with his two boats *Lion* and *Reliance*, sailed close to this island where they discovered several hundred Eskimos camped in tents.

(See Pillage Point.)

TESLIN LAKE 60°15′N 132°57′W (105–C). A large lake in the south central Yukon, straddling the Yukon-BC boundary.

This beautiful lake retains its Indian name although slightly changed: "TES-LIN-TOO" meaning "Long, Narrow Water". The first white men known to have seen the lake were "Ike" Powers, a noted pioneer prospector, and eight or nine companions who came from Juneau and up Taku Inlet and overland to the foot of the lake in either 1876 or 77. They built three boats and did a limited amount of prospecting around the lake. The next white men here were Charles Munroe and his three companions who followed Powers' route in 1880 and also prospected the lake and some of its tributaries. It was long thought that Michael Byrne of the Western Union Telegraph Company had explored north from Telegraph Creek to the foot of the lake in 1869 but opinion now is that he reached Atlin Lake.

As part of an all-Canadian Route to the Klondike, many people travelled from Glenora and Telegraph Creek 160 miles to the foot of the lake. There they built boats and sailed down to the Teslin River, on to the Lewes (Yukon) and down to Dawson. By using this route they missed the dangerous Miles Canyon and Whitehorse Rapids as well as the frightening storms of the Chilkoot Pass. The little steamer *Anglian* was built at the foot of the lake and was launched on 13 June, 1898.

Although there had been temporary settlements at the south end of the lake (in British Columbia) in 1897–98 and a HBC post there until 1903 or 04, the first trading post set up on that part of the lake in Yukon territory was built by Tom Smith in 1903 at the mouth of the Nisutlin River. He came from Dawson in the little steamer *Quick*, piloted by Captain Henry

Henderson (brother of Robert Henderson). The post was operated by Taylor and Drury for many years till about 1955 and a settlement has existed there ever since.

On maps of the 1880's the lake was sometimes called "Aklen", "Ahklen" and "Arklun". Dr. G.M. Dawson officially retained the original Indian name in 1887.

TESLIN RIVER   61°34'N 134°54'W (105-E). A major tributary to the Yukon River.

The Indians of the very early days had several names for this stream. Michael Byrne of the Western Union Telegraph Company, although he did not see the river, was told that it was the "Hootalinkwa" or "Hotaliqu". The first miners to prospect up the river from the Yukon in 1881 called it the "Iyon" after the tribal name of the natives living at its mouth. The USCGS map of 1884 used this name. Lt. F. Schwatka, US Army, while on his 1883 excursion named it the "Newberry" River, after Professor Newberry of New York. This name was never accepted or used. The Tagish Indians called it the "Nas-A-Thane" meaning "No Salmon", although there are such fish in the river and the lake. Some early maps mistakenly named it the "Tahko" River.

This was the first major tributary of the Yukon River to be prospected; fine gold was found in many of the gravel bars, but no coarse gold was ever located.

It was one of the major routes to the Klondike goldfields in 1897–98. After Teslin Lake was reached the river was clear sailing down to Dawson and all major obstacles were by-passed.

TETLIT CREEK   66°43'N 135°23'W (106-L). A tributary to the Road River.

This was named in 1962 by B.S. Norford, GSC, after the TETLIT band of Indians who live in the area.

THATCHELL CREEK   61°33'N 137°35'W (115-H). Flows into the northwest corner of Sekulmun Lake.

Recorded by the GSC field crew in 1956, this is an old Indian name meaning "Hide Scraper". The Indians for untold years came here to obtain a certain type of shale rock from which were fashioned good scrapers to work animal hides.

THETIS BAY 69°34′N 139°05′W (117-D). On the east side of Herschel Island.

Lt. Commander Charles Stockton, USN, in the survey ship USS *THETIS* charted much of the Arctic coast and the shores of Herschel Island in 1889. He named this bay after his ship and many of the island features after the whalers he found there. The bay is one of the very few safe anchorages to be found on the western Arctic coast and was much used by wintering whalers, 1885–1905.

THISTLE CREEK 63°04′N 139°28′W (115-O&N). A tributary of the Yukon River just above the mouth of the Stewart River.

In the summer of 1898 a party of eight Scottish prospectors examined this stream and found good payable gold. The two discoverers, Murdoch McIver and Robert Haddow each staked a Discovery claim on 28 September, 1898. They named the creek after the Scots nation emblem — a THISTLE. Robert Henderson bought or otherwise acquired 50% interest in McIver's Discovery claim. Their party prospected the neighbouring streams and named several of them. Thomas Barton, one of the original party, died in Dawson in 1916.

THISTLETON 63°04′N 139°27′W (115-O&N).

This small settlement and steamboat landing at the mouth of Thistle Creek was built to serve the miners working there. Sometimes called "Thistle Creek", it lasted only a few years after 1898.

THOMAS CREEK 68°11′N 140°39′W (117-B). Flows south into the Old Crow River.

Neil MacDonald, living at Old Crow, a grandson of the first Anglican minister of Fort Yukon, Robert MacDonald, stated that a local Indian named THOMAS had erected a caribou fence on this stream. It was several miles long and was used to trap the caribou to kill them. The remains of the fence still exist.

THOMAS GULCH 64°03′N 139°23′W (116-B&C). A very short stream entering the Klondike River from the south, one mile upstream from Bonanza.

D.W. THOMAS found enough gold here to stake the first claim on 20 November, 1897, but it did not pay when it was dredged in 1912–14.

THOMAS RIVER 61°33′N 129°31′W (105-H). **Joins the Anderson River to flow into the north end of the west arm of Frances Lake.**

This stream was named in July 1840 by Robert Campbell of the HBC after THOMAS Simpson, a friend of Campbell's in the company.

THOMPSON CREEK 63°55′N 135°42′W (105-M). **Flows north into the South McQuesten River.**

This was likely named by or for Ogden Pickett THOMPSON, who came into the Yukon in 1898 and spent a number of years in this immediate area. He left here in 1914 and lived at Johnson Creek in the Mayo district where he made a new and profitable discovery which he mined for some further time. He was known as a good, hard-working prospector.

THOROUGHFARE CREEK 63°41′N 137°05′W (115-P). **Flows into Vancouver Creek.**

H.S. Bostock, GSC, gave this name in the summer of 1949 because the old Conservative Trail to Clear Creek runs along the banks of this stream.

THORPE CREEK 60°02′N 125°37′W (95-C). **Flows into the Crow River.**

On 2 February, 1966, this small stream was named after William George THORPE (1892-1955) who was for many years in charge of the map collection in the Department of Lands and Forests at Victoria, BC. He was supervisor of map production for BC from 1951 to 55.

THRASHER BAY 69°33′N 139°12′W (117-D). **On the southwest side of Herschel Island.**

This bay was named by Lt. Commander Charles Stockton, USN, of the survey ship U.S.S. *Thetis*, when he surveyed the coast of Herschel Island in 1889. The name is that of a whaler which was anchored in the bay at the time.

THREE BARREL LAKE 64°56′N 136°06′W (116-A). **In the Wernecke Mountains.**

This small, one-mile-long lake was named in the early 1960's by "Pat" Callison, member of a pioneer Yukon family and a noted bush pilot. He kept a gasoline cache (storage) on the lake for his aircraft during mining exploration in the area.

THE THREE GUARDSMEN 61°11'N 137°13'W (115-H). **A group of three peaks on the south shore of Ittlemit Lake, southwest of Aishihik Lake.**

These three prominent peaks were named by miners in the 1890's who used them for landmarks. Named after the three musketeers in Alexandre Dumas' famous novel of that name, they are from east to west, Mount Athos, Mount Porthos and Mount Aramis.

MOUNT TIDD 5,563' 62°04'N 131°19'W (105-J). **About 28 miles west of Pelly Lake.**

This was named in September 1971 to commemorate Sergeant Claude Britoff TIDD, RCMP. He came to the Yukon in 1915 and served at Old Crow, Ross River, Mayo, Dawson and Fortymile until the 1940's. His entire enlistment was spent in the Yukon Territory.

TILLEI LAKE 61°46'N 129°29'W (105-H). **About 12 miles north of the west arm of Frances Lake. Drains into the Thomas River.**

Dr. G.M. Dawson, GSC, although he did not visit the lake, gave it its Indian name "TIL-E-I-TSHO" meaning "Walking Stick River". (Actually, he gave the name to the creek which drains the lake.) In 1887 he traversed this country and spoke to Henry Thibert, the discoverer of the Dease Lake goldfields in the Cassiar, who had been prospecting in this area. Thibert gave him much information on the lakes and streams of the region.

TINDIR CREEK 65°19'N 141°00'W (116-G&F). **Flows across the Yukon-Alaska border to the Nation River.**

This small creek was named in 1910 by a survey team on the international boundary. Thomas Riggs of the US was in charge. The word is an Indian name meaning "Moose".

TINTINA TRENCH 64°25'N 140°00'W (105-K, 115-P).

The GSC gave this name, meaning "Chief" in the native language, to the broad valley north of, and parallel to, the Yukon River between Fortymile and Dawson. The valley occupies one of the largest faults in the Yukon geological system. It was named by R.G. McConnell, GSC, in 1901–02. He spelled it "TIN-TIN-A".

TINY ISLAND LAKE 63°50'N 134°15'W (105-M). **15 miles east of Mayo Lake.**

H.S. Bostock, GSC, named this small lake in 1940 while investigating the area for strategic minerals for Canada's war industries.

TIZRA CREEK   67°03′N 137°30′W (116–P). Drains Whitefish Lake.

A long-known local name, "TIZRA" is a Vanta Kutchin Indian word which describes a certain type of whitefish.

TOM CREEK   60°11′N 129°02′W (105–A). About eight miles west of Watson Lake, flowing into the Liard River.

This is a long-used local name after "Liard TOM", an Indian trapper whose cabin is at the mouth of the stream. He appears in an article written about the district in the National Geographic Magazine of May 1942.

TOMBSTONE MOUNTAIN   8,200′ 64°24′N 138°40′W (116–B&C). About 33 miles northeast of Dawson at the head of the Tombstone River.

This was originally named by William Ogilvie, DLS, in 1896 after Robert Campbell (1808–1894), Chief Factor of the HBC, the discoverer of the Pelly, Lewes and upper Yukon Rivers, and builder of Forts Frances, Pelly Banks and Selkirk. It is a shaft of black rock about 600 feet wide, that rises 1,000 feet above the surrounding ridge.

The Klondikers who spread out through these valleys in their search for gold in 1897–98, having no maps of the area and unaware of its name, called it TOMBSTONE Mountain because of its singular resemblance to a grave marker.

Since that time much argument has gone on concerning its exact location. In 1968, Dr. D. Tempelman-Kluit, GSC, determined that they were both the same mountain. The Geographical Board of Canada decided to retain the miners' name. However, both before and after that date many maps, both governmental and others, still call this peak "Mount Campbell."

TOOBALLY LAKES   60°15′N 126°20′W (95–D). Two lakes on the Smith River in the southeastern corner of the Yukon Territory.

These lakes were known and fished in the 1830's to supply food for the HBC trading post at Fort Halkett at the junction of the Smith and Liard Rivers.

TOO-TSHO RANGE (See Logan Mountains.)

TORONTO CREEK   63°46′N 139°07′W (115–O&N). A tributary to Quartz Creek.

Herbert W. Savage of Toronto, Ontario, named this stream when he found enough gold on it to stake the first claim on 3 January, 1898.

TOULEARY CREEK 62°56'N 139°13'W (115-J&K). Flows into the Yukon from the east, just above Kirkman Creek.

Grant and Albert Kirkman found gold here in the summer of 1898, staked the Discovery claim on 26 July and named the creek after their home town of Tulare, California. Someone spelled the name phonetically.

TOWER PEAK 5,672' 61°17'N 133°14'W (105-F). On the north side of Big Salmon Lake.

Because of its distinctive appearance, Arthur St. Cyr, DLS, gave the peak this name in 1898 while surveying and mapping the Quiet Lake-Big Salmon River area.

TRAFFIC MOUNTAIN 6,739' 62°07'N 130°18'W (105-J). The lone peak within the junction formed by the Pelly River and Lakes.

This prominent and long-known landmark is another Yukon mystery. Although probably named about 1840 by Robert Campbell of the HBC or one of his men, and shown on a map made in 1849 and nearly all maps since, there has been no record yet found of what or whom the name represents.

TRAIL RIVER 66°40'N 134°40'W (106-L). A tributary to the Peel River.

This is the English version of the local Indian name. It is so called because the Indians ascended this stream on foot on their way across country from the Peel to the Bonnet Plume River. The stream is wild and unnavigable so all must walk the length of the river.

TRESIDDER CREEK 63°29'N 136°14'W (115-P). Enters the Stewart River about ten miles above Stewart Crossing.

In September 1941 the Geographic Board of Canada confirmed this old local name. Charles TRESIDDER was an old-timer who had trapped and lived for many years on this creek.

TRITOP PEAK 6,079' 62°13'N 137°31'W (115-I). Ten miles northwest of Mount Nansen.

About 1910 the early miners in the Mount Nansen district called this hill "The Haystack". A few years later the name was changed by a GSC survey party, ignorant of its local name and the new name was made official. The name comes from its appearance: it has three summits.

TROMBLEY CREEK   62°40′N 138°36′W (115–J&K). A small tributary to Dip Creek in the Dawson Range.

This brook was named on 16 September, 1915, during the staking rush to Rude Creek. Timothy TROMBLEY was from Québec and an active prospector in many parts of the Yukon.

TROPICAL CREEK   60°05′N 126°19′W (95–D). Flows into the Smith River, south of Toobally Lakes.

This was named by the personnel of an oil exploration company in 1949 because of the luxuriant vegetation along the banks of the stream, caused by the waters of the hot springs found there.

TRUITT CREEK   62°12′N 134°22′W (105–L). Flows into the east end of Little Salmon Lake.

This creek was named by a survey team of the US Army Corps of Engineers in the summer of 1942. Col. James J. TRUITT was in charge of location surveys for a proposed railway from Prince George, BC to Fairbanks, Alaska, which was intended to supplement or replace the Alaska Military Highway then being constructed.

Section "A" of the Trans Canadian, Alaska and Western Railway was between the above points. Section "B" was to be carried from Fairbanks to Nome, Alaska. On section "A" actual field surveys were carried out by 24 teams comprised of 556 men. They started early in May and completed the surveys by October 1942.

It was estimated that the railroad from Prince George to Fairbanks would be by way of Finlay Forks and Lower Post, BC, then to Ross River, the Five Finger Rapids and west to Fairbanks. The line was to have been approximately 1417 miles in length and estimated to cost about $111,000,000.

After the defeat of the Japanese forces in the Aleutian Islands and the successful construction of the Alaska Military Highway, the railroad project was dropped in favour of improving the highway.

The present Ross River – Carmacks Highway used these surveys as a guide to location. (See Railway Survey Creek and Truitt Peak.)

TRUITT PEAK   6,799′ 62°15′N 134°15′W (105–L). In the Glenlyon Range, at the headwaters of Truitt Creek.

Col. James J. TRUITT, US Army Corps of Engineers, was on an inspection flight of survey parties on the routes of the Trans Canadian, Alaska and Western Railway and the Canol Road in the early spring of 1942. He was returning to Whitehorse by aircraft when the pilot of the bomber they were flying allowed him to take over the controls. He had never flown an aircraft before and nearly crashed into this mountain. The pilot flew the rest of the way. After landing, the aircraft crew suggested they name this peak after him as a joking reminder of his only attempt at flying and the survey parties accepted the name. The name was later confirmed on GSC maps and was made official in 1946. The survey parties later used the name for the creek below the peak.

TUMMEL RIVER   62°47′N 135°06′W (105–L). A tributary to the Pelly River from the south.

Robert Campbell of the HBC, on his exploration of the Pelly River in the summer of 1840, named this stream after a river of the same name near his home in Perthshire, Scotland.

TURNER LAKE   66°11′N 134°15′W (106–L). West of the Peel River.

This was named in April 1973 for the new, small-scale topographical maps, after John TURNER who had been a Yukon Councillor for the Bonanza District from 1915–17.

MOUNT TURNER   65°24′N 136°14′W (116–H). East of the Hart River.

This peak was named in May 1973 to commemorate Constable F. TURNER, RNWMP, a member of the Dempster Patrol which searched for and found the lost Fitzgerald Patrol, starved to death in the Peel River country in 1911. He volunteered for this task although he was no longer a member of the force.

TUSTLES LAKE   61°43′N 129°12′W (105–H). 15 miles northeast of the west arm of Frances Lake.

This was named by Dr. G.M. Dawson, GSC, in 1887, from the Indian name "TUSTLES-TO", for which he provided no translation.

TWELFTH OF JULY CREEK   61°10′N 138°03′W (115-G&F). A tributary of Fourth of July Creek.

During the start of the rush to the Kluane Lake goldfields, Charles Racine discovered gold and staked the Discovery claim on this stream on 12 July, 1903, eight days after "Dawson" Charlie staked that of Fourth of July Creek which started the whole rush.

TWO LADDER CREEK   60°01′N 131°44′W (105–B). A tributary to the Smart (Smarch) River.

This name was given to Dorsey Lake about 1939–40. Two local Indians sank a prospect shaft for placer gold near the lake and reported that it was two ladders deep.

Dorsey Lake has regained its name and for some reason this name has been applied to this stream ten miles away.

TWOPETE CREEK   62°42′N 133°56′W (105–K). A tributary to the Tay River from the south.

J.R. Johnson, GSC, in 1935 noted this name in local use after two Swedish prospectors and trappers who lived here. Both had the given name of Peter. The mountain was named later.

TYERS RIVER   61°14′N 129°12′W (105–H). Flows into the south end of Frances Lake.

This river was named by Robert Campbell of the HBC, probably about 1840 when he was building Fort Frances. The original Indian name is not known and this is probably a Scottish name.

MOUNT TYRRELL   4,747′ 63°43′N 140°04′W (115–O&N). Between the Sixtymile and Yukon Rivers.

Joseph Burr TYRRELL (1858–1957) served the GSC from 1880 to 98 and was a noted exploration geologist in the North West Territories and the Yukon. He was born in Weston, Ontario on 1 November, 1858, and educated at Upper Canada College and the University of Toronto, where he won scholarships and graduated with distinction. He took an active part in the militia and served with the Queen's Own Rifles and later in the Governor General's Foot Guards. He was a crack shot with both rifle and pistol.

After resigning from the GSC he practised as a mining engineer in Dawson for seven years. His hobby, for which he became well-known, was researching and writing about the men of the early fur trade and their explorations in Northern Canada. He died in Agincourt, Ontario.

TYRRELL CREEK 61°55′N 138°02′W (115-G&F). A tributary to the Nisling River.

This was officially named in June 1955 after Joseph Burr TYRRELL BSc., GSC, who travelled this stream when he mapped the geology of the area, including the Nisling River, in 1898.

ULU MOUNTAIN 10,160′ 60°13′N 138°46′W (115-B&C). Ten miles southeast of Mount Kennedy.

Named after the "ULU", the Eskimo women's knife which is the symbol of the Arctic Winter Games. The peak was first climbed on 6 March, 1970, by "Monty" Alford, Louis Lambert and Jim Boyde, to celebrate the newly-established Games which embrace people from the NWT, Alaska and the Yukon.

URANUS CREEK (See Pooly Creek.)

MOUNT VAN BIBBER 6,456′ 63°02′N 135°37′W (105-M). In the McArthur Group about 35 miles south of Mayo.

This name was requested by Mrs. D.J. Fulton of Cranbrook, BC in March 1967 to commemorate her father, Ira VAN BIBBER.

Ira Van Bibber with his two brothers Theodore and Patrick, came from West Virginia to the Klondike in 1898. Ira loved the country and married an Indian wife. They trapped for three years in the then almost totally unknown Nahanni country. He became one of the best big game guides in the Yukon. He made his home for most of these years at Pelly Crossing and this mountain is in the midst of the region where he hunted and trapped. After more than 60 years in the Yukon he died, leaving many descendants to carry on his traditions.

VAN CLEAVES HILL 63°49′N 135°32′W (105-M). Six miles west of Mayo Lake.

VAN CLEAVE, prospector and trapper, lived for years at the foot of this mountain.

MOUNT VANCOUVER 15,700′ 60°20′N 139°41′W (115-B&C). A boundary line peak in the St. Elias Range.

In 1874 Professor W.H. Dall, who was with the Western Union Telegraph Company expedition as scientific director, named this peak in honour of Captain George VANCOUVER, RN, (1758-1798).

Captain Vancouver, in command of the sloop *Discovery* and accompanied by Lt. W.R. Broughton, RN, in command of the tender *Chatham*, made an exploring and surveying voyage from England to southeastern Alaska and around the world from 1790–95.

Vancouver's expedition, among other accomplishments, added a wealth of knowledge of and names to the previously ill-defined coastal features of southeastern Alaska. He respected the names he found applied by the inhabitants and traders and the nomenclature of his charts was generally accepted.

This mountain was first climbed by N.E. Odell, A. Bruce, Bill Hainsworth, Bob McCarter and Robertson on 5 July, 1949.

MOUNT VANIER 6,049′ 60°37′N 136°02′W (115-A). At the northeast corner of Kusawa Lake.

Georges VANIER, DSO, MC and Bar, MID, Legion of Honour (France), Order of Merit (US), BA, LLD, was born in Montréal on 23 April, 1888.

Vanier was educated in law at Laval University but found an early aptitude for military life. In 1914 he helped found the 22nd French Canadian Battalion, the famous "Van Doos". (In 1920 the battalion was made the Royal 22nd Regiment).

He served overseas in France from 1915–18 with high distinction, winning many decorations for bravery and losing his right leg in battle in August 1918. He continued as a soldier, attending Staff College at Camberley, England in 1922. In 1925 he was promoted to lieutenant colonel and given command of the Royal 22nd Regiment.

His diplomatic career began about this time; he was chosen as a Canadian delegate to the League of Nations in 1927 and made Minister to France in 1939, holding the post until 1942. He was a part of the highest Allied war councils and a major figure in Canadian diplomacy during the war and after.

On 3 August, 1959, he was made Governor General of Canada. He was the first French Canadian to hold the post and a popular one in all parts of the country. Serving, as always, with distinction, he died on 5 March, 1967.

VAN GORDER CREEK 62°13′N 133°22′W (105-K). A tributary of the Pelly River near Ross River.

Dell Charles VAN GORDER was born in Ord City, Nebraska on 4 March, 1876. He came to the Yukon about the turn of the century, attracted by the stories of gold.

In the early years he gravitated to the upper Pelly River country where he prospected and trapped for many years, often with Ira Van Bibber. About 1910 he became the manager of the Taylor and Drury trading post at Pelly Banks. Leaving there about 1944, he took over their post at Ross River until 1949. He retired to Teslin where he died, a respected pioneer, on 21 November, 1953. That same year Allan Kulan found a large lead-zinc-silver ore body near this creek. In June 1971 the new school at Faro was given Van Gorder's name.

His name was often misspelled "Van Gorda" and as such will be found on most maps.

VEESHRIDLAH MOUNTAIN 67°07′N 139°21′W (116-O&N). On the headwaters of Lord Creek in the Keele Range.

This is an old Vanta Kutchin Indian word meaning "dark", which describes the appearance of this hill.

VICTOR CREEK 62°38′N 138°50′W (115-J&K). A tributary to Dip Creek.

Gold was found here and a Discovery claim was staked on 16 September, 1915, by Timothy Trombley and Henry Detraz. They named it Galena Creek but the name was changed by the Mining Recorder in Dawson as there already was a Galena Creek. (See Trombley Creek.)

VICTORIA CREEK 60°32′N 137°26′W (115-A). Flows into Louise Lake, the westernmost of the Kathleen Lakes.

Peter Ehret found the first placer gold in this creek in the summer of 1902. When he recorded the Discovery claim on 24 May, the Mining Recorder, Insp. A.E.C. McDonnell, NWMP, named the stream for the occasion.

VIRGIN CREEK 60°25′N 137°26′W (115-A). A tributary to Victoria Creek, ten miles west of Dezeadash Lake.

To quote the *Whitehorse Star* of 19 August, 1905, "Thomas Laird arrived yesterday from Virgin Creek, of which he is the discoverer, in the Kluane district. He has taken out enough gold to pay good wages all summer." Laird made his find in June.

There is some evidence that an earlier prospector in the area, one William Trettin, had prospected and named the stream in 1903 during the rush to the Kluane Lake diggings.

VITTREKWA RIVER 67°00'N 135°35'W (106–L). Crosses to the NWT in the western Richardson Mountains.

In 1900 and later an Indian of this name lived on this river. The Dawson-MacPherson Patrol of the RNWMP camped at his cabin. They spelled his name "Vitchiquah", which in the Loucheaux language means "No Cry".

VOLCANO MOUNTAIN 4,063' 62°55'N 137°22'W (115–I). 11 miles north of Fort Selkirk.

Hugh S. Bostock, GSC, in 1935 reported in GSC Memoir No. 189 that "This is probably the only well preserved volcano and crater of its size in Canada."

VON WILCZEK CREEK 62°36'N 136°54'W (115–I). Enters the Yukon River north of Rink Rapids from the east.

Lt. F. Schwatka, US Army, named this stream in the summer of 1883 after Graf VON WILCZEK of Vienna, Austria, but called it a river.

The Geographical Board of Canada changed the designation to creek in July 1960 and at the same time gave the same name to the small lakes on the upper reaches of the stream.

VOREEKWA LAKES 67°08'N 138°16'W (116–O&N). Southeast of the Sharp Mountains.

These were named in 1973 as a map designation. Enquiries of the natives of Old Crow concerning the origins of the name brought the answer that it is a Vanta Kutchin word meaning "no name". (Some field man had his leg pulled on this one.)

MOUNT VOWLES 61°25'N 136°11'W (115–H). East of Aishihik Lake.

D.D. Cairnes, GSC, while mapping the geology of the area in 1910, named this landmark on the Dalton Trail after Stanley Tom VOWLES, RNWMP No. 4206. He enlisted in the force in 1904 and resigned in 1908. Most of his service was spent in this area, where Cairnes knew him.

VUNTA CREEK 67°55'N 136°33'W (116–P). A small tributary to Fish Creek, north of McDougall Pass.

This was named in the summer of 1962 by B.S. Norford, GSC, after the VUNTA Band of Indians whose trapping grounds run from here to the Porcupine River.

WALHALLA CREEK 63°07'N 138°37'W (115-O&N). Flows into Scroggie Creek.

This was known in the earliest days as the left fork of Scroggie Creek until paying gold was found in 1912 by a prospector named LeBouef. It was believed that he had been prospecting in Australia in earlier years and named this creek after the rich goldfields of WALHALLA, in the state of Victoria, Australia, which had been discovered before 1900.

MOUNT WALLACE 7,726' 61°03'N 138°34'W (115-G&F). At the southwest corner of Kluane Lake.

This mountain was named in 1960 to honour Dr. Robert C. WALLACE, past president of the University of Manitoba, former principal of Queen's University at Kingston, Ontario and distinguished scholar and geologist.

WALSH GLACIER 60°53'N 140°37'W (115-B&C). South of the Centennial Range in the St. Elias Mountains.

J.J. McArthur, DLS, of the International Boundary Survey Commission, named this feature after Supt. J.M. WALSH of the NWMP in 1900. (See Mount Walsh.)

MOUNT WALSH 14,780' 61°00'N 140°01'W (115-G&F). A boundary peak in the south St. Elias Mountains.

In July 1900, J.J. McArthur DLS, of the International Boundary Commission, named this mountain after Superintendent James Morrow WALSH of the NWMP.

Born in 1841 at Prescott, Upper Canada, Walsh was one of the original force, enlisting in 1873. After a distinguished career in the west he resigned in 1883. When the Klondike frenzy broke out he was called upon by the Canadian government, with almost unanimous public approval, to administer and govern the newly-formed Yukon Territory. He went to the Yukon in September 1897, armed with almost dictatorial powers. As well as being given the post of the Commissioner (Governor), he was handed sole command of the NWMP in the territory and appointed Supervisor of Customs and Mail Services.

Walsh spent only a year in the Yukon. Although there were many criticisms of his methods and ethics, there is no denying that, under almost intolerable conditions, he skilfully organized order out of chaos. He was ably assisted by some of the great names of the NWMP, such as Steele, Jarvis, Constantine, Wood, Belcher and others. He was hindered by honest but inefficient civil servants whose inability to cope with the huge numbers of persons flooding into the territory led to unproven charges of government graft and corruption.

He died of a stroke on 25 July, 1905 at Brockville, Ontario.

MOUNT WALTERS   3,189'   62°47'N 137°04'W (115–I). Ten miles east of Fort Selkirk.

This was named in 1971 to commemorate No. 127 Private H. WALTERS of the Royal Regiment of Canada, a member of the Yukon Field Force of 1898. He marched overland from Glenora on the Stikine River, to the foot of Teslin Lake and came by boat (rowing, not steam) to Fort Selkirk. He died here in service on 28 February, 1899, and is buried here.

MOUNT WANN   65°56'N 140°15'W (116–G&F). West of the Porcupine River.

In September 1973, this mountain was named after Clyde Gavin WANN, who organized the first commercial air service in the Yukon. He carried the first air mail between Whitehorse, Mayo, Keno, Dawson, Carcross and Atlin in 1928–30. He assisted the US Army Corps of Engineers in scouting the route for the Alaska Highway and, immediately after it was opened for public travel, built some of the first tourist services on the road at Rancheria, Morley River and Destruction Bay.

WAREHAM LAKE   63°41'N 135°52'W (105–M). On the Mayo River, five miles above Mayo Landing.

The fore-bay, or reservoir of the hydro-electric power plant here has been known locally as Wareham Lake ever since it was created, after the late Rev. G.W.N. WAREHAM, who drowned in Mayo Lake some years ago. The plant was built in 1952 to provide power for the silver-lead mines in the area.

WASSON LAKE   60°52'N 130°27'W (105–B). On the southeast side of the Simpson Range near the headwaters of the Liard River.

This small lake was named in February 1936 after Everett WASSON, the first bush pilot in the Yukon. He flew a Fairchild 71 for the Treadwell Yukon Mining Company, 1928–35. From 1935 until 1940 he was general manager and chief pilot of the WP&YR's Aviation Division.

Wasson flew the first air-search and rescue mission in Yukon history. The Burke party was lost on the upper Liard River and Wasson was called in.

On 3 November, 1930, he and Joe Walsh, an experienced Yukon prospector and guide, started the search. Due to a lack of knowledge of Burke's original destination much time was lost searching in the wrong directions.

Wasson and Walsh found the party on the banks of the upper Liard River on 6 December. After taking care of the survivors Walsh had to repair the aircraft's propellor, which had been damaged on landing. He whittled an axe handle and spliced the propellor. The repaired propellor held and the aircraft was flown to Atlin, BC. Burke had died of exhaustion and exposure shortly before the party was found. This was the first operation of its kind in the Yukon. The Dominion government awarded Wasson $1,500 and Walsh $500 for their hazardous efforts.

Wasson died of a heart attack in Alexander Valley, California in December 1958.

WATERS RIVER 67°28'N 137°01'W (116-P). Flows into the Bell River at Lapierre House.

It is probable that this river was named after Corporal WATERS of the RNWMP, who assisted the GSC in 1917 when they were mapping in this area.

MOUNT WATES 61°14'N 140°04'W (115-G&F). Southeast of the Steele Glacier in the St. Elias Mountains.

This was named by the Alpine Club of Canada in 1970, after Cyril Geoffrey WATES (1884-1946), a telephone engineer and past president of the club (1938-41). This is the south of the twin peaks, the north peak being Mount Gibson.

WATSON CREEK 63°33'N 135°07'W (105-M). A tributary of the Stewart River.

This local name has been in use since 1899, after Robert WATSON.

Watson graduated in mathematics from the University of Toronto and came to the Yukon in 1895, or 96. He was cheated out of a claim on Bonanza Creek in 1896 and was so soured that he formed a revulsion for all other men. He moved to this small stream, at that time almost totally isolated, and trapped for a living. While living here he made an intensive study of the works of Shakespeare as a source of modern slang. He died and was buried on the creek in 1905.

WATSON LAKE   60°07′N 128°48′W (105–A). At mile 635 (K1029) on the Alaska Highway in the southeastern Yukon.

Frank WATSON of Yorkshire, England started for the Klondike in early 1897 from Edmonton. Fighting his way through unmapped country he arrived on the upper Liard River in the spring of 1898. His illusions of easy gold in the Klondike were by this time completely dissipated. The country was appealing and he decided to stay in this region, to prospect and trap. He married an attractive Indian girl from Lower Post and from then on led an unrestricted and unhurried life. The upper Liard and its tributaries were his trapping and prospecting grounds while his home was on the shore of Watson Lake. The lake had been known since the 1870′s as "Fish Lake". In 1941 the area become too crowded for him when construction was begun on the airport and the highway. He moved his family a few miles north to Windid Lake.

With the building of the Alaska Highway, most of the activity in the area moved ten miles east to what was then called Watson Lake Wye, the site of the present town.

To quote the *Alaska Highway News*, Special Edition, Summer 1959, "In the spring of 1941 operations for the construction of the airport at Watson Lake were begun. First stage was the shipment of supplies by boat from Vancouver to Wrangel. It was then necessary to tranship them by riverboat and barge some 160 miles up the Stikine River to Telegraph Creek, from there by truck some 76 miles to Dease Lake but only after this section of the road had been made passable. At Dease Lake the equipment was again unloaded into barges and boats and transported down the Dease River to Lower Post on the Liard River. Here a tote road some 26 miles in length had to be built into Watson Lake to the airport site."

Two runways approximately 5,000 feet in length were built, along with administration buildings and staff quarters for both RCAF and Department of Transport personnel. The work was completed in the autumn of 1943. The project was handed over to the government by the General Construction Company Ltd., which had built it all. A post office was opened on 1 July, 1942. Watson Lake being noted for its famous collection of sign posts, it may be of interest that the first post erected was the one put up by Carl L. Lindley of Denville, Illinois, in early 1942. He was a soldier in Company "D", of the 341st Engineers, US Army.

Frank WATSON died here but some of his family still live in the community. (See Baker Lake.)

MOUNT WATSON 62°55′N 137°11′W (115-I). East of Volcano Mountain, about 12 miles northeast of Fort Selkirk.

In November 1971 this mountain was given the name of No. 125 Corporal M. WATSON of the Royal Regiment of Canada. He was a member of the Yukon Field Force of 1898. They marched overland from Glenora on the Stikine River to Teslin Lake and rowed, in boats they had built, to Fort Selkirk.

Known as Cpl. M. Watson of the RRC's, it was found after his death that he was, in reality, the Hon. M.W. St. John Watson Beresford of Creaduff House, Athlone, Ireland, a nephew of Viscount Castlemain. He was 38 years of age and had been in the service for 10 or 11 years before killing himself, accidentally, with a service revolver in the barracks at Dawson on 28 March, 1900. (See Mounts Walters, Evans, Hansen and Corcoran.)

WATSON RIVER 60°11′N 134°44′W (105-D). Flows into the north end of Lake Bennett at Carcross.

This river was named by Lt. F. Schwatka, US Army, in 1883 after Professor Sereno WATSON of Harvard University. As it was previously unnamed, Dr. G.M. Dawson, GSC, allowed the name to stand.

WAUGH CREEK 64°55′N 137°02′W (116-A). A tributary to the Hart River in the Wernecke Mountains.

The Forest Warden for this region, C.J. Shattuck, stated in a letter to the CPCGN in June 1956 that "Waugh Creek is named after a fairly ordinary man. He was a miner and promoter who started a placer mine on this creek in 1906. About $50,000 in equipment was shipped via the Mackenzie and Peel Rivers in 1909. Some doubt exists as to whether the equipment was used or abandoned en-route. At any rate Waugh took his own life by hanging, in a hotel in Chicago in May 1910 rather than admit his failure to his backers."

Harry F. WAUGH was born in New Brunswick and came into the Yukon in the spring of 1896 and was one of the first to stake a claim in the Klondike. He staked the first claim after Carmack and his party, locating No. 14 Below Discovery, while his partner, Burpee, staked No. 15 Below.

Waugh's name appears in many newspaper accounts from 1905–10 in the Yukon, all concerning his efforts to establish a viable mining operation in one of the most inaccessible and inhospitable places on the North American continent. For instance, in 1906 he and "Black" Sullivan (another Klondike original) appeared at Herschel Island with specimens of gold-bearing quartz ore and went out to Dawson on the whaler *Kar-Luk* to record their claims. He searched the country from the Ogilvie Mountains to the Arctic slope in his quest for minerals. His partners in these ventures were almost all well known Yukoners of wealth and experience, such as "Black" Sullivan, Andrew Hunker and Thomas O'Brien, who had enough faith in his ability and integrity to back him financially for years.

Waugh's last action in the Yukon was to assist the RNWMP in a long search for some lost men.

Waugh may have seemed to be of no importance, and suspect because of his willingness to gamble his own and his friends' money on such chancy ventures as looking for mines. However, his actions over the years in choosing a life of hardship in this desolate country, the regard in which he was held by his peers and his eventual suicide, all point to a man with a terrible sense of integrity and responsibility. He was certainly no "ordinary man".

WEBBER CREEK 62°03′N 137°13′W (115-I). A small tributary to Nansen Creek from the east side.

Charles and Jack WEBBER were coal miners at Carmacks before deciding to go prospecting. In 1912 they explored the Mount Nansen area and found gold on this stream.

WELLESLEY LAKE 62°21′N 139°49′W (115-J&K). This large lake is the source of the Nisling River.

Charles Willard Hayes (1859–1916), USGS geologist from 1887–1911, joined Lt. F. Schwatka, US Army, in his last expedition in 1891. The expedition, sponsored by a syndicate of American newspapers, was to explore the region between the Lynn Canal and the Copper River. Mark Russell, a noted prospector of his time, accompanied them as their guide. Their route followed the Taku Inlet trail to Teslin Lake, along the Teslin River to the Lewes, up the White River and over the Skolai Pass into Alaska and then down the Chitina and Copper Rivers.

Hayes made the first classification of the Alaskan physiographic provinces. For much of the area covered he gathered the first scientific information. He named this lake after Wellesley College in Massachusetts. The college, established in the early 1800's, was named after Lord Mornington WELLESLEY, the Duke of Wellington. The "Iron Duke" was the conqueror of Napoleon's armies in the Spanish Peninsular and French Wars.

282

WERNECKE 63°56′N 135°15′W (105-M). On Keno Hill.

This small mining camp was started in 1921 to serve the newly-found silver-lead mines of Keno Hill. It was named for Livingstone WERNECKE ME, the manager of the Treadwell-Yukon Mining Company Ltd.

Wernecke, an American mining engineer, was working at the Alaska Gatineau Mine at Juneau as a construction engineer in 1914. He was next employed as a geologist at the Alaska Treadwell Gold Mining Co. at the same place. He was the last man out of that huge mine when it caved in and sea water filled it forever in 1917.

His company had followed with interest the new finds of high-grade, silver-lead ore in the Keno Hill area and in 1919 sent Wernecke there to investigate. He bought up several promising properties which were then formed into the Treadwell-Yukon Mining Co.

By 1923 they were shipping high-grade ore to Kellogg, Idaho. In 1925 they had a mill in production. The concentrated ores were shipped by horse and wagon to Mayo Landing, by WP&YR riverboats to Whitehorse and by rail to Skagway. From Skagway the ore went by steamer to Seattle and then again by rail to Idaho. Clearly, this ore had to be very rich to pay for this expensive and costly handling and still yield a profit. Although operations were suspended from 1927–32, Wernecke, as well as managing the mines in an excellent manner, continued to explore and to send out prospectors to find more mines. He had an abiding faith that large and rich mineral deposits would be found in the mountains to the east of the Mayo district and paralleling the Yukon-NWT boundary, a theory that is now being proven correct.

The Treadwell-Yukon Mining Co. suspended operations permanently in 1942 due to the difficulty in obtaining labour and supplies during the war years. The little settlement had been abandoned about 1933 when the ore gave out in the nearby mines.

Livingstone Wernecke was killed in an aircraft crash somewhere between Juneau and Ketchikan in 1941. His death may have influenced the company in their decision to suspend all operations. The Wernecke Mountains, in whose hidden riches he firmly believed, were named at a later date in memory of this exceptional man.

WESKATAHIN 60°08′N 137°03′W (115-A). Near the site of Dalton Post on the Tatshenshini River.

The history of this Indian settlement (now abandoned) begins long before any white man ever saw it. It was the meeting place for the interior Indians and the coastal tribes to trade each year. Jack Dalton, the famous gold-rush packer, came over the old trade trail from the coast in 1890 and '91, saw this sheltered place and made it the site of his main post and head-quarters in 1894. (See Neskataheen Lake.)

WEST LAKE 63°42′N 132°22′W (105–N). Northwest of the Rogue River.

This is a local name after Runer WEST, a Swedish trapper who lived here in the 1940's.

MOUNT WESTMAN 5,905′ 64°06′N 134°11′W (106–D). East of the junction of the Beaver and Rackla Rivers.

In November 1964 this mountain was chosen to commemorate R-101306 Warrant Officer Robert Morris WESTMAN. He was born at Regina, Saskatchewan on 21 September, 1915 and enlisted in the RCAF at Van-couver on 8 May, 1941. He served in Canada and overseas and was missing, presumed killed in action, on 29 April, 1943.

WHEATON RIVER 60°07′N 134°53′W (105–D). Flows into the north end of Lake Bennett.

This river was named in 1883 by Lt. F. Schwatka, US Army, after Brevet Major General Frank WHEATON, US Army.

MOUNT WHITE 60°20′N 133°53′W (105–C). Two miles south of Jake's Corner.

William Ogilvie, DLS, during his survey of the Yukon River in 1887, named this bald hill after the then Minister of the Interior, the Hon. Thomas WHITE, who had supported the exploration and survey of the Yukon. Ogilvie had already named the White Pass after the same man.

WHITEHORSE 60°43′N 135°03′W (105–D). The capital of the Yukon Territory.

Situated at the upper limits of feasible steamboat navigation on the Yukon River and at the terminus of the WP&YR, a settlement began here in 1900. As well as controlling the shipping of the territory it became a supply and communications centre for the southern Yukon. The discovery and exploitation of the rich copper ore bodies nearby from 1899 to 1920 also helped to stimulate business and growth in the town.

Many fanciful stories have been and are told about the origin of the name

Whitehorse. It is probable that the first miners in 1880–81 saw a resemblance to white horses' manes in the white waters of the rapids. The name was in common use by 1887. The foot of the rapids made a natural stopping place for those passing through Miles Canyon and the rapids below. Few people dared these hazards with loaded boats, the majority preferring to unload and carry (portage) their goods around the dangerous waters. The boats were either let down on ropes or taken through by professional pilots. In any case this location made a good place to stop and reorganize outfits before proceeding on down the river. Most landed on the east side of the river and it was there that the first townsite of Whitehorse was surveyed in September 1899 by Paul T.C. Dumais, DLS.

The WP&YR had been granted 640 acres of land on the west side of the river for their terminus and in late 1899 laid out and surveyed a townsite which they named "Closeleigh", in honour of the Close brothers, of London England. The brothers had been instrumental in financing the construction of the railroad and the freighting operations of the company. The WP&YR, on 21 April, 1900, announced that "the name of the town is to be the old, known on two continents . . . Whitehorse."

The building of the Alaska Highway in 1942–43 assured the growth and permanence of the community. At the beginning of 1942 the population was about 500, which had increased to 8,000 by early summer when US Army Engineers and some civilian contractors arrived. This population decreased to about 3,000 by 1955 but the increasing search for oil and minerals in the north reversed this trend and it has grown steadily. The first post office was opened on 1 June, 1900, by F.W. Cane. In March 1951 the city replaced Dawson as the capital of the Yukon Territory.

The name of the town was always spelled as two words until the Geographic Board of Canada combined them on 21 March, 1957.

WHITE RANGE 60°01′N 134°29′W (105–D). On the east side of Windy Arm of Tagish Lake, near the BC boundary.

In the summer of 1899, George William Richard Montague WHITE-FRASER, DLS, DTS, BCLS, was engaged with a crew of two men in setting boundary monuments (cairns) on the Yukon-BC border between Lake Bennett and Teslin Lake. The burst of mining activity in the district had made the immediate delineation of the boundary between the Yukon and BC a necessity.

Arthur St. Cyr, DTS, in charge of the boundary survey, was following White-Fraser and cutting the actual line of the boundary, ten feet wide across country. He named this prominence after White-Fraser but when the maps of the survey were produced in Ottawa the Fraser had been dropped and it was never replaced. For a time in 1905 to 10, the period of intense mining activity, the hill was known locally as Mount Conrad and was so named on a geological map of the district. This name too was eventually dropped.

A few years ago the rest of the mountain group was included and White-Fraser Mountain, changed to White Mountain, then to Mount Conrad, is now the White Range.

WHITE RIVER 63°11′N 139°36′W (115–O&N). A major tributary to the Yukon River from the St. Elias Mountains.

Robert Campbell of the HBC in 1850 was the first white man to see this stream and named it for the colour of its water, caused by the suspension of white, volcanic ash that it carries. The Stick Indians called the river "Yu-Kon-Hini" or "Yu-Ko-Kon-Heena" and the Chilkats called it "Sand River". At the head of the stream the Tanana Indians called it the "Nasina" or "Erk-Heen" meaning Copper River.

This was the first river to be prospected in the Yukon watershed. Arthur Harper, Frederick W. Hart, A. Gestler and George W. Fitch (or Finch) spent the winter of 1873–74 on the upper part of the river. They were searching for the source of native (pure) copper described to them by the Indians. They did not find the deposits but did find placer gold prospects which were not large or rich enough to mine or to induce them back to the region the following summer.

This river is remarkable for the amount of sediment it carries down from its upper reaches. Some of it is silt, fed from the large glaciers of the St. Elias Mountains but most of it comes from an extended layer of volcanic ash through which the river flows.

Great eruptions of ash from volcanoes in the St. Elias Range took place about 900–1100 A.D. covering an area about 220 by 370 miles, reaching from Alaska into the Northwest Territories. It has been estimated that about 165 cubic miles of rock in the form of ash were deposited in some places up to 100 feet in depth. It is this ash which gives the river its colour and name.

WHITESTONE RIVER 60°01′N 137°13′W (115–A). Flows from British Columbia north into the Tatshenshini River.

This river was long known locally as "Tole" Creek after "Old Tole" who headed a prospecting party into the area in 1900 and was active here for many years afterward. When it was found that he was still living, the creek's name was changed. As he is now dead perhaps the maps will revert to the local name.

MOUNT WHITNEY 65°38′N 139°37′W (116-G&F). East of the Porcupine River.

This is a map designation name given in 1973 after Frank A. WHITNEY, who was an early principal of the Dawson Public School in 1917–18.

WILEY CREEK 61°02′N 133°47′W (105-F). A tributary of the Boswell River.

In May 1962 this stream was chosen to commemorate J-7234 Flight Lt. George William WILEY, MID. He was born on 24 January, 1922, at London, Ontario, and enlisted in the RCAF on 4 December, 1940, at Windsor, Ontario. He served in Canada and overseas and died a prisoner of war on 25 March, 1944.

WILKINSON RANGE 62°50′N 134°30′W (105-L). A small range of hills north of the Earn River.

This has been named after the WILKINSON family, two generations of whom have lived and trapped in this area.

WILLIAMS CREEK 62°24′N 136°37′W (115-I). Flows into the Yukon River five miles below Yukon Crossing.

A prospector of this name found the first gold on this stream and gave it his name in 1898. In 1907 other prospectors found quartz veins carrying good copper values on the banks of the stream, which started another rush to the area. A settlement called Boronite City was built at the mouth of the stream.

WILLIAMS CREEK 63°50′N 135°28′W (105-M). A tributary to Duncan Creek in the Mayo area.

This creek was probably named by and after Frank WILLIAMS who prospected and trapped from here east to the Mackenzie Mountains. He came in 1898, one of the first men in the district, and his name occurs often in the early news from the region. (See below.)

WILLIAMS CREEK 64°20′N 134°50′W (106-D). A tributary of the Beaver River.

This creek was also named after Frank WILLIAMS. (See above.) He assisted Charles Camsell, GSC, in his exploration of the Peel and Wind Rivers in the winter of 1904–05. Camsell held him in high regard, naming this stream for him. The mountain at the headwaters of the creek was later given the same name.

MOUNT WILLIAMS   5,585'   60°46'N 135°23'W   (105–D). South of the Takhini River.

J.D. WILLIAMS was a Canada Customs Officer at Whitehorse after the First World War. He was long active as a leader in the Boy Scout movement in the Yukon. This mountain was named in his honour in November 1973.

WILSON CREEK   60°36'N 133°30'W   (105–C). Flows into the Thirty-mile River.

In August 1952 this creek was named in memory of George WILSON, a former postmaster at Whitehorse. He was also a prospector; he found gold on this creek and mined it for several years.

WILSON LAKE   62°52'N 130°04'W   (105–J). At the headwaters of the Ross River.

This was named by Joseph Keele, GSC, in 1907 when he mapped the geology of this region. Charles WILSON prospected and trapped in this area in 1904–08 and gave Keele much assistance in his work. (See below.)

MOUNT   WILSON   7,466'   62°52'N 129°40'W   (105–I).   At   the headwaters of the Ross and Pelly Rivers on the Yukon-NWT border.

Joseph Keele, GSC, named this peak, as well as the above creek in 1907. Charles WILSON, whom most people called "Old Man" Wilson, came into the Yukon with the Klondike rush. He soon gravitated to this section of the territory where he remained. Keele appreciated his wide knowledge of the country from here to the Mackenzie valley.

He spent the rest of his life, to about 1930, searching for the Lost McHenry Gold Mine. This was a phenomenally rich deposit of placer gold supposed to be somewhere in this general area. According to Keele, McHenry was said to have been an old Dease Lake miner who penetrated this region in the late 1870's or early 1880's. He returned to Dease Lake with about 40 pounds of coarse gold and nuggets. Various reasons were given for his failure to return to his find but he gave certain friends approximate directions to the location. Many prospectors have since searched for it without success. The area of the story overlaps the Nahanni country and may be connected with the lost gold mine stories of that area.

WIND CITY 65°43′N 135°12′W (106–E). On the west bank of the Wind River about eight miles above the Peel.

In the fall of 1898 many of the gold-seekers attempting to reach the Klondike from Edmonton by way of the Mackenzie, Rat, Porcupine, Peel and Wind Rivers were caught by winter and were unable to travel farther as the rivers froze. They gathered in small groups and built cabin communities to pass the winter where they were halted.

About 70 men and women gathered at this spot. Eben McAdam, a leader, quotes in his diary, "20 September 1898. Up at seven a.m. Left for lower cache at 9:20 a.m. Back at 1:23 p.m. with last load. Have named this place Wind City. Expect about 10 shacks and about 40 men to put up in this place this winter." (*The Klondike Rush through Edmonton* by J.G. McGregor)

The settlement existed from September 1898 to March 1899. To overcome the boredom of dark winter days and to avoid friction between themselves, they organized card clubs and tournaments, choirs, lectures, concerts and outdoor sports. Only two men died of scurvy despite a lack of fresh vegetables and meat. Most continued on to Dawson in the early spring although a few returned to Fort MacPherson and on home.

WIND RIVER 65°50′N 135°19′W (106–D&E). A major tributary to the Peel River.

This river has had this name from ancient times. The Loucheaux Indians of the country called it this because of the furious winds which blow down its course almost constantly.

WIND RIVER TRAIL

This was a winter road built for truck haulage of oil-well-drilling equipment and supplies. Beginning at a point just a few miles beyond Mayo it ran north to a point on the Bell River just a few miles short of the Arctic coast.

Leo Proctor of Whitehorse was instrumental in the conception and construction of this trail and it was built by the Arctic Oilfields Transport Ltd., a subsidiary of the WP&YR. Construction was started on 12 October, 1959, and completed on 12 January, 1960, for a distance of 385 miles.

Over 3,000 tons of material moved over the road, the most northerly truck road in North America.

MOUNT WOOD 15,885' 61°14'N 140°30'W (115-G&F). In the St. Elias Range.

J.J. McArthur, DLS, while surveying the International Boundary in July 1900, named this peak after Inspector (later Commissioner) Zachary Taylor WOOD NWMP.

Wood was the grandson of the twelfth president of the United States and a graduate of the Royal Military College of Kingston, Ontario. He joined the NWMP in 1883. By 1897 he had become an outstanding officer and held the rank of inspector. Chosen to go to the Yukon, he was for a period in charge of the Dawson detachment and earned a lasting reputation for his cool, efficient and totally successful maintenance of law and order in those turbulent times. He soon rose to command the RNWMP and died in 1915.

WOODBURN CREEK 63°08'N 136°15'W (115-P). Runs into Crooked Creek, south of Stewart Crossing.

A miner of this name was the first to find gold and to stake a claim on this stream in 1915. A sizeable rush followed with the creek and others around being staked.

WOODSIDE RIVER 62°03'N 139°34'W (105-J). Flows into the Pelly Lakes.

This was named in 1909 after Major Henry WOODSIDE. He came into the Yukon in 1898 and took an active part in Dawson and Yukon political affairs. He was the Yukon Census Commissioner in 1901 and was editor of the *Yukon Midnight Sun* newspaper in the early 1900's. He was active in promoting mining exploration in the territory and spent much time in the bush. He had an anti-American bias and strongly pushed Robert Henderson's claim to be the first man to discover the gold of the Klondike. He was instrumental in having the Canadian government recognize the claim and award Henderson a pension and other benefits.

MOUNT WORTHINGTON 60°35'N 137°23'W (115-A). In the Auriol Range.

This was named in June 1968 after one of Canada's most distinguished professional soldiers, Major General Frederick Frank WORTHINGTON

CB, MC, MM, CD. He was born at Peterhead, Scotland on 17 September, 1889. Enlisting in the Canadian army at Montréal, Québec on 17 March, 1916, as a private, he won a commission in the field in France and several decorations for bravery. He enlisted again on 1 September, 1939, and was instrumental in developing armoured fighting vehicles for the Canadian and Allied armies. He organized and commanded the 5th Canadian Armoured Division until 1943. He served until his retirement on 18 March, 1943, and died on 5 December, 1967.

WOUNDED MOOSE CREEK 63°36'N 138°42'W (115-O&N). Flows north into the Indian River in the Klondike District.

There is some evidence that this stream was named by Robert Henderson when he prospected it in March or April 1895. No payable gold was found on it. The mountain at its headwaters was given the same name at a later date.

YING YANG CREEK 64°18'N 138°28'W (116-B&C). Flows into the North Klondike River from the west.

This was named in 1968 by one of the men surveying the route of the Dempster Highway.

YUKON CROSSING 62°21'N 136°29'W (115-I). On the Lewes (Yukon) River near Rink Rapids.

This little settlement was at the point where the old Whitehorse-Dawson Road crossed the Lewes (Yukon) River. During the summers a ferry operated here. A roadhouse and telegraph station were also located here. The settlement was abandoned with the end of the riverboat era and the building of the new highway to Dawson.

MOUNT YUKON 10,600' 60°58'N 140°58'W (115-B&C). In the Centennial Range of the St. Elias Mountains.

This peak was named in 1967 to honour the Yukon Territory during Canada's Centennial Year. (See Centennial Range.)

THE YUKON RIVER

The Yukon River is the focal point of Yukon history. It provided the only feasible access by itself and its tributaries to almost 70% of the territory, and for many years was the main route for people and traffic. In those days life in the territory was governed by the periods when the river was open or frozen. The summer was a time of bustling activity and the riverboats carried prospectors and freight to all parts. In the winter men settled in to mine their summer prospects, to trap in their chosen areas and above all, to pass away the long, cold, dark winter. Limited to horse and dog teams, transportation was slow and costly in the winter. The cold brought movement to a minimum.

As well as access, the river provided food. Its magnificent runs of salmon, as well as other fish, formed a major proportion of the diet of the native peoples, most of whom lived along the waterways.

The name Yukon was given by the HBC trader John Bell, who in 1846 descended the Porcupine River from the Mackenzie delta to its junction with the Yukon. He called it the "Youcon", his version of the Loucheaux Indian word"Yuchoo", meaning "the Greatest River" or "Big River". At this junction in 1847 Alexander Hunter Murray established the first HBC post on the river, Fort Yukon.

The estuary of the Yukon had been explored in 1835–38 by the Russian Glasunov, who named it the "Kwikhpak", the Aleut Eskimo word meaning "Great River". The Tanana Indians called it "Niga-to", with the same meaning.

Robert Campbell of the HBC, the first explorer of the south and central Yukon region, reached the headwaters of the Pelly (the main branch of the Yukon) in 1840 by way of the Liard and Frances Rivers. In 1848 he descended the Pelly to the Yukon River, the upper part of which he called the Lewes River and the lower part, below the junction, the Pelly. In the same year he began construction of Fort Selkirk and, floating downstream, arrived at Fort Yukon. This journey established the course and fact of a new and great trade route through the Yukon and Alaska Territories. Although he had named the river the "Pelly", he now adopted that given by John Bell and the river was known as the Yukon from its mouth to Fort Selkirk.

The GSC gives the length of the river from the foot of Marsh Lake to the Bering Sea as 1979 miles. Other authorities, using the Pelly or Teslin branches, argue for total distances of up to 2300 miles. It is navigable by large riverboats from its mouth to Whitehorse (before the bridge was built at Carmacks). It was the last major river to be explored in North America, the fourth longest, and the fifth largest in volume of water flow.

Since the advent of cheaper and more regular transport by road and aircraft the river has reverted to the wilderness and is now much the same as it was a century ago, before the coming of the white man; perhaps more so, as the native Indians who once lived along its banks have now mostly moved to the settlements. The last riverboat to carry freight and passengers stopped in 1956. However, as the main part of the "Trail of 98", the river acquired a glamour that it will never lose.

THE YUKON TERRITORY

In 1670 the Hudson's Bay Company (The Governor and Company of Adventurers Trading into Hudson's Bay) was given its charter by King Charles II of England. This charter gave them, in effect, the outright control of northern Québec, Ontario and all of what is now middle, western and Arctic Canada. To quote the charter, "The true and absolute Lords and Proprietors."

It was not until early in the 19th century that they began to realize just how vast an empire they had been given. They gradually relinquished parts of it to the established governments of eastern Canada as these governments developed and lands became colonized. With the Deed of Surrender in 1869 of Rupert's Land and the old Northwest Territories, the Hudson's Bay Company became a wholly commercial enterprise with no powers of government. After the passing of this act the Yukon was made a provisional district of the NWT, to be governed from the NWT capital at Regina.

This situation lasted until the tremendous influx of people to the Yukon after the discovery of gold on the Fortymile River in late 1886. The Dominion government, in the next few years, decided to assume a more direct role in the affairs of the territory. This was started by sending in Inspector Charles Constantine and 18 men of the NWMP in 1894–95 as well as a Canada Customs Agent. Constantine was appointed Dominion Agent for the territory. The Order-in-Council effecting this action also demarked the Yukon as a separate district of the NWT.

In 1897 the Dominion government was forced into action because of the huge preponderance of American nationals in the population of the Yukon; a figure often set at 75%. They appointed Major James Morrow Walsh as the Chief Executive Officer of the Yukon Territory (which was not yet in existence). Thomas Fawcett was appointed Gold Commissioner, Dominion Agent and Mining Recorder. T.H. McGuire was made Judge of the Court of the Yukon Provisional District.

In June 1898 "An Act to Provide for the Government of the Yukon Territory" was passed, which made the Yukon, for the first time, a separate territory. It also provided a council composed of six senior officials, all taking orders from Ottawa, with all ties to Regina severed.

In 1900 two of the councillors were elected from the general public. In 1902 all five were elected. In later years the total number of councillors was increased to seven and in the last year, to 12. The commissioner has always been appointed by Ottawa.

YUSEZYU RIVER   61°38′N 129°42′W (105–H). Flows into the north end of the west arm of Frances Lake.

Dr. G.M. Dawson GSC, on his exploration of this region in 1887, recorded this local Indian name but gave no translation. Henry Thibert, the discoverer of the Dease Lake goldfields, had explored this area in the 1870′s and gave Dawson much of his information.

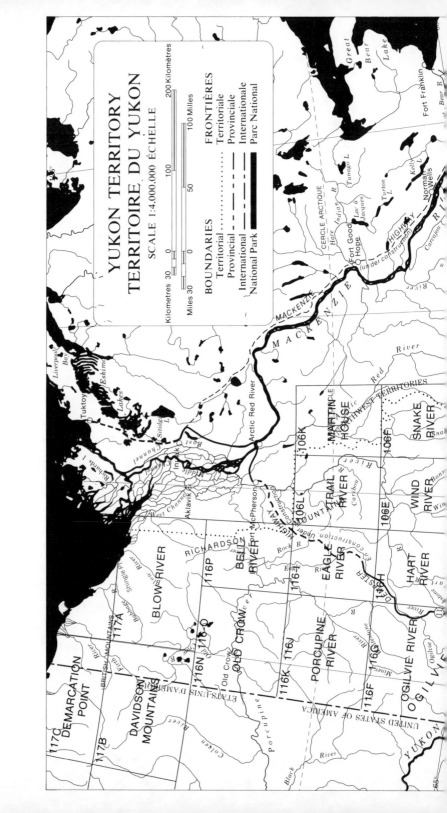

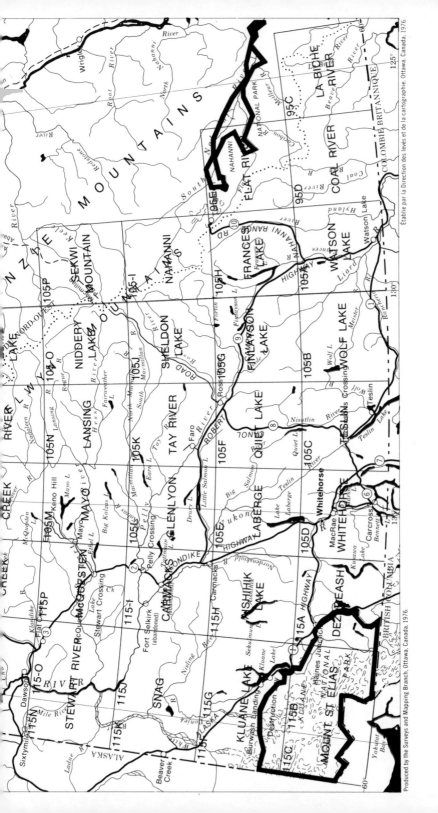

Produced by the Surveys and Mapping Branch, Ottawa, Canada. 1976.

Établie par la Direction des levés et de la cartographie. Ottawa. Canada. 1976.

NOTES

NOTES

NOTES

NOTES